Nature and the American

Hans Huth. Courtesy of The Art Institute of Chicago.

NATURE
AND THE AMERICAN

Three Centuries of Changing Attitudes

BY HANS HUTH

New Edition

Introduction by Douglas H. Strong

University of Nebraska Press
Lincoln and London

Introduction and Selected Bibliography copyright © 1990 by the University of
Nebraska Press
Manufactured in the United States of America

First printing of the second Bison Book edition: 1990
Most recent printing indicated by the last digit below:
10   9   8   7   6   5   4   3   2   1

Library of Congress Cataloging-in-Publication Data
Huth, Hans, 1892–
Nature and the American: three centuries of changing attitudes / by Hans Huth.—
New ed.
p.   cm.
Reprint. Originally published: Berkeley: University of California Press, 1957.
"A Bison book."
Includes bibliographical references.
ISBN 0-8032-7247-2
1. Nature conservation—United States—Public opinion—History.   2. Conserva-
tion of natural resources—United States—Public opinion—History.   3. Public
opinion—United States—History.   I. Title.
QH76.H88   1991   90-35727
333.95'16'0973—DC20   CIP

Originally published in 1957 by the University of California Press, Berkeley.

∞

Contents

Introduction, xv

Selected Bibliography, xli

Preface to the Bison Book Edition, xliii

Preface, xlv

1 "Axes Leap and Shapes Arise," 1

2 Scientists, Philosophers, and Travelers, 14

3 The Romantic Period, 30

4 Play and Rest, 54

5 The Poetry of Traveling, 71

6 New Eyes, 87

7 Summer Migration, 105

8 Western Reports, 129

9 Yosemite, Yellowstone, and the Grand Canyon, 148

10 City Parks and Timberlands, 165

11 The Theodore Roosevelt Era, 178

12 Conservation, 192

Notes, 213

Bibliography, 229

Acknowledgments, 239

Index, 241

Illustrations

Hans Huth   *Frontispiece*

VIGNETTES

Settlers Lumbering   1
   Pencil sketch by Joshua Shaw about 1820 (Dunbar Collection, Museum of Science and Industry, Chicago).

John Bartram's House   14
   Woodcut from William Darlington, *Memorials of John Bartram and Humphrey Marshall* (Philadelphia, 1849).

Otsego Lake, New York   30
   Woodcut from *Gleason's Pictorial Drawing-Room Companion*, I (1851), 68.

Residence of Andrew J. Downing at Newburgh, New York   54
   Woodcut from A. J. Downing, *Rural Essays* (New York, 1858).

Canalboat Crossing Over a River   71
   Woodcut (proof copy) by Alexander Robby, Philadelphia, about 1830. (Dunbar Collection, Museum of Science and Industry, Chicago).

Louis Agassiz and His Students Exploring Lake Superior   87
   Woodcut from Louis Agassiz, *Lake Superior* (Boston, 1850).

Rush for the Wilderness (Adirondacks)   105
   Woodcut from *Harper's New Monthly Magazine*, XLI (1870), 325.

A Steamboat Wooding on the Mississippi   129
   Etching by Basil Hall, from his *Forty Etchings from Sketches Made with the Camera Lucida . . . 1827 and 1828* (London, 1829).

Cotillion on a Sequoia gigantea *Stump*   148
   Woodcut from drawing by George Tirrell in [J. M. Hutchings,] *Scenes of Wonder and Curiosity in California* (San Francisco, 1861), p. 42.

The Water Terrace and the Mall, Central Park, New York   165
   Woodcut from drawing by T. Addison Richards in *Harper's New Monthly Magazine*, XXIII (1861), 294.

The Cone and Foliage of the Mammoth Trees   178
   Woodcut from drawing by George Tirrell in *Scenes of Wonder and Curiosity in California* (San Francisco, 1861), p. 47.

What Man Does to One of the Most Beautiful Gifts of Nature—The River   192
   Cartoon by Jay N. Darling ("Ding") from the Des Moines *Register*.

ILLUSTRATIONS IN TEXT

Niagara Falls 6
> Engraving after drawing by Father Hennepin, 1678, in Louis Hennepin, *A New Discovery of a Vast Country in America* (London, 1698), p. 44.

Natural Bridge, Virginia 18
> Woodcut from drawing by Porte Crayon (D. H. Strother) in *Harper's New Monthly Magazine*, XI (1855), 305.

Camp near Round Lake (Adirondacks) 51
> Woodcut from drawing by T. Addison Richards in *Harper's New Monthly Magazine*, XIX (1859), 316.

Fourth of July on the Hudson 64
> Woodcut from *Harper's New Monthly Magazine*, IX (1854), 283.

Lake Winnepesaukee 76
> Woodcut from drawing by Wheelock in Thomas Starr King, *The White Hills* (Boston, 1860), p. 67.

Artists' Excursion 85
> Woodcut from drawing by Porte Crayon (D. H. Strother) in *Harper's New Monthly Magazine*, XIX (1859), 1.

Tip-Top House on Mount Washington 93
> Woodcut from advertisement of the hotel, 1855 (Dunbar Collection, Museum of Science and Industry, Chicago).

Ascent of Mount Marcy 99
> Woodcut from drawing by T. Addison Richards, *Harper's New Monthly Magazine*, XIX (1859), 464.

On the Road to Lake George 125
> Woodcut from drawing by Winslow Homer in *Appleton's Journal*, I, July 24, 1869.

Photographer at Work in Northeastern Nevada, 1867 139
> Woodcut from photograph by W. H. O'Sullivan in *Harper's New Monthly Magazine*, XXXIX (1869), 466.

The "Three Graces," Mariposa Grove 145
> Woodcut from drawing by George Tirrell in *Scenes of Wonder and Curiosity in California* (San Francisco, 1861), p. 49.

Descending the Mountain to the Yo-Semite Valley 158
> Woodcut from drawing by George Tirrell in *Scenes of Wonder and Curiosity in California* (San Francisco, 1861), p. 89.

Shooting Buffalo on the Line of the Kansas Pacific 162
> Woodcut from *Frank Leslie's Illustrated Newspaper*, XXVII (1868), 173.

Horace Greeley at His Home in Chappaqua on His Way to Prune Trees in His Orchard 170
> Woodcut from *Frank Leslie's Illustrated Newspaper*, XXXIV (1872), 177.

Conservation Tonic 181
> Cartoon by Jay N. Darling ("Ding"), from the Des Moines *Register*.

Lumber Business   195
    Cartoon by Burr Shafer, from *Christian Science Monitor*, May 17, 1951.
Climbing in Yosemite   228
    Woodcut from drawing by George Tirrell in *Scenes of Wonder and Curiosity in California* (San Francisco, 1861), p. 128.

PLATES

1 *Niagara Falls*
    Photograph by Marta Huth, 1949.
2 *Alexander Wilson Traveling Along the Susquehannah*
    Engraving by G. Cooke after drawing by Alexander Wilson in *Port Folio*, 3d Series, II (1809), facing 147.
3 *Hadley Falls*
    Aquatint by J. R. Smith after painting by W. G. Wall, 1820, in *Hudson River Portfolio* (New York, 1825).
4 *Stagecoach near Trenton, New Jersey*
    Detail from water color by Pawel Swinin, about 1811 (Metropolitan Museum, New York).
5 *Deck Life on the* Paragon
    One of Fulton's boats on the Hudson; Fort Putnam and West Point in the background. Water color by Pawel Swinin, about 1811 (Metropolitan Museum, New York).
6 *Millpond in Maryland*
    Oil painting by an American artist, about 1790 (Hammond-Haywood House, Maryland).
7 *Landscape near Litchfield, Massachusetts*
    Detail from oil portrait of Mrs. Tallmadge by Ralph Earl, 1790 (Historical Society, Litchfield).
8 *Country Seat and Farm*
    Oil painting by an American artist, end of eighteenth century (The Art Institute of Chicago).
9 *View from Belmont Manor, Philadelphia*
    Oil painting by John Neagle, late 1820's (Newhouse Gallery, New York).
10 *John James Audubon*
    Oil painting by his sons, John W. and Victor G. Audubon, about 1841 (American Museum of Natural History, New York).
11 *Peace at Sunset*
    Oil painting by Thomas Cole, late 1820's (M. H. de Young Memorial Museum, San Francisco).
12 *Niagara Falls*
    Oil painting by Alvan Fisher, 1820 (Victor Spark, New York).
13 *On the Susquehannah*
    Oil painting by Joshua Shaw, 1839 (M. and M. Karolik Collection, Museum of Fine Arts, Boston).

14 *Kindred Spirits (Bryant and Cole)*
    Oil painting by Asher Durand, 1849 (New York Public Library).

15 *Flume in the White Mountains*
    Drawing by Thomas Cole, 1827 (Detroit Institute of Art).

16 *The Lost Balloon (near Nyack, New York)*
    Oil sketch by William H. Beard, 1880 (Lee B. Anderson, New York).

17 *William Cullen Bryant*
    Oil painting by Frank Buchser, 1868 (Staatliche Kunstsammlung, Basel, Switzerland).

18 *The Battery, New York*
    Water color by Pawel Swinin, about 1811 (Metropolitan Museum, New York).

19 *Elgin Botanical Garden*
    Sepia drawing by Hugh Reinagle, about 1812 (Stokes Collection, New York Public Library).

20 ABOVE, LEFT: *Nahant Hotel (built 1820).* ABOVE, RIGHT: *Fairmount Park, Philadelphia.*
    Both on Staffordshire china made by Joseph Stubbs, Burslem, England, between 1824 and 1829.
    BELOW: *Erie Canal*
    Bandbox covered with paper printed in colors in America about 1830 (Museum for the Arts of Decoration, Cooper Union, New York).

21 *Trenton Falls*
    Woodcut from drawing by W. Heine, half-title page of N. P. Willis, ed., *Trenton Falls* (New York, 1851).

22 *Mount Auburn Cemetery*
    Engraving by James Smillie, from Cornelia W. Walter, *Mount Auburn Cemetery* (New York, 1850).

23 *Pittsford on the Erie Canal*
    Oil painting by George Harvey, 1837 (Perry T. Rathbone, Boston).

24 *Boys Sleighing*
    Oil painting by George Harvey, 1846 (Harry Shaw Newman, New York).

25 *Fourth of July Picnic*
    Water color by Susan Merrett, about 1845 (The Art Institute of Chicago).

26 *Picnic near Mount Mansfield (Vermont)*
    Oil painting by Jerome Thompson, about 1860 (M. H. de Young Memorial Museum, San Francisco).

27 *Three Mile Point, Otsego Lake*
    Oil painting by Julius Gollmann and Louis Mignot, 1850 (New York Historical Association, Cooperstown).

28 *Smokers' Circle on Boston Common*
    Woodcut from *Gleason's Pictorial Drawing-Room Companion*, I (1851), 240.

29 *Boston Common*
   Oil painting by an unknown artist, about 1865 (The Art Institute of Chicago).

30 *Railroad in the Mohawk Valley (New York)*
   Engraving from drawing by William H. Bartlett in N. P. Willis, *American Scenery* (London, 1839).

31 *Catskill Mountain House*
   Engraving from drawing by William H. Bartlett in N. P. Willis, *American Scenery* (London, 1839).

32 *Shrewsbury River near Seabright (New Jersey)*
   Oil painting by an American artist, 1860–1865 (M. and M. Karolik Collection, Museum of Fine Arts, Boston).

33 *Daniel Webster at His Farm*
   Oil painting by an American artist, 1840–1845 (M. and M. Karolik Collection, Museum of Fine Arts, Boston).

34 *Meditation by the Sea*
   Oil painting by an American artist, 1850–1860 (M. and M. Karolik Collection, Museum of Fine Arts, Boston).

35 *Philosophers' Camp at Follansbee Pond*
   Oil painting by William J. Stillman, 1858 (Concord Free Library, Concord, Massachusetts).

36 *Camping in the Woods*
   Lithograph by A. F. Tait (Currier and Ives, 1863).

37 *Charles Loring Eliot and His Friends at Trenton High Falls*
   Oil painting by Junius B. Stearns, 1858 (Harry Shaw Newman, New York).

38 *What a Catch! (Otsego Lake)*
   Oil painting by J. G. Clonney, 1855 (M. and M. Karolik Collection, Museum of Fine Arts, Boston).

39 *Hunters' Rendezvous*
   Oil painting by Paul Weber, 1854 (Victor Spark, New York).

40 *Long Branch, New Jersey*
   Oil painting by Winslow Homer, about 1865 (Museum of Fine Arts, Boston).

41 *Pemigewasset Coach (White Mountains)*
   Oil painting by E. Wood Perry, about 1899 (Harry Shaw Newman, New York).

42 *White Sulphur Springs Hotel (Greenbrier White Sulphur Springs Hotel, West Virginia)*
   Woodcut, early 1860's.

43 *Sing-Sing Camp-Meeting*
   Lithograph from painting by Joseph B. Smith, 1838 (Harry Shaw Newman, New York).

44 *Rocky Mountains*
   Engraving from water color by Karl Bodmer in Maximilian, Prinz zu
   Wied, *Reise in das innere Nord-America* (Coblenz, 1839–1841).

45 *The Voyageurs*
   Oil painting by Charles Deas, 1845 (M. and M. Karolik Collection,
   Museum of Fine Arts, Boston).

46 *Cañon of the Grand River*
   Lithograph by J. M. Stanley from sketch by F. W. Freiherr von Egloffstein, about 1855 (*U. S. Railroad Surveys*, 1855–1860), Vol. II.

47 *Lake Tahoe*
   Oil painting by Albert Bierstadt, about 1863 (M. and M. Karolik Collection, Museum of Fine Arts, Boston).

48 *Miss Edwards at Lookout Mountain, Tennessee*
   Photograph by U. S. Signal Corps, 1863 (U. S. National Archives, Washington, D.C.).

49 *Frederick Law Olmsted*
   Photograph taken about 1860 (Frederick Law Olmsted, Jr., Palo Alto,
   California).

50 *Hunting Car, Northern Pacific Railway*
   Photograph by Frank J. Haynes, 1876 (J. E. Haynes, Yellowstone National
   Park).

51 *Bicycling at Mammoth Hot Springs, Yellowstone National Park*
   Photograph by Frank J. Haynes, 1896 (J. E. Haynes, Yellowstone National
   Park).

52 *Mammoth Hot Springs*
   Photograph by W. H. Jackson, 1871 (U. S. Geographical and Geological
   Survey, Washington, D.C.).

53 *Yellowstone Range near Fort Ellis*
   Water color by Thomas Moran, 1872 (Yellowstone National Park
   Museum).

54 *Grand Canyon National Park, Arizona*
   Photograph by Marta Huth, 1948.

55 *Mountain of the Holy Cross*
   Photograph by W. H. Jackson, 1873 (U. S. Geographical and Geological
   Survey, Washington, D.C.).

56 *Canyon of the Yampa, near Junction with Green River, Uinta Range*
   Photograph by T. H. O'Sullivan, about 1868. (U. S. National Archives,
   Washington, D.C.).

57 *Yosemite Valley from the South Rim*
   Photograph by C. E. Watkins, 1861 (Yosemite National Park Museum).

58 *Yosemite Valley from Glacier Point*
   Oil painting by William Hahn, 1874 (California Historical Society, San
   Francisco).

59 *Peshtigo Forest Fire, Wisconsin, 1871*
  Woodcut from *Illustrierte Zeitung* (Leipzig), LVII (1871), 437.
60 *Theodore Roosevelt, John Muir, and Others at Yosemite*
  Photograph by Joseph LeConte, 1903 (Yosemite National Park Museum).
61 *Interior of Cedar Cottage, Yosemite Valley*
  Photograph by H. G. Peabody, between 1890 and 1900 (Yosemite National
  Park Museum).
62 *Two Fields in Madison County, North Carolina*
  Field on left, owned by a TVA State Extension Service test-demonstration
  farmer, was formerly as gullied as the other; two years of treatment with
  phosphate and lime have produced a cover which will prevent erosion.
  Photograph from Tennessee Valley Authority.
63 *Central Park, New York*
  Photograph taken about 1950 (Park Department, City of New York).
64 *White Throne, Zion National Park*
  Photograph by Marta Huth, 1949.

Introduction by Douglas H. Strong

We live in two environments: the natural one of plants, animals, soil, water, and air, and the conceptual one of our minds.[1] Our ideas have separated us from other species, allowing us to alter the entire planet and to have a major impact on the lives of other organisms. Hans Huth focused on our conceptions of the natural environment from colonial times to the first half of the twentieth century. His *Nature and the American,* written in the 1950s, is noted for its breadth and scholarship and remains important reading for those who wish to understand how our attitudes toward nature have evolved.

Huth was a scholar, not a polemicist or environmental activist. He revealed how a number of Americans aided a growing appreciation of nature through literature, science, recreational activities, landscape design, art, and public policy. His book reflects a broad education—and his personal interest in mountaineering. It also reflects his concern for aesthetic conservation, especially the preservation of scenic lands.

Born in Germany in 1892, Huth studied in Halle, Vienna, and Berlin, where he received his doctoral degree.[2] He pursued a career as a museum curator from 1924 to 1936 before emigrating to the United States. Here he became a consultant on museum projects for the National Park Service. During the service's move to temporary headquarters during World War II, Huth joined the Art Institute of Chicago. As curator of research, he wrote a number of books, pamphlets, and articles on the decorative arts and related topics.

In the early 1940s Huth began writing reports and pamphlets for the Park Service on such topics as the protection of monuments in wartime, the preservation of mountain culture in Great Smoky Mountain National Park, and plans for the Lincoln Museum in Washington. In 1950 he wrote a more ambitious study, "The American and Nature." What most concerned him was the national park system, "which has been created through local, state and federal initiative and which is now being maintained from coast to coast as an unrivalled adornment of the western hemisphere."[3] This paper became the basis for *Nature and the American.*

This introduction brings Huth's story up-to-date, focusing, as he did, on aesthetic conservation, while also demonstrating how America's involvement in conservation has become global.

EARLY CONSERVATION MOVEMENTS

Although George Perkins Marsh and other forerunners helped foster interest in conservation in the latter half of the nineteenth century, a national conservation policy did not appear until early in the twentieth. During the presidency of Theodore Roosevelt, scientists in government bureaus warned of depletion of the nation's timber and water supplies. This led to federal management of public lands based on the principle of wise, efficient, and equitable use. Gifford Pinchot, chief of the Forest Service, instituted a system of permits and fees based on principles of "wise use" and "multiple use." This first movement peaked at the Governors' Conference in 1908, at which Roosevelt spoke of the danger of exhaustion of natural resources and called conservation "the weightiest problem now before the Nation."[4]

This early conservation movement had limitations, both in terms of the amount of land under effective management and the success of the government's programs. For example, reclamation, although intended to aid the small farmer, resulted eventually in enormous public expenditures, ecological disturbances, and water subsidies for large landowners. On the other hand, Pinchot's regulated use of resources took root and remains today the guiding principle for the Forest Service and to a lesser degree for the Bureau of Land Management (BLM), which is more permissive in its land use policies.[5]

Though national interest in conservation lagged during the difficult years of World War I and the business-oriented 1920s, it revived in a second movement under the New Deal in the 1930s. Secretary of the Interior Harold Ickes blamed shortsighted and unchecked greed for "denuded forests, floods, droughts, a disappearing water table, erosion, a less stable and equable climate, a vanishing wildlife."[6] The Franklin D. Roosevelt administration successfully used conservation to encourage employment and economic recovery while providing lasting benefits for the nation by restoring the land. Soil conservation and reforestation became important priorities, and more land was set aside for wildlife, recreation, and aesthetic purposes.

The concept of multiple-purpose use of major rivers, fostered by the conservationists of the Progressive Era, was reactivated and put into practice. The Tennessee Valley Authority became a major social experiment in rejuvenating an impoverished region. The Bureau of Reclamation became the world's largest producer of electrical power through construction of Hoover, Grand Coulee, and other huge dams in the West. Under the Taylor Grazing Act, the federal government closed the public domain to further homesteading and set up a bureau to manage the rangelands.

Although New Deal programs helped encourage economic growth, they also inadvertently set the stage for many of the environmental problems that followed World War II. For instance, parts of the West developed too rapidly for their own good. Increased revenues led to the proliferation of dams and canals, many of which proved ill-planned or unnecessary (such as Glen Canyon on the Colorado River). Unexpected by-products resulted: siltation, salinization, water evaporation, as well as loss of aesthetic resources. Communities sprang up and grew rapidly, the demand for raw materials soared, and the ecological health of the land suffered.

POSTWAR PROSPERITY

Huth wrote in the 1950s, a time of optimism in the United States. Never had the nation experienced such affluence, and never had people seemed more able to exploit the bounty of the land. They had survived World War II and emerged the world's leader. The gross national product grew at an unprecedented rate. Prosperity appeared to have no limits.

Under the Eisenhower administration, Secretary of the Interior Douglas McKay promoted resource development through transfer of the public domain to private ownership. McKay spoke for many Americans of his generation when he stated, "It took human initiative and ingenuity which could prosper only under a free system to take hold and make something out of the land and its resources."[7] The federal government had already transferred over a billion acres to state governments, corporations, and private citizens. Why stop now?

However, there were dissenters even then. Harrison Brown, in *The Challenge of Man's Future* (1954), foresaw three possibilities: "reversion to agrarian existence," a "completely controlled, collectivized industrial society," or a "world-wide free industrial society in which human beings can live in reasonable harmony with their environment."[8] Although existing trends made adoption of the third option unlikely, Brown thought it possible. World population could be stabilized and a world community could be created "in which human beings can live comfortably and in peace with each other." But with the addition of each new mouth to feed, consumption of each new barrel of oil, and loss of each additional inch of topsoil, Brown saw the problems becoming more difficult to solve. He thought the United States—with its freedom, resources, and expertise—had a responsibility to help lead the world community in finding solutions to its problems.

Most Americans saw no option to the existing system; their livelihoods depended on it. America's economy had become large-scale: big government, big corporations, and big technology—all of which had a big impact on the environment. Government centralization, fostered by the New Deal and World War II, continued with the Cold War. High levels of government-business cooperation contributed to what President Eisenhower labeled the "military-industrial complex."

As Americans moved in growing numbers to the suburbs, they welcomed the construction of freeways and shopping centers. The federal government funded an interstate highway system but did not accept responsibility for controlling air and water pollution. Oligopolies came to dominate steel, oil, and automobile production. Advanced technology permitted construction of huge oil rigs, supertankers, and petrochemical plants. Consumers purchased television sets and used energy at a record rate. By the mid-1950s, the United States, with 6 percent of the world's population, produced almost half of its goods.

The result was pollution and the deterioration of the environment. Historian Elmo Richardson lamented that when Americans were confronted by an ecological crisis, "they had nothing more to draw upon to cope with that threat than the economic materialism, the bureaucratic inertia, and the political gamesmanship practiced by the men of the Truman-Eisenhower era."[9]

THE RISE OF THE ENVIRONMENTAL MOVEMENT

How, then, in the midst of such economic abundance and apparent lack of concern for conservation, did Americans launch the environmental movement of the 1960s and 1970s? Why did Congress support extensive environmental legislation, including Clean Water and Clean Air acts, the Wilderness Act, and the National Environmental Policy Act? When did all of this activity begin?

Historian Samuel P. Hays has suggested an evolutionary process with three overlapping stages. First, a concern for the protection of the natural environment developed from the late 1950s through the 1960s. Second, from the mid-1960s into the 1970s, there emerged an interest in controlling pollution, especially of the air and water. Third, in the early 1970s, a concern for human health arose, accompanied by a rise in nutritious diets, organic gardening, physical exercise, holistic medicine, and health warnings on tobacco products.[10]

The movement reached its peak in 1969–70 with Earth Day, the passage of the National Environmental Policy Act (NEPA), and creation of the Environmental Protection Agency (EPA). Earth Day (1970), celebrated on college campuses across the nation, proved a catalyst for environmental awareness and legislation. The NEPA required federal agencies to prepare statements indicating the effects on the environment for all federal projects that might have significant environmental consequences and to consider alternatives to mitigate damage. It also provided for a Council on Environmental Quality to advise the president. The regulation of environmental quality became institutionalized with the creation of the EPA. Several national leaders contributed to the movement, including Secretary of the Interior Stewart Udall, who called attention to the "quiet conservation crisis of the 1960s."

The earlier focus on wise use of resources became secondary to protecting the natural environment from the onslaught of runaway technology and population growth. The term *conservation* gave way to *environment*, reflecting a change in values from an earlier utilitarian concern for the efficient management of physical resources to a concern for environmental quality as it affected humans and other living things.

One can only guess why this vital but diversified movement appeared. Hays believes it reflected new values and a response to a new order of threats. Affluent Americans, better educated than earlier generations, wanted more than the necessities and conveniences that had satisfied their forefathers. Many Americans, with leisure time and the security of a dependable income, became concerned about the quality of their daily lives. They protested having chemicals dumped into waterways and the air, and were concerned about the threat of pollution to the health of their families and communities. They desired outdoor recreation in unsullied natural settings, urban neighborhoods with clean air and water, and a life of physical and mental wellness.

Many credit Rachel Carson with initiating the environmental movement. After a successful career as a marine biologist with the Fish and Wildlife Service and as author of the best-seller *The Sea around Us*, she became the unexpected crusader for controlled use of insecticides and herbicides. The "miracle" insecticide DDT had proved a godsend during World War II in the control of mosquitoes, lice, and other disease-carrying organisms; farmers, householders, and gardeners used increasing amounts in subsequent years. But the growing resistance of insects to the poison and the resurgence of pest populations caused alarm. In *Silent Spring* (1962), Carson asked how supposedly intelligent human beings could "seek to control a few unwanted species by a method that contaminated the entire environment and brought the threat of disease and death even to their own kind."[11]

Carson did not oppose the use of all insecticides. She argued instead for biological and cultural controls where possible and chemical poisons only in small quantities when needed. Noting that unknown millions of people, without their knowledge or consent, had been subjected to poisons, she said: "If the Bill of Rights contains no guarantee that a citizen shall be secure against lethal poisons distributed either by private individuals or by public officials, it is surely only because our forefathers, despite their considerable wisdom and foresight, could conceive of no such problem."[12]

Her book, which caused a storm of protest from the chemical industry and agribusiness, contributed to a near total ban on DDT in the United States. Other poisons took its place, however, and most Americans returned to a state of complacency, assuming that the federal government protected them from danger. No law prevented the sale of banned insecticides, including DDT, to developing countries. Carson's warning remains prophetic: "We still talk in terms of 'conquest'—whether it be of the insect world or of the myste-rious world of space. We still have not become mature enough to see our-selves as a very tiny part of a vast and incredible universe, a universe that is distinguished above all else by a mysterious and wonderful unity that we flout at our peril."[13]

Carson was not alone. René Dubos, a microbiologist, noted the arrogance and impracticability of those who proposed eliminating all insect pests and unwanted germs. Eradication, he explained, could not succeed; humans needed greater humility and acceptance of coexistence with nature—germs included. Disease could be minimized best by improving the quality of the environment.

In the 1956 presidential campaign Adlai Stevenson criticized atmo-spheric testing of nuclear devices. Among those providing information on the dangers of fallout and strontium 90 was biologist Barry Commoner. He argued that scientists had a responsibility to provide to the public the "neces-sary facts and the means for understanding them."[14] Public awareness of the danger of nuclear fallout helped lead to the Nuclear Test Ban Treaty of 1963, in which the Soviet Union and the United States agreed to stop nuclear atmospheric testing. This was one of the early victories in the effort to save the environment "from the blind assaults of modern technology."[15] Com-moner later became an outspoken critic of the nation's nuclear power plants, "in which the rewards have been private and the huge risks . . . have been as-signed to the public."[16]

Commoner blamed the environmental crisis on the "sweeping transfor-mation of productive technologies since World War II."[17] He criticized un-bridled capitalism and the pursuit of private gain that produced new prod-ucts—such as plastics and synthetic chemicals—that could not be assimilated into the natural cycles of the environment. The solution, he believed, rested in placing social goals before private profit.

Not everyone agreed with Commoner's assessment of the problem. Paul Ehrlich, a young Stanford biology professor, argued that the explosive growth of world population was at the root of the environmental crisis. In *The Population Bomb* (1968), he outlined a frightening scenario. World popu-lation, which had reached one billion by 1850, promised to surpass seven bil-lion by the end of the twentieth century. Clearly such rate of growth could not continue long without catastrophic results. Ehrlich called for an aggres-sive "family planning" movement and draconian measures if all else failed.

Another California biologist, Garrett Hardin, warned of the "tragedy of the commons," the tendency of many to procreate beyond reason and to use the environment for their short-run advantage. Hardin saw little hope in ap-pealing to people's sense of responsibility since the majority would continue to seek their own self-interest. His solution, roundly debated, was "mutual coercion, mutually agreed upon."[18]

Controversy also surrounded publication of a computer-based study, *The Limits to Growth* (1972), commissioned by the Club of Rome, an international group of prominent industrialists, economists, and scientists. A *Time* reporter outlined its projection of world trends:

> As industrialization grows, it voraciously consumes enormous amounts of resources. Resources become scarcer, forcing more and more capital to be spent on procuring raw materials, which leaves less and less money for investment in new plants and facilities. . . . Population outstrips food and industrial supplies. Investment in new equipment falls behind the rate of obsolescence, and the industrial base begins to collapse, carrying along with it the service and agricultural activities that have become dependent on industrial products (like medical equipment and fertilizers). Because of the lack of health services and food, the world's population dwindles rapidly.[19]

The authors called for a state of equilibrium with a stable population and minimal use of nonrenewable, pollution-creating resources.

Such a suggestion angered those who believed that human ingenuity and technical ability could resolve any problem. The 1970s witnessed a counterattack by industry. Corporate America promoted a campaign to encourage development and tried to blame long lines at gasoline pumps during the oil embargo of 1973–74 on the environmentalists. While media coverage of environmental issues declined markedly after 1970 and the popularity of environmentalism ebbed on college campuses, the commitment to environmental values continued to spread through many sectors of American society.

WILDERNESS PRESERVATION

Hans Huth made no mention of toxic chemicals, acid rain, and the threat of global warming, for they had yet to come to public notice when he wrote in the 1950s. What he did, in the concluding chapter of *Nature and the American*, was emphasize his central concern, aesthetic conservation. While his book was in press, Huth noted with hope a bill introduced by Senator Hubert Humphrey to establish a "National Wilderness Preservation System."

Wilderness had been set aside in the national forest as early as 1924 (see pages 204–6). But wilderness advocates worried that administrators could declassify such areas as quickly as they could create them. They desired more permanent protection from dams, mines, and logging operations. Encouraged by a series of wilderness conferences sponsored by the Sierra Club following World War II, Howard Zahnizer, executive director of the Wilderness Society, proposed wilderness legislation that was introduced into Congress in 1956.

This marked the beginning of a protracted struggle. Only after eight years of deliberation, more than sixty bills, and eighteen hearings was a much-amended measure approved. Part of the difficulty rested with lack of public understanding of wilderness, a problem solved in part by educational efforts of the Wilderness Society, Sierra Club, National Parks Association, and other citizen groups. Moreover, the Forest Service and Park Service, which administered most existing wilderness lands, were satisfied with their customary practices and saw no need for a statutory wilderness system. Chief Forester Richard E. McCardle complained that the National Wilderness Preservation bill "would strike at the heart of the multiple-use policy of national-forest administration."[20] The Park Service thought that wilderness classification by Congress would unduly limit its own freedom of action, especially in the development of recreational facilities.

Serious objections to a wilderness system came from resource users who would be excluded or restricted in their use of public lands. The American National Cattlemen's Association, American Mining Congress, and other associations vehemently protested the "lock-up" of lands, particularly in the West. They spoke of the need for continued economic growth and development of all resources to aid national defense. The president of the Utah Cattlemen's Association summarized the view of many when he stated, "This portion of the United States has been left in a wilderness condition altogether too long now and it didn't begin to fulfill its purpose until the hand of man and his ingenuity were brought to bear upon it."[21]

Wilderness advocates, bolstered by their impressive victory in protecting Dinosaur National Monument from a dam (see page 209), countered with arguments of their own. Many were influenced by the words of the naturalist, Aldo Leopold:

> Like winds and sunsets, wild things were taken for granted until progress began to do away with them. Now we face the question whether a still higher "standard of living" is worth its cost in things natural, wild, and free. For us of the minority, the opportunity to see geese is more important than television, and the chance to find a pasque-flower is a right as inalienable as free speech.[22]

In a similar vein, Zahniser wrote, "To know the wilderness is to know a profound humility, to recognize one's littleness, to sense dependence and interdependence, indebtedness, and responsibility."[23]

Others spoke of the right of nature to exist for its own sake; the value of protecting the stability of diverse environments; the economic contribution of watersheds, estuaries, and other protected areas; the need to maintain genetic diversity; the potential to develop drugs and medicines from the storehouse of plants and animals; and the right of future generations to experience and learn from wilderness. As Nancy Newhall stated succinctly, "Wilderness holds answers to more questions than we yet know how to ask."[24]

Under the Wilderness Act of 1964, Congress set aside 9.1 million acres of national forest, "an area where the earth and its community of life are untrammeled by man, where man himself is a visitor who does not remain."[25] Based on several compromises, the act allowed for "use of the land for mineral location and development and exploration, drilling, and production." Most important, no new wilderness areas could be established without an act of Congress. This necessitated a separate battle for each additional piece of land to be designated. Passage of the Wilderness Act, though a major milestone, left unanswered how much of the public lands would ultimately be included in the system.[26]

THE NATIONAL PARK SYSTEM

Creation of a wilderness preservation system came none too soon, as resource users whittled away at the untouched lands that remained. Fortunately, the park system had expanded rapidly during the era of Stephen Mather (see pages 196–99). Then in 1933 it had gained jurisdiction over national monuments (formerly under the War Department and the Forest Service), numerous battlefields, cemeteries, memorials, and sites in the nation's capital.

Many of these areas had been set aside under the Antiquities Act of 1906 that allowed the president to establish national monuments by proclamation. This meant that prehistoric, historic, and natural features could be preserved by the stroke of the president's pen without waiting for an act of Congress (as was needed for establishment of national parks). Intended initially to protect Indian ruins in the Southwest that were being vandalized, the act was soon used by presidents to protect much larger areas such as the Grand Canyon.

The 1930s, in spite of the Great Depression, proved a time of growth for the park system. Funding for New Deal agencies, such as the Civilian Conservation Corps, employed young men to construct campgrounds, trails, roads, and other improvements on public lands. With the support of a vigorous secretary of the interior, Harold Ickes, the Park Service grew substantially and helped to encourage state park systems. The Park Service also took increased interest in historic preservation.

World War II brought gas rationing, travel restrictions, and severe cuts in the budget for the parks. Timber interests coveted the Sitka spruce in Olympic National Park; mining companies, ranchers, and others pressed to open the parks to development; the military sought training grounds for its troops. The Park Service had its hands full to protect the parks' integrity.

Visitation to national parks, which hit a low point of six million in 1942, climbed rapidly after the war to thirty-three million in 1950 and seventy-two million in 1960.[27] With steady incomes, cheap available fuel, and leisure time, Americans flocked to the parks, catching the Park Service unprepared. Author Bernard DeVoto offered the provocative suggestion that Yosemite, Yellowstone, Grand Canyon, and Rocky Mountain national parks be closed until Congress appropriated sufficient funds for their protection. Congress responded with "Mission 66," a ten-year program (1956–66) to develop park roads, visitor centers, administrative buildings, and other facilities. The Forest Service, under similar presssure to upgrade its tourist facilities, launched "Operation Outdoors," a five-year development program.

The Park Service faced a "crisis in outdoor recreation." Tourist facilities could not keep pace with demand, and urban open space dwindled with unplanned sprawl. In response, Congress in 1958 established the Outdoor Recreation Resources Review Commission (ORRRC) to study the problems and make recommendations. The Commission's report stated that outdoor recreation would triple by the year 2000, criticized the lack of a national recreation policy, and called for special efforts to meet the needs of urbanites. Congress created the Bureau of Outdoor Recreation to formulate a nationwide outdoor recreation plan and to encourage federal, state, and regional cooperation.

The Park Service scrambled to add new parklands to meet the demand. Although no new large scenic park was added for over twenty years following creation of California's Kings Canyon National Park in 1940, the service did succeed in adding several new kinds of park units: parkways, seashores, lakeshores, scenic rivers, trails, and even areas for the performing arts. Parkways gave access to scenic and historic landscapes; the Blue Ridge stretched some 465 miles through the Appalachian Mountains, connecting Shenandoah and Great Smoky Mountain national parks. National seashores, often close to urban populations, served millions of people; visitation at Cape Cod soon equaled that at Yosemite and Yellowstone combined.

At a time of proliferating dams and reservoirs, Congress authorized protection of a few selected rivers "in a free-flowing condition" under the Wild and Scenic Rivers Act. Congress also initiated a national trails system, starting with the Appalachian and Pacific Crest trails. Lake Mead, behind Hoover Dam, became the nation's first national recreation area, serving hordes from California and the Southwest who sought opportunities to boat, swim, and camp. Responding to the recreational needs of city dwellers, Congress later created the Gateway and Golden Gate national recreation areas (in the vicinities of New York City and San Francisco, respectively), more than sixty thousand acres within a two-hour drive of the homes of some twenty million people.

The 1960s witnessed impressive growth of the park system. President Lyndon Johnson and Congress set aside major scenic parks, including Canyonlands, Redwood, and the North Cascades, and created more historic sites and recreational areas. The Land and Water Conservation Fund, collected in part from park entrance and permit fees, became the most important means of financing new state and federal parklands.

Park advocates had fought successfully to protect Dinosaur National Monument from dams in the 1950s; they faced another crisis in the Grand Canyon in the 1960s. Secretary of the Interior Stewart Udall announced plans to construct two dams as part of the Central Arizona Project. One would back water into Grand Canyon National Monument and a part of the national park, and the other would end the Colorado as a free-flowing river. National citizen conservation organizations, led by the Sierra Club, the Wilderness Society, and the Audubon Society, joined forces in an unprecedented crusade to lobby to "save Grand Canyon." Environmentalist David Brower argued effectively that the dams would actually waste water, a precious commodity in the arid Southwest. Dams already existed to impound runoff, and new dams would result in extensive evaporation and seepage into porous sandstone.

Brower refused to compromise when the government suggested constructing only one small dam. As he told the Secretary of the Interior, "Mr. Udall, you are not giving us anything that God didn't put there in the first place. . . . If there are no other ways to go about getting your water, I would still say that the compromise should not be made—that Arizona should be subsidized with something other than the world's Grand Canyon, or any part of it."[28] The administration belatedly recognized that the proposed dams were not needed; when Congress passed the $1.3 billion Colorado River bill in 1968, the dams were excluded.

The Park Service's increasing emphasis on recreation distressed many park advocates, and the 1960s became a period of soul-searching. Policies that had been applauded earlier no longer gained support. As one analyst noted, "The task for environmentalists became not so much one of guiding development into its proper locations but rather one of opposing development wherever it would take place at nature's expense."[29] Author Edward Abbey, a former park ranger, complained that a campground at Arches National Monument looked like a "suburban village." He added, "The automotive combine has almost succeeded in strangling our cities; we need not let it also destroy our national parks."[30]

The suburbanization of parts of the parks was unforeseen. At the time of its origins, the Park Service had been given a dual responsibility: "First, that the national parks must be maintained in absolutely unimpaired form for the use of future generations as well as those of our own time; second, that they are set apart for the use, observation, health, and pleasure of the people."[31] In the service's early years, Stephen Mather had promoted the parks to attract visitation and solicit appropriations from Congress. With the passage of time, no one needed to tell the public about the virtues of the parks. Tourists from home and abroad came in record numbers. Parks deteriorated from overuse as the Park Service added "improvements" to meet visitor demands. Critics complained that the service had lost its focus in assuming responsibility for such a diversity of areas (natural, historical, recreational) that served quite different publics. As a result, the protection of parks and wildlife underwent intensive review.

The most influential study, prepared by A. Starker Leopold and the Advisory Board on Wildlife Management, resulted from controversy surrounding predator control and the Park Service's killing of an overpopulation of elk in Yellowstone. Leopold went beyond such questions as how to eliminate surplus animals in a national park. He questioned the use of pesticides, artificial feeding of elk and bears, and suppression of naturally occurring fires.

During the first forty years of their existence, national parks had served as game refuges, protecting animals from hunters and fire. Protection alone no longer sufficed; maintenance of habitat became recognized as the key to wildlife protection. The "Leopold Report" recommended to the Park Service "that it recognize the enormous complexity of ecologic communities and the diversity of management procedures required to preserve them." Further, it recommended that the service maintain or, where necessary, recreate conditions that "prevailed when the area was first visited by the white man." A park, according to the report, should be a "vignette of primitive America."[32] Such a policy called for personnel trained in the biological sciences.

Restoring the "primitive scene" would be difficult at best. Human use of the land over generations, introduction of exotic plants and animals, and other changes made it impossible to return to the original landscape. To recreate "a reasonable illusion of primitive America" would entail careful research and active management of parklands. For instance, Leopold called for control of grazing animals at a level that would assure the good health of the soil, vegetation, and animals of the range. He questioned the "mass application of insecticides in the control of forest insects."

He also advocated the use of controlled burning where the Park Service had overprotected the land from natural ground fires. In the groves of giant sequoias on the western slope of the Sierra Nevada, for example, older trees became endangered from abnormal accumulation of fuel around the base of their trunks, and sequoia seeds rarely germinated in areas choked with vegetation. Periodic fires cleared the debris, solving both problems.[33] Later studies reinforced Leopold's report. The ecologist F. Fraser Darling and geographer Noel D. Eichhorn, for example, stated that the one administrative principle should be "to consider first the ecological health of a park so that it shall endure for posterity."[34]

The Park Service faced a time of changing environmental attitudes, values, and policies. Should it continue its effort to accommodate visitors, a policy since the days of Stephen Mather? Should acquisition and protection of the finest scenic areas remain its chief goal? How should the Park Service meet the needs of the majority of Americans who lived in cities? These and other questions troubled service leaders.

With the new emphasis on the ecological health of parklands, the Park Service had to reconsider its definition of a national park. It wished to go beyond the "crown jewels" of scenic western parks and preserve representative samples of the diverse physiographic regions and ecosystems in the country, such as grasslands. Under new criteria outlined in the 1972 *National Park System Plan,* the service identified regions that had long been neglected for park purposes—such as the Gulf Coastal Plain, the Central Lowlands, and the Appalachian Plateau. Representative Phillip Burton of California, without much concern for the Park Service's idea of park quality or its desire to slow down and consolidate management of existing parklands, pushed an omnibus bill through Congress in 1978. It added numerous units to the park system, appropriated substantial funds for urban recreational purposes, and created a system of national historic trails. By pleasing as many members of Congress as possible, Burton's "park barrel bill" succeeded where less ambitious expansion proposals had failed.

Then, in 1980, President Jimmy Carter "consummated the greatest single act of wilderness preservation in world history."[35] He signed the Alaska National Interest Lands Conservation Act, protecting 104 million acres, an area larger than California. In one step, Congress more than doubled the area within the National Park and Wildlife Refuge systems and more than tripled the size of the National Wilderness system.

The federal government, which owned nearly all of Alaska when it became a state in 1959, had been generous in granting land and mineral royalties to the state government and land and cash claims to the native population. With similar generosity, under section 17(d)(2) of the 1971 Alaska Native Claims Settlement Act, the secretary of the interior could consider up to eighty million acres of unreserved land for addition to the nation's Park, Forest, Wildlife Refuge, and Wild and Scenic River systems. When Alaska's senators protested the "lockup" of resources and Congress failed to act by a 1978 deadline, Carter used the Antiquities Act to set aside fifty-six million acres of national monuments in Alaska. He also directed the withdrawal of millions of acres for wildlife refuges and the protection of extensive national forest land from mineral claims. Such bold action temporarily protected most of the lands that preservationists wished to save. The Alaskan Coalition, which became "the largest and most powerful citizen conservation organization in American history," representing some fifteen hundred associations and perhaps ten million members, rallied to the cause.[36]

When Ronald Reagan won the 1980 presidential election in a landslide, the environmentalists compromised with energy and development interests to gain congressional approval of legislation that Carter could sign before he left office. In the compromise, environmentalists gave up extensive acreage of proposed wilderness, accepted extensive logging in the Tongass National Forest, and left the door open for possible oil and gas exploration in the Arctic Wildlife Range. What they gained, however, was far greater. The new national park lands, according to Congressman Morris Udall, offered "the full range of nature and history in Alaska, mighty land forms and entire ecosystems of naturally occurring geologic and geomorphic processes, intricate water forms and spectacular shorelines, majestic peaks and gentle valleys, diverse plant communities and equally diverse fish and wildlife."[37]

While park advocates rested after the Alaska battle, the Park Service issued a major report, *State of the Parks 1980*, the first servicewide survey of the "threats that endanger the natural and cultural resources of the parks." Based on a questionnaire distributed to every unit in the system, the study noted that more than half the threats "were attributed to sources or activities located *external* to the parks."[38] Industrial and commercial projects and air pollution emissions presented the most common problems. For instance, expanding urban development encroached on Harper's Ferry, air pollution from pulp and paper mills descended on Olympic National Park, and industrial plants and nuclear power plant construction infringed on the Indiana Dunes National Lakeshore. "Simply stated," the report concluded, "the current levels of science and resource management activities are completely inadequate to cope effectively with the broad spectrum of threats and problems."[39]

Park Service jurisdiction ended at park boundaries. How could the service block drilling on geothermal lands of the Forest Service not far from the Old Faithful geyser basin? What could be done about acid rain in Great Smoky Mountain National Park? And how could the ecosystem of the Everglades be maintained when its natural flow of water was diverted for urban and agricultural uses? The passage of the National Environmental Policy Act and the Endangered Species, Clean Air, Clean Water and other acts provided at least some avenues by which to address these kinds of problems. But the Park Service had no solutions to the myriad problems it faced as the twentieth century was drawing to a close.

Reporter Robert Cahn, in assessing prospects for the future, stated, "What I see as the conservation challenge of the '80s is to reshape our attitudes and values and our practical approaches in such a way that we can live in an era of scarcity without ruining the life systems on which we depend."[40] Speaking of the contribution of the national parks, he argued:

Conditions in the national parks provide an early warning signal that can alert the nation to what may be happening to the natural environment as a whole. They are also the nation's best indicator of what can be called its environmental ethic. They provide a measure of the willingness of today's citizens to adhere to a set of values that includes not only appreciation of the nation's natural and cultural heritage, but a desire to share it with others and leave it unharmed for future generations.[41]

CONSERVATION IN THE 1980s

The election of Ronald Reagan initiated an acrimonious debate over the national parks and public land policies. With an optimism that was appealing to the nation's voters, Reagan pledged to "take government off the people's backs and turn the great genius of the American people loose once again."[42] To strengthen the economy, he gave private interests greater freedom to develop the land as they saw fit. The Reagan administration appointed policymakers with strong ties to extractive industries, reduced environmental standards and regulations, drove many conservation-oriented people from public service, and used the Office of Management and Budget to control the actions and policies of federal environmental agencies. When environmentalists protested, they found the doors of federal agencies closed to them.

Many protests centered on the actions of James Watt, Reagan's secretary of the interior. Watt had advocated development of public lands as director of the Mountain States Legal Foundation. He angered environmentalists in his first months in office when he proposed a speedup of mineral and oil leasing, slowed efforts to protect endangered species, advocated a severe cutback in funding for new national parks, proposed transfer of some urban national parks to the states, and argued for opening many wilderness areas to commercial use. His support of offshore drilling alienated coastal dwellers. He offended others by softening regulations for strip-mining companies, and leading a personal crusade to open vast stretches of the public lands to development.

Congress and public opinion blunted Watt's efforts. Even the "Sagebrush Rebellion," an effort by residents of several western states to gain control of public lands, proved short-lived. Leaders of the "rebellion," supported by corporate interests, argued that the extensive federal lands ought to belong to the states (where they could more easily pass into private ownership). Environmentalists counterattacked, warning of a steal of public lands. Support came from many westerners, including hunters and fishermen, who feared that lands open under federal control would be closed under state or private ownership. Reagan criticized these "environmental extremists," but his administration backed away from the transfer or sale of public lands and instead favored easing federal land use restrictions. Watt failed to build the political support he needed and had to leave office after a series of public gaffes.

Ironically, Watt's policies sparked action by citizen groups who were worried that the environmental progress of the previous two decades might be lost. Membership and financial contributions to citizen environmental associations climbed rapidly. Older, well-established groups, such as the Sierra Club, the National Wildlife Federation, and the Audubon Society flourished. The Natural Resources Defense Council and Environmental Defense Fund brought litigation to curb unwarranted assaults on the environment. Greenpeace and Earth First! used more direct action methods to influence the public. Others focused on lobbying or, like the League of Conservation Voters, told voters about the environmental records of candidates.

But the greatest activity took place at the local level, where thousands of grassroots organizations worked to prevent unwanted development and pollution. Dangers, such as toxic chemicals discovered at Love Canal in New York, aroused housewives and others whose homes and communities were threatened. As Samuel Hays stated, "People thought of environmental quality in terms of where they lived or worked or engaged in recreation."[43]

THE GLOBAL ENVIRONMENT

Although the grassroots movement helped solve local problems, Americans came increasingly to recognize that their desire for a better life also depended on protecting the global environment. The beginnings of international concern for conservation date back to the late nineteenth century, but little resulted until after World War II. Then the International Union for Conservation of Nature and Natural Resources (IUCN), created in 1948, played a leading role in encouraging global discussions. In 1960 its General Assembly concluded "that the accelerated rate of destruction of wildlife and habitat in Africa was the most urgent problem requiring concerted international effort." Formation of the World Wildlife Fund the following year aided efforts to protect endangered species. Concern about worldwide destruction of the "natural heritage" of nations extended to national parks, wilderness areas, wildlife preserves, and "to the few remaining places where the intrinsic values of natural environment, contemplation and a complete break with the rush of mid-20th century living is [sic] still possible."[44]

In Seattle in 1962, the United States hosted the First World Conference on National Parks, a meeting to encourage international understanding and support for the parks movement. Stewart Udall, who gave the keynote speech, called for a "Common Market of conservation knowledge and endeavor."[45] Ten years later, delegates from more than eighty nations met in Yellowstone to commemorate its centennial—the world's first national park. They could take heart that the park movement had spread to more than twelve hundred separate parks and reserves globally.

When the World Congress on National Parks met in Bali, Indonesia, in 1982, the delegates called for a global network of national parks and protected areas to cover all ecological regions on earth.[46] The network already included such outstanding natural areas as Australia's Great Barrier Reef, Africa's Serengeti Plain, the Soviet Union's Lake Baikal, and Venezuela's Angel Falls, as well as exceptional cultural sites such as the ruins of Angkor in Cambodia and the Mayan ruins at Tikal in Guatemala. The Swedish zoologist Kai Curry-Lindahl remarked, "The values of a global network of ecosystems preserved by national parks are manifold, but the most important one is that they will help man understand his environment and provide clues to ecological problems whose solutions may aid posterity instead of leading to disaster."[47]

International concern went far beyond national parks. The United Nations Conference on the Human Environment in Stockholm (1972) focused global attention on the need "to define what should be done to maintain the earth as a place suitable for human life."[48] The conference's report, *Only One Earth*, stated, "As we enter the global phase of human evolution it becomes obvious that each man has two countries, his own and the planet Earth."[49] Subsequent UN-sponsored meetings followed, and the United Nations Environment Programme carried on the work started in Stockholm. But as British economist Barbara Ward observed, the actions of governments rarely matched their promises.

Although the United States and other rich nations criticized developing nations for runaway population growth and waste, Ward offered a different perspective:

The peoples of North America, Japan, Britain, and the rest of Western Europe make up, together with a few oil states, the great majority of the world's rich citizens. Ours is the responsibility for the present appallingly skewed distribution of resources. The richest 20 percent, largely living in the West, have three-quarters of the wealth. The remaining three and a half billion of our fellow citizens must make do with the last quarter that remains.[50]

The problem was how to reconcile the desire of the rich countries to maintain the advantages they had already acquired and the need of the poor nations for economic development. Shortly before his death in 1965, Adlai Stevenson addressed the issue eloquently:

We travel together, passengers in a little spaceship, dependent upon its vulnerable reserves of air and soil; all committed for our safety to its security and peace; preserved from annihilation only by the care, the work and, I will say, the love we give our fragile craft. We cannot maintain it half fortunate, half miserable, half confident, half despairing, half slave to the ancient enemies of man, half free in a liberation of resources undreamed of until this day. No craft, no crew can travel safely with such vast contradictions. On their resolution depends the survival of us all.[51]

Poor people, seeking to survive, cut down trees, overgrazed grasslands, plowed marginal land, and crowded into congested cities. Rich people, seeking to enhance their standard of living, used new technologies that left a residue of toxic chemicals and waste in the biosphere. Each nation, rich and poor, sought its own survival and prosperity with limited concern for its neighbors.

Assessments of the deteriorating situation varied widely. At the beginning of the 1980s, the United States issued *The Global 2000* Report to the President, the first federal study of global environmental conditions. It concluded: "If present trends continue, the world in 2000 will be more crowded, more polluted, less stable ecologically, and more vulnerable to disruption than the world we live in now. Serious stresses involving population, resources, and environment are clearly visible ahead. Despite greater material output, the world's people will be poorer in many ways than they are today."[52] In contrast, Julian Simon and Herman Kahn wrote in *The Resourceful Earth: A Response to Global 2000:* "We are confident that the nature of the physical world permits continued improvement in humankind's economic lot in the long run, indefinitely."[53] Who was correct, and how could experts so disagree? The debate continued.

Following a request from the General Assembly of the United Nations, the World Commission on Environment and Development issued *Our Common Future* (1987), a vision of earth as seen by astronauts:

> From space, we see a small and fragile ball dominated not by human activity and edifice but by a pattern of clouds, oceans, greenery, and soils. Humanity's inability to fit its doings into that pattern is changing planetary systems, fundamentally. Many such changes are accompanied by life-threatening hazards. This new reality, from which there is no escape, must be recognized—and managed.[54]

The Commission, with representatives from the United States and twenty other nations throughout the world, pondered how to deal with such recent events as the leak from a Union-Carbide pesticide plant in Bhopal, India, that killed over two thousand people and injured or blinded more than two hundred thousand; a drought-triggered crisis in Africa that affected some thirty-five million people, killing perhaps one million; a nuclear reaction explosion at Chernobyl in the Soviet Union whose nuclear fallout swept around the globe; and the poisoning of the Rhine after a warehouse fire in Switzerland released chemicals, solvents, and mercury. In developing countries, in less than three years, diarrheal diseases caused by bad drinking water and malnutrition resulted in the death of perhaps sixty million people (mainly children). Beyond immediate problems loomed global challenges for the twenty-first century—desertification of productive farmland, destruction of forests in the tropics and elsewhere, acid rain falling far from its place of origin, global warming from the burning of fossil fuels, depletion of the planet's protective ozone layer from various industrial gases, nuclear winter.

Some blamed global military expenditures, which had reached one trillion dollars annually and consumed income needed for other purposes. President Eisenhower, a generation earlier, had recognized the problem: "Every gun that is made, every warship launched, every rocket fired signifies, in the final sense, a theft from those who hunger and are not fed, those who are cold and are not clothed. This world in arms is not spending money alone. It is spending the sweat of its laborers, the genius of its scientists, the hopes of its children."[55]

More recently, Lester Brown of the Worldwatch Institute stated that global military expenditures "exceeded the incomes of the poorest half of humanity." Weapons research alone, employing more than half a million scientists, cost more than what was spent "on developing new energy technologies, improving human health, raising agricultural productivity, and controlling population."[56]

Many Americans began to question the relative merits of expenditures for military security versus environmental security. As the World Commission pointed out, global military spending in the mid-1980s of $2.5 billion *daily* could be directed to other purposes. A plan to save the tropical forests, for example, would cost $1.3 billion annually—equivalent to a half-day of military expenditures; contraceptives for all women desiring family planning and not yet receiving it would cost an additional $1 billion annually—equivalent to ten hours of military spending.[57] As one critic stated caustically, "Military bands cost more than the appropriations for the Peace Corps."[58]

Recognizing that present trends left "increasing numbers of people poor and vulnerable, while at the same time degrading the environment," the World Commission asked, "How can such development serve next century's world of twice as many people relying on the same environment?"[59] The key was "sustainable development." This would depend on better management of technology and social organization, greater equity in sharing global resources, effective citizen participation in decision making, a harmonious balance between population and the resource base, and living within the planet's ecological means. The Commission concluded:

> sustainable development is not a fixed state of harmony, but rather a process of change in which the exploitation of resources, the direction of investments, the orientation of technological development, and institutional change are made consistent with future as well as present needs. We do not pretend that the process is easy or straightforward. Painful choices have to be made. Thus, in the final analysis, sustainable development must rest on political will.[60]

In a series of annual volumes entitled *State of the World,* Lester Brown and the Worldwatch Institute warned that an expanding global economy, based on cheap energy and advancing technology, undermined the natural resource base on which all people depend. For example, acidity in the soil may have no apparent harmful effect until it passes a certain threshold—then certain species die. Many scientists warned of an irreversible climatic change if carbon dioxide doubles in the atmosphere. In brief, the earth's biological systems were becoming less able to support themselves. "Once the sustainable yield threshold is crossed," Brown stated, "further population growth has a double-edged effect, simultaneously expanding demand and reducing the supply."[61] The Sumerian civilization in Mesopotamia, the Mayan civilization in Guatemala, among others, may have been early victims of the surpassing of such thresholds.

At the same time Brown noted that "every threat to sustainability has been successfully addressed by at least a few countries."[62] He told of growing international cooperation and the sharing of information. For instance, the international scientific community proposed a "Global Change" program to study the physical, chemical, and biological processes that support life on earth. The estimated cost of this vital program would equal ten hours of global military expenditures.

The United States could play a vital role in such programs, if it reevaluated its priorities and if it had the political will. The nation's need for a consistent policy on family planning was a case in point. For years its leaders supported the United Nations Fund for Population Activities and the International Planned Parenthood Federation. Then the Reagan administration withdrew support. This action puzzled recipients, for reduced family planning led to more unwanted children and more abortions. Population growth also led to greater poverty, starvation, instability, illegal immigration, and environmental deterioration. An ideologically based policy, using the argument that "free enterprise is the best contraceptive," failed to respond to the realities of life in poor nations. Education and economic opportunities for women, parental expectations of survival of children, among other things, could significantly aid in reducing the size of families.

At the end of the 1980s, it was difficult for Americans to avoid thinking about global environmental concerns. *Time, Newsweek,* and *National Geographic* ran feature articles on the plight of planet earth. *Time* senior editor Thomas Sancton placed responsibility on a personal level:

No attempt to protect the environment will be successful in the long run unless ordinary people—the California housewife, the Mexican peasant, the Soviet factory worker, the Chinese farmer—are willing to adjust their life-styles. Our wasteful, careless ways must become a thing of the past. We must recycle more, procreate less, turn off our lights, use mass transit, do a thousand things differently in our everyday lives. We owe this not only to ourselves and our children but also to the unborn generations who will one day inherit the earth.[63]

Everyone's behavior needed reassessment. As California ecologist Raymond Dasmann confessed, "I am a gasoline junky still, although I know it is not right that I should be burning up the highways going from here to there, but it is hard to kick the habit."[64] Conservationists, like their neighbors, consumed more energy and resources than the global ecosystem could sustain.

Corporations had a more obvious impact on the environment. In 1989 news reached Americans of a mammoth oil spill in Alaska when the oil tanker *Exxon Valdez* ran aground, blackening hundreds of miles of shoreline and killing countless birds, fish, and marine mammals. Shortly before, the Argentine ship *Bahía Paraíso* had sunk off the Antarctic coast, fouling a rookery of Adelie penguins. No place was safe. Following public outrage over the oil spills, pollster Louis Harris suggested that in the nineties the United States might have a president "chosen and elected with a pro-environment stance as his primary identification."[65] Certainly politicians in Europe were scrambling to embrace the environmental cause as voters supported "green" candidates.

The 1990s hold both promise and a sense of foreboding. Donella Meadows, one of the authors of *Limits to Growth,* spoke candidly:

I don't know if we are running into the limits to growth, or if they are still ahead, or if we have surpassed them and are only now getting signals that we have gone too far. No one knows. The only certainty is that we are closer to them than we used to be. The global warming, the dying trees, the polluted waters are not a surprise, not bad luck, not minor inconveniences that can be quickly fixed. They are powerful lessons about how a finite planet responds to a species that refuses to set its own limits.

That is our choice—to set our own limits rather than have the planet set them for us. A good way to start would be by questioning our vague sacrosanct goal of growth. Growth of what? For whom? For how long? At what cost? Paid by whom? Paid when?[66]

Dasmann noted that people had once lived in harmony with the local ecosystem on which they depended, but today, "biosphere people" utilize resources far from their shores.[67] For example, "Oil from Saudi Arabia fuels the machines and makes the fertilizers and pesticides which allow marginal land in West Africa to grow a crop of cocoa for Switzerland to make into chocolate which is flown on American-made airplanes to Singapore for distribution in Southeast Asia."[68] Dasmann called for greater local and regional self-sufficiency and an end to destructive "exploitation of other people, places, and living communities."[69]

The ecologist Marston Bates, like Hans Huth, believed that attitudes influence our behavior toward the land. As Bates argued, "It is through his
ideas that man has shifted from being just one more species in a biological
community into becoming a sort of geological force, altering the whole sur-
face of the planet and affecting one way or another the lives of all other organisms." Bates saw room for hope: "Our very survival is threatened by the
consequences of some of our ideas. But if we made them, can't we change
them? All we need are some good ideas, and if we are half as clever as we like
to think we are, this should be possible."[70]

Huth ends *Nature and the American* by stressing the importance of "the
mind and the way we have trained it to be receptive to the beauties and
wonders of God's creation." Herein lies our future. Will we view the planet as
an irreplaceable ecosystem in need of protection from our expanding population and the effects of our technology? Or will we continue down a path of
procrastination, enjoying the fruits of nature's bounty today while leaving to
our children the consequences of our folly? Such concerns grow naturally
out of those of Hans Huth and reveal the continuing relevance of *Nature and
the American* to our own day.

Notes

1. The term *conceptual environment* was coined by Marston Bates in *The Human Environment,* Horace M. Albright Conservation Lectureship (University of California
School of Forestry, 1962), pp. 8–9. The author is grateful to Thomas R. Cox, Maxine
and Michael McCloskey, Alfred Runte, and several friends and family members who
read an earlier draft of this chapter and offered helpful suggestions for revision.

2. Biographical material was obtained from Eileen Harakal, executive director of
public affairs, Art Institute of Chicago.

3. Hans Huth, "The American and Nature," *Journal of the Warburg and Courtland Institutes* 13 (1950): 149.

4. *Proceedings of a Conference of Governors in the White House, Washington, D.C., May
13–15, 1908* (Washington: Government Printing Office, 1909), p. 3.

5. Formed in 1946 when the Grazing Service and General Land Office merged, the
BLM gained its multiple use, sustained yield guidelines under the Federal Land Policy
and Management Act of 1976. The BLM and the Forest Service administer the largest
areas of federal lands.

6. Harold L. Ickes, *The New Democracy* (New York: W. W. Norton, 1934), p. 19.

7. Gladwin Hill, "M'Kay Emphasizes U.S. Lands Policy," *New York Times,* November
3, 1953; sec. 1, p. 25.

8. Harrison Brown, *The Challenge of Man's Future* (New York: Viking Press, 1954), p.
264.

9. Elmo Richardson, *Dams, Parks and Politics* (Lexington: The University of Kentucky Press, 1973), p. 201.

10. Samuel P. Hays, "From Conservation to Environment: Environmental Politics

in the United States since World War II," *Environmental Review* 6 (Fall 1982): 14–41, and Hays, *Beauty, Health, and Permanence: Environmental Politics in the United States, 1955–1985* (Cambridge: Cambridge University Press, 1987), pp. 52–62.

11. Rachel Carson, *Silent Spring* (Boston: Houghton Mifflin, 1962), p. 8.

12. Carson, pp. 12–13.

13. Rachel Carson, "Of Man and the Stream of Time," graduation address delivered at Scripps College, Claremont, Calif., 1962, p. 8.

14. Barry Commoner, "The Fallout Problem," *Science* 127 (May 2, 1958): 1025.

15. Barry Commoner, *The Closing Circle* (New York: Alfred A. Knopf, 1971), p. 56.

16. Barry Commoner, *The Poverty of Power* (New York: Alfred A. Knopf, 1976), p. 112.

17. Commoner, *The Closing Circle*, pp. 12, 177.

18. Garrett Hardin, "The Tragedy of the Commons," *Science* 162 (December 13, 1968): 1247.

19. "The Worst Is Yet to Be?" *Time* 99 (January 24, 1972): 32.

20. U.S. Congress, Senate Committee on Interior and Insular Affairs, *National Wilderness Preservation Act, Hearings on S. 1176*, 85th Cong., 1st sess., June 19–20, 1957, p. 93.

21. U.S. Congress, Senate Committee on Interior and Insular Affairs, *National Wilderness Preservation Act, Hearings on S. 4028*, 85th Cong., 2d sess., November 12, 1958, p. 755.

22. Aldo Leopold, *A Sand County Almanac* (New York: Oxford University Press, 1949), p. vii.

23. Howard Zahniser, "The Need of Wilderness Areas," *Living Wilderness* 21 (Winter–Spring 1956–57): 40.

24. Ansel Adams and Nancy Newhall, *This Is the American Earth* (San Francisco: Sierra Club, 1960), p. 62.

25. *United States Statutes at Large*, 78: 891.

26. Twenty-five years later, to the surprise of many, the wilderness system had expanded to include 474 units covering 91 million acres of federal land, including 57 million acres in Alaska. "The Power of Wilderness," *Los Angeles Times*, April 16, 1989. BLM lands offer the best opportunity for wilderness expansion in the 1990s.

27. *The National Parks: Shaping the System* (Washington, D.C.: U.S. Department of the Interior, National Park Service, 1985), p. 42.

28. "Regional Disputes, Lobbying Shape Colorado River Bill," *Congressional Quarterly Weekly Report*, no. 44 (November 1, 1968), p. 3024.

29. Ronald A. Foresta, *America's National Parks and Their Keepers* (Washington, D.C.: Resources for the Future, 1984), p. 61.

30. Edward Abbey, *Desert Solitaire* (New York: Ballantine, 1968), pp. 51, 59.

31. *Report of the Secretary of the Interior, 1918*, 65th Cong., 3d sess., H. Doc. 1455, p. 110.

32. "Report of the Advisory Board on Wildlife Management," *National Parks Magazine* 37 (April 1963): special insert, II, III.

33. The policy of allowing natural fires to burn did not always meet with public understanding or acceptance, witness the Yellowstone fires of 1988.

34. F. Fraser Darling and Noel D. Eichhorn, *Man and Nature in the National Parks:*

Reflections of Policy, 2d ed. (Washington, D. C.: Conservation Foundation, 1969), p. 35.

35. Roderick Nash, *Wilderness and the American Mind*, 3d ed. (New Haven: Yale University Press, 1982), p. 272.

36. Nash, p. 299.

37. *Alaska: Administrative History, The National Park Service and the Alaska National Lands Conservation Act of 1980* (U.S. Department of the Interior, National Park Service, 1985), p. 239.

38. *State of the Parks: A Report to Congress* (U.S. Department of the Interior, National Park Service, 1980), pp. vii, viii.

39. *State of the Parks*, p. 36.

40. Robert Cahn, *The Conservation Challenge of the 80s*, Horace M. Albright Conservation Lectureship (University of California, College of Natural Resources, Department of Forestry and Resource Management, 1980), p. 2.

41. Robert Cahn, "Quelling the Storm: What It Will Take," *Christian Science Monitor*, June 18, 1982, p. 12.

42. C. Brant Short, *Ronald Reagan and the Public Lands: America's Conservation Debate, 1979–1984* (College Station: Texas A & M University Press, 1989), p. 42.

43. Hays, *Beauty, Health, and Permanence*, p. 529.

44. *IUCN Bulletin*, New Series, No. 1 (August 1961), pp. 1, 2.

45. *First World Conference on National Parks* (Washington, D.C.: U.S. Department of the Interior, National Park Service, 1962), p. 8.

46. Jeffrey A. McNeely and Kenton R. Miller, eds., *National Parks, Conservation, and Development: The Role of Protected Areas in Sustaining Society* (Washington, D.C.: Smithsonian Institution Press, 1984), p. 761. UNESCO, under its Man and Biosphere Program, had established a network of global ecosystems for study; it also sponsored the Convention for the Conservation of the World Cultural and Natural Heritage.

47. Kai Curry-Lindahl, *The Global Role of National Parks for the World of Tomorrow*, Horace M. Albright Conservation Lectureship (University of California School of Forestry and Conservation, 1974), p. 15.

48. Barbara Ward and René Dubos, *Only One Earth* (New York: Ballantine, 1972), p. xiii.

49. Ward and Dubos, p. xviii.

50. Barbara Ward, "A Decade of Environmental Action," *Environment* 24 (May 1982), pp. 4–5.

51. Hugh Nash, ed., *Progress As If Survival Mattered* (San Francisco: Friends of the Earth, 1977), p. 11.

52. *The Global 2000 Report to the President*, vol. 1 (Washington, D.C.: Government Printing Office, 1980), p. 1.

53. Julian L. Simon and Herman Kahn, eds., *The Resourceful Earth: A Response to Global 2000* (Oxford, England: Basil Blackwell, 1984), p. 3.

54. World Commission on Environment and Development, *Our Common Future* (Oxford: Oxford University Press, 1987), p. 1.

55. Nash, *Progress As If Survival Mattered*, p. 274.

56. Lester Brown, *State of the World 1986* (New York: W. W. Norton, 1986), pp. 196, 199.

57. World Commission, *Our Common Future*, p. 303.

58. "The Economy: Hangover from a Spending Spree," *The Washington Spectator* 13 (June 1, 1987): 1.

59. World Commission, *Our Common Future*, p. 4.

60. *Our Common Future*, p. 9.

61. Lester Brown, "Crossing the Threshold," *Environment* 21 (October 1979): 13.

62. Quoted in A. Kent MacDougall, "Worldwatch Spotlights Future Ecological Crises," *Los Angeles Times*, July 14, 1985, sec. 5, p. 1.

63. Thomas A. Sancton, "What on Earth Are We Doing?" *Time* 133 (January 2, 1989): 30. See also William F. Allman, "Rediscovering Planet Earth," *U.S. News and World Report* 105 (October 31, 1988): 56–68; *National Geographic* 174 (December 1988): 766–945; and *Scientific American* 261 (September 1989): 46–174.

64. Raymond Dasmann, *The Threatened World of Nature*, Horace M. Albright Lectureship (University of California, College of Natural Resources, Department of Forestry and Conservation, 1976), p. 6.

65. Kevin Phillips, "The Green Wave to Meet a World of Poison," *Los Angeles Times*, May 21, 1989, sec. 5, p. 1.

66. Donella H. Meadows, "Futures Terrible and Terrific," *Los Angeles Times*, January 29, 1989, sec. 5, p. 1.

67. Dasmann, *The Threatened World of Nature*, p. 6.

68. Jeffrey A. McNeely, *National Parks*, p. 2.

69. Dasmann, *The Threatened World of Nature*, p. 9.

70. Bates, *The Human Environment*, p. 9.

Selected Bibliography

Literature on the environment since World War II is vast. Only a few references useful to this chapter are mentioned here. Valuable bibliographies include Ronald J. Fahl, *North American Forest and Conservation History: A Bibliography* (Santa Barbara, Calif.: ABC-Clio Press, 1977), and Mary Anglemyer and Eleanor R. Seagraves, *The Natural Environment: An Annotated Bibliography on Attitudes and Values* (Washington, D.C.: Smithsonian Institution Press, 1984).

Two excellent environmental anthologies, representing viewpoints in the 1960s and 1980s respectively, are Paul Shepard and Daniel McKinley, eds., *The Subversive Science: Essays toward an Ecology of Man* (Boston: Houghton Mifflin, 1969), and Donald Worster, ed., *The Ends of the Earth: Perspectives on Modern Environmental History* (Cambridge: Cambridge University Press, 1988). Biographical sketches of environmentalists are contained in Paul Brooks, *Speaking for Nature* (San Francisco: Sierra Club Books, 1980), and Douglas H. Strong, *Dreamers and Defenders: American Conservationists* (Lincoln: University of Nebraska Press, 1988).

Several books and articles on wilderness, wildlife, and the national parks are illuminating: Roderick Nash, *Wilderness and the American Mind*, 3d ed. (New Haven: Yale University Press, 1982); David Brower, ed., *Wildlands in Our Civilization* (San Francisco: Sierra Club, 1964); John Ise, *Our National Parks: A Critical History* (Baltimore: Johns Hopkins, 1961); Dyan Zaslowsky, *These American Lands: Parks, Wilderness, and the Public Lands* (New York: Henry Holt and Co., 1986); Thomas R. Dunlap, *Saving America's Wildlife* (Princeton: Princeton University Press, 1988); Joseph L. Sax, *Mountains without Handrails: Reflections on the National Parks* (Ann Arbor: University of Michigan Press, 1980); Robert Cahn, "Our National Parks," a five-part series in the *Christian Science Monitor*, beginning June 14, 1982; Ronald A. Foresta, *America's National Parks and Their Keepers* (Washington, D.C.: Resources for the Future, 1984); *National Parks for a New Generation: Vision, Realities, Prospects* (Washington, D.C.: Conservation Foundation, 1985); *The National Parks: Shaping the System* (Washington, D.C.: U.S. Department of the Interior, National Park Service, 1985); Alfred Runte, *National Parks: The American Experience*, rev. 2nd ed. (Lincoln: University of Nebraska Press, 1987); and Hal Rothman, *Preserving Different Pasts: The American National Monuments* (Urbana: University of Illinois Press, 1989).

For discussion of the environmental movement of the 1960s and 1970s, see Donald Fleming, "Roots of the New Conservation Movement," in Fleming, ed., *Perspectives in American History* (Cambridge: Harvard University, Charles Center for Studies in American History, 1972), 6: 7–91, and Samuel P. Hays, *Beauty, Health, and Permanence: Environmental Politics in the United States, 1955–1985* (Cambridge: Cambridge University Press, 1987). Also, see Garrett De Bell, *The Environmental Handbook: Prepared for* the First National Environmental Teach-in (New York: Ballantine, 1970), and David L. Sills, "The Environmental Movement and Its Critics," *Human Ecology* 3 (January 1975): 1–41.

Global environmental issues are discussed in Barbara Ward and René Dubos, *Only One Earth* (New York: Ballantine, 1972); Erik P. Eckholm, *Losing Ground: Environmental Stress and World Food Prospects* (New York: W. W. Norton, 1976); Richard J. Barnet, *The Lean Years: Politics in the Age of Scarcity* (New York: Simon and Schuster, 1980); Robert Allen, *How To Save the World: Strategy for World Conservation* (Totowa, N.J.: Barnes and Noble, 1980); Lester R. Brown, *Building a Sustainable Society* (New York: W. W. Norton, 1981); Andrew Goudie, *The Human Impact on the Natural Environment* (Oxford: Basil Blackwell, 1986); World Commission on Environment and Development, *Our Common Future* (Oxford: Oxford University Press, 1987); and Lester Brown, *State of the World* (New York: W. W. Norton), published annually since 1984.

Two works that discuss environmental prospects for the United States in the 1990s are *State of the Environment: A View toward the Nineties* (Washington, D.C.: Conservation Foundation, 1987), and Peter Borrelli, ed., *Crossroads: Environmental Priorities for the Future* (Washington, D.C.: Island Press, 1988).

Periodicals and newspapers contain a wealth of information. For historical articles, see the *Journal of Forest History* and *Environmental Review*. Current environmental issues are discussed in *Worldwatch, Amicus Journal, Environment,* and numerous other journals published by environmental associations.

—Douglas H. Strong

Preface to the Bison Book Edition

THIS BOOK WAS written at a time when pioneers in conservation had limited influence, the dangers of pollution were only beginning to be recognized, and the word *ecology* had to be looked up in the dictionary to be understood. Today all that is changed. Surely every responsible person, public agency, and industrial establishment is convinced that action, total concerted action, is essential to guarantee the survival of mankind. Public opinion has been aroused all over the world, and, indeed, the only idea today about which there seems to be consensus among all nations is the importance of conservation.

The United States has been accused of wasting and polluting earth, air, and water more than any other country. And it is true that the abundance of natural resources offered the pioneer has been wantonly and shamelessly depleted by ruthless exploiters and industrialists. Yet in 1864 an American was the first in any country to raise his voice in protest against the abuse of nature. George Perkins Marsh was the man who placed the fundamental issue of conservation before the conscience of mankind in a thoroughly documented book originally entitled *Man and Nature*. (The second edition, published in 1874, was called more accurately *The Earth as Modified by Human Action*.) As American minister to united Italy in 1861, Marsh took advantage of the opportunity to study the territory around the Mediterranean Sea. Here he observed the destruction of the harmony of nature and became convinced that the devastation perpetrated by the Romans had been an important reason for the decline of the Roman Empire. Marsh was farsighted enough to bring the results of his study to the attention of his native country as a warning that must be heeded.

In the same spirit Frederick Law Olmsted, another early American conservationist, was the first to advance the idea of placing certain areas under government protection. His success was attested in the bill, signed by President Abraham Lincoln on June 29, 1864, designating Yosemite "for public use, resort and recreation, [to be] held inalienable for all time." This was the first time that a national government set aside land for the purpose of conservation. As Aldo Leopold put it in 1949, such moves spring from a consideration of what is "ethically and esthetically right." But earlier Marsh had asked for more, and it is only today that the reasons for his demands are beginning to be fully recognized.

First published in 1957, *Nature and the American* was intended to show the early development of conservation as it was rooted in American tradition. Although the movement began with only limited goals, it led to important work and legislation through the 1950s. During the next decade we were inundated by an outpouring of information and scientific knowledge, and it continues to overwhelm us in the seventies. These recent developments present material outside the scope of the present work. Many problems remain unsolved and are controversial or lie in the realm of trial-and-error investigation. The road to organizing world society and controlling it by reason is still uncharted. But it is hoped that this book, which relates the basic facts about conservation as they line up within the pattern of American civilization, will be a stimulus for positive action in the future.

HANS HUTH

Carmel, California

Preface

IN THIS BOOK an attempt is made to present the basic developments which led to the conservation movement in this country. These developments, which spread over three centuries, were both causes and effects of changes in the American point of view with respect to nature. Only as it seems necessary to complete the story are present-day conservation problems discussed. Some ideas presented here were outlined earlier in my essay "Yosemite: The Story of an Idea," and were treated more extensively in a paper called "The American and Nature" (see Bibliography).

To Mr. Horace M. Albright I feel most deeply indebted: over the years he has given me not only encouragement and moral support but also helpful counsel from the wealth of his knowledge, particularly that acquired in the course of his extraordinary activities in all fields of conservation.

A grant from Resources for the Future has made possible the reproduction of the many paintings and drawings that form an important part of this book. I therefore wish to express my gratitude to the president of that corporation, Dr. R. G. Gustavson, for taking so great an interest in my work.

I owe many thanks to Mr. Frederick Law Olmsted, Jr., who generously opened his private archives and gave me access to his father's papers as well as to his own, and also through letters let me share in the rich experience of a lifetime spent in conservation work and landscape planning.

The recent director of the National Park Service, Mr. Newton B. Drury, as well as the present director, Mr. Conrad L. Wirth, gave me ready access to all facilities of the National Park Service and helped me in many ways; for this aid I am very grateful. Whenever I visited national forests or parks, the rangers always received me, as they do every tourist, with unvarying cordiality, and they never failed to assist me and answer my questions with patience. My thanks go to these many rangers.

I am grateful to Mr. Frederick B. Adams, Jr., for permitting me to quote from the "Logbook" of Charles Tracy, owned by the Pierpont Morgan Library. And to everyone else who supplied information, allowed me to reproduce illustrations, or assisted me by reading and commenting on my manuscript and thus gave me opportunities to improve my work I wish to express my grateful appreciation; particularly to Mr. Lee B. Anderson, Miss Sarah R. Bartlett, Mr. Arnold Bergsträsser, Mr. David R. Brower, Mr. Victor H. Cahalane, Miss Mary Bartlett Cowdrey, Mr. John F. Doerr, Mr. J. F. Doherty, Mr. Henry H. Eddy, Mr. H. Raymond Gregg, Mr. Calvin Hathaway, Mr. J. E. Haynes, Mr. William H. Hees, Miss Harlean James, Mr. Howard Mumford Jones, Mr. Herbert E. Kahler, the late Herbert Kellar, Mr. Waldemar Kaempffert, Mr. Ronald F. Lee, Mr. George Marshall, Mr. C. W. Mattison, Mr. Beaumont Newhall, Mr. Harry Shaw Newman, Miss Stella G. Obst, Mr. Stanley Pargellis, Mr. Charles E. Peterson, Mr. Charles Porter III, Mr. Carl P. Russell, Mr. Paul Scheffer, the late Walter Schönichen, Mr. Paul Shepard, Miss Julia D. Sophronia Snow, Mr. Victor Spark, Mr. Eduard Steichen, Mr. Rudolf Wittkower, and Mr. William Zimmermann, Jr.

My very sincere thanks are due Miss Helen Perce, who with loyal care and keen perception shepherded the manuscript and helped me avoid many a pitfall.

It was a pleasure to work with the University of California Press, which produced this book in the best possible way, and I feel particularly grateful to Miss Dorothy H. Huggins of that Press for her most careful editing of the book.

I dedicate this book to my wife, as a token of my gratitude for the inspiring ideas she contributed, for the stimulating discussions we had on the topic of this book, and for the photographs she provided.

While this book was in press, Senator Hubert H. Humphrey (Minnesota) introduced bill S. 1176 in Congress, on February 11, 1957. This bill provides for the establishment of a "National Wilderness Preservation System" composed of areas of public land which are to retain their natural primeval environment and influence and which "shall serve the public purposes of recreational, scenic, scientific, educational, conservational, and historical use and enjoyment by the people in such manner as will leave them unimpaired for future use and enjoyment as wilderness." If this bill is enacted, this as well as the policy of the National Park Service expressed in *Our Heritage, a Plan for Its Protection and Use: "Mission 66"* (Washington, 1956) and of the National Forest Service stated in the U. S. Department of Agriculture pamphlet *Operation Outdoors* (see Bibliography) will be of the utmost importance for the future pattern of public use of protected areas under government management.

HANS HUTH

Nature and the American

Man is naturally a wild
animal . . . taken from the woods,
he is never happy . . . till he
returns to them again.

—*Benjamin Rush*[1]

1

"Axes Leap and Shapes Arise"

MAN's love of nature is now taken for granted. The desires expressed by Carl Sandburg in the following lines are today common to many people:

> Sea sunsets, give us keepsakes.
> Prairie gloamings, pay us for prayers.
> Mountain clouds on bronze skies—Give us great memories.
> Let us have summer roses.
> Let us have tawny harvest haze in pumpkin time.
> Let us have springtime faces to toil for and play for.
> Let us have the fun of booming winds on long waters.[2]

Along with this appreciation of natural beauties has come a realization that the treasures nature bestows on mankind must be widely shared, not

VIGNETTE: Settlers Lumbering.

hoarded for the use of a few. However, unless natural resources are used and distributed in accordance with man's needs and without undue waste, few of these treasures will be left to enrich the lives of future generations. This thought was made popular about 1908 when Theodore Roosevelt and Gifford Pinchot introduced a new slogan: "Conservation." The word was first used in its present sense about 1875, at the time the American Forestry Association was started.

In colonial days and in the years following them in which the pioneers pushed the frontier farther west, the situation had been very different. Then the breaking of ground was all important and the broadaxe was considered the most essential tool. Later, the axe was even accepted as the appropriate symbol of the early American attitude toward nature. The most profound impression received by observers traveling in this country in the eighteenth and nineteenth centuries was invariably that made by the extraordinary success with which enterprising Yankees were settling the lands west of the eastern seaboard. It was a revelation to these travelers to find cities in areas which only recently had been Indian territory, uncultivated plains or virgin forest. To be sure the travelers did not entirely overlook scenic spots; they compared the Hudson River Valley with the valley of the Rhine and paid due respect to Niagara and even to Trenton Falls, and later to the great wonders of the West. However, in descriptions of the country, emphasis was unfailingly concentrated upon westward expansion, and the standard story centered on the frontiersman's untiring efforts to fell primeval forests in his rapid strides to clear the ground. Receding timber stands were accepted as a matter of course, and whatever loss might result from the removal of a few trees appeared overbalanced by the increase of farmland and the growth of cities. The supply of timber was apparently inexhaustible, and most of the vast expanse of the West was still unexplored. There was no fear that the abundance would not last or that the day would come when the diminution of natural resources would result in a very critical situation.

Before anyone envisaged this disastrous possibility, the tremendous achievements of the settlers throughout the latter part of the nineteenth century stood out as the marvels of the age. In the vigorously flourishing New World it is not surprising to find Walt Whitman glorifying the material development of his century as progress, in spite of all the evil consequences which this kind of progress had generated. Quite as one would expect, the author of the "Song of the Broad-Axe" (1858) exalts pioneers as heroes in this hymn dedicated to the early settlers. Thoughts of this kind reach their culmination in "Give Me the Splendid Silent Sun" (1865). Here, after a good deal of heart searching, Whitman rejects "the quiet places by the woods" though he has no intention of seeking a place in the "splendid silent sun"; instead, he asks for "Manhattan faces and eyes forever." Written in the same spirit, the "Song of the Redwood Tree" (1874) asserts that the tree must "disappear" so that it may "serve" to "build a grander future."[3] If such utilitarian ideas about the natural forests of his country prevailed in the mind of one of the greatest American poets of the century, one can scarcely blame John Ruskin for telling Charles Eliot Norton in 1858: "I have just been seeing a number of landscapes by an American painter of some repute; and the ugliness of them is wonderful. I see that they are true studies and that the ugliness of the country must be unfathomable."[4]

But anyone who gauges Whitman's attitude toward nature only by his intense reaction to the singularly expansive forces of his period has failed to grasp the cosmic character of his thinking. No one ever had deeper appreciation of the grandeur and unique character of the American scene than Whitman. Yet he continually stressed and tried to interpret the intimate relationship between man and nature. In a poem published in 1855 he says:

> I tramp a perpetual journey (come listen all):
> My signs are a rainproof coat, good shoes, and a staff cut from
> the woods,
> No friend of mine takes his ease in my chair,
> I have no chair, no church, no philosophy,
> I lead no man to a dinner-table, library, exchange,
> But each man and each woman of you I lead upon a knoll . . .
> . . . pointing to landscapes of continents and the public road.[5]

Viewing creation from his all-embracing standpoint, Whitman regards the world as a great ensemble; to him no subject is too profound and there is no form of nature that does not deserve respect. Yet, though Whitman accepts this status as the supreme law, the lines quoted earlier from "Give Me the Splendid Silent Sun" seem to express thoughts inconsonant with this conception. But Whitman did not care about such contradictions: "let one line of my poems contradict another" he wrote in 1856.[6] This cleavage of opinion corresponds to the general public attitude of the period, wavering between neglect of nature and respect for it. But the very fact that Whitman's genius finally succeeded in overcoming this dual nature of his feelings makes him appear as the beacon of a new era which learned to regard as axiomatic the unity and mutual dependence of man and nature.

In our day it has become a matter of common knowledge that we no longer are permitted to choose between the destruction of natural resources and their conservation; instead it is imperative that we take measures to keep all factors in balance. Some of the most important forces which have encouraged love of nature and respect for it will be discussed in the following pages. What started this movement and how it began to play its part in American life will also be studied. Not all branches of this movement flowed vigorously, and some dried up. But the great stream flows on steadily, and a well-developed tributary system promises to make it even stronger as time advances. No power could ever divert the increasing support public opinion is giving to the idea of bringing nature and man into a harmonious relationship.

The life of the early pioneer obviously did not conduce in him a friendly attitude toward his surroundings, which from the moment he landed on the shores of the new continent were full of hidden dangers. Yet even the earliest descriptions of the virgin land contain passages indicating that some of the newcomers felt that the new country was actually a pleasant place.

There is, for example, the report by Captain Arthur Barlowe of his approach in 1584 to the region which is now the state of North Carolina: "we smelt so sweet, and so strong a smell as if we had bene in the midst of some delicate garden abounding with all kinds of odoriferous flowers, by which we were assured, that the land could not be farre distant."[7] In 1626 George Percy, the youngest of the Earl of Northumberland's eight sons, traveling in the new continent thus described his impressions: "we traced along some foure miles . . . the ground all flowing over with faire flowers of sundry colours and kindes, as though it had been any Garden or Orchard in England . . . We kept on our way in this Paradise."[8] Another commentator, Thomas Morton, in 1637 praised New England—"the new English Canaan," as he called it—to the disadvantage of Virginia, asserting that "the bewty of the country, with her naturall endowements"[9] surpassed the other colonies. However, in 1650, Edward Williams declared that Virginia was "of so delectable an aspect, that the melanchollyest eye in the World cannot look upon it without contentment."[10] In all these descriptions the sight of colorful flowers, the fragrance of a few berries, or a glimpse of an orchard or a spring of sparkling fresh water seem to have been sufficient to catch the imagination of the narrator and prompt him to describe his observations in the fanciful terms of his age.

Although this pattern gives the illusion that the writers were lovers of nature, albeit only of some of its small rural charms, it must not be forgotten that these descriptions were more or less stylized accounts made to glorify the possibilities awaiting the settler in the new country. Narratives were written or published as a kind of prospectus to catch the eye and mind of potential settlers, or more particularly of sponsors who might conceivably take an interest in colonial affairs. Captain John Smith came close to this purpose by stating plainly in 1612 that Virginia is a "nurse for soldiers, a practice for mariners, a trade for merchants, a reward for the good, and that which is most of all a businesse (most acceptable to God) to bring such poor infidels to the true knowledge of God and His Holy Gospell."[11]

What were the actual feelings of settlers can be deduced from the manner in which they blazed their way and made no compromises (see vignette). They rejected everything in nature that was not of immediate and practical use—a philosophy which is expressed in a little poem published in 1692:

> In such a Wilderness. . . .
> When we began to clear the Land . . .
> Then with the Ax, with Might and Strength
> The trees so thick and strong . . .
> We laid them all along . . .
> Which we with Fire, most furiously
> To ashes did confound.[12]

The matter-of-fact approach of the Reverend Johannes Megapolensis, who visited Cohoes Falls in 1644, is equally significant. Because of the noise of the falls the clergyman could hardly hear his companions talk. The water, though clear as crystal and as fresh as milk, boiled and dashed as if it were raining, and the trees looked as if they were standing in the rain. Yet, taking no delight in the extraordinary sight, the visitor was impressed only by the obvious consequences of the fall of so great an amount of water.[13] Another case in point is John Josselyn's description of the view from Sugarloaf Mountain in Connecticut, in a work published in 1672. Josselyn speaks of a "rude heap of massie stones" from which one could see "the whole country round about . . . northward [it is] daunting terrible, being full of rocky hills as thick as mole-hills in a meadow, and cloathed with infinite thick woods."[14]

Perhaps the peak of all these descriptions is to be found in the account by Father Hennepin, the first man to report about Niagara Falls. In 1679, profoundly impressed by the spectacle (see text figure and pl. 1), Hennepin wrote:

> . . . a vast and prodigious Cadence of Water which falls down after a surprizing and astonishing manner . . . At the foot of this horrible Precipice, we meet with the River Niagara . . . The Waters which fall from this vast height, do foam and boyl after the most hideous manner imaginable, making an outrageous Noise, more terrible than that of Thunder; . . . dismal roaring may be heard above Fifteen Leagues off.[15]

In none of these descriptions are the aesthetic qualities of nature ever considered; but we could hardly expect it to be otherwise. The writers never praise nature but tell us in straight terms that it is uncouth. Thus Michael Wigglesworth states that outside the settlements there was (in 1662) nothing but

> A waste and howling wilderness,
> Where none inhabited
> But hellish fiends, and brutish men
> That Devils worshipped.[16]

Niagara Falls, 1678

To the student of the situation in Europe at that time, this attitude is not surprising. There on the beaten tracks the traveler usually encountered no difficulties other than those caused by bandits or bad roads. But occasionally he would have to face the dangers and hardships of nature as the settlers of the New World did. For instance, in crossing the Alps on the way to or from Italy, a traveler might meet a variety of disasters caused by inclement weather, precipices, wolves, washed-out roads, or sudden torrents. In short, all sorts of dangers brought by the elements and other natural causes could come upon the traveler and give him the feeling of being in a "howling wilderness." Reacting to such "awful" experiences, seventeenth-century travelers in Europe, like their contemporaries in America, complained about the ordeals they had to undergo in passing through the "strange, horrid and fearful crags and tracts." John Evelyn's diary provides an interesting illustration of this. His sensitive mind was always ready to admire some valuable piece of art, but when on his route across the Alps he came face to face with the majestic scenery, he was unable and unwilling to evaluate aesthetically the impact of this experience. He heard a "terrible roaring of waters," precipices seemed to him nothing but "harbors for bears and wolves," wayside cottages he thought were "miserable," and the road passed through "horrid mountains."[17] Evelyn, in Europe, reacted in just the same way as the clergyman who visited Cohoes Falls, or as any other traveler of the period. Any aspects of nature which differed from the accustomed sights near cities or country places inspired in the beholder nothing but awe and dislike. Only the peaceful sight of fertile land stretching away through a valley delighted a traveler and rewarded him for the perils he endured as he journeyed through the mountains.

The Puritans' stern outlook on life not only was in keeping with this uncompromising attitude toward the vicissitudes of nature but went even beyond it. They disapproved of outdoor sports and of hunting for pleasure, which might have strengthened ties between man and nature. Strictly adhering to the doctrine that "what is not useful is vicious," men like Cotton Mather denounced any frolic. Even the celebration of May Day by setting up a Maypole, which gave city people a rare opportunity to gather leisurely in the open air, was regarded with disapproval because of the heathen antecedents of this festivity (see chap. 4).

A possible exception to the general rule is found in the attitude of Jonathan Edwards (1702–1758), the prominent Calvinist pastor of Puritan stock who belongs to the generation after Cotton Mather. But Edwards, in spite of his deeply poetic nature, could not completely disengage himself from the line of Puritan thinking. As a small boy he had become strongly interested in the sciences, and throughout all his life he professed his great regard for nature. In order to communicate with God in prayer, the child sought solitary places in the woods because he felt that only there could he worship. After Edwards become a minister he wrote some passages which are outstanding in their praise of the beauties of nature. Yet we must realize that these were conceived merely to explain these glories as the "shadows of the excellency of the Son of God . . . When we are delighted with flowery meadows and gentle breezes of wind . . . we see only the emanation of the sweet benevolence of Jesus Christ." The text goes on to praise fragrant roses, crystal rivers, and murmuring streams, the light and brightness of the sun, the golden edges of an evening cloud, and the blue sky. All these are lovely in God's creation, but there are "many things wherein we may behold His awful majesty;

in the Sun in his strength, in comets, in thunder, in the hovering thunder-clouds, in ragged rocks and the brows of mountains."[18]

Figures of speech such as this were common in the otherwise plain Puritan writings, but somehow they sound different when Edwards uses them, because they seem to be expressions of genuine emotion. They make us feel that Edwards is on the verge of including in his admiration those natural features of "awful" character which had been despised in Evelyn's age. However, his mind is not yet properly prepared to do so, primarily because Edwards was a Puritan, but also because there was no philosophical system which provided categories and definitions which could be applied to these new conceptions. Only in one way could Edwards accept the "horrors" of nature and discover their hidden beauties, and that was by acknowledging them as metaphors or similes for acts of God. It is only to the unphilosophical or unreligious person that certain "awful" features in nature always will remain "uncouth."

From some of his writings first published by Perry Miller in 1948, Edwards' attitude toward nature seems even more progressive than one might conclude from his previously known works. Attempting to reconcile Newton's principles with the accepted relationship between the natural world and the "City of God," Edwards penned notes which he called *Images or Shadows of Divine Things.* In these he uses typological examples in describing works of nature and thereby reveals that his observation was so keen that, according to Miller, his "Visage of Spring" gives a more accurate picture of the season "than all the poetry of Whittier and Longfellow." In "The Beauty of the World" Edwards not only extolls certain obvious qualities to be found in nature, but he also praises the hidden beauties, and in passages such as the following he shows an awareness of the harmony of the universe:

> It is very probable that the wonderful suitableness of green for the grass and ... the colours of flowers, consists in a complicated proportion that these colours make one with another, either in their magnitude of the rays, the number of vibrations that are caused in the atmosphere, or some other way. So there is a great suitableness between the objects of different senses ...

Even more revealing than any other passage is the one with which he concludes this paper:

> ... almost all men, and those that seem to be very miserable, love life, because they cannot bear to lose sight of such a beautiful and lovely world. The ideas, that every moment whilst we live have a beauty that we take not distinct notice of, brings a pleasure that, when we come to the trial, we had rather live in much pain and misery than lose."[19]

Hidden in Edwards' papers, these ideas were not published until long after his death. They certainly show that in spite of the strait jacket of Puritanism, there were men in New England capable of thinking in patterns of a new type.

Turning from New England to the South, we find an entirely different situation. Seldom concentrated in sizable townships, plantations and settlements were widely scattered. Here, owners of large estates as well as small farmers, living under the mild tutelage of the Anglican Church, were wont to shape their lives according to their own desires. Plantation owners vied with each other in surrounding their manors with gardens and orchards, cheerfully following the advice, "Dwell here, live plentifully, and be rich." Colonel William Byrd (1674–1744), the owner of "Westover," sets forth the ideal goal of the Southern country gentleman: "A library, a Garden, a Grove, a Purling stream are the Innocent scenes that divert our Leisure."[20] Such simple desires show the modesty of the demands made upon nature; yet they also indicate that there were no puritanical restrictions on the use of leisure time or on any pleasant relationship between man and nature. Certain administrative policies common to both South and North were helpful in gradually bringing to the minds of the people recognition of the nonutilitarian values of their environment. In Williamsburg, besides private gardens for each man, there were common gardens which were set aside for the growing of hemp and flax at a very early period; and in Boston the area now called the Common was purchased in 1634 by the community to be used as a field for military training and as a cow pasture. Although these areas were set aside originally for utilitarian purposes, in time they became places of recreation for later generations. In Philadelphia, William Penn's extraordinary foresight created a city plan providing for a future sound development of the city as far as was humanly possible. His goal was a green and always wholesome country town, one which would be "a great part of the settlement of this Age."[21] Penn's all-embracing mind resented the wasting of natural resources even at a time when bountiful riches made it appear ludicrous to ask for the protection of these resources. In 1681, before he had ever seen the country granted to him, Penn included in the "Conditions and Concessions" to be agreed upon between administration and settler the stipulation that, "in clearing the ground, care be taken to leave an acre of trees for every five acres cleared."[22] Also, Penn was decidedly opposed to "burning the land which is arable, because it nurses idleness."[23] In 1682 Penn arrived in the new colony, very significantly called "Pennsylvania," and was more than ever resolved to protect the woods "adorned with lovely flowers" which might even have improved the "gardens of London best stored with that sort of Beauty."[24] He made efforts to "prevent people's cutting wood and especially timber off from other men's lots"; and foreseeing the scarcity that would quickly follow, he "did appoint a woodsman who was instructed to grant such trees as belonged not to any private person and in such numbers as the case deserved."[25] This probably is the earliest known instance in this country of the employment of a forester to prevent mismanagement of timber. More than two hundred years were to elapse before this became a recognized practice.

After the heroic age of the seventeenth century had passed and while the colonists were settling down to take stock of the achievements of the early pioneers in wresting their farms and cities from the wilderness, the pattern of the intellectual life predominantly shaped by Christian ideals underwent basic changes. This evolution was due to various currents of thought transmitted from Europe. The most important of these were deism and rationalism, systems which aimed to build up a natural religion or religious opinions in general on the basis of reason and tended to revise the prevailing ideas concerning the relation of mankind to the universe. The spiritual force of deism continued to inspire those American thinkers of the nineteenth century who undertook to revise man's attitude toward nature.

The minds of many colonists were influenced by the deistic teachings of the Earl of Shaftesbury. His philosophical writings, or at least the essence of his teachings, reached the colonies through various channels. It is quite possible that some books presenting these teachings were in the library that Bishop Berkeley bequeathed to Yale College, for it contained many works by rationalist writers. Colonists with perceptive minds must have been amazed at passages by Shaftesbury which sounded as though they had been written when the author was in a situation similar to that in which the inhabitants of the New World found themselves. This passage from "The Moralists," for instance: "The wilderness pleases. We seem to live alone with Nature. We . . . contemplate her with more delight in these original wilds than in the artificial labyrinths and feigned wildernesses of the palace." Or another passage:

> I shall no longer resist the passion growing in me for things of a natural kind, where neither art nor the conceit or caprice of man has spoiled their genuine order by breaking in upon that primitive state. Even the rude rocks, the mossy caverns, the irregular unwrought grottos and broken falls of water, with all the horrid graces of the wilderness itself, as representing Nature more, will be the more engaging, and appear with a magnificence beyond the formal mockery of princely gardens.

What a difference between this appreciation of the beauty of nature and the old way of denying oneself the enjoyment of nature in order to gain the grace of God, and of feeling great awe of Him when observing the "fearful" aspects of His creation. To those emerging from the dark age of Puritan tutoring, Shaftesbury's maxim "Far be it from us ... to condemn a joy which is from Nature"[20] must have sounded like a leitmotiv to guide the spirit into a more promising and delightful future. Besides the works of Shaftesbury, writings of his emulator Alexander Pope were widely read in the colonies.

Now that deism was the basis of a new appreciation of nature above and beyond its practical use, and its aesthetic values were recognized, it became essential to find appropriate terms to be used in the reclassification of those elements in nature which hitherto had aroused awe and fear as evidences of God's power or had been considered insignificant and unworthy of any studious attention.

Edmund Burke filled this need with his "Philosophical Enquiry into ... the Sublime and Beautiful," published in 1756. This bold attempt to set up principles in a field of inquiry in which there had been only timorous approaches toward analysis of the factors involved was entirely successful. Speculative minds were now provided with devices for making accurate inquiries into the sentimental disposition of man toward nature. The mainspring of such research was Burke's postulate that the Sublime, specifying the strongest emotion of which the mind is capable, should be ranged in a category coördinated with the Beautiful. According to Burke, the Sublime, though distinguished from the Beautiful, is perfectly consistent with it. Among the properties of the Sublime he lists "objects of great dimension," "vastness," and "darkness." This elevation and classification of the Sublime, as well as the clear definition of the Beautiful, was eminently helpful to those observers who had been giving their attention to the wonders of nature without being able or even daring to establish any consistency between their impressions and the traditional reasoning and expression of thought.

After Burke had established his categories in the realm of aestheticism, still finer definitions were needed to describe newly perceived abstract values. Perhaps the most important idea, and certainly the one to be discussed most widely, was the idea of the "picturesque." This term, from the French, had been a part of that language since the seventeenth century. Pope had taken it up and had used it occasionally to indicate in a general way the pictorial quality of an object. The term acquired specific significance after William Gilpin published his essay "Upon Prints" in 1768. In this he first established the principle that a scene or picture has beauty if it conforms with the rules of painting.

Gilpin devoted most of his life to determining the various factors which made up the picturesque. For this purpose he undertook a thorough study of nature, "examining the face of a country by the rules of picturesque beauty" and observing "immediately from the scenes of nature as they arise."[27] Gilpin was the first to offer a method which made it possible for the spectator to make precise definitions of all that was to be perceived in nature. Guided by Gilpin's numerous books, his readers trained their eyes to recognize aesthetic values nobody had noticed before. Their impressions represented a new kind of factual information for which there was a distinct need. This was now transformed into painting, prose, poetry, or some other medium, to describe the various phases of nature's appearance. Gilpin's discovery was a prelude to the ideas that were popular in the romantic period, which began in the early eighteenth century. Although during this era imaginative forces gained strength and reason gave way to sensation and emotional power, Gilpin's method of analyzing nature was not entirely forgotten. It was even retained by romanticists, like Mrs. Ann Radcliffe, when they sketched their lofty visions of true or imagined landscapes. Although Gilpin was an English writer who had not been interested in the Western Hemisphere, he definitely deserves a place in this study since it was he who in many ways gave vision to the eyes of those who looked upon the American scene. There is no proof that Gilpin's works were widely read in this country immediately after they were published, nor is it even very probable that they were. But it is known that William Combe's satire on Gilpin, "The Tour of Dr. Syntax in Search of the Picturesque," first published in *Ackermann's Political Magazine* (1809–1811), was popular here, and at least three editions of it were published in Philadelphia soon after it was published in book form in London in 1812. Poe knew Gilpin, as did Hawthorne, Thomas Cole, Thoreau, and Emerson, and Gilpin's theories remained popular throughout the first half of the nineteenth century.

Before we can attempt to study the romantic feeling that spread throughout the country at the beginning of the century we must first find out in what form of literature the philosophic ideas carefully formed and expressed by the English writers of the eighteenth century were used in the interpretation of nature. It would seem that poets would have been among the first to adopt the new ideas, but as a rule no traces of Pope's deism, Burke's definitions, or Gilpin's elucidations are to be found in either the everyday prose or the ordinary poem of the day. Taken at its face value, much of this literature expresses an enthusiasm for nature, but actually the writers' feeling for nature was quite superficial. Both the prose and the poetry are the work of hacks, who tried to follow European examples but succeeded in doing so only in a pedestrian way. Alamode stylists conventionalized commonplace sentiments which did not spring from any really intimate relation with nature. Their products were printed in magazines, of which the *American Magazine; or a Monthly View of the Political State* was the first (1741) to be published in this country. These new periodicals soon were in demand; most of them were short-lived, however, and were quickly replaced by others. Nearly all contained poetry of a sort; but most of the odes, elegies, and pastorals were deplorable in both form and content. Here is an example from "Evening, a Pastoral," printed in the rather distinguished *New York Magazine* in 1795:

> The milk-maid's pail is fill'd with luscious cream,
> While youth and vigour in her visage beam;
> ... The lads and lasses all have quit the plains
> And nought but dreariness and me remains.[28]

Probably the only real poet of the period was Philip Freneau, whom H. H. Brackenridge introduced in his *United States Magazine* in 1779, assuming that "the public must be pleased with everything from that gentleman."[29] Although Freneau's personality was indeed outstanding, his poetry, as well as eighteenth-century poetry in general, is disappointing because it reveals very little about the matters we are concerned with here.

2

Scientists, Philosophers, and Travelers

WHEN scientists began to tell about their explorations of the country, the general attitude toward nature took on a new aspect. The foremost of these scientists was John Bartram, the "king's botanist" and the creator of the first botanical garden in North America, which he established in 1730 close to his charming house on the banks of the Schuylkill near Philadelphia. Bartram is known primarily through his correspondence with the English naturalist Peter Collinson, and through a few of his travel accounts. Although their subject matter is important, his writings make rather dull reading. Beyond factual observations about the gathering of seeds and about the Indians he met on autumnal trips which took him thousands of miles into the back country, as far north as Lake Ontario and south to South Carolina, Georgia, and Florida, this great botanist

VIGNETTE: John Bartram's House, near Philadelphia, 1849.

rarely ever jotted down his personal impressions of the grand showpieces of nature which he saw. Yet it was he who inspired his son William not only to observe but to love nature. An interview John Bartram is supposed to have given to a Russian traveler gives an insight into his character. In reality, St. Jean de Crèvecœur wrote the piece as a tribute to his friend. The Frenchman had been strongly impressed by Bartram's forthright character and his practice of sharing with his friends his all-embracing love and understanding of nature. An inscription Crèvecœur discovered on a greenhouse revealed the spirit of his host.

> Slave to no sect, who takes no private road,
> But looks through Nature, up to Nature's God![1]

The shrubs Bartram set out and the trees he planted still shade the house (see vignette) he built with his own hands at Kingsess, now a suburb of Philadelphia. The site, on an eminence which slopes down to the banks of the winding Schuylkill, even today makes us forget the industrial establishments that spread over the entire neighborhood. Every plant in Bartram's country retreat testifies to his love of nature, though he did not give adequate expression to his feelings in print.

Bartram spent most of his life in studying botany and was the most eminent man in his field. There were a number of other persons of his time who also approached nature as scientists, not so much because they nurtured any scholarly ambitions as because they enjoyed a study which brought them into contact with the unexplored wilds of their country. Cadwallader Colden, who had been a surveyor general, retired to "Coldenham" near Newburgh on the Hudson in 1739 at a time when this neighborhood was still not safe from Indian attacks. Here he delighted in botanical research. His daughter Jane, too, was intensely interested in botany and became an amateur botanist of rather wide reputation. Another ardent lover of nature, Humphrey Marshall, followed Bartram's example and in 1773 established a botanical garden at his place in Marshallton, Pennsylvania, the second botanical garden in America. Marshall also published a list of species of American trees and shrubs and was considered an authority on this subject. Samuel Vaughan turned to him in 1785 when he sought advice about the trees to be planted in State House Square in Philadelphia. All these men and William Byrd, Benjamin Franklin, and Thomas Jefferson, to mention some of the foremost, knew each other and constantly exchanged views, particularly at meetings of the American Philosophical Society and in its publications.

Franklin had been the driving power in establishing the American Philosophical Society, which he regarded as one of the most powerful media for spreading scientific knowledge. Since his youth, "nature philosophy" had held his interest; later experiments which allowed him to study the secrets of nature became the great passion of his life, for he felt that much "useful knowledge might be acquired by such work." Franklin's insight and genius helped to allay some of the age-old fears of the dangers of water and fire. Franklin taught himself to swim, a pastime which in his day was rather unusual, and he even tried out, quite successfully, fins of his own construction. His continuous efforts to recommend swimming not only as a useful exercise but as a character builder did much to popularize this sport. More impressive was his invention of the lightning rod, "for drawing the electric fire from clouds by means of pointed rods of iron erected on high buildings."[2] Also of importance was his invention of the "Pennsylvania fireplace," a description of which Franklin published in 1744. The "Franklin stove," by making it possible for firewood to be utilized far more economically than before, opened an entirely new line of thought, that of conserving natural resources.

Throughout his entire life Franklin attempted to carry out ideas that aided in harmonizing the relation between man and nature and in bringing about improvements in general living conditions. Even when he lived in Paris, Franklin was busy with affairs at home which, though they seemed trifling to others, he knew to be of importance. Thus, he tried to help John Bartram and Humphrey Marshall in their efforts to exchange seeds and plants with botanists and horticulturists on the continent; and at another time he recommended planting trees in all the streets of Philadelphia. Although Franklin was deeply interested in nature, it is questionable whether he had any inclination toward the romantic or aesthetic appreciation of its beauties.

One of Franklin's fellow "nature philosophers" was Dr. Nicholas Collin, rector of the Swedish Church in Philadelphia. As a member of the American Philosophical Society he delivered a remarkable paper on April 3, 1789, entitled "An Essay on Natural Philosophy and Its Relationship to the Development of the New World." Discussing rural economy, Dr. Collin put in a strong plea for the conservation of forests:

> Our stately forests are a national treasure, deserving the solicitous care of the patriotic philosopher and politician. Hitherto they have been too much abandoned to the axes of rude and thoughtless wood-choppers.... In many parts of this country a preservation and encrease of the timber for fuel and domestic uses render these queries important....

The speaker then enumerated several queries, such as "What trees are of the quickest growth? And he went on to advise proper care of forests, even to the point of considering their ecology. Admitting that the practical use must be considered first, Dr. Collin invited the owners of wooded lands to regard them as principal ornaments of their country; and while they clear a part for the purposes of agriculture, leave those hills crowned with towering pines, and stately oaks. . . . is it not then deplorable, that so many American farmers daily destroy what their offsprings of better taste will deeply regret! this evil might in a great measure be lessened by a *treatise on ornamental* planting . . .[3]

This paper was printed in the *Proceedings of the American Philosophical Society* and must have come to the attention of most of the scientists of the country. Possibly some of the ideas expressed in it influenced the later writings of such men as Benjamin Rush and Timothy Dwight.

Another prominent scientist of the period was the colorful Charles Willson Peale, the founder, owner, and curator of the first natural history museum of importance, established in Philadelphia in 1785. There had been an earlier American Museum containing some objects of scientific character, more or less a curio cabinet of little consequence, which had been established by Pierre Du Simitière in 1774 and was maintained by him until his death in 1784. At that time Peale took over a number of the exhibits and classified them in his museum according to species, conforming to the exacting standard expected of a member of the American Philosophical Society. It is difficult to exaggerate the influence this museum and the branch established in Baltimore in 1796 exerted during the more than half a century they existed. A small part of the museum is shown in the portrait which Peale painted of himself lifting a curtain of one of its rooms and inviting the visitor to come in. Almost no traveler to Philadelphia would forego the opportunity of seeing the mastodon bones Peale had excavated and the animals he had preserved. A stuffed buffalo even gave a faint idea of the appearance of the herds of bison which were still grazing the western prairies. According to the words on his signboard, Peale invited his visitors to go through "the great school of nature," and with "the book of Nature open, explore the wondrous world, an institute of laws eternal."[4] The stimulus given by the museum to the movement to acquaint the public with nature in general and the scenery and natural history of this continent specifically was extraordinary, especially in a day when visual education was scarcely known. Following Peale's example, some citizens of Cincinnati founded the Western Museum of Science in that city in 1815. The managing directors of the museum felt confident that it would receive all the aid that public-minded fellow citizens "might feel disposed to give them."[5]

Peale's versatility in the sciences and arts was not usual. After all, toward the end of the eighteenth century it was not necessary to be a specialist in order to be recognized as a man of science. Thomas Jefferson, with a general knowledge so vast as to be considered spectacular, was

Natural Bridge, Virginia

regarded as one of the outstanding scientists of his day. He advocated vigorously that science must be made the "corner stone of our Republic" and wrote from Paris to Joseph Willard, the president of Harvard College: "What a field have we at our doors to signalize ourselves in. The botany of America is far from being exhausted, its mineralogy is untouched, and its natural history or zoology totally mistaken and misrepresented. . . . It is the work to which the young men you are forming should lay their hands."[6] Eight years earlier, by publishing his *Notes on the State of Virginia* (1781), Jefferson had already proved himself an authority on natural history. This comprehensive treatise aroused enormous interest and was reprinted many times. Although the facts pertaining to natural history comprise only a small part of its contents, they are of great importance because some of them correct earlier misconceptions. There are also passages which deserve attention because they illustrate a new attitude toward the physical universe and therefore must be considered as milestones in the progress of a better understanding of nature. Most remarkable, perhaps, is the passage in which Jefferson praises the Natural Bridge:

> If the view from the top be painful and intolerable that from below is delightful in an equal extreme. It is impossible for the emotions arising from the sublime to be felt beyond what they are here; so beautiful an arch, so elevated, so light and springing as it were up to heaven: the rapture of the spectator is really indescribable.[7]

In evaluating this emotional outburst we must not forget that the Natural Bridge ranked among the great sights of the country, along with Trenton Falls, and a little later, Mammoth Cave. The bridge and the falls had always been highly regarded and considered to be on a par with Niagara Falls. Ever since they had first become known these places had been visited by sightseers because they were thought of as curiosities and freaks of nature, and their strangeness, dreadfulness, or awesomeness never failed to impress the visitor. Jefferson, however, brought up an entirely new point. Although he could not help thinking of the view from the bridge as "painful" and "intolerable," he considered the view from below it "delightful." From this description we can see just what it was that affected the spectator's emotions. It is easy to comprehend why Jefferson, the architect, extolled the aesthetic qualities of an arch, and particularly this one, "springing up to heaven." This passage could not have been written without a knowledge of Burke's definitions and inquiries into the origin of the sublime. Such lines of thought link Jefferson with Burke, but Jefferson's interest in aesthetic ideas connect him also with the romanticists, whose interest in nature was primarily an aesthetic one. His capability of creating impressive images of sites which caught his imagination indicates that his generation had become sensitive to visual impressions and at the same time had developed a suitable literary form in which to present impressions received. The description of the spot near Harpers Ferry where the Potomac breaks through the Blue Ridge is a perfect example of this newly won literary power. Here there was

> perhaps one of the most stupendous scenes in nature. On your right comes up the Shenandoah ... to seek a vent, to the left approaches the Potomac, in quest of a passage also. In the moment of their junction, they rush together against the mountain, rend it asunder, and pass off to the sea ... the mountain being cloven asunder, she presents to your eye, through the cleft, a small patch of smooth blue horizon, and an infinite distance in the plain country ... This scene is worth a voyage across the Atlantic.[5]

One of the men with whom Jefferson had many contacts was William Bartram. In 1806 Bartram recommended Alexander Wilson to Jefferson as a man who could suitably be employed in the investigation of Louisiana natural history. And again it was William Bartram to whom the proprietor of "Monticello" turned when he needed strawberries or other plants for his garden. Like Jefferson, Bartram belonged to the generation growing up after the middle of the eighteenth century which was widening its outlook with new ideas about natural phenomena. Indeed, there was a great difference between the spiritual habitat of William Bartram and that of his father, John. Born in 1739, William seems never to have ventured beyond the orbit of "Kingsess" and the atmosphere of that country place, except when he accompanied his father or when he explored the wilds of Florida. Yet the great journal that he kept during his five years of travel through the South differs in every respect from the writings of John Bartram, which were in the classic style and showed evidence of a rigid spirit. Not that either of these men loved nature less than the other, but they were at variance in their relationship to nature. It is here that we glimpse the difference in the attitude of the two generations.

A detailed analysis of William Bartram's accounts of his travels affords ample proof that he was much influenced by Pope, Burke, and the Lake poets. Bartram was also deeply religious, though he was no pantheist. God to him was still the Creator, and though he was somewhat in doubt about the force which animates nature, he did believe that there are immanent principles which guide creation. Unrestrained love of nature gave Bartram the ability to conjure up scenes of dramatic quality which cause him to appear as a truly romantic writer of great individuality and almost make us forget that he stands on the shoulders of earlier English writers. Trained by his father, William Bartram was a keen observer; he invited his countrymen also to behold with him "as yet unmodified by the hand of man, ... the unlimited, varied, and truly astonishing native

wild scenes of landscape and perspective." Deeply emotional, Bartram
was keenly sensitive to "vastness" and he would lose himself completely
"amidst sublimely high forests, awful shades." It cannot be doubted that
Bartram's feelings were true and sincere; they were the genuine sensations
of an artist and did not arise from any superficial aesthetic enthusiasm.
There is something of heartfelt worship and the belief in the immanence
of the creative principle within nature in Bartram's description of a sunset
as it appeared to him after he had roamed all day on his "sylvan pilgrimage." "How glorious the powerful sun, minister of the Most High . . . leaves
our hemisphere . . . tinging the fleecy roseate clouds, now riding far away
on the eastern horizon; behold they vanish from sight in the azure skies!"[9]

William Bartram traveled in the southern states from 1773 to 1777, but
his book was not published until 1791. In the following year it was reprinted in London and soon was translated into several European lan-
guages. In America, Bartram's book was appreciated only by that elite
group of his countrymen who had already found in nature a source of
delight; it did not immediately bring about an increase in the general
enthusiasm for nature, nor did it induce any prominent writers to emulate
its author. Abroad it was a different story. The Lake poets of England
became well acquainted with Bartram's *Travels;* and Chateaubriand, who
had roamed the New World himself, was so entranced with Bartram's
descriptions of scenery that he used elements from the *Travels* in his own
Atala and *René*. In time these two novels became world famous and
aroused enthusiasm in both hemispheres because of their exotic flavor,
which appealed strongly to the romantic taste of the period.[10] Even after
many years, Carlyle, under the spell of Bartram, wrote Emerson that the
wonderful eloquence in his *Travels* should impel all American libraries
"to provide themselves with that kind of book . . . as a kind of future
biblical article."[11]

As it happened, in this period a Frenchman became a leading authority
on American matters on the basis of a slender book published in London
in 1782. This was St. Jean de Crèvecœur, a nobleman who in 1769 had
established himself as a farmer not far from New York. For years after the
publication of his *Letters from an American Farmer* the work was regarded as a fundamental source book. This is indeed understandable,
since probably few men of his time knew the American territory as thoroughly and loved the country as well as did this native of France who was
elected an honorary freeman of New Haven and was made a member of
an Indian tribe. To Crèvecœur it always remained strange that "you
should have in England so many learned and wise men, and that none
should ever have come over here to describe some part of this great field
which nature presents."[12] Crèvecœur became rather quickly allied with

kindred spirits in the country of his choice. His farm, "Pine Hill," made him a neighbor of Cadwallader Colden; and in 1770 he wrote his famous essay on John Bartram, who had received him into the large circle of his friends.

It has often been said that the picture Crèvecœur gives of American life and its natural surroundings is too idealized. To some extent this may be true of certain passages which were added to the second French edition of the *Letters*, prepared at the time Crèvecœur returned to France. But the truth remains that his sympathetic descriptions of natural scenery and his directness in reporting his observations and impressions are outstanding characteristics of his writings. Although William Bartram's more lyrical manner of writing differs from Crèvecœur's forceful style, both men were lovers of nature. Their descriptions of the natural landscape and its effect on their emotions were sound beginnings in the development of nature interpretation and set an example for future naturalists. Their ideas about nature had a greater influence on the minds of later generations than did the thoughts of the English poets from Campbell to Coleridge. In "Ant Hill Town" Crèvecœur very likely expressed not only his own thoughts but those of men like Colden, the two Bartrams, Humphrey Marshall, and others.

> How I hate to dwell in those accumulated and crowded cities! . . . I always delighted to live in the country. Have you never felt at the returning of spring a glow of general pleasure, an indiscernible something that pervades our whole frame, an inward involuntary admiration of everything which surrounds us? 'Tis then the beauties of Nature, everywhere spread, seem to swell every sentiment as she swells every juice.[13]

One of the feelings that Crèvecœur was instrumental in passing on to those who lived in his time or immediately after him was the great happiness that he always felt when in the woods.

Although it is known that the Lake poets of England were influenced by Crèvecœur's idealistic attitude, his development of nature appreciation in this country has not been studied. In demonstrating how the farmer is affected by changes in nature, Crèvecœur shows directness, simplicity, and grandeur which even foreshadow Whitman: "A great thunderstorm; an extensive flood; a desolating hurricane; a sudden and intense frost; an overwhelming snowstorm; a sultry day, each of these different scenes exhibits singular beauties even in spite of the damage they cause."[14] Written in 1769, thirty-five years before Alexander Wilson composed "The Foresters," these amazing lines betray no fear of nature, nor do they show delight in pastoral amenities. It is the stalwart pioneer who speaks, but his voice seems to have an entirely new ring. Here is not only great admiration for nature but perhaps also the beginning of a feeling that man can render himself independent of nature's evils. In this country Crèvecœur's writings seem to have been completely forgotten throughout the nineteenth century. For instance, in none of Donald Grant Mitchell's books, such as *Wet Days at Edgewood* (1884) or *American Lands and Letters* (1898), is there any hint that the author was acquainted with Crèvecœur. This is astonishing because Mitchell, another farmer-writer, whose works were widely read, surely would have been receptive to Crèvecœur's progressive ideas.

As scientists came more often in contact with nature they became increasingly appreciative of opportunities afforded by virgin woods, savannas, and unmapped lakes; perhaps in these could be found species of fauna and flora never before recorded. The Bartrams and Crèvecœur were but a few of the distinguished men in that continually enlarging group of nature enthusiasts comprised of learned men and amateurs of both sexes. In the minds of these progressive persons, traditional, dogmatic limitations vanished and prejudices were abolished. An entirely new relationship began to be established between man and nature, and even though the relationship was felt only by small groups of people it actually made for a better understanding of nature. This understanding, however, was not widespread, and the time was not yet ripe for a general revision of man's behavior toward nature.

A case in point is the work of Philip Freneau, an early author of a number of poems on nature and Indian lore, who was generally called the "father of American poetry." A comparison of Freneau's poems "The Dying Indian" (1784) and "The Wild Honey Suckle" (1786) with the dialectic exercises of alamode stylists who populated sylvan grounds with evanescent damsels of Greek ancestry reveals a definite progress in his receptiveness to impressions emanating from the New World. Being a traveler and a seafaring man, Freneau was a keen observer and noticed small as well as large natural features. Also, as a deist, he was well equipped to speculate on themes such as the "uniformity and perfection of nature." Paraphrasing Pope, whom he considered one of his masters, he states (1815):

> No imperfection can be found
> In all that is, above, around,—
> All, nature made, in reason's sight
> Is order all, and *all is right*.[13]

Freneau's deistic optimism, however, was counterbalanced by ancient fears; the sea's abyss was still a watery grave, and the wild honeysuckle, though a lovely plant indigenous to America, was after all only a symbol of transience and death. This kind of pessimism haunts much of Freneau's lyrics and lessens their value as pure homage to nature. A comparison between some of William Bartram's hymnlike passages and Freneau's reasoned, intellectual poetry demonstrates that Bartram's ideas were advancing toward nineteenth-century pantheism as found in Emerson, while Freneau's reflections were still expressive of standard eighteenth-century sentiment and were of a far more transitory character.

The foregoing evaluations, far from disparaging Freneau, merely indicate the limitations of this man of keen sensitivity who undoubtedly had the most poetical mind in America before Bryant and, like him, took notice of the physical world in which he lived. It need hardly be added that during the early years of the republic general circumstances were so unfavorable to anything not concerned with the practical needs of life that James Madison certainly expressed the general opinion when he stated that instead of pure poetry "something more substantial, more durable, more profitable befits our riper age."[16] In spite of such limitations, deism as professed by Freneau was one of the starting points for the later romantic interpretation.

One of the key figures in the movement toward a better understanding of nature, and one who deserves special attention, is Alexander Wilson. As a scientist Wilson has been remembered, but as a poet and writer he has been undeservedly forgotten. It may be that his lyrics were never really popular, but because of his radiant personality Wilson in his day had considerable influence in making his contemporaries aware of the beauties of nature. The title of his great epic poem, "The Foresters, Description of a Pedestrian Tour to the Fall of the Niagara in the Autumn of 1804," gives us an insight into the attitude of this enthusiast for the natural wonders of his adopted country. Wilson well knew that the thing for which he was striving seemed quixotic to most of his contemporaries, but this did not prevent him from following his own designs and enjoying the "sight of the green meadows, the singing of birds, the fragrance of flowers and blossoms," which were in great contrast to "the burning streets, the growling oyster men, the stinking sewers and polite company of Philadelphia." In this frame of mind Wilson began his journey to Niagara (see pl. 12). He spent two months on the 1,300-mile trip, traveling, without regard for the hardships, "through deep snow, almost unhabited forests or over stupendous mountains," knee-deep in mud over many miles of his road, until his boots were finally reduced to legs and upper leather and his pantaloons were in a sad plight. By December he was back in his sunny home near Grays Ferry and sat down to tell his story:

> Sons of the city!
> Come roam with me Columbia's forests . . .
> Where scenes sublime shall meet your wandering view . . ."[17]

Wilson's poem, published in the Philadelphia *Port Folio* won immediate success. With a sincerity and deep feeling for which there had been scarcely any precedent, except perhaps in William Bartram's *Travels,* the epic told of deep shades, sky-encircled lakes, lone hermit streams, the hunter's cabin, enormous cataracts, and many other wondrous sights. Wilson was intensely aware that these scenes were new to song and that his was a "path untrod before." But though he was willing and eager to explore the matchless western world, he occasionally felt lost in the "awful silence of the unemployed waste" and was awed by the rocks and stones covering the country, which he said "grinned horribly."[18] Passages such as these reveal that Wilson, whose happier concept of nature was in conflict with the awe-filled moods common in earlier times, definitely stands between two epochs. By softening those feelings of awe and fear Wilson rendered a great service to the following generation and opened a new path to the enjoyment of nature.

Wilson had been a traveler and wanderer all his life. In his native Scotland he had peddled Paisley weavings and his poems at the same time; in this country he settled down on the shore of the Schuylkill not far from the spot where John Bartram had created his earthly paradise. Bartram became Wilson's tutor and helped him find his real vocation by aiding him to develop the artistic talent which later enabled him faithfully to record the American birds. After the publication of his first volume of the *American Ornithology* (9 vols.; 1808–1814) Wilson continued his wanderings up and down the seaboard states from Savannah to Portland. He penetrated into remote places to sell subscriptions for his bird books, and though they were priced at $120.00 a set, he managed to sell 458 copies. Wilson became a well-known figure and the most eloquent advocate of love of nature. Through his work in ornithology Wilson discovered that man's great interest in bird life is based on the fact that man and bird appear to have habits and feelings in common. Frequently commenting on such ties in the letterpress accompanying his engravings, Wilson was able to create interest in his subject and make it attractive to the public. The steadily increasing number of correspondents who were eager to supply Wilson with information about birds shows that his ideas and observations were known throughout the country.

The extraordinary popularity John James Audubon (see pl. 10) has gained in recent years makes it difficult to realize that in their own time Wilson was far better known than Audubon, who came into general public view much later. It was not until 1840, after the octavo edition of his *Birds of America* had been published, that Audubon's fame spread. By this time Wilson's volumes and the later volumes by Prince Lucien Bonaparte had acquainted the public sufficiently with American ornithol-

ogy to make the subject extremely popular. Interest had also been aroused
by a number of other publications. Therefore one cannot say that Audubon's work contributed anything extraordinary to the general knowledge
about American birds. But certainly Audubon's work was superior artis-
tically to that of Wilson, and his often quite fanciful descriptions were
well suited to increase and spread interest in wildlife. Indeed, Audubon
was one of the most tireless explorers of this country and allowed no
obstacles to interfere with his firm resolve to make a pictorial record of
as many of the birds of America as possible. "It was the spectacle of
birds and the idea of birds which fascinated him, . . . he loved them more
as one might love . . . a wonderful mechanism than as creatures with whose
individual lives he was concerned."[19]

Although Audubon was serious in his study of wildlife, he was not
averse to having an occasional joke at the expense of others. Once he
made a fool of a traveler who visited him in the West, by telling him tall
stories about an as yet unheard of species of fish. This man, who undoubtedly was an eccentric, had a name with a strange ring, Constantine Samuel
Rafinesque-Schmaltz.[20] Born in Turkey, Rafinesque lived from time to
time in Italy, Sicily, Philadelphia, and Lexington when he was not making
his thousand-mile exploring tours through the backwoods of America,
studying the flora and fauna. The results of these studies, published in
magazines, seemed so meritorious to European learned societies that they
bestowed many honors on him. Rafinesque must be considered one of the
most advanced spirits of his time, contributing to the stimulation of interest in American science and dissemination of knowledge about it. His
presence in the Middle West must have been especially stimulating to
those who were aspiring to learning and scholarship yet were handicapped
by circumstances of isolation.

Rafinesque's four hundred papers scattered through the magazines of
the period give favorable account of the quality and quantity of papers
made accessible to the public through the many periodicals that were
being published at this time. Essentially differing in quality from contributions to the "department of poetry," articles on natural history and
travel were with few exceptions sent in by experts. The public reached
through these periodicals was much larger than the actual number of
subscribers, for every copy was undoubtedly handed around among
friends and neighbors. The most widely read publications were the *Columbian Magazine*, the *American Museum*, the *Massachusetts Magazine*, the
New York Magazine, and the *Port Folio;* but there were others, like the
Boston Magazine and the *Ladies' Magazine*, which are of interest because
they specialized in articles on travel and nature. Among the regular con-
tributors were William Byrd, Dr. Benjamin Rush, Dr. Samuel L. Mitchell,

William Bartram, and Alexander Wilson. These journals frequently offered "embellishments" as additional features: landscape engravings, for instance, which usually pictured popular sites such as the Natural Bridge, Niagara Falls, Grays Ferry, and occasionally a country seat or a lesser known place, such as the Juniata River. Though most of these were rather uninteresting illustrations, topographical in character and lacking in charm, they were of value as a start toward acquainting readers with the American scene.

Some new books on travel received additional publicity by being reprinted in part in magazines. Though a great number of these travel books were written by foreigners, they shed some light on the natural features most highly esteemed by many Americans, because what these travelers saw or were led to see reflected to some extent what their hosts felt would be worth their while. Their comments were discussed with great interest and thus contributed to the shaping of public opinion.

There was, for instance, Andrew Burnaby, an Englishman who traveled in America in 1759–1760 and published an account in 1775. Like most of the other travelers, he displayed increasing amazement at the natural wonders he saw. The aesthetic points of view expressed in the third edition of Burnaby's descriptions (republished in 1798) lead us to believe that he may have reviewed his records after taking notice of William Gilpin's remarks on the principles of picturesque beauty first published in 1768. On viewing the falls of the Pawtucket River in Massachusetts, Burnaby expressed regret that the erection of two or three mills had "taken very much from the beauty of the scene; which would otherwise be transcendentally elegant," for he thought the falls were "by far the most romantic and picturesque" of any he had seen. When he was on top of the Blue Ridge, he was delighted with the scene which opened before him, and he describes the view as he would a stage setting. Sylvan scenes "far from the bustle of life" attracted him and fascinated him far more than any of the more utilitarian sites. But Burnaby, too, followed convention and experienced the "emotion" always mentioned by travelers who visited such famous sites as the Natural Bridge in Virginia and the falls of the Rappahannock, Potomac, and Passaic.[21] In appraising the traveler's appreciation of popular attractions it is well to be cautious. All these sites had a "curio" value of long standing which had little to do with their aesthetic merits. Every traveler inspected landmarks just as he did any man-made curiosity or freak of nature; therefore in appraising "raptures" one must distinguish between the visitor's delight in a curiosity and his possibly growing appreciation of the scenic value. A great traveler who thought and wrote along lines related to those of Bartram and his friends was the New Englander Timothy Dwight, who was president of Yale from 1795 to his death in 1817. Such an attitude should not seem strange coming from the author of "Greenfield Hill," an early product of romanticism. Though we know that this poem reflects John Dyer's "Grongar Hill," Dwight's descriptions of his travels are entirely his own, and the narratives of his journeys throughout New England contain delightful passages of true lyrical value mirroring his interest and impressions of his native land. Wandering through the Catskills (1804) he occasionally "passed a cottage; and heard the distant sound of an axe, and of a human voice. All was grandeur, gloom and solitude." As he approached the falls they appeared to him thus:

> The mountains on either side were steep, wild and shaggy, covered almost everywhere with a dark forest, the lofty trees of which approached nearer and nearer to each other as the eye wandered towards the bottom. . . . All beneath seemed to be midnight, although the day was uncommonly bright and beautiful; and all above a dreary solitude, secluded from the world . . . This magnificent current, after dashing upon a shelf, falls over a second precipice . . . when it vanishes in the midnight beneath . . . A cloud of vapour, raised by the dashing of this stream . . . rises above the forests . . . On the bosom of this elegant volume of mist appears . . . a succession of rain-bows, floating . . . down the valley, and reluctantly . . . yielding their place to others.[22]

Dwight was especially attracted by the Catskills, but he was enthusiastic about the northern lakes also; for instance, when he noticed the pleasing arrangement of a train of islands in Lake Winnepesaukee, a site completely unknown to the ordinary traveler of his day. He describes his native New England with great ardor and records with pride that someone thought that he was the first person who had ever traveled through New England simply from curiosity. This, certainly, was not entirely true, for the eminently "curious" John Bartram had already been in the Catskills in 1753; but it is true that Dwight's reports of the wonders of the Catskills and other sites later to become famous were the first noteworthy ones. Even before Dwight started on his wanderings in the Catskills another group of curious travelers had ventured to explore the White Mountains. The well-known minister Manasseh Cutler, in the company of Jeremy Belknap and some other gentlemen, had gone there in 1784. This group derived a certain satisfaction from the "noble effects" which the mountains presented. But, making observations from the summit of the Sugarloaf Mountain, they were not concerned so much with "most extensive prospects" as they were with the physical reasons for the cloud formations which they beheld.[23] The feelings of the Cutler company resemble the impressions which the traveler Robert Hunter reported after he had visited Niagara the year before (1785). He felt that "the rapids as you approach them are dreadful to look at. . . . roaring noise, wild-looking islands . . .

dreadful fall of water..."²⁴ And he was "thunderstruck at the grandeur and magnificence of such an awful sight." By comparing Cutler's and Hunter's remarks with passages in Wilson's "Foresters" and Dwight's *Travels,* we recognize a difference in the attitudes of the two pairs of authors. In an interval of about twenty years a change had taken place and a new era was soon to begin which would be characterized by a fresh, romantic mood and an eager acceptance of the offerings of nature.

3

The Romantic Period

IN THE early summer of 1817, Dr. Peter Bryant, the father of William Cullen Bryant, found in his desk the manuscripts of some poems which his son had placed there. William Cullen was then practicing law at Great Barrington. His father, pleased and excited about the poems, took them to friends in Boston who published the *North American Review*. The Boston gentlemen were amazed, and one of them, Richard H. Dana, stated that "no one on this side of the Atlantic is capable of writing such verse."[1] All agreed, however, that the two poems, "Thanatopsis" and "Fragment," should be published in the *Review*. Their publication was the first literary recognition of an entirely new approach to the contem-

VIGNETTE: Otsego Lake, New York.

plation of nature[2] and was one of the milestones in the history of American poetry. Bryant, of course, had found the books of James Fenimore Cooper and Robert Southey in his father's library and knew them well. In his early youth he had explored the countryside and the woods still surrounding his father's home at Cummington, and these also had captured his imagination. Bryant's poems reflect his boyhood impressions. "Collateral objects and appearances," as Wordsworth had once called those sources of influence which build up the mind,[3] had made their imprint on Bryant throughout his formative years. Bryant's sincerity and purity deeply impressed Dana and caught the attention of the public.

Once before, in 1808, Bryant had been in the public eye because of his *Embargo*, a volume of satires against Jefferson's administration. Now, in 1817, he was at the beginning of a career which was to last for more than half a century and make him one of the most influential and representative figures of his age. Dana's doubts and astonishment are understandable when we compare Bryant's poems with the poetical platitudes published in the "departments of poetry" in the current magazines. Although a new generation had grown up since Freneau's "Dying Indian" was published in 1784, no one had written anything resembling it, nor had Freneau fulfilled the promise of presenting a new conception of nature that had been suggested by his earlier works. The poet throughout his declining years was enmeshed in politics, but otherwise lived almost entirely in the past, even to wearing to the end of his life (1832) the small clothes and buckled shoes of an earlier period.

The difference between the old and the new generations is apparent if we realize that Wilson's poem "The Foresters" was published in the *Port Folio* in 1809, and that Bryant wrote "Thanatopsis" not more than two years later. In the first half of the nineteenth century English literature had a deep influence on the literary life of America. The Lake poets— Samuel Coleridge, Southey, and particularly William Wordsworth—were widely read, and Sir Walter Scott and Lord Byron were also in high favor. The influence of these English writers was far stronger than that of Jean Jacques Rousseau or any of the other French writers. Howard Mumford Jones has shown that Bryant, for instance, was influenced largely by Wordsworth and not as one might imagine by Rousseau.[4] Inclined to abandon himself to his emotions, Bryant did not relate his conception of nature to any social philosophy. But when Bryant read Wordsworth for the first time, "a thousand springs seemed to gush up at once in his heart, and the face of Nature, of a sudden, appeared to change into a strange freshness and life."[5] Nor did Wordsworth's influence cease before the middle of the century. As late as 1851 John Greenleaf Whittier hailed Wordsworth in a poem which included the following stanza.

How welcome to our ears, long pained
By strife of sect and party noise,
The brook-like murmur of his song
Of nature's simple joys.[9]

Nevertheless, foreign influences of this kind did not remain unchallenged. Strong nationalistic ideas developed in America in the first quarter of the nineteenth century. Discussions of literary problems were carried on principally in the magazines. The most distinguished forum was the Philadelphia *Port Folio*, which enjoyed an unusually long life, from 1801 to 1827. English literature was in favor in that city and was much eulogized. The first editor, Joseph Dennie, being a stout Federalist, praised the stilted poems of Timothy Dwight and John Trumbull but did not mention the writings of Freneau, the Jeffersonian. One of the magazine's most important contributions to literature was the publication of Wilson's "Foresters" through ten issues, from 1809 to 1810. The magazine was also notable for the large number of illustrations it carried. In 1809 the publishers even promised to include in each volume an engraved plate of an American scene, because this country afforded the pencil "an inexhaustible abundance which for the picturesque effect cannot be surpassed in any part of the Old World. We invite the artist and the amateur to furnish us with sketches and accompanying descriptions.'" Stimulated by the *Port Folio* and similar publications, such as the *Monthly Anthology*, published in Boston, the Baltimore *Portico*, and even a *Western Review and Miscellaneous Magazine*, printed in Lexington, Kentucky, there gradually emerged all over the country a group of writers who reported their direct observations of nature. In order to justify his impressions, an early writer on nature would quote a romantic poet, such as Scott. He would perhaps tell of a traveler who entered a forest at a late hour and heard there the sound of a bugle. This is a truly romantic scene, the writer thinks, because the situation reminds him of a novel by Scott he has just read. Another admirer of scenery wishes that he had "the pencil of a Radcliffe"[8] to give life to his description. Although this kind of comparison had a sentimental ring and certainly indicated that the author had read extensively, it foreboded trouble in the form of long-drawn-out argument. The question to be disputed for many years was, how does the scenery of America compare with that of Europe? In spite of many dissenting opinions, it was eventually recognized that the great rivers, lakes, and mountains of this country were as "noble" as those of other lands, and that, since they differed in some ways from those anywhere else, they should be given special consideration.

Bryant, of course, was a strong supporter of those who preferred the beauties of American scenery, so much so that when he visited Italy for the first time, in 1834, he was "less struck with the beauty" of the Italian scenery than he had expected. The mountains seemed more picturesque, perhaps, but even "if the hand of man had done something to embellish the scenery, it has done more to deform it ... the simplicity of natural scenery, so far as can be done, is destroyed."⁹ From these remarks it is easy to imagine that Bryant must have delighted in sauntering through the Catskills and along the Susquehanna after he became associate editor of the New York *Evening Post* in 1826.

At the time Bryant came to New York in the middle 1820's, James Fenimore Cooper was still enjoying his early fame and glory. *The Spy* and *The Pioneers* had been published, and the author was extremely popular. The large circle of Cooper's friends known as the Bread and Cheese Club met regularly at the Washington Hotel. Here Bryant, Fitz-Greene Halleck, James Kirke Paulding, and other writers mingled with artists such as John Vanderlyn, Samuel Morse, William Dunlap, and Thomas Cole. The apogee of Cooper's fame had been reached on that February day in 1823 when *The Pioneers* was published and 3,500 copies were sold by noon, extracts having previously been printed in the newspapers. This demand did not continue, and the novel had no more than average success; but *The Pioneers* proved to be the beginning of a new literary style, just as "Thanatopsis" had been a fresh start in poetry. Although we are not here concerned with Cooper's art as a novelist, his new way of describing the American scene and discussing problems connected with it is of great interest.

Cooper had grown up in the country. His daughter, Susan Fenimore Cooper, tells us that "his first childish recollections were all closely connected with the forests and hills, the fresh clearings, new fields, and houses on the banks of the Otsego. From the first bow and arrow, kite and ball, to later feats in riding, fishing, swimming, skating, all were connected with his highland home."¹⁰ Inspired by such experiences, Cooper set the scene of his novel at Otsego, and he never wearied of bringing this beautiful spot to the attention of the public. One of the devices he used was to lead his reader up a mountain overlooking the scene to be described. He used the same device in *Notions of the Americans* (1828) and *Home as Found* (1838). In both works there are unsentimental but entirely captivating descriptions that seldom contain such words as "grandeur," "sublime," or "picturesque," which were indispensable in earlier travel accounts. When Cooper had Judge Templeton look upon Otsego Lake for the first time, "not an opening was to be seen in the boundless forests, except where the lake lay, like a mirror of glass. The water was covered by myriads of the wild fowl that migrate with the changes of the season ...

I saw a bear with her cubs descend to the shore to drink."[11] By the time
Home as Found was written, the view had changed considerably. The
lake was still nestled in woods and hills, but there were "farms beautifully
relieved by patches of wood, in a way to resemble the scenery of a vast
park or a royal pleasure ground . . . all was teeming with the fruit of
human labor, and yet all was relieved by pieces of wood."[12] Anyone standing today on one of the hills above Otsego Lake, such as the one from
which Samuel Morse painted his "View from Apple Hill,"[13] can feel something of the atmosphere Cooper created (see vignette). It is easy to imagine
the deep impression made in the literary circles of the 1820's by this new
voice, ringing so true and bearing so direct an appeal. The general public,
however, was not strongly affected by it. The popular demand was for
descriptions of action, such as the killing of the panther in *The Pioneers*.
Cooper knew this well and dared to say so in *Home as Found*. In this we
are told that a picnic held in the middle of "native wildness" can be enjoyed only by intellectual persons. Therefore, two members of the party
with minds more simply organized call this kind of entertainment stupid
and nothing but "outlandish dog-in-the-mangerism."[14]

But to point out ways to enjoy nature was only a minor purpose in
Cooper's writings. What was far more important to him was the problem
of balancing the household of nature. Cooper, of course, used no such
word as "conservation"; yet in building up the story of *The Pioneers* he
employs the idea that man should govern the resources of nature by
certain principles in order to conserve them. Chapter after chapter deals
with man's waste of the treasures nature has provided for him. When
flocks of pigeons are being shot down wantonly, Leatherstocking is sure
that "the Lord won't see the waste of his creatures for nothing, and right
will be done to the pigeons, as well as others, by and by." Hauling in
great quantities of bass with dragnets "is fearful expenditure of the choicest
gifts of Providence." Above all, it is the woodchopper to whom Cooper
makes an appeal. Forests are felled "as if no end could be found to their
treasures, nor any limits to their extent. If we go on in this way, twenty
years hence we shall want fuel." Here Cooper follows in the footsteps of
his father, Judge William Cooper (see chap. 8), who had warned much
earlier that a day would come when there would be few trees left for
firewood and lumber. Cooper's treatment of the relationship between man
and nature makes apparent the moral problem involved in this relationship. Certainly not everyone would be willing or able to follow Natty
Bumpo on his flight from the evils of mankind to "the loneliness of the
Catskills." When Edward asks Natty, "What see you when you get there?"
he answers: "Creation, all creation, lad, . . . how should a man who has
lived in towns and schools know anything about the wonders of the

woods? ... and none know how often the hand of God is seen in the wilderness, but them that rove it for a man's life."[15]

Although Cooper knew that most people must struggle to get along in whatever circumstances and places they find themselves, whether it be New York, Otsego, or a settlement on the border of the prairie, he sensed that unless some steps were taken to limit the exploitation of nature's resources there would not be enough of these resources for future generations. Strangely enough, this theme of which Cooper makes so much has hardly been touched upon in the reviews of *The Pioneers* from the earliest to the one by D. H. Lawrence.[16] That these undertones would escape Mark Twain's cruel dissection of Cooper's "literary offences" might have been expected, in spite of, or because of, the manner in which Mark Twain unleniently examines his literary victim with a yardstick and a timepiece.[17] Mark Twain takes pigeon shooting, bass fishing, and tree felling as the natural consequences of new settlements. He considers Judge Templeton's arguments against the unnecessary cruelty and apparent waste of "precious gifts of nature" to be unrealistic, and believes that the life extolled by Natty Bumpo was doomed in view of Yankee progress, which was desirable. In the light of Cooper's strong and continued arguments for the conservation of natural resources, we must accept him, along with Dr. Nicholas Collin, as one of the very early authorities who had the vision to realize that even the seemingly inexhaustible riches of the New World were limited.

In the popular discussion about the distinctive character of the American scene Cooper definitely took sides. He regarded the view across the valley of the Mohawk which he describes in *Notions of the Americans* as "completely an American scene, embracing all that admixture of civilization, and of the forest, of the works of man, and of the reign of nature, that one can so easily imagine to belong to this country."[18] In his old age and after many years of disappointment in American life, Cooper, for the last time, expressed his ideas about the American scene in "American and European Scenery Compared." Here we find that Cooper is no longer much interested in the aesthetic problems concerning the American scene; he simply points out that the Rocky Mountains "must possess many novel views" though the accessories are necessarily wanting, for "a union of art and nature can alone render scenery perfect." Yet Cooper admits that "the mountain scenery of the United States, though wanting in grandeur ... is not without attractions that are singularly its own."[19] It is strange to think that this late essay, which is restrained in its treatment of nature, was written by one whose earlier word paintings of the phenomena of nature Balzac considered to be on the highest possible level.

Like two giants, Cooper and Bryant opened the path for the early nineteenth-century approach to nature. Cooper's influence in this respect comes mainly from works published between 1823 and 1841; Bryant's works continued to affect public opinion until the 1870's.

Sharing the general strong nationalist feelings, Bryant, about 1839, complained that so many Americans went to visit Wales or Scotland instead of "the Western shore of the Hudson," which was "as worthy of a pilgrimage across the Atlantic as the Alps themselves." To inspire the public, Bryant provided the *Evening Post* with descriptions of his trips to the Palisades, the Delaware Water Gap, the Catskills, and the Berkshires. Taking biscuits and apples along, he put up at wayside inns and workmen's cottages. He delighted in living the life of a vagabond and wrote blissful accounts of these jaunts and sent them to his paper. Washington Irving called these essays "essentially American," and Emerson maintained that Bryant "first, and he only made known to mankind our Northern nature—its summer splendors, its autumn russets, its wintry lights and glooms." Bryant's poems were first published in 1821; their intrinsic value and enduring influence is evidenced by the fact that an edition was brought out in 1846 for a new generation of readers. At the celebration of Bryant's seventieth birthday in 1864, fourteen years before he died, Emerson stated that there was "no feature of day or night in the country which does not, to a contemplative mind, recall the name of Bryant,"[20] and James Russell Lowell hailed the dean of American poets in stanzas like this:

> The voices of the hills did his obey;
> The torrents flashed and tumbled in his song;
> He brought our native fields from far away . . .[21]

When Bryant died in 1878, Curtis said of him: "whoever saw Bryant, saw America."[22] (See pl. 17.)

Though dwarfed by Bryant and Cooper, a number of their contemporaries explored and interpreted the American scene. For example, there was James Kirke Paulding, Washington Irving's most intimate friend, who owed his early fame to their common enterprise, the publishing of the *Salmagundi* papers, "to interest the young, inform the old and castigate the age." Paulding was a nationalist who unceasingly ridiculed John Bull and praised his own country. As youths, he and Irving had roamed the countryside around Tarrytown and along the banks of the Hudson. To restore his failing health, Paulding later traveled in the South and published an account of his journey. This lively book, in which descriptions are intermingled with political digressions, drew quick attention, though the route Paulding followed was not a fashionable one. From Williamsburg, Paulding went up the Pamunkey River and across the Blue Ridge toward the upper waters of the Shenandoah, in order to visit the various hot springs in that region. In "no part of the world," according to Paulding, could "the pure admirer of nature be more easily and variously gratified," and that was why Americans should travel through their own country. At the sight of the Natural Bridge, Paulding felt that "Jefferson deserves ill-will of every traveller in this part of the world, by having in his Notes on Virginia . . . given a description of this bridge, so provokingly happy, so inexcusably correct, that none can expect to rival him, and therefore the less I say about it the better."[23]

Paulding, in his *Backwoodsmen*, published in 1818 as an offer to the "neglected mass of this our western clime," attempted to picture the life of the settlers in Ohio, and though the book was decidedly a failure, it shows that some interest was being taken in the purely American subject of the opening up of western lands. In 1828 the publication of a satire, *The New Mirror for Travellers*, by Paulding, is evidence that traveling had already become a custom worth poking fun at. In this book Paulding took a disdainful attitude toward fashionable watering places and made innumerable gibes at Saratoga and Ballston. *The New Mirror* was republished in 1868—a rather astonishing revival for a parody which ridiculed the fashions and manners of a period forty years earlier.

When Paulding's friend Washington Irving went to England in 1814 as representative of his family's business enterprise, he had already earned some fame as the co-author of the *Salmagundi* papers and the author of *Diedrich Knickerbocker's History of New York* (1809), but this was nothing compared with the immediately and lasting success of *The Sketch Book*, published in installments in 1819 and 1820 from manuscripts which Irving sent home from England. Not only did this book carry the full-hearted blessing of Sir Walter Scott, but Lord Byron even avowed that he knew it by heart. In this country it was given unanimous recognition, and Richard H. Dana wrote in the *North American Review* that Irving's scenery was so true that "the bright and holy influences of nature fall on us."[24]

The Sketch Book contains only two pieces with direct bearing on the American scene, "Rip van Winkle" and "The Legend of Sleepy Hollow," but these two stories are as pure and full of vigor as a noble vintage wine. In the author's account of himself, Irving shows that he was intimately acquainted with the fine scenery of his own country and had first begun to be familiar with it in his early youth. How great an impression the scenery made on him is indicated by a memoir he wrote in 1851, forty years after his boyhood experiences.

> The scenery of the Hudson, the Kaatskill Mountains had the most witching effect on my boyish imagination. Never shall I forget the effect upon me of the first view of them predominating over a wide extent of country, part

wild, woody, and rugged; part softened away into all the graces of cultivation. As we slowly floated along I lay on the deck and watched them
through a long summer's day.[25]

Braced with such sentiments and cognizant of the rich lore of America's
English past which still lingered on, Irving resolved to endow the natural
scenery of America, which was full of youthful promise, with the "stored
and poetical association" needed to vie with the charm and beauty of
the Old World. Irving's magic wand indeed turned the Catskills, "clothed
in blue and purple" or sometimes gathering "gray vapours about the summits," into fairy mountains. After Irving had settled Henry Hudson with
his crew in the wilds of the Catskill Mountains and had made Ichabod
Crane at home in the cove of Sleepy Hollow, there never again could be
any thought of "uncouth" mountains, and the "howling wilderness" of the
seventeenth century was discarded forever. Irving had made an enormous
advance toward bridging the gap which still existed between man and
nature, though it was growing narrower from generation to generation.
These were entirely new vistas Irving had opened up, and, as if responding
to his call, artists began to people the amphitheater of the Catskills and
the banks of the Hudson. They came there to paint what Rip van Winkle
beheld when he looked down from the site of present Catskill Mountain
House and saw at a distance "the lordly Hudson, far, far below him,
moving on its silent but majestic course, with the reflection of a purple
cloud, or the sail of a lagging bark, here and there sleeping on its grassy
bosom, and at last losing itself in the blue highlands."[26]

In view of Bryant's and Irving's obvious achievements and the recognition they had gained in this country and abroad, literary circles were
shocked by an article published in the *Foreign Quarterly Review* in February, 1844, which, repeating Sydney Smith's diatribe of 1820, stated once
more that there was no national school of poetry in the United States.
Naturally, the papers of the day went into "severe paroxysms of wrath."[27]
Yet there were those who agreed with the writer of the article, though
they maintained that this lack of poetry was a misfortune rather than a
fault. As George Templeton Strong, the diarist who portrayed New York
life from 1835 to 1876, put it, there was neither a "legendary past nor a
poetic present. Large mountains, extensive prairies, tall cataracts, long
rivers, millions of dirty acres of every cosmographical character"[28] did not
provide a basis for poetry. Strong's description shows how little even a
man who was the proud owner of a fine library and who had traveled
extensively in New England and along the Hudson really knew about
the American scene in general. And not until artists and photographers
had made pictorial records of the little-known treasures of the continent
was this situation likely to change.

Before considering those artists who were the first to portray the glories of the Hudson River valley and the mountains and shores of New England, we must turn to the earlier colonial painters, not because of any rich inheritance of landscape paintings left us, but rather to clarify some of the doubts which exist concerning their work. The view has been expressed that painting in all its branches, including landscape painting, flourished in colonial times and that there is a flood of evidence to corroborate such statements.[29] Certainly "landskips" are mentioned in many documents such as wills, inventories, artists' obituaries, sign painters' advertisements, and the like. However, in most of these it is impossible to ascertain whether the landscapes were painted by artists in America or were imported, or perhaps were only engravings. But even though landscapes are mentioned in accounts of picture exhibitions, which were first held toward the end of the eighteenth century, the canvases exhibited were probably in no way comparable to the landscapes produced by artists of a later period, such as those of the Hudson River school. Since no proof of the existence of an American Richard Wilson has been found, we must assume that eighteenth-century landscapes by native American painters were topographical views, or portraits of particular places, so to speak. In canvases of this type there seems to have been no attempt to re-create a part of nature, though some of them are rather captivating because of naïve or imaginative qualities somewhat akin to those in certain kinds of contemporary painting. Undoubtedly, more than a few landscape paintings were made in colonial times, though only a small number have been handed down to us. Those that have survived are mediocre, though some of them may excusably be called primitive. In any history of American painting the daubings of an early period must be separated from the paintings of trained artists who consciously followed, or at least attempted to follow, an artistic calling. Alice Winchester and Jean Lipman have very successfully done this in their book *Primitive American Painting* (1951), and such a distinction should also be made whenever the history of academic American landscape painting is being discussed. An early landscape in the Worcester Museum, for instance, was done by one of the itinerant sign painters or journeyman artists who advertised: "Landscapes for Chimney Pieces of all Sizes: Likewise Drafts of . . . Houses in Colours or Indian Ink."[30] Many paintings of this sort are naïve representations of actual views, or copies of prints showing views of country seats or city and harbor prospects. When Ralph Earl went to Bennington, Vermont, in 1798 to paint portraits of the Van der Spiegel family, he too painted the view from the house. The landscape painting, however, had little charm, though it probably satisfied the owner and served its purpose as a record. A number of portraits by Ralph Earl (see pl. 7), Joseph Steward, James

Peale, and others show landscape details in the background. These, too, are either topographical renderings of buildings and sites associated with the sitter, or fanciful displays of foliage and trees which leave doubt whether the scene is American or one copied from a European print. An examination of the topographical views (see pls. 6, 8) that have come down to us, important historical documents though they may be, shows that not one of them depicts luxuriant and vast scenes of the kind that prompted William Bartram and Alexander Wilson to express themselves in terms of high admiration based on understanding and deep emotion.

In view of the Puritan attitude toward enjoyment of worldly pleasures (see chap. 1), it is very unlikely that landscape painters could have made a living or would have sold even a small number of landscapes in New England in the seventeenth century, or even in the eighteenth before the time of Jonathan Edwards, about the middle of the century. In the South, where more liberal thinking prevailed, it would have been even more difficult to sell such paintings, since the plantations were scattered. Charleston and courthouse meeting places, such as Williamsburg, could have offered but slim opportunities for a professional landscape painter. Besides, wealthy plantation owners, if they were ambitious, would not have been satisfied with anything but the best. The colonial squire, like his English cousins who adorned their mantelpieces with portraits by Sir Godfrey Kneller, or who cherished a Salvator Rosa to throw "Italian light on British walls," wanted paintings that would add to his prestige, or at least the nearest thing to paintings which could be had at less expense—copies of famous works of art.

In the seventeenth century nobody in the American colonies felt the need for pictures showing the uncouth state of the countryside. In Holland, however, the situation was quite different; the country was well cultivated and the burgher was proud of it and was eager to have it pictured from many different angles and as factually as possible. As the eighteenth century approached, the landscape of colonial America became even more unsuitable for reproduction. In Justus Engelhardt Kühn's portraits appears what was considered the ideal background—views of parks or gardens arranged in formal style. Joseph Blackburn's and William Williams' outdoor portraits of a later day show backgrounds in the informal English park style. These suggest theatrical backdrops rather than American landscapes, even though occasionally a topographical view of New York is visible through wings formed by park trees.

Even in England no one would have cared for realistic landscapes; Gainsborough in one of his letters asserts that "with regard to *real views* from Nature in this country, he has never seen any place that affords a subject equal to the poorest imitation of Gasper [Poussin] or Claude

[Lorrain]."[31] It should also be remembered how poorly Richard Wilson's efforts at landscape paintings were rewarded. Under such circumstances it would be useless to look for sentimental landscape painting in the New World before the early nineteenth century. It was only then that a few connoisseurs began to regard the American landscape as either a "noble" subject or one of sufficient "grandeur" to make it worth the painting. Although by this time the terms "sublime" and "picturesque" were not unknown in polite society, they were not yet generally applied to the American scene. Gradually, however, an evolution took place during the years of transition at the end of the eighteenth and the beginning of the nineteenth century. This is well illustrated by the story of four English painters who came to make their fortunes in America after the conclusion of Jay's treaty between Great Britain and the United States in 1794.

These four painters—George Beck, William Groombridge, Francis Guy, and William Winstanley[32]—though fairly competent in their profession, were in no way outstanding artists and certainly had no predilection for romantic discoveries. What makes them interesting so far as our subject is concerned is the reaction of the general public to their paintings. At the time these men worked, the public was beginning to acquire some knowledge of the immense scenic wonders secluded in the upper valleys of the great rivers and the inaccessible mountains. These Englishmen lived in or near Philadelphia, Baltimore, and New York and had to work hard to earn their meager living. They painted what was in demand—topographical views, country seats of wealthy gentlemen, and perhaps now and then a canvas for a mantelpiece. Only occasionally did they essay a scene of the outdoors in the style of the ideal landscapes of Claude Lorrain. Two of them, George Beck and William Winstanley, were so fortunate as to attract the attention of George Washington, who bought some of their views of the Hudson River and the Falls of the Potomac. Indeed, the president recommended Winstanley, "a celebrated landskip painter," to the Commission of the District of Columbia, pointing out that he might paint the Grand and the Little Falls, the passage of the Potomac through the Blue Ridge Mountains, the Natural Bridge, and other "grand objects." If any subjects were to be suggested these were the ones to be expected, because paintings of landscapes were deemed worth while only if they represented prominent or unusual features and were done in the grand manner. Winstanley's and Beck's paintings of the American scene acquired by George Washington thus show a definite relation to traditional European landscape painting.

Washington's commissions were highlights in the lives of the artists, who otherwise were compelled to use the most ingenious devices to sell their pictures. But even forced sales, such as raffles after art shows held at inns, were insufficient to change the general "Siberian climate" for artists, or to make the public desirous of buying landscapes. Eventually, Groombridge and Beck and their wives took up teaching in order to earn enough money for them to live on. Winstanley painted portraits and eventually returned to England. Guy succeeded in making a precarious living by interesting the public in some novel technical drawing devices. Though all these landscapists had definite artistic qualifications which would have enabled them to depict nature truthfully, they were frustrated by lack of support.

Thomas Birch (1779–1851), another Englishman, was more fortunate than his compatriots, perhaps because he specialized in marine scenes as well as the usual topographic views. Some of his marine paintings are dramatic and in some ways express that romantic taste which sought the unusual. Occasionally Birch also painted a landscape or a winter scene in a rather lyrical manner, from which it can be assumed that he might have done more of this kind of work during his early career had it been in greater demand. Birch's paintings, like those by Jacob Hoffman, Archibald Robertson, and many others whose names have now been forgotten, were engraved for the *Columbian Magazine,* the *New York Magazine,* or the *Massachusetts Magazine.*[33] In the story of the painters' discovery of the American scene, all these men figure as the vanguard.

Of greater stature, however, than all these minor painters was that American who gave promise of being the greatest artist of the period, though tragedy prevented the full development of his artistic powers. This was Washington Allston. A Harvard graduate, traveler, and cosmopolite, Allston was at home in London, Paris, and Rome, where he frequented elite circles and associated with the most brilliant writers and artists of the day. Coleridge, who became his lifelong friend, was among them, as were Shelley, Keats, Madame de Staël, and scores of others. It seemed as though destiny had chosen Allston to plant the seed of romanticism on American soil. Imbued with idealism of European stamp and extremely sensitive to the particular character of the New World, Allston set an example for American landscape painting of a higher order than anything which had been done before. In 1804 Allston produced his first great romantic paintings, "The Deluge" and "The Thunderstorm at Sea." Unfortunately, only a few more pictures, though these were of impressive character, such as "Elijah Feeding the Ravens,"[34] were to come from his brush. Although these in some respects suggest the work of Claude Lorrain and Jacob van Ruisdael, they show Allston's own imaginative power and have a serenity that is also entirely his own. When Allston's creative powers ceased, he still remained a forceful teacher. He did much to bring to the fore the kind of American landscape painting that helped to make more intimate the relationship between man and nature. It was Allston who marked out the route Cole was to follow when he went to Europe. He admonished Cole never to lose his love for nature, and told him that "the young artist should study nature and pictures together,"[35] an advice Cole did not fail to follow when he went abroad to study Turner, Poussin, and Salvator Rosa.

Contemporary with Allston's early works were some paintings by John Trumbull and John Vanderlyn that treat Niagara Falls as a scene of grandeur worthy of the brush of a romantic painter and one which could be represented in the grand style. Vanderlyn, who had been befriended by Allston, is supposed to have been the first artist to paint Niagara, which he did in 1802. Trumbull, though of an older generation, painted a series of waterfalls in 1808 in which he included Niagara. He intended to use his Niagara sketches as material for a panorama which was to be executed in London, where such showpieces were then fashionable. Perhaps Vanderlyn had the same intention, for he painted a panorama of the park of Versailles, which he showed in New York in 1815. When later, in 1826, he executed a large painting of Niagara, it differed from his earlier conception. His first sketches had been close-up studies showing dramatic aspects of the falls. In the 1826 version the falls are pushed back and the foreground is filled with the rotting trunks of trees, in one of which a hawk is perched. A lonely mood pervades the whole picture and gives it a typically romantic feeling. This change in style, however, did not originate with Vanderlyn. In the quarter of a century between the two conceptions, American landscape painting had become popular and had taken a turn toward romanticism. Vanderlyn was ready to adopt the romantic style though he was not close to the leaders of the school of American landscape painting that had begun to develop.

Before we turn to Thomas Cole, the leader of the new school of romantic painting, let us consider briefly some other painters, in various sections of the country, who worked along rather independent lines. These artists eked out their living principally by painting portraits. Differing from their predecessors who also had been portraitists and who had painted topographical views on the side, John Neagle (see pl. 9), Ezra Ames, and several others became interested in nature itself and painted natural scenery for their own delight, though they may have been stimulated by descriptions of nature which they had read in travel books or magazines. Their landscapes were unsophisticated and the painters made no attempt to make them fashionable; yet there must have been a small number of art lovers besides the artists themselves to whom this new subject had some appeal.

One of these painters who rose to fame from anonymity was Thomas Doughty. In 1820 Doughty gave up the leather business, in which he had been successful, and listed himself as "landscape painter." From his early youth he had been enthusiastic about the outdoors. His first pictures of American scenes, including some illustrations for Cooper's *Pioneers*, were shown in the Philadelphia exhibitions of 1822 and 1824 and were welcomed immediately. At the New York Academy exhibition of 1826 the critic of the *New-York Mirror*[36] pointed to Doughty's work as "the most beautiful in the room," although three of Thomas Cole's pictures were exhibited in the same show. A painting depicting the Rocky Mountains, perhaps one of those exhibited in New York and apparently the earliest known picture painted by Doughty, was reproduced in the *Port Folio* of March, 1822. Doughty had never seen the Rockies. But Titian R. Peale and Samuel Seymour had accompanied the expedition led by Major Stephen Long from Pittsburgh to the Rockies in 1819–1820, and Seymour had done "numerous landscape views, exhibiting the characteristic features of various parts of the country besides many others of detached scenery."[37] One of the few drawings by Seymour included in the London edition of the report of the expedition published in 1822 served as a model for Doughty, who must have seen Seymour's drawing before it was published. Although Doughty was reasonably successful, he never was as famous as Thomas Cole, who became the undisputed leader in romantic landscape painting, the movement later known as the Hudson River school.[38]

Cole began his career at the age of twenty-four when he came to New York in the spring of 1825. This was indeed a propitious time. In the fall of that year, the opening of the Erie Canal, which extended from Lake Erie to the Hudson River, gave New York an opportunity to expand its trade. Governor De Witt Clinton had conceived the daring idea of digging the "big ditch" and had carried it through with success. Besides being versed in business and practical matters, Clinton took a deep interest in art and was one of the most active promoters of the American Academy of the Fine Arts, a forerunner of the National Academy of Design. The first exhibition held by the American Academy in 1816 was opened with a speech by Clinton. At this time none of the novels of Irving or Cooper had been published, nor had Cole or Doughty shown the public any of their romantic landscapes. The thoughts expressed by Clinton in his speech anticipate sentiments later expressed by these romanticists. According to Clinton, the artist's imagination "must derive its forms . . . from the country in which he was born . . . can there be a country in the world better calculated than ours to exercise and to exalt the imagination . . . Here nature has conducted her operations on a magnificent scale . . . this wild, romantic and awful scenery . . ." Clinton was inclined to believe also that the fine arts "ought to receive the encouraging smiles of public beneficence," and that a wealthy nation must be friendly to those arts "which

Plate 1.   Niagara Falls. Photograph by Marta Huth, 1949.

*Plate 2.   Alexander Wilson Traveling along the Susquehanna.
From drawing by Wilson, 1809.*

Plate 3.   Hadley Falls. From painting by W. G. Wall, 1820.

Plate 4. Stagecoach near Trenton, New Jersey. Detail from water color by Pawel Swinin, ca. 1811.

Plate 5. *Fulton's* Paragon *on the Hudson. From water color by Pawel Swinin, ca. 1811.*

Plate 6. Millpond in Maryland. Painting by an American artist, ca. *1811.*

Plate 7.   Landscape near Litchfield, Massachusetts. Detail from painting by Ralph Earl, 1790.

Plate 8. Country Seat Painting by an American artist. ca. *1800.*

*Plate 9. View from Belmont Manor, Philadelphia. Painting by
John Neagle, late 1820's.*

*Plate 10.   John James Audubon. Painting by his sons, John W. and
Victor G. Audubon,* ca. *1841.*

Plate 11.   Peace at Sunset. Painting by Thomas Cole, late 1820's.

Plate 12.   Niagara Falls. Painting by Alvan Fisher, 1820.

Plate 13. On the Susquehanna. Painting by Joshua Shaw, 1839.

*Plate 14.   Kindred Spirits (Bryant and Cole). Painting by Asher
Durand, 1849.*

Plate 15. Flume in the White Mountains. Drawing by Thomas Cole, 1827.

Plate 16.   The Lost Balloon (near Nyack, New York). Painting by William H. Beard, 1880.

*Plate 17.   William Cullen Bryant. Painting by Frank Buchser,
1868.*

Plate 18.   The Battery, New York. Water color by Pawel Swinin,
ca. *1811.*

Plate 19. *Elgin Botanical Garden. Drawing by Hugh Reinagle,*
ca. *1812.*

Plate 20.   ABOVE, LEFT: *Nahant Hotel.*
ABOVE, RIGHT: *Fairmont Park, Philadelphia.*
Both on Staffordshire china, 1824–1829.
BELOW: *Erie Canal. American printed paper on
bandbox, ca. 1830.*

Plate 21. Trenton Falls. From drawing by W. Heine, 1851.

*Plate 22.   Mount Auburn Cemetery. Engraving by James Smillie,
1850.*

Plate 23.   Pittsford on the Erie Canal. Painting by George Harvey, 1837.

Plate 24.   Boys Sleighing. Painting by George Harvey, 1846.

Plate 25. *Fourth of July Picnic. Water color by Susan Merrett,*
ca. *1845.*

*Plate 26.   Picnic near Mount Mansfield (Vermont). Painting by
Jerome Thompson, ca. 1860.*

Plate 27. Three Mile Point, Otsego Lake. Painting by Julius
Gollman and Louis Mignot, 1850.

Plate 28.   Smokers' Circle on Boston Common. Woodcut, 1851.

Plate 29. Boston Common. Painting by an unknown artist,
ca. 1865.

Plate 30. Railroad in the Mohawk Valley. From drawing by William H. Bartlett, 1839.

*Plate 31.   Catskill Mountain House. From drawing by William
H. Bartlett, 1839.*

*Plate 32.   Shrewsbury River near Seabright (New Jersey). Painting .
by an American artist, 1860–1865.*

Plate 33. Daniel Webster at His Farm. Painting by an American artist, 1840–1845.

*Plate 34.   Meditation by the Sea. Painting by an American artist,
1850–1860.*

*Plate 35. Philosophers' Camp at Follansbee Pond. Painting by
William J. Stillman, 1858.*

Plate 36.   Camping in the Woods. Lithograph by A. F. Tait, 1863.

Plate 37.   *Charles Loring Eliot and Friends at Trenton High Falls.*
Painting by Junius B. Stearns, 1858.

Plate 38. What a Catch! (Otsego Lake). Painting by J. G. Clonney, 1855.

Plate 39.   Hunters' Rendezvous. Painting by Paul Weber, 1854.

Plate 40.   Long Branch, New Jersey. Painting by Winslow Homer,
            ca. *1865.*

Plate 41. Pemigewasset Coach (White Mountains). Painting by
E. Wood Perry, 1899.

Plate 42.   White Sulphur Springs Hotel (West Virginia). Woodcut, early 1860's.

Plate 43.   Sing-Sing Camp Meeting. From painting by Joseph B. Smith, 1838.

Plate 44.   Rocky Mountains. From water color by Karl Bodmer,
1831.

Plate 45.   The Voyageurs. Painting by Charles Deas, 1845.

Plate 46. Cañon of the Grand River. From sketch by F. W. Egloffstein, ca. 1855.

Plate 47.   Lake Tahoe. Painting by Albert Bierstadt, 1863.

Plate 48.   Miss Edwards at Lookout Mountain, Tennessee.
Photograph by U. S. Signal Corps, 1863.

Plate 49.   Frederick Law Olmsted. Photograph about 1860.

Plate 50. Hunting Car, Northern Pacific Railway. Photograph by Frank Jay Haynes, 1876.

Plate 51. Bicycling at Mammoth Hot Springs, Yellowstone
National Park. Photograph by Frank Jay Haynes,
1896.

Plate 52.   Mammoth Hot Springs. Photograph by W. H. Jackson, 1871.

Plate 53.   *Yellowstone Range near Fort Ellis. Water color by*
Thomas Moran, 1872.

*Plate 54.   Grand Canyon National Park, Arizona. Photograph by
Marta Huth, 1948.*

Plate 55. Mountain of the Holy Cross. Photograph by W. H. Jackson, 1873.

*Plate 56.   Canyon of the Yampa, near Junction with Green River,
Uinta Range. Photograph by T. H. O'Sullivan,
1867– 1869.*

Plate 57. *Yosemite Valley from the South Rim. Photograph by*
C. E. Watkins, 1861.

*Plate 58.   Yosemite Valley from Glacier Point. Painting by
William Hahn, 1874.*

Plate 59.   Peshtigo Forest Fire,Wisconsin. Woodcut, 1871.

*Plate 60.   Theodore Roosevelt, John Muir, and Others, Yosemite.
Photograph by Joseph LeConte, 1903.*

Plate 61.   Interior of Cedar Cottage, Yosemite Valley.
Photograph by H. G. Peabody, after 1890.

Plate 62.   Two Contrasting Experimental Fields in Madison County, North Carolina, ca. 1950.

Plate 63.   Central Park, New York. Photograph, ca. 1950.

*Plate 64.   White Throne, Zion National Park. Photograph by
Marta Huth, 1949.*

polish and refine society."[39] With extraordinary insight Clinton fostered
two ideas which were to become fundamental throughout the forthcoming
development of American painting. The first was the recognition of the
American scene as an appropriate subject for the artist. Since national
pride and self-reliance had developed rapidly in the period following the
War of 1812, the public accepted this conception with no great difficulty.
The second idea was a greater challenge. The proposition that society, or
perhaps the state, should accept the responsibility of giving the artist
adequate recompense for his work was an issue which would have been
strongly disputed by an earlier generation represented by men like Roger
Sherman, who had denied in Congress that the government should assume
obligations of this kind. But times had changed; commissions for painting
the rotunda of the Capitol had been given, and many similar commissions
were to follow.

Clinton's interest in art, stimulated perhaps by some of his artist friends,
such as John Trumbull and Samuel Morse, was shared by many of his companions. Among these men from various walks of life were Robert R. Livingston, the former ambassador to France; Dr. David Hosack, the founder
of the New York Botanical Garden; Gulian C. Verplanck, the historian;
and Robert Fulton, the engineer and inventor. Considering that this enlightened circle was intent upon furthering the newly sprouting literature
and arts, it is easy to imagine the favorable reception given to Cole's and
Bryant's paintings in New York in the early 1820's. Theoretical interest
was backed up by practical assistance; art patronage was found both
in New York and in smaller cities. Cole, for one, was given important commissions in Hartford and Baltimore. In most of his work he was allowed
to follow his own ideas, his patrons being perfectly willing to subordinate
their own desires to his. Perhaps Cole was the first painter to be in so
favorable a situation. From the moment he had the good fortune to sell
pictures of the highlands of the Hudson River valley to John Trumbull,
William Dunlap, and Asher B. Durand, he was permitted to paint whatever he wished.

Cole was self-taught, but he had studied a great deal and was never a
naïve painter. Since his youth he had been an avid reader; he had known
the New World from books and travel descriptions even before he had
left England and come to America with his father in 1818. After his arrival,
the young artist immediately took stock of the surroundings to which he
had been brought. He learned to know the Ohio country and Pennsylvania
intimately and took extended walking trips across the Alleghenies. With
almost no money and in the company of a friend, he trudged along the
highways and byways, fortified by nothing but a flute, which he played
lustily to chase away any fears which might have beset him and his com-

panion on their march toward the unknown wilds of the country. There was always a sketchbook in his knapsack. Early sketches still exist which show his close observation of living trees, rotten stumps, and foliage. Like Bartram, Bryant, and all the other nature enthusiasts, Cole trained himself early to observe closely. For instance, he studied a tree from its root to its top where it lost itself in the sky, and made sketches of it from various angles. He always brought home such sketches and from them composed his pictures (pl. 15). Though Cole traveled much in later life, his Catskill home was the place where he felt secure and where he believed he really belonged. Here with a full view of the mountains from his own piazza, he felt as though nature had spread a banquet before him from which he might feast. His delight in the natural beauties of the region prompted him to remark that "the painter of American scenery has indeed privileges superior to any other. All nature here is new to art."[40]

The widespread admiration Cole enjoyed was based not only on his ability as a painter but also on his high ethical standards and deep religious feelings. His biographer, the clergyman and poet Louis Noble, doubts whether Cole's pictures, which after all were the acknowledged basis of his fame, "show the greater part of the man . . . they reveal less of his soul than did what may be called his wood-and-field talk." From his early youth Cole had been deeply impressed by Wordsworth's philosophy, and at a time when the public was most receptive to this philosophy, Cole through his pictures and his personal influence became one of Wordsworth's strongest advocates. Intense communion with nature derived from Wordsworth's religious and moral idealism was expressed in every one of Cole's paintings (see pl. 11). The beginning of Cole's career coincided with the Boston publication of Wordsworth's poetical works in 1824. After Cole had painted his early mountain scenes, some of them definitely associated with American history, he in 1827 painted his "St. John Preaching in the Wilderness." Although the mountain background of the picture is based on studies of natural scenes, the impact of the picture lies in the figure of St. John, through which Cole expresses the idea that "the wilderness is yet a fitting place in which to speak of God," because "the pathless solitudes are congenial to religious musings."[41] Cole's attitude was the opposite of that of the early Renaissance painter who liked to paint a landscape but felt that he must include in it a subject considered more worthy, such as "The Flight into Egypt." With the years, Cole's work increasingly took on dogmatic purpose; the symbolism in his pictures, which he now grouped in cycles, began to weigh down his representation of natural features. Although it is now believed that Cole overreached himself in these grandiose schemes, it should not be forgotten that his paintings were greatly admired in their time and that his allegorical scenes were regarded as well-justified interpretations of the relationship between man and nature.

Almost as soon as the merit of Cole's work was generally recognized, the public began to take an interest also in the work of Asher B. Durand. Recognizing Cole's talent immediately, Durand bought one of Cole's very early pictures. Unlike Cole, who made mere sketches when he faced his "subjects," Durand painted carefully finished studies which he later used in composing his pictures in his studio. It is evident, therefore, that his conception of nature differed from that of Cole. Durand was content to represent the outward aspect of some site as he would the face of someone whose portrait he was painting, but without idealizing it. Lacking the genius and intuition of Cole but perhaps surpassing him in faithful rendition, Durand set an example which weaker followers emulated, with the result that much of American landscape painting of the period lacked sensitivity and eventually the public lost interest in it. Durand came perhaps closer to Cole's conception in the canvas which shows Bryant and Cole as "kindred spirits" in the admiration of nature (pl. 14). The painting was ordered by Luman Reed, the great art lover, to commemorate Cole's death. Perhaps this canvas, which was painted in 1849, marks the apogee of romantic painting. Before romanticism had run its course, many other capable artists entered upon successful careers—John W. Casilaer, Frederick E. Church, J. F. Cropsey, Henry Inman, J. F. Kensett, W. S. Mount, and Alexander H. Wyant, to mention a few. The pattern set by Cole did not change essentially for at least another decade; and a number of painters followed it much longer (see pl. 18). About the middle of the century certain new forces came into play; among these were influences from abroad which tended to change the outlook of the American landscapists.

Before Durand took up landscape painting, he had won recognition as an engraver, especially as an engraver of landscapes. In 1830 he had launched an ambitious serial publication, *The American Landscape*. It was not the first venture of its kind. The engraver John Hill had previously published two similar series, one made from paintings by Joshua Shaw, an English painter who had come to America (see pl. 13). The plan for these *Picturesque Views of the American Scene* (1820) was to present scenes which Shaw would paint in a number of states in order to show "our lofty mountains . . . the unexampled magnitude of our cataracts, the wild grandeur of our western forests . . . unsurpassed by any of the boasted scenery of other countries." These striking features of nature, he said, "have rarely been made the subjects of pictorial delineation."[12] The assertion that Shaw had visited a great number of states to provide these views was a slight exaggeration, because the one plate showing a western scene,

"The Falls of St. Anthony," was painted from a colored view made by a "Captain Watson of the British Navy." Since only three issues, containing twenty attractively colored plates, were published, the series apparently was not as well received as Hill had hoped it would be. He then made engravings from paintings by William G. Wall which were published between 1821 and 1826 as *The Hudson River Portfolio* (see pl. 3). Dedicated to the beauties of the "American Rhine," these prints proved quite successful. Durand was the next to bring out a series of this kind: in 1830 he published *The American Landscape;* it was of folio size and contained steel engravings of landscapes by his friends. In the prospectus of this portfolio, Bryant had expressed the hope that there would be no want of taste in the community to insure the most successful results.[48] But unfortunately Durand was never able to produce more than the first issue, which contained a reproduction of Cole's "Winnepesaukee Lake," painted in 1827. This was the lake that Timothy Dwight had found singularly beautiful a quarter of a century earlier. In spite of the failure of Durand's publications, his work was popular until the very end of the romantic period, because of its extraordinary realism combined with a touch of romantic sentiment.

The various kinds of engravings and lithographs used for illustrating books made this period especially rich in the publication of almanacs and albums containing reproductions of paintings by Thomas Cole, Asher B. Durand, Thomas Doughty, Henry Inman, Alvan Fisher (see pl. 12), and many others now forgotten. Quantities of books of this new species, carrying colorful titles such as *The Atlantic Souvenir, The Talisman, The Token,* and *The Snow Flake,* were offered to the American reading public, who loved to place elegant keepsakes on the drawing-room table. During the period these miscellanies were in vogue—that is, between 1825 and 1865—more than a thousand different titles are supposed to have been published. Many of the novels, lyrics, essays, and "embellishments" contained in these volumes had to do with nature in some form or other, and thus these almanacs aided in popularizing the ideas of romanticism.

Beyond their original purpose, engravings in almanacs and similar publications were used as patterns for Staffordshire pottery and other works of the decorative arts (see pl. 20). Cole's pictures were special favorites of the decorators of British blue ware and pink ware which were produced in quantities from the early 1820's on. And among the so-called scenic wallpapers imported from France after 1834 there was a set called "American Scenery" which showed views of Niagara Falls and the Natural Bridge as well as other subjects.[49]

Beginning in the 1820's, the holding of art exhibitions became a regular practice in many cities, and a number of periodicals printed reviews of these shows. This new institution demonstrated that American painters were discovering the beauty of their country, and it became one of the most important factors in arousing general interest in the arts. Magazine writers even pointed out that the paintings by American artists were aiding in the formation of a national character.

An entirely new way of distributing and popularizing works of art was devised in 1839 when the American Art Union was established.[45] Following a European pattern which had originated in France and was copied in all European countries, the Art Union published engravings from American paintings and encouraged artists in general by handing out well-paid commissions. Although the Union was very successful along these lines, after a period of ten years, it had to stop this kind of activity because it supposedly violated lottery laws.

As the half-century mark approached, the romantic movement was still strong, though it had lost its initial impetus and freshness. Cole, instead of worshipping mountain sunrises, was now laboring over his didactic picture cycles, and Bryant was becoming a cosmopolite, preparing for publication accounts of his travels abroad. Painting in the romantic style was commonplace, just as sentimental feeling was hackneyed by writers of various degrees of competence. When Mrs. Anna Jameson, an English writer, visited America in 1837 she

> was struck by the manner in which the imaginative talent of the people had thrown itself forth in painting, the country seemed to me to swarm with painters. . . . Some I found looking at Nature, and imitating her in her more obvious external aspects, with such a simplicity and earnestness, that their productions, in spite of most crude and defective execution, fixed attention.[46]

In spite of this general willingness of American painters to follow romantic trends there were some widely discussed questions for which there seemed to be no clear-cut answer. For instance, "Was it true that the American scene was inferior to the European one because it still lacked sufficient historical or legendary associations in spite of all the literary and artistic efforts which had been made for decades?" and "Was artistic interpretation justifiable without pertinent associations?" The sting Sydney Smith had given to American arts and literature in the *Edinburgh Review* of 1820 had been forgotten, and his question "Who was reading American books and considering American pictures?" was still being asked again and again. The painful controversy was kept up through many a critical book written by Europeans traveling in this country, and it always caused endless discussions. Whether American writers and painters should follow European romantic trends or write and paint in a style peculiar to America was indeed a crucial issue. No less than Goethe, who had been closely following the development of the New World, recognized the problem in his poem addressed to the United States in 1827.

America, you're better off than
Our continent, the old.
You have no castles which are fallen
No basalt to behold.
You're not disturbed within your inmost being
Right up till today's daily life
By useless remembering
And unrewarding strife.
Use well the present and good luck to you
And when your children begin writing poetry
Let them guard well in all they do
Against knight- robber- and ghost-story."

Similar advice had come from Chateaubriand, who had roamed the forests of America himself: "Il n'y a de vieux en Amérique, que les bois enfants de la terre, et la liberté, mère de toute société humaine; cela vaut bien des monuments et des aieux."⁴⁸ Both men emphasized the theory that traditions and historical associations do not and need not exist in the New World, and that man, being a free agent, should shape his own patterns of creating and living.

Washington Irving, not heeding such counsel, established the bowling green of Hudson's crew so firmly in the Catskills that every thunderstorm in the Hudson River valley to this day brings to mind the picture he created. Writers in all parts of the country soon followed his example. They peopled lonely glades with Indian maidens, and described the wrath of the Indian gods. Undoubtedly, all such associations did make for a closer approach of man to the yet unexplored strongholds of nature; but the question remained: Could any friendly relationship between man and nature be established without the existence of such associations, and how did the situation compare with that in Europe?

Cole tried to give an answer in his first lecture about the American landscape, which he delivered at the American Lyceum in New York City in 1835. Constantly searching for the picturesque, he had become aware of the "sublimity of untamed wilderness and the majesty of the eternal mountains." Affinity with such manifestations of nature alone justified his paintings, he felt, and gave them their distinctly American character. He told his listeners that it was their apathy which made them unappreciative of the beauties of external nature, that it was not true "that American scenery possessed little that is interesting or truly beautiful, and that being destitute of the vestige of antiquity it may not be compared with European scenery . . . it has features, and noble ones unknown to Europe." Wildness was most characteristic feature of the American scene. There was also a union of the picturesque and the sublime, and of grandeur and loveliness, the sublime melting into the beautiful. One after another, Cole praised the water, the falls, river scenes, forests, and the seasons; then in conclusion he said that the home scene was by no means destitute of historical and legendary associations.

Obviously Cole was not able to make all his points emphatic, because his world was only New England. He had never visited the Great West

Camp near Round Lake (Adirondacks)

with its vast prairies and magnificent mountains. The natural features he appraised were in the East, and the categories he ascribed to them were pertinent to the East and were not essentially different from those used by European romanticists. Cole's contention that there were American associations which made it worth while to paint the home scene proved precisely that he felt that the work of the artist needed these associations for its justification. Yet he made the astonishing statement, "American associations are not so much of the past as of the present and the future— and in looking over the uncultivated scene, the mind may travel far into

futurity . . ."[49] This indeed is an indication of the cleavage in Cole's mind.
He had a serious desire to penetrate to the heart of the American scene
and value it on its own merit, and at the same time he depended on
romantic ideas that were related to those of his fellow romanticists in
Europe. Throughout Cole's lifetime no decisive answer was given to these
questions, though definite ideas about the problem were occasionally expressed. For instance, Robert Gilmore of Baltimore, an exceedingly sensitive art collector and one of Cole's patrons, made it known that he preferred "real American scenes and compositions," with their natural effects
"so pleasing and spirited as the artist can feel permitted to do without
violation of its truth."[50] Edgar Allan Poe pointed very definitely in 1844
to these "real" American scenes; he wrote of

> the gorgeous interior scenery of some of our western and southern dis-
> tricts,—of the vast valley of Louisiana, for example,—a realization of the
> wildest dreams of paradise. . . . In fact, the real Edens of the land lie far
> away from the track of our most deliberate tourists . . . No fiction has ap-
> proached it. . . . And *beauty* is, indeed, its sole character. It has little, or
> rather nothing, of the sublime.[51]

A decade later, George William Curtis expressed the thought that there
was a positive want of the picturesque in American scenery and life, but
went on to say that there should be another level of comparison than the
one ordinarily used. "Picturesqueness should not be the yardstick . . .
Space and wildness are the proper praises of American scenery. . . . We
have only vast and unimproved extent, and the interest with which the
possible grandeur of a mysterious future may invest it."[52]

Judged by these definitions, the situation of the American landscapist
appears to have been an extremely difficult one. In the long run, the picturesque, fleeting in its nature, could not provide him with any suitable or
dependable subject matter; even less to be depended on were moral implications such as those suggested by some of the titles of Cole's late pictures.
Living on a continent which, in the European sense, had no past and therefore presented no need for the artist to revolt against academic and conservative forces, the American artist was left without the stimulating controversies which moved European romanticists. What inspiration, then,
did he need to bring out his progressive spirit and stir him to action?
Edgar P. Richardson answered this question very ably by adapting a
phrase from Palladio: "Earth, air, water, self-mastery and the belief that
the voices of sentiment and intuition speak the final words on these great
themes."[53]

To study nature, to rely on his own resources when he had the urge to
visualize what he had seen or to express what he felt—that indeed became
the vocation of the American painter, as it was to be that of the scientist

and writer. The names of the painters Worthington Whittredge, George Inness, and Winslow Homer come to mind; and of the writers Henry Thoreau, John Burroughs, John Muir, and Thomas Wolfe, all of whom wrote at a later date, at a time when man's friendship with nature was much more deeply rooted.

4

Play and Rest

THROUGHOUT colonial days, hunting and fishing were the most common ways of enjoying the outdoors, but even these pleasures were greatly restricted in some places. In New England they were permissible only so far as they were necessary for a livelihood; as mere pastimes they were undesirable, according to the Puritan way of thinking. Beyond the limits of New England the situation was somewhat different. In places where the upper classes still clung to English tradition, hunting and fishing—that is, "sports"—were much in favor. Frequently companies were organized in

VIGNETTE: Andrew J. Downing's House at Newburgh, New York.

which open-air activities of this kind were performed as social functions. In Philadelphia there still exists the "Fishhouse," officially known as the Schuylkill Fishing Company of the State in Schuylkill, which was founded in 1732. In 1759 Andrew Burnaby visited the company on its grounds in what is now Fairmount Park and was pleasantly surprised by the beauty of the club gardens "which, together with the walks and fine groves . . . form a most beautiful and picturesque scene." Here both men and women gathered to "divert themselves with walking, fishing, going up the water . . . [and] in winter . . . it is usual to make sleighing parties."[1]

In the South, wild-fowl shooting, deer hunting, and riding after hounds were important sports; indeed, the social life of a southern gentleman was not complete without fox hunting. George Washington, who was president of the Virginia Jockey Club and one of the most accomplished riders of his day, boasted of running a pack of hounds so close that it could be covered with a blanket. Although he had to neglect his hunting establishment during the Revolutionary War, Washington began hunting again after Lafayette presented him with a pack of swift French hounds. The President loved to start before sunrise and follow the hounds across the countryside in the bracing morning air.

In the North, as we learn from the diary of the wealthy New Yorker Philip Hone, written during the early part of the nineteenth century, sailing and fishing parties were leisure-time pleasures. Hone with much delight tells of the trout he and his sporting friends caught off New York and Boston.[2]

In general, one gets the impression that hunting and fishing as sports were for the recreation of only the upper strata of society. The ordinary citizen did not often indulge in sports, and conservative persons considered them rather reprehensible. A typical article in the *Massachusetts Missionary Magazine* in 1803 asserted that the golden days of youth spent in the pursuit of sports were a prodigal waste, that sports were not fit for a Christian, and that such activities counteracted the design of all religious institutions.[3] Deeply prejudiced against outdoor sports, the serious American businessman believed that they were the frivolous pastimes of irresponsible young men. Indeed, in the early 1830's there was a shady connotation to the term "sportsman" which implied an enjoyment of gambling dens rather than the pleasures of outdoor life. How long such prejudice lasted in certain New England circles may be gathered from the Beecher sisters' books on "domestic economy" published under varying titles since 1842. In all of these, including the one which was kept in print at least until 1873 under the title *The Housekeeper's Manual*, it was stated in one form or another that "hunting and fishing, for mere sport, can never be justified."[4]

In spite of these prejudices, by the end of the eighteenth century there had already been some persons who regarded all kinds of fishing, fowling, and hunting as healthy pastimes which had a beneficial influence on the temper of man and made him more amiable and so more useful. Progressive men like Benjamin Franklin and Dr. Benjamin Rush recommended all outdoor recreation, including swimming. Even some of the periodicals tried to further sports and outdoor activities. Among these there was the *American Farmer,* in which lines such as the following could frequently be found:

> Come, thou harmless recreation
> Holding out the Angler's reed,
> Nurse of pleasing contemplation
> By the stream my wandrings lead.[5]

But the really great change of opinion came in the late 1830's when an Englishman, Henry William Herbert, writing under the pen name "Frank Forester," began a series of essays and books on fishing and hunting. These publications did a great deal to rid the ordinary American of his bias against sports. Gradually it was recognized that Herbert's writings stimulated in his readers a very strong desire for the life of the hunter and fisherman and the public acquired an understanding of what it really meant to be active in field sports. After young Americans of all classes began to learn the rules of fair play and gentlemanly behavior in outdoor sports, public opinion did an about-face and the hunter came to be looked upon as a skilled woodsman, truly representative of his country. Herbert's beliefs and hopes now were coming true; that is "if our American men could be drawn from their offices ... to forest and field, they would be benefited, physically, morally, and mentally, and come to enjoy a larger existence."[6] Long after Herbert's death his sporting books were reprinted again and again; the most famous, *Field Sports,* published in 1848, went through more than twenty printings. This man, well in advance of his time—"Our Frank," as he was called by a large fraternity of genuine sportsmen—indeed deserves his name as the father of American woodcraft literature.

Winter sports were always much in popular favor except, of course, with the Puritans. The burghers of New Amsterdam probably enjoyed skating just as much as their cousins in Holland, and had there been in colonial America a painter like Hendrick van Averkamp, who pictured the skating, merrymaking crowd on the ice of Dutch canals, some painted records of the period might have been preserved. In Pennsylvania, Governor Mifflin was known as one of the best skaters of his time. When the Delaware River froze about New Year's Day, Philadelphians had ox roasts on the river; throngs of "skaters of all colours and sizes mingled together," and the governor as well as "a black Othello" called attention to their "high Dutch" skating and the figures they cut on the ice.⁷ Gay sleighing parties were popular in many parts of the country and in New England after the beginning of the nineteenth century (see pl. 24). Snow seldom fell in the South, of course, but when it did come, the people eagerly seized every opportunity for sleighing; country inns were kept open at night, dances were held, and fiddlers went along in the sleighs.

This development of sports should not be given too much credit for the increase of interest in nature, for certainly not every participant in a moonlight sleighing party become a devotee of nature, nor did hunters necessarily become avid readers of Bryant's poetry. Nevertheless, the increased participation in outdoor sports throughout the nineteenth century must have contributed in some measure toward bringing man closer to nature than he had been before.

Let us now turn from sports to the recreational facilities offered by cities, and to some of the problems of city planning. Before the industrial upheaval in the second quarter of the nineteenth century, the cities of America were not crowded and usually had more open spaces than those of Europe. Ever since the earliest settlements were started along the eastern seaboard, gardens had been an essential part of cities, though the type of garden depended on where it was and the spirit in which it was created. The Puritan garden was a closely fenced plot designated for useful purposes. The gardens in New York and Pennsylvania were likewise utilitarian, though the Pennsylvania gardens invariably had more flowers, such as lilacs, roses, snowballs, pinks, and of course tulips. In the South, the vast plantations always included areas for the culture of fruit, vegetables, herbs, and flowers. Some sections were set aside for purposes of pleasure; these were very much like the places that have been recreated at Mount Vernon, Stratford, and Williamsburg. In the days of Governor Berkeley, about 1641, every colonist in Virginia who owned a hundred acres was expected to plant a garden and an orchard and protect them with a fence. In Savannah each freeholder had a lot in town and five acres of land beyond the commons, to be used as a garden. Charleston, too, was famous for its gardens. Actually, most cities had an abundance of small and large gardens. To what extent these gardens were sometimes developed may be gathered from the fact that in eighteenth-century Princetown, one amateur patterned his garden after Alexander Pope's garden at Twickenham. The banks of such rivers as the James, the Schuylkill, and the Hudson were embellished with manors and country houses, the summer retreats of wealthy townsmen (see pl. 8). In 1759 Burnaby described "Belvedere," one of the places owned by Colonel Byrd, as situated in "a prodigious extent of wilderness" through which the river wound majestically.⁸ William Dunlap, too, was enchanted when he saw the banks of the Patapsco River adorned with "many delightful villas, and snug retreats with all the attention to decoration and delight which is usual in the neighborhood of populous towns."⁹ When the traveler Thomas Twining visited Philadelphia in 1795, he called on William Hamilton at his country home, "Woodlands," which was close to the city. The extensive grounds which surrounded it were "tastefully laid out along the right bank of the Schuylkyl," and the company took pleasant walks amid a variety of wild and cultivated shrubs and trees, which even included a gingko tree.¹⁰ William Hamilton was an intimate friend of Jefferson, and the two men exchanged ideas on gardening and landscaping. In 1806 Jefferson wrote Hamilton that he would soon return to "Monticello" in order to devote all his time to improving his estate, but that he had no intention of transforming the grounds in accordance with the current fashion; the unique mountainside with which he had to deal would be treated in a "disposition analogous to its character." Accordingly, he would use only indigenous plants and trees.¹¹ In planning his garden to suit the topography and natural conditions of the region, Jefferson anticipated the solution of a problem which would not be generally recognized as such until much later, when the writings of Andrew Jackson Downing and his successor Frederick Law Olmsted brought it to the attention of the public.

Although Jefferson's advanced idea for the arrangement of "Monticello" was almost unique, there were numbers of country seats in all parts of the country which had been developed in the conventional manner of landscaping favored in England. Visitors who described the environs of the large cities never failed to praise the appearance of the estates there, which provided city businessmen with the pleasures of rural life.

The great mass of the population, however, if they wished to enjoy the invigorating power of fresh air had to do so in more humble ways. When William Penn established the city of Philadelphia in 1682, he ordered that the city be laid out with five open squares of eight to ten acres each. These were to be graced with trees, and nothing was to be built on them except, perhaps, few public buildings. Penn even directed that each private house should "be in the middle of the breadth of his ground" so that there would be room for "gardens &c." He intended that Philadelphia should "be a green country towne which might never be burnt and might always be wholesome."¹² By the year 1700 the city was regarded as pleasant indeed, and its air as "most delicate." In the course of time, however, the city became crowded and the old plan was no longer followed; house lots and public squares were smaller, streets were narrower, and some of the squares instead of being planted with grass and trees were used as burial places. New streets were not lined with trees, because insurance companies refused to insure houses which had trees in front of them. Much to the displeasure of the inhabitants, this practice continued until 1784, when the Second Mutual Fire Insurance Company, later popularly called "the Green Tree," began to accept clients who wished to plant trees in front of their houses. Very appropriately, the company adopted as its symbol a plaque showing a tree and placed it on the houses of their policy holders. By and by Italian poplars were planted along the streets, and François and André Michaux remarked that they made the houses appear "elegantly rural."[13] By the end of the century, Centre Square was the largest green space left inside the town. Besides this there was a small area behind the State House, which had been developed as a park and was even equipped with Windsor settees and garden chairs. When Robert Hunter saw this park in 1785 he found it "pleasing beyond description . . . Philadelphia will be the first city in the world . . . the state house is infinitely beyond anything I have either seen in New York or Boston, and the walk before it does infinite honor to Mr. Vaughan's taste and ingenuity in laying it out."[14] The Reverend Manasseh Cutler was equally enthusiastic in his praises of the park. "Ornamented with trees and walks," he wrote, it was "a display of rural fancy and elegance . . . where Hogarth's line of beauty was verified." But during the 1820's this public walk fell into disfavor, probably because the neighborhood had deteriorated. Then Gray's Inn on the Schuylkill became known as a fashionable resort. Its grounds, laid out in the English romantic style, by Samuel Vaughan, offered excursionists scenes "romantic and delightful" beyond description, including arched bridges in the Chinese style. The garden was "improved and embellished by art, and yet the art was so blended with nature as hardly to be distinguished from it"; the place seemed enchanting to the Reverend Mr. Cutler.[15]

When the new water system was introduced in 1801 after the yellow fever epidemic had ravaged the city in 1793 and again in 1798, a pumping station was set up on the "Faire Mount" near the Schuylkill. The building was of monumental character, with steps and terraces to accommodate visitors. By 1828 an area of twenty-four acres surrounding the waterworks was acquired by the city and arranged as a pleasure ground for the public. This marked the humble beginning of Fairmount Park (see pl. 20), which now comprises about four thousand acres. Rather significantly, both N. P. Willis and Philadelphia's faithful chronicler John F. Watson observed that the public did not take advantage of such comforts—perhaps, according to Willis, because "as a people, we have no habit of amusement in America. Business and repose are the only states of existence we know [and] . . . our health suffers from distaste for places of public relaxation and resort."

Watson noted as late as 1842 that there were "thousands of our citizens who have never visited [the waterworks at Fairmount Park] and many of them have been first induced to visit them from hearing them extolled by people at a distance."[16] This indifference is confirmed by Poe, who stated: ". . . it was not until Fanny Kemble . . . pointed out to the Philadelphians the rare loveliness of a stream [the Wissahiccon] which lay at their own doors, that this loveliness was more than suspected by a few adventurous pedestrians of the vicinity." Poe had every reason to know, for during many hours of rambling he had discovered for himself the surroundings of Philadelphia as he did later the environs of New York, where he fell in love with the banks and meadows of "Manhatta." In those days, he would certainly have been pleased with "a bivouac in the open air,"[17] with a knapsack as a pillow and his hound as a sentry.

Before turning from Philadelphia, we should note the activities of one man, the unpretentious proprietor of a seed store on Second Street, whose fame spread far beyond the limits of the city. His name, Bernard McMahon, was familiar to every botanist in the country, including Jefferson, who not only ordered seeds from McMahon but sought his advice and confided to his care a good part of the seeds that the Lewis and Clark expedition had sent back. If anyone could classify and raise plants from this miscellany of western seeds it was McMahon. In his store connoisseurs met and discussed botany, and availed themselves of the precious reference library conveniently placed for their use. McMahon's real claim to fame, however, lay in his publication of *The American Gardener's Calendar*, in 1806. This was the first handbook based completely on American experience and not adapted from English publications. The *Calendar* was full of practical information and came in good time to aid the townspeople whose growing wealth made it possible for them to improve and beautify their gardens. Eleven editions of it were published. The book stimulated innumerable garden lovers to acquire a sounder knowledge of gardening. Influenced by McMahon, Philadelphians enriched their gardens "by such new things as, altheas, seringas, cocoras, geraniums, verbenas and numerous new varieties of roses," and "many new . . . tulips and other bulbous roots."[18] With efficient waterworks, improved city squares, spacious Fairmount Park, and intensified private initiative, Philadelphia was once more regarded as a model city.

Boston suffered by comparison, for it was not considered as beautiful as Philadelphia, except perhaps for the views from Beacon Hill. As early as 1716 old Judge Samuel Sewall, a horticulturist of sorts, complained that the charming gardens and walks which he had enjoyed in his youth had vanished. Practically the only large green space left in the city was the Common, which had been set apart as a pasture in 1639 and was so used until 1830, when landscaping of it was begun. After the Mall—Tremont Street of today—was laid out in 1789 it became a fashionable promenade, first lined with poplars and later with elms. In spite of such an asset, Timothy Dwight stated in 1810 that the Bostonians did not have as much breathing space as they needed, because the city had not been suitably planned. Presenting his readers with an improved plan, which Dwight himself had devised, he said he hoped that "on these open grounds the inhabitants might always find sweet air, charming walks, fountains refreshing the atmosphere, trees excluding the sun . . . presenting to the eye . . . objects found in the country. Yet many large centers are utterly destitute of these appendages."[19] Nevertheless, Sophie Amelia Peabody, aged twenty years, after walking along Beacon Street in 1829 wrote in her diary, "I . . . could but just keep my feet upon the sidewalk, so bubble-like and baloony were my sensations. The full, rich foliage, the hills, the water inflated me. Oh that Common—that Eden in Miniature."[20] In the 1840's after the Common (see pl. 28) had been arranged as a small park, smoking was forbidden except in one small specified corner, where by special dispensation from the mayor, the sinners were allowed to enjoy the air and pollute it at the same time.[21] In 1857 the Common was still a lovely place. A distinguished New York gentleman taking a walk there at that time noted, "A more lovely walk than the Mall is not"; but, he added, "Pity the Common is not genteel."[22]

In New York, the Battery (pl. 18) and the Bowling Green, stripped of their military character after the Revolution, were the grounds enjoyed most by the public. When the Reverend Mr. Cutler visited the Mall in 1788 he found it thronged with "a vast concourse of gentlemen and ladies constantly walking a little before sunset."[23] About 1820, even in the daytime, "businessmen in dull times left their stores not far off and resorted occasionally to the Battery, to inhale some of its invigorating sea-breeze and bask in its genial sunshine."[24] In 1834 the Battery was still beautifully kept, but it had become unfashionable and was left to nursery maids and their charges, and eventually it became the haunt of immigrants leaving Castle Garden, the point of immigration. At that time the chronicler Philip Hone wrote in his diary that he had not promenaded on the Battery for seven years, and commented "what a beautiful spot it is, yet we citizens of New York . . . seldom enjoy it."[25] Between 1807 and 1812, Elgin Garden, established under the leadership of Dr. Hosack on the site of present Rockefeller Center, came into favor as a public botanical garden (see pl. 19); but the place was badly mismanaged and soon lost its attraction. Instead, walks around Weehawken, not far from Hoboken, became popular, and the Elysian Fields, also near Hoboken, became one of the most fashionable resorts for ladies and children. Fresh summer breezes made the crossing of the river very enjoyable, and the resort with its lawns and trees offered pleasant and happy hours. Here Philip Hone loved to take walks with the ladies of his family, and distinguished guests such as Fanny Kemble were entertained by the Pacific Society. The magnificent view from this spot across the Hudson toward Manhattan may still be enjoyed in the painting by E. C. Coates now owned by the New York State Historical Association at Cooperstown. Such rural pleasures and outdoor recreation would put anyone "on the road to health although he may not be in search of it."[26] Unfortunately, in the 1840's commercial progress destroyed a great deal of the Hoboken countryside and, according to Asher Durand, the rural districts were more and more "invaded by roughs, the inevitable canker of public grounds contiguous to our great cities,"[27] and the once lovely sites were devastated.

Obviously in western cities the facilities for public outdoor recreation increased as the cities developed. When Margaret Fuller saw Chicago in 1843 it was still a western outpost, a "portal to the prairie," and a harbor which offered excitement only at the time a boat arrived with immigrants and freight. An afternoon's drive "near the blue lake, between the low oak-wood and the narrow beach," let her forget the city and gave her an "anticipation of the beauty of the prairies." On the banks of Rock River, a few days later, Miss Fuller saw a "double log-cabin" which seemed to her "the model of a Western villa. Nature had laid out before it grounds which could not be improved."[28] As for Chicago itself, she mentions no city improvements there, although one year before she came some far-sighted citizens had deeded a square to the city—the lot now called Washington Square, where soapbox orators hold forth—on condition that it be planted with trees and enclosed "with a handsome post and board or picket fence within five years and kept enclosed forever for use as a Public Square."[29] Very likely, at the time Miss Fuller saw it in 1843 nothing had yet been done to improve the site, for, as Mrs. Caroline Kirkland remarked on another occasion, "indifference to ornament and amusement which is a permanent characteristic of our people" would have prevented a public square of this kind from "undergoing any other treatment than it would receive by chance."[30]

In the much older city of St. Louis the situation was entirely different. By the 1840's a number of handsome buildings had been built, and a fashionable drive, passing by country seats and through copses, tufts, and shrubbery led to the Prairie House. In the shady garden of that establishment one could cool off with ice cream. One might then drive on to the Sulphur Springs, which offered "walks quite refreshing to the tired and heated citizen." Farther east in Cincinnati, the "Queen of the West," there was even greater elegance, in spite of Mrs. Frances Trollope's constant complaints. Here the fashionable evening drive along the river was crowded by an assembly of carriages and handsome riders enjoying a breeze.[31]

On certain days almost the entire population in various parts of the country went on gay outings. One of the oldest of these holidays, May Day, had been approved in King James's *Book of Sports,* published in 1618, though the early Puritan authorities did not agree to celebrate it, and Governor John Endicott of Massachusetts in 1628 had a Maypole cut down. Two centuries later, frolics of this kind were no longer considered sinful, and for Bostonians May Day became one of the occasions when "hundreds of the refined citizens" planned "pedaneous excursions" in order to witness "the glorious spectacle of a rising sun."[32] In Philadelphia on May Day young lads would walk into the country to gather flowers. In many places parties were made up for picnics and family gatherings, and flutes or fiddles were taken along to add to the gaiety. At one time a legal fight to obtain rights to certain picnicking grounds (see pl. 26) aroused a nation-wide clamor and heated debates. This was in Cooperstown, New York, where James Fenimore Cooper tried to claim—but finally lost his right to—the property on "Three Mile Point" (see pl. 27), a spot where his father had for many years allowed the people of Cooperstown to go for their outings.

The Fourth of July (see pl. 25) was another day when everybody joined in great outdoor celebrations, such as the one shown in the picture of Centre Square in Philadelphia crowded with merrymakers, painted by John Krimmel in 1812.[33] In 1846 Walt Whitman made some astute observations about the manner in which different groups celebrated Independence Day. The crowd at Old Fort Greene (now Prospect Park in Brooklyn), which was on an elevated ridge and commanded a fine view, was "quieted, refined by the poetic repose of Nature," and " 'behaved' after a method that would not have been unseemly in the parlors of nobles." In complete contrast there were the goings on in New York City in one of the open spaces. Here were about 30,000 people, and "amid dust, danger, obscenity, confusion, deafening din, an atmosphere of pulverised impurities, women frightened, children screaming, rampant vileness, precocious sin, and every phase of the iniquity which springs from the root, civilization— there went off *their* fireworks."[34]

Whitman's remarks, like those of Durand quoted earlier, give us an idea of the vulgarity that was becoming prevalent in New York parks, and also in the parks of Philadelphia, Boston, and other large towns. Existing recreational areas were becoming less and less sufficient to meet the needs of the constantly enlarging cities. By 1853 the total area of open spaces scattered throughout New York had been narrowed to 117

Fac-Simile of Mr. CRAYON's unfinished Sketch of the Palisades—in the possession of Miss PUFFIN.

Young Gentleman from London pronounces the Scenery "Very Fair."

Mr. PUFFIN entertains the ladies on the Promenade Deck—

—While AUGUSTUS and FRANK step down to try a Mint Julep—

—And Mr. CRAYON attempts another Sketch.— Stranger giving his views on the Nebraska Bill.

Fourth of July on the Hudson

acres. Similar unfavorable conditions were common to all large cities, though smaller cities, such as New Haven, Hartford, and even Washington, had not yet begun to be too crowded. The need for reconditioning the lungs of these cities was recognized early enough, but the questions what kind of steps should be taken and who would take the initiative were not soon answered. Besides, an unexpected problem had arisen. Because public grounds had become crowded and had acquired an offensive atmosphere, the better class of people began to avoid such places. When travel conditions improved, these people found it pleasanter to leave town and go to summer resorts. Civic-minded men, however, looked askance at this new custom because to them it seemed undemocratic.

In order to remedy the situation and provide more space for recreation, Boston had made a beginning by landscaping its "cow pasture" in 1830. New York, however, was not yet prepared to take such a step. The need for a park, a place where exercise could be taken and the refreshing breezes could be enjoyed in the evenings of the sultry months, had been recognized as early as 1785. In that year "Veritas" published a letter in the *New York Packet*,[35] setting forth this public demand and suggesting that a competition be held among artists and art lovers for the best plans for the improvement of the city. Nothing came of this farsighted suggestion, and for many years only small and feeble efforts were made to accommodate existing spaces to the needs of the New Yorkers. About 1836 William Cullen Bryant had begun discussing the park idea in his family circle. Finally, on a hot day in July, 1844, he took a long walk through New York to explore the possibilities for a future park on ground as yet unbroken. As a result, he wrote an editorial on July 3 for the *Evening Post* under the title "A New Park." Bryant pointed out that forty years earlier every artisan had been able to get to the open country in half an hour, but now Manhattan was in imminent danger of losing its last chance to acquire territory suitable for recreation and pleasure grounds. By this time, farsighted men everywhere were aware of this need for open green spaces in cities. For instance, James Jackson Jarves in 1844 recommended for Honolulu: ". . . as the town increases . . . a central spot should be reserved and trees planted for this purpose. It is highly necessary for the comfort and health of all classes that ventilators, or lungs, as these squares have been called, should be left in all cities."[36] Bryant's proposal for New York aroused public interest, and the pros and cons were weighed for years; there were many heated discussions before it was finally carried into effect. However, before examining the details of this park project, let us investigate the beginnings of the park idea in this country.

European parks originated in the lands which princes and nobles had enclosed for hunting, such as the Forest of Fontainebleau and the lands at Richmond on the Thames. The Common in Boston was developed from plots of ground set aside primarily as pasture lands. Later these served as grounds for parades and recreation. As time went on, it was not possible to conserve all these grounds; some were given up entirely and others were reduced in size and thus became inadequate to satisfy the needs of the public. Pierre L'Enfant's grandiose plan for Washington, which originally provided ample space for malls and parks, for example, was scrapped at a very early date. (In 1909, however, the old plan was resurrected.) Fortunately, the frequency with which city rulings forbidding building in certain open spaces were broken was paralleled by a movement which, once it started, rapidly gained extraordinary popularity all over the country—the establishment of scenic cemeteries.

The man who probably originated the idea was a prominent citizen of Boston, Dr. Jacob Bigelow (1786–1879). Bigelow, a physician, may have become aware of the impolicy of burials under churches or in churchyards close to the abodes of the living, through a study of European literature on the subject. Or as an enlightened hygienist and public-minded citizen, he may have seen potential danger in the usual burying places, most of which were in a "sad, neglected state, exposed to every sort of intrusion, with scarcely any tree to shelter their barrennesses." In any event, he waged a war to do away with the old burial customs and in November, 1825, called a meeting to advocate the establishment of a cemetery outside the city. Among his friends who aided him in the project were influential men such as Joseph Story, John Lowell, Edward Everett, and Daniel Webster. It took five years to put the plan into effect. In the meantime a useful and valuable preliminary step was taken: the Massachusetts Horticultural Society was founded in 1829, and the members of this society soon merged with the advocates of the rural cemetery. Suitable grounds were found at Mount Auburn, and on September 24, 1831, the first scenic cemetery was consecrated. Situated four miles from Boston, Mount Auburn Cemetery (see pl. 22) was "the first example in modern times of so large a tract of ground being selected for its natural beauties and submitted to the processes of landscape gardening to prepare for the reception of the dead."[37]

The establishment of Mount Auburn struck a chord which reverberated throughout the entire country. In his consecration address, Judge Joseph Story spoke of being deeply touched by the "solemn calm, as if we were in the bosom of the wilderness . . . a spectacle well fit to excite in us a noble emulation."[38] Whether or not the Père-Lachaise in Paris served as an example is not definitely known. It is a fact, however, that by 1828 about eight Americans had been buried in the Père-Lachaise, and that a year after Dr. Bigelow initiated his movement, the *Atlantic Souvenir* published a traveler's impressions of this vast sanctuary which presented "the appearance of a wide and variegated garden ... where trees and shrubs conceal and disclose wild romantic beauty, tombs and temples."[39] An English traveler remarked in 1833 that Mount Auburn had been laid out in imitation of the Père-Lachaise. To a certain degree this is true, but there was one great difference. The Père-Lachaise was an old, established garden which, after being dedicated to a new purpose, remained more or less as it had been; Mount Auburn, however, was a spot of natural beauty which had been selected with the intention of conserving its original aspect. It was believed that the necessary changes, such as the appropriate placing of monuments, would not detract from the natural beauty of the area but would actually enhance it. The popularity of the cemetery increased rapidly; an English traveler wrote in 1834 that "parties of pleasure come hither from the city in great numbers,"[40] sometimes at the rate of six hundred visitors a day. Fanny Kemble, too, mentions that Mount Auburn was a favorite trysting place.[41] It was for good reasons, then, that the critic Theodore Dwight suggested that cemeteries be planned "with reference to the living as well as the dead, and should at once be convenient and pleasant to visitors."[42] The founding of scenic cemeteries at New Haven in 1833, New York and Philadelphia in 1836, and in many other places in the next few years shows that the idea was being rapidly accepted in all parts of the country.

After this it was only logical that a further step be taken to establish park areas dedicated to the living alone, on the scale of the cemeteries rather than of the city parks, all of which were small and most of which were of formal character. Here the romantic ideal of the picturesque bore fruit; the images which writers and painters had for so long conjured up were at last realized. A park was no longer to be thought of as an accumulation of malls, as it might have been had the New York Battery or the Boston Common been used as the pattern. The new kind of park was thought of as a work of art, though "only the simple and the natural"[43] were used in its design. In addition, it was intended to provide refreshment and recreation on a large scale for the constantly growing population.

There is no evidence that when William Cullen Bryant tried to interest the people of New York in the idea of a public park he was influenced by the cemetery movement. But we can more or less take it for granted that the author of "Thanatopsis" and "An Indian at the Burial Place of His Father" must have been deeply impressed by the rural cemeteries which were developing throughout the country. Bryant was joined in his efforts by Andrew Jackson Downing, the great landscape architect, who rose to prominence in 1841 at the age of twenty-six, after he had published his book *Treatise on the Theory and Practice of Landscape Gardening*.

Downing's life and work were of definite and lasting influence; his book immediately became a classic and was "invaluable to the thousands in every part of the country who were waiting for the masterword which should tell them what to do to make their homes as beautiful as they wished."⁴⁴ Even John Lindley, the English botanist who later tried in vain to introduce the name *Wellingtonia* for our *Sequoia gigantea*, considered the book excellent and thought that "our American brethren, so far from being behind us in skill, enthusiasm or execution, seem to be taking the lead most decidedly."⁴⁵ As Bernard McMahon four decades earlier had provided for the modest needs of the middle class of his time, Downing now gave his countrymen what they needed when larger funds were available for more expansive undertakings.

Downing lived at Newburgh-on-the-Hudson in a rural home he had designed in the Elizabethan style (see vignette), surrounded by a charming garden of some six acres. He gave advice to clients on Long Island and along the Hudson, as well as to the government in Washington; he published books and edited *The Horticulturist*. Brilliant in society and admired wherever he went, he was one of the outstanding figures in the cultural life of his time. On July 22, 1852, Downing with his family embarked on the *Henry Clay* to sail down the Hudson to New York. Trying to outrace a ship of a competing line, the *Henry Clay* caught fire and foundered. Although his family was saved, Downing drowned in an attempt to rescue some of the passengers.

Downing's treatise on landscape gardening was "adapted to North America." Like the Bartrams and Jefferson, Downing aspired to study the American scenery and add to the general knowledge of its characteristics. In spite of the importance of his work and the fact that he had much to do with fostering the national taste for the outdoors and interest in the natural scene, no one has yet written Downing's biography.

In Downing's judgment, as expressed in the October, 1848, issue of *The Horticulturist*, France and Germany were ahead of America, as far as social life and customs were concerned, for the public parks and gardens there were frequented by people of all classes—the king, the shopkeeper, and the artisan. This was especially true in Munich, where the so-called English Garden, which still thrives, had been laid out in 1790 by Count Rumford, who was none other than the American-born Tory and scientist Benjamin Thompson. Downing felt that the common enjoyment of public grounds would result in social freedom and an easy intercourse among all classes, which was as yet unknown in either England or America. He advocated the establishment of large public parks with room for everybody; if they were made attractive, he said, all classes would come and enjoy the new outdoor recreation they offered. Downing saw a confirmation of his ideas in the use to which the scenic cemetery was being put: "people seem to go there to enjoy themselves, and not to indulge in any serious recollections or regrets."[46] The public park, according to Downing, would promote more general good will than any lecture on the philosophy of happiness. He therefore planned to "talk, write, preach to all . . . about it . . . till some good experiment of the kind is fairly tried in the country."[47]

In July, 1849, Downing took up the theme once more and wrote about public cemeteries and public gardens. "If 30,000 persons visit a cemetery in a single season, would not a large public garden be equally a matter of curious investigation?"[48] he asked. With so large a number of visitors the success of a public park in New York or Boston would be assured. According to Downing, it was the duty and should be the policy of republics to further the taste for parks and gardens which *all* may enjoy. After Mayor Ambrose C. Kingland launched the final proposal for a park in New York, Downing wrote his last essay on the subject in August, 1851. He said that at least five hundred acres (Central Park now actually comprises 840 acres) should be allotted to the park so that it would be a breathing zone large enough to accommodate the future growth of the population. "Plant spacious parks in your cities," he wrote, "and unloose their gate as wide as the gate of morning to the whole people."[49] With such eloquent advocates as Bryant and Downing, the proposal for a public park in New York was well received, and in 1851 the first act was passed authorizing the acquisition of some of the necessary land. But years of struggle embittered by political enmities still lay ahead. These came to an end only when Frederick Law Olmsted (see pl. 49), in spite of fierce opposition to his appointment, was made superintendent of the project and soon afterward won the competition for the best plan for the park. Finally, the appointment of Olmsted in 1858 as architect-in-chief of the park, with orders to carry out his own plan, ended all existing difficulties and initiated a new era. Olmsted had been a friend and pupil of Downing and also had garnered experience in Europe. After some years of fruitful work in establishing Central Park (see pl. 63), Olmsted, finding that he and the park authorities were not in agreement on some matters and that difficulties had been placed in his way, gave up his position in May, 1863. He then immediately accepted another position as superintendent of the mining estate of General John C. Frémont in Mariposa County, California. In the light of later events, this shifting of Olmsted's position from New York to California, which proved to be only temporary, must be regarded as a very fortunate coincidence. Olmsted's resignation appears like the closing incident of the first act of a drama. After an intermission the actor of the leading role will return and the action will resume and will lead to an unexpected climax.

Before taking up Olmsted's later career (which will be discussed in the chapter on Yosemite) let us examine some of the factors which helped to make the general public responsive to nature and more thoroughly enjoy American scenery. In the descriptive report accompanying his winning plan for Central Park, Olmsted had announced that he would bring to the tired workers of New York, "a specimen of God's handiwork that shall be to them, inexpensively, what a month or two in the White Mountains, or the Adirondacks is . . . to those in easier circumstances."[50]

This promise might have been little heeded had not traveling for pleasure in various parts of America become rather common. Indeed, Frederick Law Olmsted many years later (in 1880) stated that Downing's writings introducing the park movement "could not have obtained the public attention they did, nor have proved the seed of so large a harvest, but for their timeliness, and a condition of expectancy in the soil upon which they fell."[51]

5

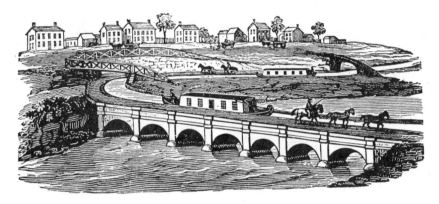

The Poetry of Traveling

UNTIL transportation facilities were vastly improved it was impossible for many persons to see and enjoy those beauty spots of American scenery which writers of the second half of the eighteenth century had described in glowing terms. Only wealthy or important people owned carriages, and only on rare occasions did they use them for traveling. Even traveling by mail coach or stagecoach (see pl. 4) was prohibitive to most persons because of the expense. In addition, mail coaches, moving continuously night and day, permitted only a minimum of comfort, though extra or passenger stages did at least stop for the night at inns and thus gave travelers an opportunity to rest in relative tranquillity. When the painter William Dunlap and his friends took a holiday jaunt to Passaic Falls in 1797 they hired two carriages for the trip and met no one on the road except for a few charabancs filled with merrymakers. Because of the

VIGNETTE: Canalboat Crossing Over a River.

holidays these were packed with rustic beaux and belles who were not at all interested in nature; instead, they crowded into public houses as fast as they could.[1]

Before 1825, horseback was the popular means of traveling. This was the most convenient and least uncomfortable method by which to ride over the badly kept roads, such as those between Boston and Albany, Boston and Philadelphia, and Washington and New York. Even the National Road (today U. S. Highway 40) from Baltimore to Cumberland and Wheeling (the future great artery to the West which had reached the Ohio in 1818) was for a good two-thirds of the way filled with deeply worn ruts. Therefore, in the 1820's when the canal age came into being, traveling by waterways (see vignette and pls. 5, 23, 32) came as a great relief, and people began to think of a journey as a pleasure instead of an ordeal. During the decade between 1827 and 1837, after the opening of the Erie Canal, travel by boat was so much in vogue that "a man who had not traveled on it, was considered a homebody."[2] Compared with horseback, transportation by water did offer many and great comforts. True, the new canalboats moved at the slow pace of four miles an hour, but as compensation they provided sleeping and dining facilities. *The Traveller's Guide,* by George H. Davison, the standard guide for travelers in the Atlantic states in this period, informs us that "the recent and gigantic internal improvements in the northern and middle states, and the development of new and highly interesting natural scenery, together with the increased facilities for travelling," greatly augmented the number of tourists who undertook "what has been usually denominated the fashionable or Northern Tour."[3] One of the famous trips took passengers up through New York State to a place on Lake Ontario from which Niagara Falls could be conveniently visited. For "8 dollars you can go, in four days, 200 miles without a jolt or the least fatigue, and employ the whole time in reading, writing, rational conversation, amusement or viewing the most interesting region of the globe," with scenery "alternately picturesque, beautiful and sublime."[4] Certainly it must have been a thrilling experience to sail through the new and thriving cities of Utica, Palmyra, and Rochester and to see unbroken wilds just outside the towns. Mrs. Caroline Gilman, the poetess, gives a moving description of how the crowd "rushing to the [Niagara] Falls," after mounting the canalboat, formed a group in the middle of which somebody read a story so touching that the ladies wept. Later, everybody admired the sunset, and most of the passengers felt that the trip was a very unusual experience.[5]

N. P. Willis, the fashionable chronicler of the 1830's, states in one of his essays that tourists coming along the Erie Canal were eager to discover the unhackneyed beauties of silent lakes and vast forests, and that they

experienced most of their "romantic raptures" on the route from Schenectady to Buffalo.⁶ Theodore Dwight, a Hartford publisher and nephew
of Yale's Timothy Dwight, said he was thankful that "our canals often
introduce us to the hearts of forests; the retreats of wild animals are almost
exposed to our view." Though "our scenery, history and biography attract
more attention than they once did," he added, many are brought up unfit
to enjoy them and despise those who like to "frequent our wild scenes
and to enjoy the beauties of nature."⁷

Yet, by and by, canal travel was found to have some drawbacks. Even
De Witt Clinton, the originator of the Erie Canal, realized as early as
1820 that the "conveyance of passengers will be principally by land, and
of commodities by water, after the prevailing curiosity to visit the canal
is gratified."⁸ Clinton was right. In the early years the number of passengers
traveling over the Erie, the Chesapeake and Ohio, and other canals in
Pennsylvania was enormous, and the elegant boats were greatly admired.
But by the end of the 1830's, this kind of slow traveling was no longer
popular; meals seemed tedious, mosquitoes bothersome, and the constant
cry of the captain, "Look out for bridge," a complete nuisance. Dickens'
complaints about his canalboat trip in 1842, published in *American Notes*,
were undoubtedly well founded. But however unfavorably the public
may have regarded the canalboat, it is certain that this mode of travel
had introduced some conveniences and had even made traveling the
fashion. Easily accessible places on the seacoast, such as Nahant near
Boston and Long Branch near New York, had been frequented by travelers
since the end of the eighteenth century, and spas such as Virginia Hot
Springs and Ballston had attracted visitors long before the Revolution.
Travelers to these places had gone to recover their health, or perhaps
to avoid the city during the hot season. By the end of the 1830's the situation had changed. Entirely unknown regions were being opened to the
public, and travelers were having their first experience of taking inland
trips in a leisurely fashion. Traveling costs were no longer excessive. Railroads, with trains traveling at about fifteen or twenty miles an hour, came
into use, and elegant steamboats began to ply the lakes and rivers. These
new types of conveyance found people ready and willing to avail themselves of the splendid opportunities to explore the countryside and visit
the little-known lakes and mountain valleys, the beauty and sublimity of
which had been extolled by poets, writers, and painters for many years.
A steadily increasing throng was now discovering the romance of travel.
The title of a book by Mrs. Caroline Gilman, *The Poetry of Travelling in
the United States*, published in 1838, is significant of the mood in which
the new custom was being adopted. To the traveler and lover of nature,
Beauty and Nature seemed to be more or less synonymous and poetry

appeared to be the adequate means of conveying the feelings aroused by the sight of a tree or a cloud. So long as those impressions or feelings could not be interpreted and supplemented by observations made by discerning minds and eyes, perhaps poetry was the best means of expressing them. Wordsworth's strong influence had much to do with this attitude. Another writer who felt that nature appreciation was closely linked with poetry was the famous Mrs. Sarah J. Hale, the editor of *Godey's Ladies' Book*. According to Mrs. Hale, many travelers who could be sensitive to natural beauties had not yet taken to touring the country because they had no intellectual or poetical associations with the scenery.[9] This may be one of the reasons that Irving's efforts to imbue the American scene with "associations" were valued so highly.

In 1840 Willis published a book called *American Scenery*, which was profusely illustrated with plates done from drawings by the skillful English draughtsman William Bartlett, who had traveled with him over the United States in 1837 and 1838 for the express purpose of providing these illustrations. They included more than one hundred illustrations of "transatlantic Nature." According to Willis' introduction[10] they were picturesque, but he intended them to feed the imagination of the future rather than call up associations of the past; in fact, all external objects, he believed, should be looked at as exponents of the future. The sight of a valley, with its abundance of virgin growth, should give rise to thoughts of villages that would soon sparkle on its hillsides, and a speculating traveler could with his pencil calculate how much the population would increase in ten years. For the artist there was all the rich country, especially the river scenery, which surpassed everything to be seen in all other lands.

In spite of Willis' promises of "new" aspects to be opened up and glimpses of future developments, his letterpress for the most part offers only some vague ideas about progress and expresses only trivial romantic feelings. Legends, events, or personal stories of the past are tied up with the sites illustrated, in an attempt to make them worthy of attention by reason of their historical associations. Although Willis' book was published in many editions, it does not stand out in any way from the mass of picture albums produced in this period. It is valuable, however, as a gauge of the standards of the period, and it is also enlightening because the route taken by the artist and reporter was the same as that usually taken by travelers of the 1840's when they wanted to get away from the city and enjoy the country.

From New York there was always the standard trip by steamboat up the Hudson River valley to Albany, which could be interrupted by a jaunt in the stage going up to the Catskill Mountains. On the route from Albany to Boston, traveled by railroad and stage, Mount Holyoke could be visited, and this place might serve as a point of departure for a trip by stage up the Connecticut Valley, or for a visit to the White Mountains. From the mountains, travelers could take the stage to Boston and on the way visit Lake Winnepesaukee. Those who stayed at Saratoga would consider an excursion to Lake George as a matter of course. Hardy travelers who were not limited in their time or means could proceed westward by the Erie Canal to Oswego and take either a boat or the Utica and Schenectady Railroad to Buffalo. Coming back they might enjoy seeing Genesee Falls near Rochester. Although in 1834 these falls were still regarded as a spot of magnificence and natural beauty, man was already "doing all he could to mar them."[11] Travelers who did not venture as far as Lake Ontario would at least take a look at Trenton Falls (see pl. 21), which had been known since about 1805. In 1822 a house had been built near these falls, for the use of the increasing number of visitors, which proudly displayed a signboard, "Rural Resort." Mrs. Gilman was "overwhelmed" when she inspected the falls and declared that all the pictures she had seen of them previously had been nothing but mockeries. Other visitors, for some strange reason, compared the scenery with that of the Alhambra, and most of them agreed that it was more delightful than that of any of the other romantic resorts and contrasted the falls with the awe-inspiring Niagara.

New Yorkers regarded Passaic Falls as the most conveniently situated natural spectacle. Sightseers from Philadelphia would avail themselves of the new Columbia Railroad to go west toward Harrisburg, though this method of transportation did not become popular until a decade later when travelers began to explore the Wyoming Valley and the Juniata River. The Natural Bridge in Virginia was the greatest attraction south of Baltimore. To reach it, the traveler would ride by stagecoach down the Shenandoah Valley, and occasionally one would take a side trip to visit Washington's tomb at Mount Vernon. Mrs. Gilman went into ecstasies when she described the Natural Bridge: "This stupendous structure . . . in all its mighty grandeur, in its overpowering wildness, in all that vastness which causes the mind almost to lose itself . . . sublime reality . . . we gazed into the abyss . . . we looked from a dizzy height . . . an awful chasm yawned beneath."[12] We should, perhaps, allow for a little purposeful exaggeration in this description, since Mrs. Gilman was a southern lady and might have intended to stimulate interest in the Virginia gem.

In the list of sites visited in the 1830's and 1840's, omissions are as significant as inclusions. It is apparent that recognition came much later to southern beauty spots than to northern ones. This was because Southerners, as well as everybody else, were becoming accustomed to travel to the northern resorts to escape the summer heat. These resorts became popular one after another as they were discovered by the public. When a spot be-

Lake Winnepesaukee, White Mountains

came too crowded, visitors pushed farther north or northwest; Mount Desert and the Adirondacks were therefore late to come into the favor of the public.

One of the first of the mountaintops to be frequented by tourists was the summit of Mount Holyoke, where a building to accommodate travelers was built as early as 1821. In 1837 two or three thousand tourists visited it. From the summit the "richest view in point of cultivation and fertile beauty" afforded ample compensation to tourists, "whose patronage of ginger beer and sunrises maintains a shanty and a hermit on the top, and keeps in repair a series of scrambling but convenient ladders at the difficult points . . . of the fashionable climb."[13] Several views from the top showing the "oxbow" of the Connecticut River were painted or drawn by Cole and others. From many of these pictures engravings were made, and the engravings in turn were copied by painters. All these views made the public familiar with the enchanting panorama.

Going up the Hudson, the traveler enjoyed "scenes imparting to the beholder all the charms of novelty, with the highest emotions of the sublime."[14] However, these trips did not exactly commend themselves to contemplative souls. Boats were crowded, and during the height of the season the steamer carried some seven or eight hundred people, who swarmed over it "with lapdogs, crammed baskets, uncut novels and baggage."[15] Many persons would leave the boat to go up into the Catskills. There the place to stay was Pine Orchard, later named the Mountain House.

Being readily accessible from New York, the site had been well known since Cooper described the view in his *Pioneers* and Irving's Rip Van Winkle had pointed out the magnificent 1,400-foot drop down to the Hudson River valley. After the first shelter for tourists was erected in 1823, by the Catskill Mountain Association, the stream of sightseers began. In the following year, the original shack was replaced by a more substantial building, which thereafter was enlarged several times and, after 1832, was embellished with a portico of thirteen Corinthian columns. According to Talbot Hamlin, the historian of the period of Greek Revival,

> the hotel remains an impressive monument to the luxuries of summer vacations a century ago, and there is a certain superb daring, a true sense of scale and composition, an almost breathtaking quality in its long horizontals and its sweeping colonnade crowning the precipitous cliff. It is a perfect expression of the joining of the two great enthusiasms, for Greece and for nature; a wedding, unexpectedly successful, of Stuart and Revett with the Hudson River School painters.[16]

Pine Orchard "attracted the attention of all classes of men, and still continues to draw to it numbers of those who are fond of novelty, and especially of the sublime and romantic scenery in which it abounds." The prospect from the plateau (see pl. 31) showed "more diversity than is to be found in any other part of the State or perhaps the United States."[17] Undoubtedly Cole's paintings and views reproduced in engravings and on china had much to do with spreading the fame of this unique place. Here nature lovers were awakened every morning to enjoy the sunrise. Conditions had changed since Timothy Dwight's travels through the Catskills in 1804. At that time he had only occasionally seen a cottage, and the mountains "seemed to shut out the few inhabitants of the valley from the rest of mankind,"[18] as they do in Switzerland. By 1826 the wonders of the Catskills had become so famous that the *Atlantic Souvenir* published an article exhorting Americans not to "leave this native land for enjoyment, when you can view the rugged wildness of her mountains, [and] admire the beauty of her cultured plains."[19] Six years later Theodore Dwight visited the Mountain House and described the sun rites:

> As soon as I could perceive the first blush of dawn I dressed and hastened to the roof of the hotel, to watch the approach of the day . . . there was more sublimity to be feasted upon every moment that passed, than some people witness in their whole lives. What a groveling soul that must be which prefers a morning slumber to such a sight.[20]

In the 1840's visiting the Catskills became a fad. The Mountain House grew into a luxurious hotel, and a semidaily stage ran between the Hudson River and the resort, where thousands of transients went to enjoy the novelty of this "eagles' nest" and the delicacies the dining room offered, such as "turtle soup, ice cream, Charlotte Russe and other fashionable dainties."[21]

Because Lake George—or Horikon, the old Indian name romantic writers liked to use—was only a day's ride from Saratoga, its loveliness was discovered early. As early as 1776, during the war, John Trumbull's taste for the picturesque had here received "a splendid gratification."[22] In 1826 Thomas Cole went all the way up to Ticonderoga and, while staying with the Pell family, made sketches for his impressive view of Mount Defiance, a picture still owned by the family of his hosts at Ticonderoga. Until the 1840's, except for such occasional visitors, no one visited Lake George except the few who were enterprising enough to leave the Saratoga crowd behind for a couple of days. They stayed overnight at the Lake George Coffee House at Caldwell and took one of the daily boat trips on the lake, which was frequently compared with Loch Katrine. In the 1850's a few public houses were opened on the western shore. The Lake House had a reputation for elegance and good company, and Lyman's Tavern catered to those who enjoyed beautiful scenery and loved quiet.[23] The eastern shore, however, remained a comparative wilderness for a long time.

Much of the early interest in the White Mountains was due to Ethan Allan Crawford, a stalwart American mountain pioneer, who was called the "Keeper of the Mountain." Crawford's home at the top of Franconia Notch was open to all travelers. Although he had not intended his house to become an inn, public demand and his interest in functioning as a mountain guide practically forced him in the 1820's to take lodgers. He even enlarged his house when it seemed necessary, a venture which later ruined him. Crawford became the host of nearly every traveler desirous of climbing the White Mountains. To please his friends and clients, he and his men even cut a path to the summit of Mount Washington in 1819. This effort was rewarded by a steadily increasing number of visitors. In 1821 two ladies came, the Misses Austin from Boston, who wished to be—and undoubtedly were—the first women to climb to the summit. Crawford had organized the ascent to Mount Washington with great care, establishing a camp on the way, which was well equipped with blankets, food, and all the needs of mountaineers. In 1824 he even placed on the summit a sheet of lead on which visitors could inscribe their names with an iron pencil. This proved to be a time-saving device, since previously those who indulged in the age-old practice of name scribbling had to use a hammer and chisel. It became "fashionable for ladies attended by gentlemen to visit this place both for health and amusement." Crawford had crowned his efforts by erecting some rude stone huts at the top of the mountain. The visitor, arriving at the summit, could

> look over the whole creation with wonder and surprise as far as the eye could extend in every direction, and view the wonderful works of God! Every large pond and sheet of water was plain to be seen . . . until the sun had got up so high as to cause a vapor to rise from the waters; this, also, was grand to see; the commencement of the little vapor, which would grow larger and larger until it made a cloud and entrenched the view.[24]

How much the sensitive visitor was impressed and overawed by the view we may gather from the words of one traveler: "the sensations which affect the corporeal faculties, as one views these stupendous creations of Omnipotence are absolutely afflicting and painful . . . too sublime and overwhelming to be described."[25] In 1826, the year in which this visitor saw the White Mountains, nation-wide attention had been given to the region. A landslide in Franconia Notch had buried the fleeing inhabitants of the Willey cottage; but the place itself, as if by a miracle, had escaped disaster. For many years after the landslide, the Willey place was a spot of general interest and attracted visitors to the White Mountains.

Thomas Cole stayed at the Crawford House when he traveled in the White Mountains in the spring of 1827. He carefully recorded his impressions in a sketchbook[26] for further use in his Catskill studio. At least two paintings based on these sketches are now known, one in the Museum of Historic Art in Princeton and one in the Wadsworth Atheneum in Hartford. Cole climbed Mount Chocorua, "a steep and terribly laborious journey" over pine and gnarled birch heaped together in the wildest manner. Upon reaching the summit he was rewarded by a sublime prospect on every side, with glistening silver or dark blue lakes, and clouds casting shadows. Yet the artist felt that "with all its beauty the scene was one too extended and maplike for the canvas." He ascended Chocorua "not for sketches . . . but for thoughts; and for these this was truly the region."[27]

When the traveler Charles Lanman climbed Mount Washington in 1844, he felt that painters would appreciate the very wild and diversified mountain scenery that came into view during the ascent from Crawford's, but that "the prospect from the summit of Mount Washington will most excite the soul of the poet."[28] Both Cole's and Lanman's remarks reflect a truly romantic feeling. Overcome by emotion in the face of the sublime aspect of nature, painter and writer escape into philosophical reasoning.

One of the popular features of this period which must not be forgotten were groups of singers, who usually traveled as families. Those that specialized in songs of sentimental and romantic character were particularly popular. Outstanding among these entertainers was the Hutchinson family, numbering thirteen singing brothers and sisters and, in the next two generations, even more cousins. Coming from Milford, New Hampshire, and familiar with the scenery of New England, the Hutchinsons loved to acquaint the rest of the country with the beauties of their home territory. Their family anthem was "The Old Granite State," which resounded with "wild mountain singing," emancipation, teetotalism, and liberty. Other songs of theirs dramatized the glories of the mountains, as we may gather from titles such as "Hark! Above Us on the Mountains," "I'm a Child of the Mountain," and lines such as these from "The Mountaineer":

> I climb up the craggy mountains
> And inhale its balmy airs
> I drink at the sparkling fountain
> And laugh at the world and its cares.[29]

In the summer of 1844 the Hutchinsons went on a summer jaunt to the White Mountains. In order to provide adequate transportation for this family enterprise it was necessary to charter a stagecoach and extra carriages. Combining vacation pleasures and concert performances, this was a memorable tour. The men pitched tents at night, the ladies slept in farmhouses. Full enjoyment of the outdoors in the daytime and concert work and singing in hotels at all times made these strenuous holidays. The climax came when the Hutchinsons rode up Mount Washington. Before they rested on the summit they joined in the song

> We stood upon the Mountain Height
> And viewed the valleys o'er . . .

On their return to Fabyan's Resort, before the Hutchinsons retired to their rooms to relax their stiff limbs, the less adventurous summer guests showered them with praise and admiration. The exploits of this summer provided many good topics which the Hutchinsons offered to audiences throughout the country during the next season.[30]

In 1837 Charles Fenno Hoffman had done some early exploring in the Adirondacks and had prophesied that "a few years hence [the Adirondacks] will become as favorite as Lake George, Trenton Falls and Niagara."[31] This prophecy did not exactly come true, since the opening up of the area for temporary visitors did not take place until the 1850's. In the 'thirties, any visitor who ventured into the dense forest had to depend on lumbermen for guidance, and there was scarcely a shanty in which he could stay. One of the few places to offer shelter was the Newcomb Farm, southwest of Sanford Lake, owned by Steuben Hewitt; another was a place that belonged to John Cheney. These men were famous hunters and guides who traveled with the adventurous artist or sportsman wanting to climb Tahawus Mountain (now called Mount Marcy) or to glide up Long Lake in a canoe. Thomas Cole, who visited the Adirondacks in 1845, was one of the early travelers to penetrate them in such company. When Louis Noble, a minister who also was a nature enthusiast, wrote a biography of Cole in 1852 he asserted that "a jaunt through [the Adirondacks] . . . will ordinarily subject the tourist to more privation and fatigue than almost any other he can take in the United States."[32] At that time, wolves, bears and mountain lions were still roaming the forest. Although Cole's excursion proved to be one of the wildest and most exciting he had ever undertaken in quest of the picturesque, it turned out to be enjoyable and satisfying. It is significant that Cole, like other American writers, compared what he saw to European scenery; Long Lake seemed to him to resemble Lago Maggiore, and Tahawus was comparable to Mont Blanc.

The earliest sightseer to visit Mount Desert Island was apparently Thomas Doughty. Unfortunately the only evidence of his visit is a painting of the lighthouse on Desert Rock which Doughty sent to an exhibition in London in 1836, and from which an engraving was later made. Cole was another early visitor on the island. In August, 1844, he met his friend Henry C. Pratt and with him traveled up the Penobscot and finally to the heart of Mount Desert. There they found a village in which there was not even a tavern.[33] Although the roads were extremely bad, the two men visited many other parts of the island. They enjoyed the delightful woods of fir and cedar and thought that Sand Beach on the eastern extremity of the island offered the greatest coast scenery they had ever seen.

Charles Lanman visited the Adirondacks in 1845 soon after Cole was there. Lanman was a writer and painter, and above all an enthusiastic traveler. For a period of almost thirty years he had made innumerable tours, visiting almost every nook and corner of the United States. His books, now almost completely forgotten, ran into many editions and were greatly enjoyed by the public in this country and in Great Britain as well. Joseph Henry, Henry R. Schoolcraft, and George P. Marsh were among his closest friends; he knew William Cullen Bryant well, visited Cole in his Catskill retreat, and exchanged letters with Washington Irving and Edward Everett. Born in Michigan and familiar with the canoe since his childhood, Lanman began traveling in the early 1840's. He pushed up the headwaters of the Mississippi, down the Saguenay, and up the Potomac. On foot and on horseback he frequently crossed the Alleghenies and explored the Great Smokies. He was at home on the St. John and the Chattahoochee, the St. Lawrence, and the Potomac. His travel books, which might well stand as guide books, are written in a lively style and are interspersed with descriptions of the important persons with whom he became acquainted. At Fort Snelling he met the army officers and the painter Seth Eastman (see chap. 8); in St. Louis he came across another painter, Charles Deas; and in New England he went to see George Marsh and Daniel Webster at their country places. Lanman's books stimulated many a traveler to set out on explorations of his own. Frequently Lanman wrote of Indian lore; and it is obvious that he, like Willis and Irving, endeavored to supply a background of association for the natural scenery which the American tourist was only beginning to appreciate. In 1847 Lanman penetrated into the dense woods of Maine and traveled up the Penobscot and to Moosehead Lake, though almost everyone else shuddered when the Penobscot was mentioned, because of the "remembrance of the acrid blasts that have swept over the country from that quarter."[34] He may have been stimulated to visit the Penobscot by Thoreau, who had published an account of his 1846 trip to Mount Katahdin in the *Union Magazine*.

More fortunate than Thoreau, Lanman was able to gather his essays, first published in magazines and journals, into "summer books," a type of literature that was the vogue in the 1840's and 1850's. The great popularity of these books is ample evidence of the enormous increase of interest in the outdoors. Many of these publications were trivial in content and were written in the romantic vein, which had begun to lose its appeal. There was still, however, much charm in the freshness with which the author viewed nature, and in the joy that he felt at the swift approach of a train to a mountain or a lake. Only a few of these reporters, such as Charles Lanman or T. A. Richards, traveled south; and Theodore Winthrop was one of the few who went all the way to the Pacific Coast.

The Midwest was visited by Charles Hoffman, the first editor of the *Knickerbocker Magazine,* who set out alone on horseback to explore the Ohio Valley, eastern Missouri, Illinois, and Kentucky. Enchanted by the beauty of the country, he asked, in a *Winter in the West:* "Why are there none to sing her primeval glories in our land? . . . There is a singular joyousness in a wilderness. The subduing hand of cultivation . . . could add nothing here."[35] Edgar Allen Poe, who knew and admired Hoffman, reviewed the book in a very appreciative way. He believed that the work deserved its popularity because it contained nothing "of the cant of the tourist for the sake not of nature, but of tourism."[36] Judge James Hall, the Cincinnati publisher, was favorably impressed by Hoffman and naturally was glad that an Easterner of literary reputation should praise the country he himself was trying to interpret to eastern minds. Among those who followed Hoffman's call was Mrs. Caroline Kirkland, who established her household near Lake Michigan in an obscure village and wrote a book to which she gave the title *A New Home—Who'll Follow?* (1839). The author admitted freely that this book, like another which she wrote soon afterward called *Forest Life* (1842), was full of "Rip van Winkleism." Indeed, it contained all the incongruities one might expect from a lady living in the wilderness yet trying to do some pleasant "crayoning" in the style of Willis. Although it seemed unfortunate to Mrs. Kirkland that settlers were regarding the forests' "earthborn columns" only as timber, she thought that "the felling of a great tree has something of the sublime in it."[37] Only two years later (1841) *A Summer Journey in the West* was published by a Mrs. Steele, who stated that her friends had urged her to write it because her book might be useful to immigrants. Her book does contain some basic information about the country and a reliable report of an interview with her friend Henry R. Schoolcraft, on Mackinac Island. In it, she definitely states, she set down not "notes by the way" or "crayoning" or "pencil sketches," but rather—and here she is pointing to a new age—"perfect Daguerrotype likenesses" of all she saw.[38]

The majority of the travel books of the period deal with New England and New York State. One of the more typical accounts is that of George W. Curtis. His book *Lotus-Eating: A Summer Book,* charmingly illustrated by Kensett, was composed of letters to the editor, originally published in newspapers in the early 1850's. In a comparison of the Rhine and the Hudson, the American river does not fare too badly; in another essay, Lake George is contrasted with Lake Como, a comparison which seemed to Curtis like contrasting a beautiful country cousin with an elegant courtier.

Letters about life in the Catskills and visits to Trenton, Niagara, Saratoga, and Nahant contained in Curtis' work are written in a slightly satirical vein, ridiculing some of the foibles of townspeople on summer vacation. Curtis dares to confess that he did not get up to see the sunrise at the Mountain House, in spite of the bright Sunday morning, because he preferred to sleep.[39] In general, the book is written in a nostalgic mood; the author apparently was only mildly interested in nature, and only as far as it was compatible with his indulgence in art and literature. We are indebted to Curtis for another book (published in 1863) composed of papers which Theodore Winthrop left unpublished at the time he was killed in the Civil War. It carries the title *Life in the Open Air,* taken from the principal essay describing a trip from the Catskills to Mount Katahdin and down the Penobscot which Winthrop made accompanied by the painter Frederick E. Church, in the early 1850's. This record is full of exuberance and the joy of traveling, as one would expect from the youthful author of *The Canoe and the Saddle* (1862), one of the earliest popular books to give Easterners some knowledge of western nature and adventure.

In the early 1850's the manner in which Americans established a relationship with the wilderness scenes began to conform to a pattern. Artists and writers would invade hitherto untraveled parts in the northern states, occasionally in the Midwest, and rarely in the South. Usually with considerable effort and by really "roughing it," these men penetrated the woods and explored lakes and mountains as far as their meager means allowed and lodging facilities—lonely farm houses, lumbermen's cabins, or tents and grounds for camping—permitted. After they returned to studio and desk their sketchbooks and notebooks provided them with materials for paintings and glowing accounts of "summer jaunts." Scores of the paintings were then reproduced and published in magazines or almanacs and became as widely known as many essays or poems. No author, it seems, ever tired of describing the sublimity and the grandeur of the scenery and the enchantment produced by it. Perhaps what the public expected and liked—or was at least supposed to like—is brought out most clearly in the critics' reviews of Lanman's first work, *Essays for Summer Hours,* published in 1841. Although this book was in reality a rather unimportant collection of superficial nature studies, Bryant found that it was written "with a vein of poetic embellishment"; another reviewer thought it "harmoniously blended, a contribution to our elegant literature," containing "picturesque views and moral reflections," and commended it for not disturbing the reader with paradoxical statements. The old idea of the picturesque was perhaps never more often discussed than in this period. To a certain extent even Thoreau was fascinated by it; he really felt grateful to Gilpin for elaborating upon this subject.

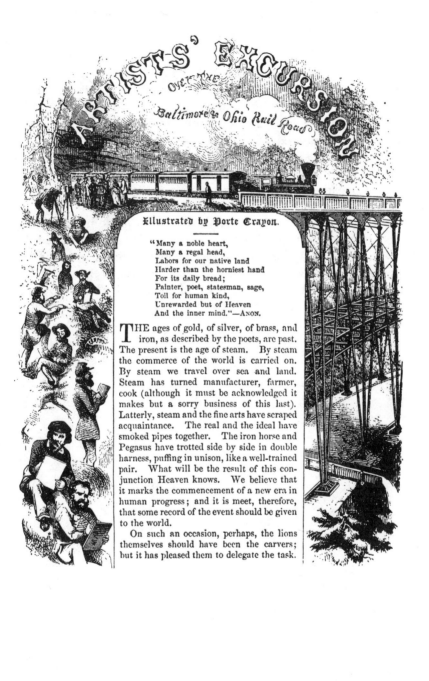

ARTISTS' EXCURSION

over the Baltimore & Ohio Rail Road

Illustrated by Porte Crayon.

"Many a noble heart,
Many a regal head,
Labors for our native land
Harder than the horniest hand
For its daily bread;
Painter, poet, statesman, sage,
Toil for human kind,
Unrewarded but of Heaven
And the inner mind."—ANON.

THE ages of gold, of silver, of brass, and
iron, as described by the poets, are past.
The present is the age of steam. By steam
the commerce of the world is carried on.
By steam we travel over sea and land.
Steam has turned manufacturer, farmer,
cook (although it must be acknowledged it
makes but a sorry business of this last).
Latterly, steam and the fine arts have scraped
acquaintance. The real and the ideal have
smoked pipes together. The iron horse and
Pegasus have trotted side by side in double
harness, puffing in unison, like a well-trained
pair. What will be the result of this con-
junction Heaven knows. We believe that
it marks the commencement of a new era in
human progress; and it is meet, therefore,
that some record of the event should be given
to the world.

On such an occasion, perhaps, the lions
themselves should have been the carvers;
but it has pleased them to delegate the task.

> To prose it here, to verse it there
> And picturesque it everywhere

became a literary mannerism used to brighten many a poem or essay.
Finally, a railroad company, the Baltimore and Ohio, capitalized on the
search for the picturesque by using a charming and original publicity
device. In 1857 the company invited writers, painters, and photographers
to board a special train equipped with the utmost comforts of the day—
sofas, a piano, a bar, and even a darkroom for the photographers. By way
of Harpers Ferry and Martinsburg, along the "Picturesque Line of
America," a slogan still in use in the 'eighties, the gay crowd moved to St.
John, the train stopping whenever the gentlemen wished to take pictures
or make sketches. Among the twenty artists who made merry over Ca-
tawba cobblers, champagne, and deviled crabs were Asher Durand, John
F. Kensett, and N. P. Willis. After a very lively evening spent at Berkeley
Springs, the travelers went on as far as Wheeling, then returned to Baltimore.[40] There could have been no better demonstration of the poetry of
traveling than this joint undertaking of artists and railway company to
interest the public in American scenery.

6

New Eyes

WHILE the public was experiencing the romance of traveling and reading—or at least glancing through—pleasantly embellished summer books, Emerson in Concord was mapping a program of another kind. His journal for 1835 carried this statement:

> If life were long enough, among my thousand and one works should be a book of nature whereof Howitt's *Seasons* should be not so much the model as the parody. It should contain the natural history of the woods around my shifting camp for every month in the year. It should tie their astronomy, botany, physiology, meteorology, picturesque, and poetry together. No bird, no bug, no bud, should be forgotten on his day and hour. . . . Nothing is beautiful alone. Nothing but is beautiful in the whole.[1]

VIGNETTE: Louis Agassiz and His Students on Lake Superior.

Two more years were to pass before Emerson was able to acquaint the public with the essence of this proposed work, his philosophy of nature, the first to be outlined by an author in this country. When the slim volume entitled *Nature* was published in 1835, Carlyle immediately recognized its cardinal importance and told Emerson that he thought that this book represented the "Foundation and Ground-plan"[2] of his future work. However, what the great historian could not foresee was that eventually this essay would be regarded as the philosophical constitution of transcendentalism,[3] and that it would be a source of some of the main future trends of thought. In fact, profound changes in the American attitude toward nature would be brought about through its influence. But these changes did not take place immediately. Sentimental literature was still read for decades after Emerson's essay was first published, and it is only just to admit that at least some of that literature channeled public interest in the direction of nature appreciation. Yet it gradually became apparent that the current of romantic sentimentalism could not keep up its force indefinitely unless a more rational and more substantial basis could be found for it. Rational minds would soon reject worn-out classifications such as sublimity, grandeur, and picturesqueness for interpreting the relationship between man and nature; and the kind of shallow moralizing found in polite literature would not be tolerated much longer by men who were confronted with the realities of a new way of life.

In *Nature* Emerson opens his discussion by demanding that we have "our own works and laws and worship," in order that we may "enjoy an original relation to the universe." He also expresses his reverence for creation and his deep belief in a mystical union with God through nature. Burdened with an emotional inheritance of romantic character, Emerson did not easily bridge the chasm which William Bartram had believed to exist between man and nature, but he finally succeeded in doing so and found an "occult relation between man and the vegetable." In order to answer the question "To what end is nature?" Emerson found that it was necessary to look "at the world with new eyes." All the facts in natural history taken by themselves have no value, he believed, but united with human history they are full of life, and that is why the knowledge of natural history infinitely aids the growth of spiritual force. The philosopher concluded that "behind nature, throughout nature, spirit is present," and that "spirit, that is, the Supreme Being, does not build up nature around us but puts it forth through us." This view, he says, "animates me to create my own world through the purification of my soul."[4]

That Emerson's essay was a beginning of his work rather than a final judgment, and was an expression of his intuitive feelings rather than an exposition supported by proof, becomes clear in the final chapter where

Emerson introduces the orphic poet who foretells the future because "a dream may let us deeper into the secret of nature than a hundred concerted experiments." Apparently not caring to prove his doctrine, Emerson advanced the idea that "nature is not fixed but fluid. Spirit alters, molds, makes it. . . . Build therefore your own world." In a second essay on "Nature," published in 1844 in his second series of essays, he amplifies the subject without indicating any change in his views.

The number of contemporaries who were impressed by the views of this transcendentalist was small—only a few hundred copies of the book were sold—but response came swiftly in reviews from all over the country, a sure sign that Emerson's thesis had aroused interest in certain circles throughout the nation. Now that his philosophical foundation was firmly laid, Emerson went on to acquire experience within the realm which he had chosen for exploration. Fortunately he was able to leave the details of this work to Thoreau, who devoted his life to the task.

Although Emerson could never have found the time or energy to study a dry catalogue of facts, he was intent to use "new eyes," the term he had coined in his essay. The following entry, dated October 13, 1837, appears in his journal: "New Eyes. What is, appears, Go out to walk with a painter, and you shall see for the first time groups, colors, clouds, and keepings, and shall have the pleasure of discovering resources in a hitherto barren ground, of finding as good as a new sense in such skill to use an old one." Not content to acquire merely a new function for his eyes and perhaps get some close knowledge of unrelated facts, Emerson was determined to draw moral implications from his way of studying nature. Adapting Gilpin's theory of "searching for the picturesque" to his own newly won conceptions, Emerson applied it in a new and unconventional way. "Our hunting for the picturesque is inseparable from our protest against false society." Generally speaking, this idea was not new, since literature of the romantic movement had expressed somewhat similar thoughts; but coming from Emerson and founded on his intimate study of nature, the idea was a novel and an important one.

It focused on the beginning conflict between the traditional way of life and industrialism. Earlier the romanticists had rebelled against city life, but had done so because the remote in time and subject or the picturesque in natural scenery had been the center of their interest. In the 1840's when social changes were imminent, difficulties caused by industrialism demanded the attention of the thinkers. Now transcendentalist belief in self-reliance and individualism, coupled with the conviction that man is directed by divine reason, furthered the adjustment of the relationship between man and nature. This widespread and sincere belief, which was mainly the result of Emerson's influence, was more firmly established than any of the ideas current in the early days of romanticism.

Many persons were led to adopt this new way of thinking, through the efforts of one man, Louis Agassiz, the great Swiss scientist, whose arrival on these shores in 1846 was strikingly opportune. Distinguished in the field of scientific research, Agassiz was also a great teacher. Indeed, he became the greatest teachers' teacher in the nation as far as science was concerned; the period between 1840 and 1870 has been called the age of Agassiz. It was he who made science fashionable. He imbued students (see vignette) and future teachers with his enthusiasm and imparted to them his meticulous method of exploring nature. In an age when public lectures, institutes, and summer schools were the vogue, Agassiz was able to influence a far wider public than the circle of his Harvard students. Instead of giving his pupils lessons to learn, he advised them to "read Nature." Very much in Emerson's spirit, Agassiz asserted that it was his duty to open eyes which "cannot see" to the wonders of God's creation. A born collector, Agassiz considered museums indispensable in all educational efforts and promoted their establishment whenever possible. At Harvard in 1860 he established the Museum of Comparative Zoology, designed to show the history of living creatures from the dawn of life to the present. The Agassiz tradition was apparent in 1876 when the National Museum in Washington was reorganized by its first two directors, Spencer Fullerton Baird and George Brown Goode, both of whom had been greatly stimulated by Agassiz. This museum was an outgrowth of James Smithson's gift to the nation in 1826, "to found at Washington an establishment for the increase and diffusion of knowledge among men." It had been established in 1846, with the primary objective of promoting science both through research work and the collection and display of museum specimens. Under the guidance of the first executive secretary, Joseph Henry, who remained in office for thirty-two years, collections had not degenerated into mere curiosity shows as had those of the earlier science museums which had been established in a number of cities. The scientific status of the proposed national museum, however, was threatened in 1865 when even men like Horace Greeley, William Cullen Bryant, and Henry Ward Beecher sponsored a petition to put Phineas T. Barnum at the head of the new institution. Fortunately this idea of making it a "pleasant and attractive place of public amusement"[8] was unsuccessful, because, as time went on, it became common knowledge that Barnum and "humbug" were synonymous.

The situation was definitely saved when Baird and Goode reorganized the museum on a sound basis. Their museum, as well as the one developed in New York, the American Museum of Natural History, was exemplary, and it offered scientific learning suited to the tastes and needs of the nineteenth century, in which large numbers of people began to explore the American scene in many directions.

Accounts of the exploits of these travelers or poetic interpretations of their experiences were accepted by magazines like *Harper's* (established in 1850) and the *Atlantic Monthly* (established in 1857). The short-lived *Dial* (1840–1844) had set the example by publishing such pieces as Thoreau's "Natural History of Massachusetts" and Emerson's "Wood Notes," and even Ellery Channing's poems. The majority of contributions of this kind printed in serious magazines in the middle years of the nineteenth century differed widely from the facile meditations printed in the popular keepsakes and annuals of an earlier day. The generation coming to maturity in the 1840's was indeed preparing to study nature rather than to contemplate it or to enjoy merely the outward aspect of it. As Emerson wrote in his journal,

> . . . a perpetual solicitation of man's faculties to read the riddle is made by the prominence and the beauty of the mountains and the streams under the sun and moon, meeting him everywhere in his daily walk. . . . these monuments of nature and pyramids of the elements, by the side of this silent procession of brute elements, is the poem of man's life.[9]

As if to answer the desire for popular education and to make people "see," a book with a strange title, *The Scene-Shower*, was published in 1844. Significantly, the author, Warren Burton, was a Swedenborgian minister who had been a classmate of Emerson at Harvard. His utopian idea of establishing a "school of scene-showing" which would educate the public to be properly sensitive to landscape beauty was never carried out, although this was the type of education the public seemed to need. Another scheme in which Burton took part, however, did materialize, though from its beginning it seemed utopian to most transcendentalists, in spite of the fact that it was started by some of the prominent members of their group.

George Ripley, the Boston minister, and his wife had spent a couple of summers on a farm near West Roxbury, Massachusetts. Here Mrs. Ripley had found "entire separation from wordly care and rest to the spirit," enjoying "birds and trees, sloping green hills . . . hayfields and nut trees on the green knoll nearby," while the minister lay "for hours on green banks, reading Burns and whistling to the birds, who sing to him."[10] From this idyll, Ripley had conceived the idea of establishing the Brook Farm community (1841). The minister and some of his friends planned to manage the entire farm and supply the labor as well. Enjoyment and satisfaction were to come from this sharing of the labor, and from intellectual intercourse, which was to be cultivated. Emerson and some of his close friends refrained from joining the group; but the more than one hundred associates, including Nathaniel Hawthorne, Warren Burton, George William Curtis, and many others, most of whom did not actually live at the farm, tried hard to make a success of the undertaking. How strange the manual work which had to be performed seemed to most of the members we may gather from an entry in one of Hawthorne's notebooks: "After breakfast, Mr. Ripley put a four-pronged instrument into my hands, which he gave me to understand was called a pitchfork . . . we all three commenced a gallant attack upon a heap of manure." In spite of these difficulties, Hawthorne was confident that he would "make an excellent husbandman,—I feel the original Adam reviving within me."[11]

As time went on and the economic difficulties of the early 1840's did not subside, the laborers at Brook Farm became involved in Fourierism and its drastic schemes to reform society. Since Ripley became one of its most devoted adherents, his original idea of living an ideal life close to and following the laws of nature came to an end. With growing tension inside the group and much mishap, the Brook Farm experiment was faced with unsurmountable difficulties and had to be abandoned in 1845. It shared the fate of similar ventures, such as Economy, the settlement of the Rappists, and New Harmony, the community founded by Robert Owen and William Maclure. If anything, the failure of Brook Farm proved that it was impossible for a group of idealists to establish a new way of life which would overcome the difficulties resulting from the growing complexity of living conditions.

City dwellers undoubtedly were growing increasingly fearful of being engulfed by industry and being cut off from the trees and the fields and other natural beauties characteristic of rural areas. These fears are reflected in some of the remarks of travelers who during their short holidays sought refuge in the tranquillity of the countryside, or perhaps even in the wilderness. When the youthful Francis Parkman went to the White Mountains with a friend in 1841, his chief objective in going so far was to have "a taste of the half-savage kind of life necessary to be led, and to see the wilderness where it was as yet uninvaded by the hand of man." The idea of writing the history of the American forest,[12] which he also had in mind in taking this trip, unfortunately was never carried out. Emerson, too, dreamed of writing a book which, along with many other topics, should contain the natural history of the woods.

During these same years Thoreau was nurturing similar plans. He had appeared suddenly on the literary horizon and had gradually moved into the orbit of Emerson. There he performed the task of bringing to the minds of his fellow men some understanding of nature, a duty which Emerson had felt to be his but for various reasons had been prevented from fulfilling. Thoreau accepted the challenge that Emerson had addressed to the American scholar in 1837. He had become aware of this summoning after he had read *Nature*, but there was another call in this address which made him listen: "So much of nature as he is ignorant of, so much of his own mind does he not yet possess. . . . 'Know thyself,' and . . . 'Study nature' become at last one maxim."[13] Another passage in *Nature* also stirred him. "The reason why the world lacks unity, and lies broken and in heaps, is because man is disunited with himself. . . . It will not need, when the mind is prepared for study, to search for objects. The invariable mark of wisdom is to see the miraculous in the common. . . . So shall we come to look at the world with new eyes."[14] There seems to

Tip-Top House on Mount Washington (New Hampshire)

be an answer to this in one of the great passages in Thoreau's essay "Ktaadn," which tells of his reflections when in 1846 he traveled into the heart of Maine: "Think of our life in nature,—daily to be shown matter, to come in contact with it,—rocks, trees, wind on our cheeks! The *solid* earth! The *actual* world! The *common sense! Contact! Contact! Who* are we? *where* are we?"[15]

When Thoreau died Emerson bade good-bye to his friend and disciple, saying that Thoreau had "dedicated his genius with such entire love to the fields, hills and waters of his native town, that he made them known and interesting to all reading Americans, and to people over the sea."[16] We must not let the directness with which Thoreau followed his chosen way from the beginning to the end, never compromising and rarely ever groping on his path, mislead us into thinking that no obstacles impeded his progress; we must not forget the difficulties he had to overcome and

the pitfalls his sagacity led him to avoid. For instance, he knew well of
the works of two British writers, William Howitt and William Gilpin,
and was considerably influenced by them; yet he knew better than to
copy their style. Howitt had been a poor country boy and had grown up
with romantic ideals. With his wife, Mary, he had roamed the Lake District, and he and Gilpin were staunch admirers of Wordsworth. Howitt's
Book of the Seasons, as Mary Howitt told her sister, contained

> original sketches on every month, with every characteristic of the season,
> and a garden department which will fill thy heart brimful of all garden
> delights, greenness, and boweriness. Mountain scenery and lake scenery,
> meadows and woods, hamlets, farms, halls, storm and sunshine—all are in
> this most delicious book grouped into a most harmonious whole.[17]

Although the author had had difficulty in finding a publisher for it, the
book proved an enormous and lasting success after it came from the press
in 1836. Emerson became acquainted with it and regarded it not as an
inspiration but rather as a "parody" of what he had planned to write
himself. Thoreau felt the same way about it. He disdained to "write
Howittish"[18] and learned to avoid doing so; but he did approve of the
literary form of the *Book of the Seasons* and preferred to shape his own
work in this way rather than in the scientific manner of Gilbert White,
the author of *The Natural History and Antiquities of Selborne.*

About Gilpin's works Thoreau felt somewhat differently. He did not
become closely acquainted with them until 1852. From then on he read
them with much enthusiasm, not so much because he agreed with Gilpin's
ideas, but because he appreciated his genuine interest in nature. In spite
of his enthusiasm, Thoreau remained completely independent, though he
studied carefully Gilpin's conception of nature. He disapproved of Gilpin's
emphasis on the aesthetic aspect of nature, and of his disregard of the
spiritual and ethical issues. Perhaps also he sensed that Gilpin had insep-
arably coupled sentimentality with his idea of the picturesque. In any
event, sound critical judgment prevented Thoreau from accepting Gilpin's
superficial sentimentalism, though most of his contemporaries had done
so and had frequently used his phraseology—unsuccessfully— to brighten
their prose. Thoreau, however, gained from his study of Gilpin, for it gave
him greater ability to appreciate and perceive the beauty of nature.

In spite of Thoreau's excellent preparation, his first publication, *A Week
on the Concord and Merrimack Rivers* (1849), failed to sell. What was
the reason for this failure? Possibly the author's learning seemed ostenta-
tious and that which was really new in the book passed unperceived.
Among the few people who recognized its value was Bronson Alcott. "The
book is purely American, fragrant with the lives of New England woods
and streams, and could have been written nowhere else ... [It is filled

with] sinewy vigour. It preserves to us whatever of the wild and mystic remains to us along our brooksides."[19]

When *Walden* appeared in 1854, the situation had changed. The life Thoreau had lived at Walden Pond for everyone to see had appealed to many people for various reasons. Thoreau's book showed deep wisdom and strong confidence of finding God in nature; besides, there was humor in it, and Yankee thrift. There were many who were comforted by Thoreau's marked resistance to the world as it was beginning to take shape in the 1840's. Opposition to materialism, the search for the inner life combined with a direct appeal to nature, made the book attractive to a great and diversified circle of readers. Thoreau made himself the mouthpiece for his generation, and *Walden* has continued to influence succeeding generations. As Henry Seidel Canby expressed it, "the full significance of *Walden* has never been felt until today . . . and because it records one great individualist's heart-felt and brain-felt experience, it is still eloquent."[20]

However valuable in theory transcendental doctrines had been in the development of the philosophy of nature as formulated by Emerson, without Thoreau's work in observing nature these ideas would never have received that kind of specific interpretation which made it possible for a widespread public to absorb them. Lowell's characterization of Thoreau's work as strawberries from Emerson's garden[21] is not only unkind but fails to take into account the fact that had it not been for Thoreau some of the seed sown by Emerson would not have borne fruit. Emerson engaged in philosophical speculation, whereas Thoreau provided detailed information gathered under the stimulating influence of transcendentalism. And he offered it in a form which he had shaped to suit his needs—the nature essay. Compared with the travel accounts I have already discussed, Thoreau's essays introduced a new way of presenting information about nature. In them, instead of romantic sentiment, superficial enthusiasm, or a quest for novelty, there is genuine inspiration, realistic style, unfailing perception, and above all a deep feeling for and understanding of every small bit of God's creation. Somehow Thoreau seems to have made himself a part of nature and to have learned more from it than all the scientific observers had learned by rationalistic study. With his thoughts and observations as an example, Thoreau's followers continued to emulate the nature essay throughout the second half of the nineteenth century.

One of those stimulated by Thoreau was his close friend Nathaniel Hawthorne, who felt that "Nature in return for his love seems to adopt him as her especial child, and shows him secrets which few others are allowed to witness."[22] The walks and talks Hawthorne enjoyed with Thoreau definitely turned Hawthorne's mind to a closer attention to nature and resulted in his writing such studies as "Buds and Bird Voices," which was first published in 1843 and was later incorporated in his *Mosses from an Old Manse* (1846). Certainly Thoreau did not turn Hawthorne into a scientist, but through his influence Hawthorne became a keen observer. Perhaps most of his observations were confined to the view from his study window, but they enabled him to compare happenings from the drama of nature with events in human life. In this he no doubt was influenced by Emerson's transcendental idea of interpreting human history through natural history. Here again we see the effect of the interrelation of the works of Emerson and those of Thoreau.

One year after *Walden* came out, Henry Ward Beecher published some essays under the title *Star Papers* (1855). This collection differs essentially from the summer books of the day. Surprisingly unpretentious, Beecher made an effort to show his readers the good life by teaching them how to enjoy a quiet vacation in Connecticut. In Woodstock there was no tavern, and the place was so quiet that only a few persons selected it as a vacation spot. "Trouting" all alone by a mountain stream was an experience which Beecher found so different from any other and so enjoyable that he felt every man should try it at least once. Nature is a minister of happiness, he believed, and it is through nature that the soul seeks and sees God. In the thickets of the forest man should feel truly at home. Though we are impressed by the glory and grace of single trees, we must not overlook the beauty of the forest as a whole. Sound knowledge and true love of nature form the basis of the book; observations on the grandeur and sublimity of nature like those offered by the romanticists find no part in it.

Whether Beecher's attitude was due to the influence of Thoreau or to that of transcendentalism is a question which can hardly be answered. It is enough to say that Beecher's widely read book was a step on the right way toward establishing sound relationships between man and nature.

In 1858 a summer camp was established in the Adirondacks which was presided over by Emerson and was later known as the "Philosophers' Camp." Ever since his student days at Harvard when he had roamed through "Sweet Auburn," Emerson had been fond of outings, though usually he got no farther than Walden Pond. When occasionally he took a short holiday, the beauties of nature made a deep impression on him. "We saw stars shine, we felt the awe of mountains, we heard the rustle of the wind in the grass, and knew again the ineffable secret of solitude . . . it was nearer to nature than anything we had before,"[23] he recorded of one such experience.

The idea of camping out in the wilderness of the Adirondacks had been forwarded by W. J. Stillman, who had explored the Adirondacks in the previous year. It may be that Stillman had been stimulated by a little book called *The Adirondacks; or, Life in the Woods,* written by the prolific writer I. T. Headley and first published in 1849. In it the author told about going to the Adirondacks to improve his health. Stillman had studied landscape painting with Frederick Church, and later, when he went to England in 1849, Ruskin had befriended him. Returning home in 1852, Stillman became the art critic for the New York *Evening Post,* and in 1855 he helped found *The Crayon.* In his autobiography and in an earlier essay Stillman explained that he originally went to the Adirondacks because he felt that "going into the desert might quicken the spiritual faculties." But then he found that the "wilderness" factor was not really necessary, that art did not depend on any particular subject, and a dull life in the backwoods was not essential to artistic creation."⁴ In his youth, when he had studied art, landscape painters had roamed the wilderness of the northern states in search of the picturesque. But later Stillman and many others of his generation became more fascinated by "the solitude and savagery of the [woods] than by anything paintable he found there." Thus, the generation after that of Cole discovered that aesthetic appreciation of nature imbued with romantic sentimentalism and centered in the picturesque was no longer essential. There is no denying that Stillman came under the spell of the unbroken wilderness, as did Thoreau, but he no longer preferred to enjoy it by himself. Instead, he wanted his friends to join him in his new experience and gathered round him men in various fields of science. Presided over by Stillman, who was unsurpassed as a moderator, they benefited tremendously from their many new observations and the rational discussion of them. Stillman painted the group at this outing and thus provided a valuable record of the memorable gathering (see pl. 35).

The philosophers set out for their vacation in August, 1858. Among the eight men who joined Emerson and Stillman were Louis Agassiz, James Russell Lowell, and Judge Ebenezer R. Hoar. Longfellow had been invited, but when he heard that even Emerson was going to carry a rifle he refused to take part because he felt sure that somebody would be shot. Thoreau, however, who had decided to travel in Maine that summer, was not invited, and undoubtedly this man who loved solitude would hardly have fitted into the gay company. To Emerson the enterprise must have been a singular experience, judging from his comments in his poem, "The Adirondacs," a "journal" dedicated to his "fellow-travelers." At Follansbee Pond, north of Long Lake, these "ten scholars, who wonted to lie warm and soft," slept "on the fragrant brush," in a shanty roughly built of bark. Here these "polished gentlemen," now "associates of the sylvan gods," were made "freemen of the forest laws." They "tried their rifles at a

mark, . . . trode on air," and . . . "contemned the distant towns." But when
the turmoil of the day was over, Emerson felt that

> The spiritual stars rise nightly, shedding down
> A private beam into each several heart. . . .
> Suns haste to set, that so remoter lights
> Beckon the wanderer to his vaster home.

After this experience the poet expressed once more what he had envisioned
and expressed two decades earlier in *Nature*, "the greatest delight which
the fields and woods minister is the suggestion of an occult relation between man and the vegetable."[25]

But Emerson was not the only one who had a good time, as we learn
from Charles Eliot Norton, who visited Lowell immediately after his
return from the trip. Norton found Lowell

> very well and in capital spirits, having just returned from a wild camping-
> out journey in the Adirondack mountains. He had been cutting paths
> through woods in which no paths had ever been made before, he had shot
> a bear that was swimming a lake, he had seen heards of wild deer, and
> measured pine trees whose trunks three men could not clasp round; and
> all this in the midst of superb and unusual scenery. Our American semi-
> civilization is all round this tract, but has not yet penetrated into it.[26]

Many years later, Stillman gave a colorful account of the journey,[27]
showing how Emerson's personality stood out even in that distinguished
circle. Stillman, himself a great woodsman endowed with the instinct of
the *coureurs de bois,* testified that each member of the party was elated
and cleansed by the experience of living close to nature. As Emerson put
it, in this Paradise,

> Some mystic hint accosts the vigilant,
> Not clearly voiced, but waking a new sense
> Inviting to new knowledge, one with old.[28]

The ten philosophers intended to repeat the successful adventure but
never did so. Soon even the campsite was forgotten, and Adirondack
guides would point to various places as the spot where Emerson and the
other gentlemen from Boston supposedly had camped. To the men who
shared this summer camp, the experience was more than just an outing.
To Emerson, the main figure of the group, it meant a rich harvest of
sensations which he never before had felt. For the others it was a wholesome and unforgettable experience. And for those who had heard of it
but had not taken part in it, the camp became a legend.

Camping (see pl. 36) in the Adirondacks came into vogue in spite of the
fact that lumbermen were making devastating inroads into forests which
had never before been touched by the axe. Winslow Homer was perhaps

Ascent of Mount Marcy (New York)

the last to sketch the guides who had known the Adirondacks in the days when the Emerson party had roamed the wilderness.

James Russell Lowell is known to have had an antipathy to Thoreau, which seems strange for the author of "My Garden Acquaintance," a genuine nature essay. His antagonism may have been founded on his reaction to Thoreau's disregard of what Lowell considered to be the full life—the kind of life he had shared with his philosopher companions at Follansbee Pond. The extremism of Thoreau's views may have been another reason for Lowell's dislike. In spite of his dislike of Thoreau, Lowell was discerning enough to appreciate the excellence of his writing. He considered Gilbert White's *Natural History and Antiquities of Selborne*, as compared with Thoreau's book, "dry as a country clergyman's meteorological journal in an old almanac."[29]

Although prejudices handicapped Lowell in his judgment of Thoreau, he clearly saw the weakness of romantic sentimentality expressed in popular summer books. For instance, he did not hesitate to disparage, at least slightly, N. P. Willis, who was lionized by many people:

> . . . Willis' shallowness makes half his beauty.
> His prose winds along with a blithe, gurgling error, . . .
> 'Tis a narrowish strip, but it is not an artifice;
> 'Tis the true out-of-doors, with its genuine hearty phiz . . ."[30]

As the editor of the *Atlantic Monthly* from its founding in 1857, Lowell willingly sponsored as many articles about nature as he could. Among the most important authors whose work he accepted, two deserve special attention—Wilson Flagg and Thomas Wentworth Higginson. Actually, Flagg was not a discovery of Lowell's. He had written essays for the *Boston Weekly Magazine* as early as 1839 and 1840, and these he had collected in his *Studies in the Field and Forest*, published in 1857, in order to "foster in the public mind a taste for the observation of natural objects and to cultivate the laws of nature."[31] Some of the subjects treated by Flagg were very uncommon; he has, for instance, a chapter on "Sounds from Inanimate Nature," in which there are subtle investigations of melodies peculiar to the seasons. Other chapters are concerned with "Colors and Fragrance of Flowers," and "Music of Insects." Flagg also was one of the early students of ecology, profoundly believing "that each species performs certain services in the economy of nature which cannot be so well accomplished by any other species,"[32] and therefore demanded preservation of what now we call habitat groups. Essays on bird life published in the *Atlantic Monthly* in 1858 established Flagg's reputation as an expert in this field. In all his numerous books and essays Flagg tried to acquaint the public with facts about nature which he had gained from his precise observation. In spite of his sincerity and obvious sensitivity, he irritated Thoreau, who thought that "he is not alert enough. He wants stirring up with a pole. He should practice turning a series of somersets rapidly."[33] The public apparently disagreed with Thoreau's views and did not regard Flagg as a pedestrian writer.

Thomas Wentworth Higginson, like Flagg, came into prominence as an essayist through pieces published in the *Atlantic Monthly;* his "April Days" was printed in that magazine in 1861. Higginson owed much to Emerson and Thoreau; yet he was an independent thinker and had a keen spirit which made him take action whenever he felt the occasion demanded it. Caring nothing for the opinions of small-minded citizens, he was one of those who made every effort to liberate the abolitionist John Brown. During the Civil War he took command of a colored regiment and was successful despite the prophecies of his friends that he would fail. Higginson declined transcendentalism, as far as it seemed exaggerated and only pretended love of nature, for he found that in the early days of the movement "this mental chlorosis reached such a height as almost to nauseate one with nature." Although he conceded that this situation might be exceptional and transitory, he still believed that Emerson overrated the importance of natural objects. According to Higginson, "the simple enjoyment that may be crowded into one hour of sunshine" was all that counted. Nature, he thought, was not didactic but simply healthful. A great bicyclist and oarsman, Higginson valued nature mainly as a means for gaining or maintaining health. This was a new idea and it helped to bring about a more harmonious relationship between men and nature. In addition to being interested in the practical side of human intercourse with nature, Higginson paid considerable attention to its aesthetic value. Always a vigorous fighter for ideas, he never ceased to promote "habitual cultivation of outdoor habits."[34]

Another outdoor man, a great mountaineer and follower of transcendentalism who deserves a place close to Higginson, was Thomas Starr King. King was a disciple of William Ellery Channing, the famous Unitarian minister, and was one of the great propagators of the Unitarian faith. During the War he fostered the Union cause in New England and also in California, to which state he went in 1860. A lover of nature and a follower of Emerson and Thoreau, King published a book about his wanderings in the White Mountains under the title *The White Hills* (1860). If Warren Burton had established his "school of scene-showing" mentioned previously, King's work might have served as its textbook. In it King outlines the natural history of the area and accompanies the reader on his trip through the mountains. Without imposing his own sentiment, he describes the scenery in a lucid and highly animated way. Quoting freely from Emerson's *Nature* and Thoreau's *A Week on the Concord and Merri-mack Rivers,* King tries to induce the reader to take his time when he travels, and to stop for observations. Most summer travelers "bolt the scenery, as a man, driven by work, bolts his dinner ... Sometimes ... they will *gobble* some of the superb views between two trains, with as little consciousness of any flavor or artistic relish, as a turkey has in swallowing corn." Sometimes "people go into New Hampshire with such apathetic eyes, that they have no relish for richness of landscape, or for mountain grandeur. There is no *smack* in their seeing ... To learn to see is one of the chief objects of education and life." Possibly with William Gilpin in his mind, King urges the traveler to observe minutely "the hues and harmonies of a landscape at different times of the day, and under widely different conditions of air and cloud and light." A journey of this kind, he says, should result in "a purer delight in art, and an intelligent patron-age of it."[85] Unfortunately, King's life was short. He wrote a series of articles on Yosemite, which were published in the Boston *Evening Tran-script* in 1860 and 1861, and he had intended to write a book on Yosemite and perhaps one on the Sierras, but he died in 1864 without having written either. The method of presentation used in his White Mountain book, however, was not only enjoyed by his contemporaries but was copied by many a later writer.

Throughout the 1870's, facts about nature had been spread widely by the authors already discussed, and the information provided by earlier natural scientists, such as André Michaux, John James Audubon, and Thomas Nuttall, had been incorporated in popular books. This amplifi-cation and interpretation of scientific matters had been carried out to such an extent that, at least in the East, it was no longer easy to find facts about nature that were of general interest and that had not already been reported. When John Burroughs first began to write, there was little "news" to make headlines for nature essays. However, he set a new standard for the nature essay, which soon occupied a definite niche in literature.

As the "grand old man" in his field and the "seer of Slabsides," Burroughs personally interpreted nature to more than one generation, and his books are still fresh in our memory. Within his creative lifetime, which spanned more than half a century, he was not only a contemporary of Thoreau and Whitman but lived through World War I. By the time Burroughs died in 1919, his nature studies had become known to the entire nation. In the preface of the 1895 reprint of his *Wake-Robin* (first published in 1871) Burroughs could truthfully state that the reader and he "understand each other very well already."[86] Indeed, during the first two decades of the twentieth century, Burroughs was the accepted guide in matters of the out-of-doors.

Burroughs' first nature essay, "With the Birds," was published in the *Atlantic Monthly* in 1865 and was soon followed by others. In the review of his *Winter Sunshine* (1876) in *The Nation*, Burroughs was called "a sort of reduced, but also more humorous, more available, and more sociable Thoreau."[37] With success assured, Burroughs established himself on a farm in New York State. Later he withdrew occasionally to his secluded retreats, "Slabsides" and "Woodchuck Lodge." From these places he traveled to near and far places, occasionally in the company of such friends as Theodore Roosevelt, Thomas Edison, and Henry Ford. Burroughs never thought of himself as a scientist, but he did assert that he had explored the facts of nature with the freedom of love and old acquaintance and had never taken any liberties with them. He brought home to the ordinary man unadulterated, realistic facts about nature and also gave him inspiration; this was Burroughs' extraordinary accomplishment.

Burroughs gave the nature essay its definite form after it had gone through a formative period in which it had assimilated romantic and transcendental ideas. Burroughs always felt, however, that he did not owe much to Thoreau. Certainly he did not share Thoreau's mystic longings. No desire to recapture "hound, bay horse and turtle dove" is evident in any of his writings. Nor was he attracted by the wilderness. Among the many photographs of Burroughs, the most characteristic are those which show him kneeling to examine some flower growing in his path, or watching birds and clouds while looking at the sky from his lodge. Burroughs did not really care for these phenomena as such, but rather was interested in the way they were correlated and the manner in which they fitted into the universe. Man in harmony with nature was Burroughs' concern; in fact, he believed that "man can have but one interest in nature, namely, to see himself reflected or interpreted there." Bound to the universe, "every creature must take its chance, and man is no exception." Burroughs achieved the apogee of nature writing. He was more successful than anyone else had been in capturing the minds of the public and injecting into them deep affection for nature seasoned by genuine understanding. He knew well that a part of his success was based on his putting "personal feelings and attractions into subjects of universal interest."[38]

After reading a number of works by John Muir, Burroughs became "tired of his writing"; he said that Muir was "crazy about trees and wild scenes," and called him "mountain-drunk." But after Muir's visit with him, Burroughs felt differently. He sensed immediately that here was a "poet, prophet, man of science—a wonderful fellow. There's a far-away look in his face and eyes as if he saw the heights and peaks beckoning to him."[39] Thus it would seem that Burroughs never had felt "mountain-drunk," nor had he apparently ever been greatly impressed by the spectacle of the

Far West. He had gone to California merely to enjoy the warmth, which
did him good in his old age; but the serene atmosphere of the High Sierra
never seems to have tempted him. Yet Burroughs seems to have sensed
very well that his emulator Muir, officiating "in the high temples of the
great Sierra Crown,"[40] in a manner differing from his own, was creating
new aims and new ideals.

7

Summer Migration

THE discussion of the work of Burroughs and Muir has greatly
advanced one phase of our story and has brought it down almost to our
own time. It seemed best to follow this particular path since the conception of nature of both these men stemmed directly from Emerson
and Thoreau and continued and expanded the trends which came from
Concord. But in keeping on the narrow ridge along which our path traveled

VIGNETTE: Rush for the Wilderness (Adirondacks).

we did not touch certain other fields which now must be explored. We have followed the romantic traveler and watched him discover the beauties of the country. Traveling was a characteristic approach to nature in the second quarter of the nineteenth century, but it was not the only one; there were many and varied ways in which townspeople could become acquainted with the American scene. Most of these can be grouped under the general heading "summer migration." A great exodus and redistribution of the American people takes place every summer and, in some regions, in other seasons as well. Although the crowds of summer migrants have increased with the years, people have tried to get away from the city during the sultry season ever since improvements in transportation made traveling easier, in the early part of the nineteenth century. Summer migration is not peculiar to this country, however. European city dwellers enjoy summer peregrinations as much as exhausted Manhattanites or Chicagoans, though the type of vacation they prefer varies according to the country. The sign *Clôture annuelle* found on French shops during the month of August means that the proprietors have gone into the country to visit their relatives. English businessmen may choose to go to the seashore, and Germans have always loved to travel as far afield as possible.

The average American family found a somewhat different solution of their need for a change of scene and air, especially after the automobile became available to most wage earners. The entire family was loaded into the car, along with an assortment of clothing and equipment for summer sports and for keeping house in a cabin rented in some beauty spot. Or members of the family were distributed in various camps, roughing it according to age and preference. Today, seashore and mountains offer innumerable accommodations of all kinds to summer people in all income categories. Holidays spent outdoors have become an important factor in everyone's life. How did the American variety of vacation and enjoyment of the great outdoors originate, some may wonder. And how did it become an outstanding trait in the American way of life?

Even in the eighteenth century, when traveling was difficult, spas had attracted a number of visitors, who went there for their health. Throughout the nineteenth century, spas and baths continued to attract increasing numbers of visitors because the greater ease of traveling encouraged many people to take the waters, and life at the resorts was, or at least seemed to be, rather entertaining. By 1857 the big Saratoga hotels could accommodate twelve hundred guests each. Some of the more elegant hotels also provided cottages which gave the more select guests a touch of rustic life. At Saratoga, life moved in well-worn ruts—much as it did in the city. A lady would rise, dress, go down to the spring, drink the waters to the accompaniment of music of a band, walk around the park, greet friends, chat, drink the waters again, breakfast, see who came in on the train, take a siesta, walk, and have a little small talk with groups of ladies and gentlemen. A gentleman would perhaps smoke on the stoop, play billiards, go to the bar, and gamble,[1] ad infinitum, until the "cure" came to a happy consummation. Sometimes the more enterprising would ride down four miles to the lake to eat trout prepared by an old settler and served on his piazza. A trip to Lake George required as much exertion as anyone was able to stand. To romantic observers like the Reverend Timothy Flint, who loved the primitive forms of society he had found on the western frontier, the kind of life at Saratoga about 1825 showed definitely that the American character had recently undergone some unfortunate changes. Any lover of the country would find cause for regret in "the rapid strides in extravagance and luxury society was taking."[2] Social routine at Saratoga was indeed becoming interminable, there was little time to enjoy the surroundings of the place, and in spite of much genteel talk about the beauties and charms of the spa, visitors were rather indifferent to the natural scene. A young New York lawyer, George Templeton Strong, after his visit to Saratoga in 1841, made this entry in his diary:

> O Saratoga, Saratoga—if proof demonstrative be wanted of fashion's omnipotence, truly thou dost furnish some four thousand unanswerable arguments! It's my first visit, and I devoutly hope my last. A mean little country town . . . an immense wilderness of hotels—like stray cabbages in a potato patch . . . such confusion as would be thought wholly unendurable in town.[3]

At White Sulphur Springs—today Greenbriar White Sulphur Springs, West Virginia, the renowned watering place of the South—the situation was somewhat different. In ante-bellum days it had been the most favored retreat of Southern society, from the Gulf states to tidewater Virginia, and in spite of the wealth and elegance of its clientele, it had remained very simple. Visitors lived "in cabins built of square logs, whitewashed, and disposed in a range just on the skirts of a little lawn, so that they have all the air of a rural village."[4] Although a hotel was built in 1854, the "rustic routine" of the cabin system remained in vogue, and the summer guests spent happy weeks there, all knowing one another.

About 1860, however, in the anxious months that preceded the War Between the States, the atmosphere of the summer resorts became less serene. Even in these gay surroundings Southerners felt that they were treated worse by their countrymen in the North than by any foreign enemies. Southern papers exhorted Virginians to stay at home and spend their money among their fellow Southerners. As a consequence, a number of new watering places opened up in the South along the Mississippi Gulf coast. After the war, many of these resorts lost their clientele, but prosperity came back in the late 1870's. Although at that time there was an influx of Northerners, the springs stayed "intact from the presence both of the *nouveau riche* class and of Messrs. Rag Tag and Bobtail," and the old tradition of good company was perpetuated.⁵ "Old White," as the hotel used to be called, existed until 1913 (see pl. 42), when it was replaced by the present establishment, which has carefully preserved the delightful assembly of cabins on the wooded border of the site. The new development is managed by the Chespeake and Ohio Railroad, which penetrated into the valley of the New River in the early 'sixties, supplanting the old stages which plantation society had used. Another new development of the postwar period took place in Florida. Dormant cities, such as Thomasville, Jacksonville, and St. Augustine, began to attract attention as winter resorts and rapidly increased their seasonal population. In the 'seventies the foundations were laid for the establishment of Florida as a great vacation land.

Although White Sulphur Springs and all the other Virginia springs always maintained their character as rural resorts in accordance with the wishes of their conservative visitors, the spas of the North were more willing to accommodate everyone—both the old society and the throngs of newcomers trying to climb, by mingling with the fashionable crowd, to higher social rank. Many critics did not believe that the recreation offered by such resorts, which were frequented almost exclusively by the wealthy, was appropriate for a nation which worked hard and played little. By 1853 Charles Loring Brace, a professor living in New York and a friend of Frederick Law Olmsted, asserted that "those most useless trips to crowded watering-places must be dropped for something—cheering, healthful, boyish—or we shall be a nation of dyspeptics." Instead, one should take cheering mountain walks, "to let the full almost unconscious enjoyment of scenery pour into the heart."⁶ Although Brace was in general undoubtedly right, there was at least something to be said for the spa. It did offer a change of climate and health-giving waters, and there was a certain beneficial regularity in the daily life, all of which helped improve the health of worn-out businessmen and gave them a change they otherwise would not have had. A sojourn at a watering place at least convinced city dwellers that to leave town for a while was a wholesomely beneficial experience.

After the middle of the century many city people became rather anxious to improve their health and living conditions. The park movement, initiated by Bryant, was one of these efforts to cope with the situation. Bryant himself, with his strong physique, appeared an ideal apostle of any movement of this kind, and it was only natural to seek his advice about the proper mode of living. William Howitt, the English naturalist, who was much disliked by Emerson, was also consulted. Both Bryant and Howitt gave their versions of the "early to bed" principle of keeping sound, and both stressed that exercise in the out-of-doors was of the greatest importance for the well-being of the human body. Their answers to questions about health were duly published in a series of tracts issued for the benefit of young men, under the title *Miniature Herald of Health,* and may even have done some good. The public had just begun to realize the importance of the efforts Francis Lieber and Charles T. Follen had made in the late 1820's to popularize swimming and gymnastics in this country. As might have been expected, Walt Whitman, for one, pointed out that "young fellows . . . should be in the habit of daily spending an hour or two in some out-door game or recreation. The body and mind would both be benefited by it."' There certainly was a great need for such improvement, if we are to believe the editor of *Harper's Monthly,* who thought that the American youth of his time was a sad-looking creature, "pale, pasty-faced, narrow-chested, spindle-shanked, dwarfed face—a mere walking manikin to advertise the last cut of the fashionable tailor."⁸

With so much attention being paid to the subject of health, it was natural that active sports should become popular. Henry W. Herbert and his follower Elisha J. Lewis had so successfully revived interest in outdoor sports that trips to hunting or fishing grounds were no longer regarded as extravagant. In the 1850's, numbers of sportsmen of the rod and gun joined in hunting trips (see pls. 37–39) to the wilderness areas of New York State, frequently organized by the North Woods Walton Club, which exploited the lakes of the Moose River in the Adirondacks. The opening of the Erie Railroad in 1851 made the northern lakes and the hunting grounds along their shores easily accessible. Lake Erie could now be reached by a seventeen-hour ride, in the course of which the train passed through scenery which could "scarcely be excelled on the entire continent for beauty and sublimity," though this, as we know, was a claim also made by the Baltimore and Ohio. The train inaugurating the Erie line carried President Fillmore and Daniel Webster (see pl. 33) among the number of illustrious guests. While most of the dignitaries rode in the passenger cars, Daniel Webster, who hated to be in a close car of this kind, rode in the open air on a flatcar. Through the first day of the trip he sat there on a rocking chair which had been mounted on the flatcar so that he "might better enjoy the scenery." This incident and a speech Webster gave in 1847 at the opening of the Northern Railway to Grafton, New Hampshire,' shed some interesting light on his attitude toward certain developments in this age of transition. Like some of his farsighted contemporaries, the great statesman acknowledged that railroads were useful, and he expressed his belief that they would help to create prosperity. He had seen many changes in the course of his lifetime, he told his audience. As a boy he had loved to roam over New England on country roads and byways leading to his favorite haunts; later he had seen the development of great turnpikes and the introduction of canals. Taking advantage of both, he had enjoyed the beauties of the countryside in an entirely new fashion. Then the time had come when he was able to establish a country home at his beloved Marshfield, where he could hear the rolling of the ocean. Now he was speaking to honor the railroadmen who, he felt assured, were inaugurating a new and prosperous era. Yet, he dared to say, "railroad directors are utilitarians in their creed and in their practice . . . their business is to cut and slash . . . if they can find a fair reason to run a tunnel under a deep mountain.they are half in raptures." To be sure, railroads were necessary, but they would destroy much of what he loved and what was essential for man's well-being. In Webster's day this was a courageous attitude to take and one which could be assumed publicly only by a man of his stature. Since Webster was one of the idols of his period, his opinion carried considerable weight and probably was shared by many of his compatriots. Thus Webster, rocking on top of his flatcar, admiring the country vistas like any tourist and traveling on a railroad established for strictly utilitarian purposes, appears as a symbol of trends which in his era were still far apart but in a later day would become reconciled.

The idea of vacationing and traveling for pleasure had taken hold of the minds of the people of the nation; it no longer was peculiar to those who lived along the eastern seaboard. Naturally, Westerners liked to go East and visit the spas in Virginia or New York State. But at the end of the 1860's St. Louis people went also to places like Madison-on-the-Lakes, which boasted an unusually well equipped hotel and served as an excellent focal point for fishing expeditions. New Yorkers were particularly attracted by the wilderness areas, and so during the 'sixties the Adirondacks at last came into fashion and soon were thoroughly explored. Scarcely penetrable at the time of the Philosophers' Camp, they became almost crowded by the 1870's, particularly after William H. H. Murray published in 1869 a kind of guide called *Adventures in the Wilderness; or, Camp Life in the Adirondacks*. Edwin L. Godkin in *The Nation* welcomed this type of book because it might lead "a good many people to forsake watering places and loafing and try the shanty life of hemlock-bough beds." But he made it very clear that this particular book, unfortunately, was written as if in falsetto; it was screeching, loud, and altogether vulgar; "the author was making a fool of himself."[10] Nevertheless, as a result of such publicity, townspeople were intruding into the "wilds" wherever they thought they might find them, but without laying aside their need for urban comforts. When they were disappointed in what they found, they did not hesitate to voice their displeasure; this was enough to generate antagonism against their kind among the country people. In 1870 the editors of *Harper's* must have felt that the "cockneyism" shown in the rush for the wilderness warranted attack. They printed a long, illustrated (see vignette) satirical article entitled "The Raquette Club," in which, of course, Murray's all too fanciful guide played an important role.[11]

But there were those who were eager to give their families the pleasure of a vacation without having to take cheap quarters in a dingy boarding house or to spend huge sums at one of the big resort hotels. A good solution to this problem was given in an article published in *Scribner's Monthly* in August, 1874, entitled "The Tent Under the Beach," which highly recommended camping. A group of eight or ten families had joined in such a camping enterprise, much to the satisfaction of everyone. Thirteen tents had been pitched, providing for dining room, kitchen, and bedrooms, and two servants with carts had foraged food from nearby villages. Everything had functioned smoothly, including the care of the children, who had been quite happy. In June of the next year, just before vacation, *Scribner's* again took up the subject and stated that "camping out" was "rapidly growing in favor." The magazine suggested that tents might be pitched on the beaches of Virginia, in the White Mountains, on the Minnesota plains, in the Unaka range, or on the shores of Hudson Bay. Anyone who is "above conventionality" and who has "a lucky drop of vagabond blood" in his veins,[12] the article said, would heartily enjoy this kind of vacation. A guide to "popular resorts" published in 1874 by the painter-writer John B. Bachelder, even made "camping out" the subject of a whole chapter and recommended it as a sort of woodman's or frontier life. All this shows definitely that the idea of the Philosophers' Camp was embraced and popularized by groups which, though completely different, had in common an appreciation of nature. Godkin, in *The Nation*, took every opportunity to foster trends of this kind. When Major John M. Gould published a manual on *How to Camp Out* in 1877, Godkin praised it highly and even censured physicians for not recommending enough exercise in the open air. Instead of prescribing rest from business, he said, they should insist that the patient walk from New York to Niagara, or urge him to help the Appalachian Club build its trails.[13]

The 1860's and 1870's saw the introduction of a number of summer sports, as well as the custom of camping out. Croquet, for instance, began its career in 1866. Now it is considered a rather mild form of outdoor exercise; but in those days it was taken quite seriously, and the first national convention of croquet players was held in Chicago in 1879. The game appealed to many people because it was played outdoors and it also offered an opportunity for courting. It was a mild introduction to the age of increasing physical freedom for women. Tennis, which began to be played about 1874, was a far better game than croquet and required more skill. It, too, was suitable for summer flirtations. The bicycle in its turn became the favored vehicle for country excursions for nature lovers and other kinds of lovers. But neither the "boneshaker" popular about 1869 nor the high-wheeled bicycle introduced in the 1870's proved a really great success; not until the low "safety" wheel was introduced in the early 1880's did bicycling become a craze. This reached its peak about 1900, when the popularity of the bicycle began to be challenged by the first automobiles. The *Wheelman,* which began publication in 1882, appealed to those to whom the bicycle offered a convenient means of relaxation in the out-of-doors. Its columns abounded in articles giving information on how to plan trips, records of successful bicycle tours to Virginia and to Yellowstone Park (see pl. 51), and even an account of coasting down slopes of the Rocky Mountains.

The majority of urban workers were unable to go so far for their recreation or take interesting bicycle trips the costs of which it was difficult to budget ahead. For these people a nearby seaside resort was the most suitable vacation spot and offered a variety of possibilities suited to a wide range of incomes.

Even in pre-Revolutionary days, seabathing had not been unknown. Philadelphians and New Yorkers would go out to the beach in a Jersey wagon, taking provisions along, and either get home as best they could or find residents near the shore who would give them shelter for the night. But only men took part in this strenuous sport; it was far too rough for females. After the Revolution, Old Point Comfort, Long Branch (see pl. 40), Cape May, Rockaway Beach, and similar places were developed. These beaches were so much frequented by Southern gentry, Philadelphians, and New Yorkers that soon after 1810 it was necessary to build special boardinghouses. For the most part built on lonely beaches, they were constructed in a simple manner; nobody cared much about discomforts as long as everybody became "salted and pickled with sea air." A Philadelphia diarist, Jacob Hiltzheimer, reported in 1795 that he took swims somewhere near Long Branch with families of his acquaintance, even including the ladies." This was rather unusual, for as a rule men and women frequented the beach at different times. In Massachusetts, sea bathing seems to have been taken up somewhat later. The first cottage at Nahant (see pl. 20), a spot frequented by Bostonians, was built in 1817; but this beach, unlike others, gained popularity quickly. It was not long before most people thought that being exempt "from all the usual family concerns of housekeeping or business is a state which a care-crazed man of business should be glad to arrive at," and that if "the closely confined city drudge" would "visit a sans-souci establishment and abandon his mind," it "would make him a more ethereal being."[15] In 1820, when the French scientist Jacques Milbert visited Nahant, he was astonished to find many taverns in the place, and the resort frequented by "a crowd of delicate women . . . most scantily dressed and risking to get sick because of the sharp winds . . ."[16] Sea bathing for women was not customary before the end of the 1820's, and when women did enter the water they were undoubtedly dressed far more fully than those Milbert had seen promenading; the five-piece bathing suit remained in vogue throughout the nineteenth century.

The growth of Nahant deserves some study, for it is typical of the development of other places. In the eyes of some writers, ethical standards were lowered by the questionable moral conduct displayed in Nahant, where women were allowed to play billiards and show a degree of independence elsewhere unheard of. Theodore Dwight, however, took a different view and stressed more positive points. He believed that children brought up to admire the false glitter of wealth would be imbued with new and better ideas if they would listen to the "monitory voice in the sea . . . which affects the old and even the accustomed mind with awe . . . and makes an impression no human power . . . can ever entirely deface." Dwight also recommended "resting places arranged on the most advantageous points of view," where the harried man of business might gaze in admiration on the horizon and indulge "in reflection ennobling to a mind borne down with daily cares." The association of men and women on the beaches, he felt, would foster in them an appreciation of nature; and interesting talks about the natural and real beauty of the place would replace conversation about fine dinners and good wine, and everyone would depart in far better mental health than when they came. The mind of a person who took a dip into the waves would thereafter be especially well prepared for useful meditations, it was believed (see pl. 34), for "how little like a man does a man feel in such circumstances when he is plunged into an element foreign to his nature."[17] Pious hopes of a moralist observing the beginnings of the movement to enjoy the outdoors! Many changes in fashion and in taste were to come before the attitude of the public toward the seaside or any other part of the outdoors became stabilized.

In the early 1840's, the days of N. P. Willis, Nahant was full of bustle and life and provided a stylish background for stories of the period; but in the 1850's it lost its leading role to Newport. One of the reasons for this may have been that at Nahant there was no escape from the ocean, which surrounds the promontory and makes its overpowering might felt on all sides. But it is more likely that the change was due to a development common to many resorts. Visitors, especially the more affluent ones and those

who had been coming to the resort for many years, became tired of living
in hotels which had become too large to suit their taste and also were
catering to newcomers in society who were not acceptable to the earlier
inhabitants. Many of these wished to have their own cottages, in order to
be independent and have an opportunity to draw social lines wherever
they saw fit. Since at Nahant there was not sufficient space for expansion,
society turned to Newport. The ocean was not quite so overwhelming
there; Curtis even called it a luxury, for there was so much space that
cottages could be built far away from the roar of the sea.[18]

In the days in which Nahant was becoming famous as a resort, some
Cambridge professors had chosen the old city of Newport for their summer
residences. The theologian Andrews Norton, Charles Eliot Norton's father,
for instance, was one of those who built summer homes in the city. Even
as late as the 'sixties, when Henry James settled in Newport, his family
found the place very agreeable. As his son (also named Henry) wrote
later, James maintained that this place was "the one right residence, in all
our great country, for those tainted, under whatever attenuations, with
the quality and the effect of detachment. The effect of detachment was the
fact of the experience in Europe."[19] This seems to indicate that Newport
was undergoing a development of a kind peculiarly its own. One of those
with whom the Jameses associated for a short while was William Morris
Hunt, who had opened a studio in Newport in 1856. After a stay of a few
years, however, resenting the burden of social obligations at the resort,
Hunt left for Boston in 1862.

Social activities at Newport had been very handsomely initiated by a
fancy-dress ball given at the opening of the Ocean House in 1846, for
which the subscription tickets were ten dollars each. With standards of
this kind established, Newport developed steadily until the end of the
century. The clique which formed finally became so exclusive that it was
said newcomers were not admitted to the inner circle until they had been
there at least four seasons, and some never succeeded in entering it. When
Henry Adams went to Newport in 1868 and tried to be fashionable, "he
failed as fashion" and turned away disgusted by its social routine.[20] Two
years later, Henry James spoke disparagingly of the vanities of Newport,
and added that he did not wish to be suspected "of the untasteful heresy
of meaning primarily rocks and waves rather than ladies and gentlemen."[21]
A milder judge, Thomas Wentworth Higginson, was slightly amused by
Newport activities; he thought it rather pleasant "to see some opulent
citizen in his first kid gloves. His new-born splendor stands in such brilliant
relief against the confirmed respectability of the 'Old Stone Mill.' "[22] Since
social life of the superficial kind meant so much to Newport residents, one
can imagine that Charles Eliot Norton was little inclined to establish a

summer home at Newport as his father had done. Instead, he went out to Ashfield, where he found "the old classical ideal of a pleasant home in a smiling country with books, friends, children, dogs, horses, fields, a garden and trees."[23]

After Nahant had yielded the social palm to Newport, it once more reverted to "freedom from the fury of fashion" and became a place where "Grecian gaiety upon the sea" could be enjoyed and sensible people could live with the sea and sky and yet not lose "that pleasant social intercourse, which has a secret sweeter than the sea or the sky can whisper."[24]

Although conditions occasionally changed throughout the years, and fashion might rule out one place in favor of another, bathing places on the shore continued to thrive along the whole Atlantic coast. Among the multitude of these beach resorts there are two which deserve special attention because of their unusual development: Appledore, one of the Isles of Shoals, and Mount Desert, an island on the coast of Maine.

A disgruntled politician, Henry B. Laighton, obtained an appointment as lighthouse keeper on one of the Isles of Shoals and swore never again to put foot on the mainland. After he retired, he decided to start a summer hotel on Appledore. He erected a four-story building with eighty sleeping rooms and spacious halls and piazzas; placed a few advertisements in the Boston, Newburyport, and Manchester papers; and opened the hotel for business on June 15, 1848, without the slightest knowledge of who might come. From the very first, however, Laighton's venture was successful; not only did guests arrive, but he acquired a very special clientele. By chance, a former Harvard man, Levi Thaxter, had taken a liking to the Laightons and had spent a winter at the lighthouse teaching the Laighton children. When the hotel was opened, Thaxter returned, and one after another his friends, the elite of Boston, appeared. James Russell Lowell, Thomas Wentworth Higginson, J. Mason Parker, Nathaniel Hawthorne, and many others came and felt at home on Appledore. In 1851 Levi Thaxter married Celia, the daughter of his host. Brought up on the Isles, highly sensitive to their peculiar beauty and with her whole being deeply rooted in their lore, Celia Thaxter developed a poetic mind and expressed her ideas about the sea and other forms of nature surrounding her in poems which had a wide appeal. Everyone who met her was enchanted with her rich personality, and she herself took delight in the gay life which developed on Appledore. Until the end of her life she spent nearly every summer on the island, and each summer saw an increase in the number of her admirers. Sometimes Celia shared the honors of the court with John Greenleaf Whittier, who adored her, and whose friends adored him. From his home at Amesbury, Whittier would imagine that he saw the evening sun flash on the windows of Appledore (ten miles out at sea), and thinking

of Celia Thaxter and her poems about Appledore he wondered what the
island "would be without thee—a mere pile of rocks, I imagine, dead as
the moon's old volcanic mountains. Thee have given them an atmosphere."[25]

In 1879 William Morris Hunt visited Appledore and was put up in the
Thaxter cottage. The painter was a sick man when he arrived, but no one
anticipated the outcome of his visit. As Mrs. Thaxter told a friend later,
the suffering man passed his days on the sunny piazza in the sweet summer weather, "watching the glowing colors in the little garden or the
beautiful sea and sky," listening to music, chatting pleasantly with friends,
and feeling appreciated by all. Then one day he disappeared. When he
was found he was dead, lying on the edge of the reservoir, where a fit of
vertigo had brought his life to an end.[26]

The last painter who joined the Appledore circle was Childe Hassam,
who painted on the island for several years and also illustrated Celia Thaxter's book, *My Island Garden*. As time went on, a hotel on nearby Star
Island, built in 1873, was taken over by Celia's brothers, who managed
the place on Appledore, and with this accommodations for as many as
fourteen hundred guests were possible. After Celia Thaxter died in 1894,
things began to change. Now that the central figure of that small universe
was gone and many of her friends had also passed away, the old company
began to break up. The story of old Appledore came to an end after nearly
half a century of spirited life. Interest in the island had been extraordinarily stimulated by Celia Thaxter and the inner circle of her friends,
and the throng of summer guests who came to the Isles of Shoals when
she was alive must have returned home more appreciative of the beauties
of nature and with a better understanding of their natural surroundings.

Mount Desert Island in Maine had been visited in 1844 by Thomas Cole.
His pupil Frederick Church was the next artist to visit there, and very
likely it was through Church that the island became known for its singular
beauty. Church must have become acquainted with Mount Desert between 1844 and 1854. As it happened, his intimate friend Theodore Winthrop was studying law in New York with Charles Tracy in 1855, and it
was undoubtedly he who advised Tracy, later father-in-law of J. Pierpont
Morgan, to select Somesville on Mount Desert for a summer sojourn in
August and September, 1855. This was in the nature of a major undertaking, for Tracy brought his entire family and a number of friends also,
among whom were Church and Winthrop. All together there were twenty-
six persons—and a piano. This company filled Somes Tavern and another
house to capacity and required a goodly number of the inhabitants of
Somesville to do household chores. The logbook which Tracy kept of this
jaunt describes in detail the activities of the company. Time passed very

quickly, with boating, fishing, riding, and tramping during the day, and backgammon in the evening, as well as rehearsals in preparation for Sunday services. The presence of Church and Winthrop contributed greatly to the entertainment of the group. Winthrop, handsome and gay, had returned from Panama and the Pacific Coast not long before, and no doubt was full of western adventure stories. Church, thoroughly familiar with the island, interpreted the scene admirably. He would paint and draw and show his sketches while the company sat around the fireside. Then Winthrop would recite poems he had composed. As the climax of the vacation there was an ascent of Mount Newport, some 1,060 feet, from the summit of which could be seen the coast of Maine. Tracy was "smitten with all the wide, wide blue Ocean as the most grand, most impressive, most beautiful and yet most fearful of all the things in the complete prospect . . . old as the world and yet as fresh and living as if newly finished . . . time and showers and frost have seared these old rocks . . . but the sea is unchanged." After the company returned to New York, Tracy ended his logbook with the remark, "this ends an expedition which has been interesting, instructive and often exciting in a very high degree. It will be the fund of story and conversation for years to come. The children come back broader and browner and stronger than they went. So it all ends well!"[27]

In 1858 Robert Carter, a Washington journalist who worked for the New York *Tribune*, passed a few days on Mount Desert Island when he was on a summer cruise up the coast of New England. Carter landed at Bass Harbor and then worked his way across to Bar Harbor. Boarders were taken by a number of people on the island, though lodgings were not to be had in all villages. According to Carter, Mount Desert had already become a favorite resort for artists and for a number of summer loungers. He believed that the matchless natural beauty of the island should now be developed by persons with a cultivated taste. If a program of judicious reforestation could be put into proper effect, he thought, the island might become a place of pilgrimage dear to all lovers of the beautiful and sublime in nature.[28] In only a few years the island became well known for the "goodly company at Mt. Desert—wise men of affairs, accomplished men of letters, artists, students, fair women and bright girls . . ."[29] But soon people of a different kind began to invade the island. This might have been foreseen because it had been predicted that when "the needed capital determines to invest, and the newspapers open their trumpet throats to proclaim Mount Desert and 'all about it,' the armies of summer pilgrims will commence the mighty march to grand and glorious Mount Desert."[30]

In 1880 a group of Harvard students pitched their tents in a more remote part of the island, on Somes Sound. The students liked the place so much that they returned the next summer. Among them, and indeed the one who initiated the plan was Charles Eliot, a great nature enthusiast, who later earned renown as a landscape architect and an associate of Frederick Law Olmsted. Eliot prevailed on his father, Charles William Eliot, the president of Harvard College, to buy some property for a summer home on Somes Sound. A friend of the president, Bishop Dean of Albany, followed suit immediately, and before long other friends had established themselves. There is little need to stress the great difference between this group and the "cottagers" of Newport. Stimulated by the efforts and example of the Eliots, the settlers took great interest in conserving the natural background of the island and were unwilling to have it spoiled by unsuitable buildings. In 1903 this group formed an association "with the object of raising, holding, and appropriating for public use such lands which by reason of historic interest or scenic beauty were suited for a public monument." After securing title to this area, the association, under the active leadership of George B. Dorr, offered it in 1916 to the nation as a national monument. Thus originated the first national park east of the Mississippi, and one which had been created not from the public domain but by the foresight and sacrifice of public-minded citizens.[31] Independent of these conservation-minded persons there was a fluctuating mass of summer boarders which crowded the island and its flourishing hotels. By 1900 Bar Harbor had become one of the most fashionable resorts in the country.

Nahant, Newport, Appledore, and Mount Desert may serve as examples of the general development of beach resorts; the stages in their development were more or less the same for all. Scenes of natural beauty became popular as a result of their being observed and appreciated by some discriminating persons. Visitors would come in greater and greater numbers until they created an unwieldy and sometimes annoying crowd. As a consequence, the more sensitive or the more exclusive of them would then try to protect themselves against the others. The outcome of the battle depended on specific local conditions.

Vacationists who could not afford a holiday on the coast or at some inland resort in the early 1850's had the opportunity to join some of the Methodist camp meetings, such as those at Ocean Grove and Round Lake in New Jersey and Eastham in Massachusetts (see pl. 43). Camp meetings had flourished in the sparsely settled areas of Kentucky and Tennessee since 1799. There in beautiful surroundings campgrounds established in the early days attracted people from far and near to come and worship and enjoy community life in good, neighborly fashion. The sounds of sacred music, "rising on the stillness of a summer night blended with the voices of the forest till it was the lightest task of fancy to hear the song of angels in the dying cadences . . . Here was a harmony—not of art, but that wild, uncultured beauty in which Nature adorns herself with flowers or tints the autumn leaf."[32] However delightful this sounds, it is well to remember that these early gatherings did not always appear quite so attractive and tasteful to other reporters; Mrs. Trollope, for instance, or even less easily offended persons.

In recent years in parts of the Southwest needs like those in old Kentucky have found a similar solution. Ranchers living far from towns and cities seldom have an opportunity to attend religious service. In 1940, cattlemen in southern Arizona arranged for a nondenominational church gathering at a beautiful site called Nogal Mesa. Here stockmen within a radius of a hundred and fifty miles camped together for four days. Since then, more meeting places have been arranged in Wyoming, Colorado, New Mexico, Arizona, and Texas. The gatherings take place in the open under a fine, tall ponderosa pine or a white oak. As an old-timer put it, "We got us a church that grows bigger and better every year. . . . there couldn't be a prettier temple any place 'cause God made this one Hisself."[33]

Although the goal of the early church gatherings had been the fostering of Christian principles, the meetings held in the East in the late 1850's tended to promote healthful recreation also. But conditions under which these camps were established differed entirely from those in the West, and a number of defects developed in the eastern camps. These camps often became extremely congested and so overcrowded that the sanitation facilities were far from adequate. Yet in spite of such shortcomings the institution of these camps was the beginning of recreation for those people who otherwise would never have had a chance to enjoy any open-air vacation. It should be remembered that about the middle of the century bricks and mortar were closing in on townspeople, and the contrast between the life of laborers in the towns and the farmers in the country had never been greater. That the idea of gathering kindred spirits in camps was sound and was becoming well-rooted in American life is proved by the fact that it became commercialized; meeting grounds were advertised as suitable places for conventions. A typical meeting place for such outings was Harmony Grove near Framingham, Massachusetts. Here in 1852 citizens were offered "a day of pleasant recreation among woodland and lake scenery." On a fifteen-acre lot[34] one could find an elevated platform for speakers, a natural amphitheater, cricket grounds, and superior accommodations of all kinds for parties. The Chautauqua movement, which adopted some of the features of the camp meetings, and which also had originated in Methodist circles, deserves mention here mainly because one of its fundamental ideas was to carry on its activities in beautiful natural surroundings in order to stir its followers to respect God's creation and learn to understand it better.

The problems presented by mass-meeting areas and seaside watering places differed considerably from those of inland resorts. Anyone wishing to enjoy the surf could find ample opportunity to do so at a cost commensurate with his means. But for anyone with the Catskill Mountain House, Franconia Notch, or even a secluded valley in Pennsylvania as a goal, it was a different story. Not everyone could afford such places; but even disregarding the cost, the appeal of these places differed greatly according to the individual tastes of the visitor.

As we have seen, after public attention had been directed toward a specific fall or mountain peak, visitors streamed to these places. Perhaps one or another spot, such as Trenton Falls or Mount Holyoke, might lose popularity in time; but in general, once the reputation of a place had been established, visitors would continue to pour into it, and hotels would be built to keep pace with the growth in popularity. For instance, the White Mountains region, as mentioned earlier, was first brought to the attention of the country by the Willey catastrophe in 1826, and for many years stories and poems kept memories of the disaster alive. In 1837 Hawthorne published his *Twice-told Tales,* including "The Great Carbuncle," a story from the White Mountains. This he followed up with another story, "The Great Stone Face," published in the *National Era* in 1850. Whittier, in his "Bride of Pennacock," published in 1844, described the scenery in the very heart of the region, and three years later his "Mary Garvin," a poem about the Saco River, was printed. Always faithful to the White Mountains, Whittier returned summer after summer to Bear Camp River House at West Ossipee, to Intervale, and to Holderness. Many of his poems were written in this vicinity; the one which perhaps became most popular was *Among the Hills,* written in 1867. In fond recollection of the hills, where he felt himself closer to God than anywhere else, Whittier tells his impressions of a "Sunset on the Bearcamp," a "Storm on Lake Asquam," "The Wood Giant," and perhaps the strongest of them all, "Chocorua's tall defiant sentinel . . ."

All these poetic renditions, as well as the paintings by Cole, Durand, Casilaer, Kensett, Samuel Colman, Daniel Huntington, and Benjamin Champney, to mention but a few, gave the public an excellent idea of what the region was like. As a climax came Starr King's book *The White Hills,* a classic in every respect, written by an author whose work was certain to be welcomed in all parts of the country.

In the years since Mount Washington (see frontispiece) first became known in the early 1820's, its fame had risen steadily, and it had attracted more and more visitors. The stone huts erected by Crawford on the summit had quickly fallen into disrepair after he had left the area, but the bridle path completed in 1840 remained usable for a long while and served the rude Tip Top House, which was run as an inn for a short time. Next to come were the first Summit House and the second Tip Top House (see illustration in chap. 6) opened in 1852 and 1853. But in spite of all the apparent comforts which were offered, a trip to the rugged White Mountain area was generally thought of as only "being well suited for young lovers and romantic fools." As for "old gentlemen, they should stay in their comfortable town house."[35] Things became easier in 1869 after the cog railway was built up the mountain. The Franconia Notch region saw the establishment of the Lafayette House as early as 1835; the Flume House with one hundred rooms followed in 1848, and the Profile House in 1853. To answer the needs of visitors to these prospering enterprises, a narrow-gauge railroad was built in 1879.

Other resorts, too, prospered; but as the crowds increased great shortcomings became noticeable. Many newcomers lacked even the rudiments of education, to say nothing of any preparedness for the surroundings into which a quick train ride from Boston or New York plunged them. Indeed, the vacationist behaving in an awkward or ridiculous manner in his unaccustomed surroundings was a standard subject of cartoons of the day. Little wonder, then, that the more cultivated persons looked for ways to avoid the uncouth and plebeian during their vacation time.

One way to escape from the crowd was to build a summer home. This was not a new idea, for in the eighteenth century, country estates were common in the vicinity of flourishing cities. The southern countryside had been justly famous for opulent plantation houses, as well as manors, but the style and purpose of these early country seats differed from those built in the period which we are now considering. In the eighteenth century a country seat had been either a place to which a gentleman retired after serving his country—most likely the hereditary home of his family, such as Madison's "Montpelier"—or a place near the city, such as William Hamilton's "Woodlands." In either case it was maintained in grand style and differed only in scale from the country estates of the landed gentry in England.

As early as 1813 Timothy Dwight envisioned the time when "it will not be thought necessary to place a country residence in the purlieus of a great city, or desirable to look for the pleasure of rural life in the neighborhood of the dwellings of market people and the stalls of butchers." And Dwight mentioned a number of beauty spots which he thought were "fitted to become rich and delightful residences of men," though at that time most of the country homes of the wealthy inhabitants of New England were not far out in the country.[36] In 1818 another traveler through New England wrote: "the genuine country seat has not yet made its appearance, in the four states which I have seen."[37] But in the decade between 1820 and 1830 the change came, and country seats on the Hudson, on lakes, and in other outstanding beauty spots became fashionable.

The term "country seat," or rather "country home" or "country cottage," as after a while it was preferably called, now took on a different connotation. Not only did the style of the country seat frequently change, but persons of a different kind from those who had once lived on the outskirts of the towns began to occupy them. It may not be too far-fetched to suppose that in a measure Sir Walter Scott's "Abbotsford" had set an ideal for which it seemed worth striving. Scott had achieved this by means of his pen. American authors or artists, possibly with this in mind, strove to obtain a pleasant and somewhat similar abode, though perhaps one not quite so lofty as "Abbotsford" and better "adapted to North America," as Andrew Downing expressed it.

The painter Thomas Cole was the first to reside both summers and winters in the Catskills, and in so doing aroused the curiosity of the public. Later, Washington Irving's "Sunnyside," overlooking the Hudson, caught the imagination of his readers. In a letter to the editor of the *Knickerbocker Magazine*, in March, 1839, Irving set forth his reasons for retiring to the country. "Here, then, have I set up my rest, surrounded by the recollection of early days . . . with that glorious river before me . . . which has ever been to me a river of delight."[38]

Although Poe was never fortunate enough to establish a real country residence, his imagination built a huge one. It is likely that Downing's book on landscape gardening, published in 1841, kindled Poe's fancy and stimulated him to write his "Landscape Garden," which was published in October, 1842, in the *Ladies' Companion*. In 1847 Poe incorporated this fragment in a more extended story entitled *The Domain of Arnheim*. Stimulated by William Beckford's imaginative creation at "Fonthill," described in *Vathek*, and also by an anecdote in the travel accounts of Prince Hermann von Pückler-Muskau, a great German landscape gardener, Poe tells the story of a man who fell heir to a vast sum of money and established a landscape garden because that kind of enterprise offered "the most magnificent of opportunities." Poe goes on to describe this vast creation with all its exuberant beauties. Two years later (1849) he published "a pendant" to this study under the title "Landor's Cottage." This time, inspired by his own experience, he idealized the cottage at Fordham which he had discovered on one of his walking tours in 1846. This modest place tucked away in charming surroundings appealed to Poe so much that he rented it. The cottage still exists, though in 1913 it was moved a short distance from its original location.[39]

After Willis built his first country place, "Glen Mary," on the Susquehanna, Poe hoped that with tranquillity and leisure Willis would accomplish a good deal in this Arcadia. Unfortunately, Willis had to give up this place "under the bridge"; but he later established another country seat, "Idlewild," which became one of the most famous of the romantic Hudson River retreats. By this time Audubon had retired to a place on the outskirts of New York, where fawns and even an elk roamed. The spot chosen by Henry William Herbert ("Frank Forester") was beside Mount Pleasant Cemetery, just out of Newark. There he built "Cedars," a place that became well known to all hunting men. When Thoreau took up his abode at Walden in 1845, he said, "I wished to live deliberately, to front only the essential facts of life, and see if I could not learn what it had to teach, and not, when I came to die, discover that I had not lived."[40] Daniel Webster selected Marshfield as his home because it was close to the sea, which he loved, though not perhaps as others loved it. As he told his friend Samuel Goodrich, "I cannot pick up sticks and pebbles along the shore. I can never forget the presence of the sea. It seems to speak to me and beckon to me. The mystery of its depths, the history of its devastations crowd the mind with lofty images."[41] When Emerson passed a summer vacation in New Hampshire, staying with Ethan Allen Crawford, he wrote in his journal (1832): "The good of going into the mountains is that life is reconsidered . . . you have opportunity of viewing the town at such a distance as may afford you a just view."[42] Susan F. Cooper published an entire collection of poems under the title *Rhyme and Reason of Country Life* (1855).

So many prominent men retired to the country that living in the country became the fashion, particularly since Downing had set the pattern for this mode of life in his *Cottage Residences*, published in 1842, and in a number of later publications. In addition, books such as *Homes of the American Authors* (1853) and *Homes of the American Statesmen* (1854) and a vast number of essays on the subject familiarized the public not only with the idea of living in the country but also with that of living in country style and enjoying it. The businessman in New York, which had experienced a tremendous growth in commerce, was thus prompted to build an Italian villa on the shores of the Hudson or establish a fashionable "cottage ornée" on Long Island. Businessmen of Boston and of Philadelphia did likewise.

Undoubtedly the movement was a healthful one and gave city dwellers a means of escaping the misery of town life in the summer, which, as the Autocrat of the Breakfast Table maintained, represented "a peculiar force of suspended existence, or semi-asphyxia."[43] Unfortunately, difficulties developed when people who tried to comply with the demands of fashion found that their bank accounts were not commensurate with their plans. In 1853 *Harper's Magazine* mentioned "out-of-town houses for working

men which are springing up in every direction . . . in villages along the
Hudson, the East River, and Staten Island."⁴⁴ However, Downing, scared
by "the rapidity with which cottages and villa residences were increasing
in the country," warned against acquiring such country homes if the
costly burden could not be carried easily.⁴⁵

Many people were disappointed after they found out that a country
place was difficult to maintain and was a great luxury for anyone who did
not have a good deal of money or had had no experience in making such
a place pay. There was an added drawback. This was something for which
the term "cockneyism" was invented.

Shortly before the middle of the century critics complained vigorously
about this "ism." Gentleman-hunters who roamed through upstate woods
were disgusted to meet some "New York cockneys," "flaunting their ban-
ners of the awkward squad, proclaiming to the world with protuberant
pride that they are the veritable backwoodsmen—rather doing it, rather
astonishing the natives, they think. And so they are."⁴⁶ "Cockneys" invaded
the fashionable bathing places and made them unsuitable for "nice"
people. Worst of all, there was the cockney who went to live in the country
and thereafter disturbed the peace of mind of every person of discrimina-
tion living near him. It was not that anybody objected to the newcomers
because of their lack of wealth. On the contrary, cockneys were usually
rather wealthy people. The real trouble with them was that they felt
they could impose their taste—or, as the others thought, their lack of
taste—on a somewhat recalcitrant community. Men like Downing and,
somewhat later, Godkin, the editor of *The Nation,* saw a real danger in
this kind of influence. From the point of view of a good democrat it
seemed that a cancerous growth was overrunning the countryside and
spoiling a way of living which had theretofore been healthy and normal.
This was happening not only in small places conveniently near the large
cities but also in more remote resorts in all parts of New England.

Most of these resorts had been discovered by some artist who had found
lodging with an obliging farmer, and who, because he admired the scenery,
endured the roughness of the accommodations and the coarseness of the
food and came again and also recommended the place to friends. Thus
encouraged, the farmer gradually developed a liking for the new business
and, trying to improve it, improved his manners. By and by the hills in
the vicinity would acquire colorful names, a soda fountain perhaps would
be installed, and the farmer might even become a prosperous innkeeper.
This process was slow in some places; in others the resort would mushroom. Many of the customers who had been coming to a place for several
years would eventually buy a small piece of ground one year and build
a summer cottage the next. Little by little there came to be more summer

cottagers than summer boarders, and soon there would be more summer people than "natives." As long as the cottagers were recruited from the sincere nature lovers, even if they were poor, things were not so bad. But if the cockney variety of summer visitor turned up, the atmosphere was definitely spoiled. The cockneys would build summer houses and

On the Road to Lake George (New York)

also would usurp more and more space in the hotels, sending prices up and making life unbearable for the old-timers. As a result, the boarders who had been coming to the resort for many years went out in search of a new Canaan. Time and again this cycle repeated itself, until these fugitives from the cockney influence found themselves close to the northern borders of the United States. As a consequence they began to venture west and soon went as far as it was possible to go in the 1860's and 1870's with the limited means of transportation available. Then the problem arose: What would happen when there was no longer any place to go to avoid the crowd pushing its way out of the cities? Godkin thought that eventually these poor fugitives might be found "in out-of-the-way places along the American coasts, often in the Alps or . . . Norway . . . but they will find no summer resorts which can have for them the charm of Frenchman's Bay or Newport Mountain."[47] William Dean Howells described very accurately this development, which began for the most part after the Civil War, in *The Landlord at Lion's Head*, published in 1897. These people who suffered from being constantly dispossessed he characterized as "middle-aged maiden ladies from university towns, living upon carefully guarded investments, young married ladies with a scant child or two . . . college professors . . . literary men or women . . . clergymen . . . an agreeable bachelor . . . Such people are human, refined, appreciative, sympathetic."[48] This is indeed a rather impressive list of those vacationists who used to visit the beauty spots of New England in the 'seventies and 'eighties. They did not go there because it was fashionable, but because they loved nature and needed to be close to it, even though living in these places was not very convenient or comfortable. These people were not sentimental, nor were they looking for any startling or romantic scenery. They had all read their Starr King, Henry Ward Beecher, Thomas Wilson Flagg, and John Burroughs, and they had learned to use their eyes. In his novel *The Landlord at Lion's Head* Howells introduced a neighborhood farmer who undertook to arrange walks for summer visitors, which he called "tramps home to nature." Like the ranger of a future day, this man taught his pupils how to become acquainted with nature instead of speculating vaguely about its romantic aspects. As if to underline this concept he had even arranged a small "trailside museum"—a term which had not yet come into use—along the brim of his hat, where he kept flowers and fungi of the area ready to help him answer the questions of his clients.

There is, of course, no reason to suppose that all nature lovers were interested only in biological and scientific facts. Those who had an inclination toward literature and painting were eager to become acquainted with the natural background of the poems they had read and the pictures they had seen, and with the men and women who had written the poems or painted the pictures. For instance, Whittier himself was as popular as his poems which praised the beauties and the historical background of New England. When he resided at the Bearcamp River House in West Ossipee, New Hampshire, it was "nearly filled with relatives and friends of the poet and these reunions were occasions full of enjoyment to him."[49] There were times, however, when these hordes proved too much even for him. He would try, not always successfully, to evade his admirers by going to Holderness, or to Wakefield, or some similar place. Many of

Whittier's poems, such as the "Sun on the Merrimac" and "The Laurels," as well as his presence at the "Laurel parties" held between 1861 and 1878, brought fame to the Merrimac River and attracted visitors to this part of "Whittier Land" long after June boating trips up the river to enjoy the "Laurel grounds" in full bloom had been discontinued.

Another cult centered around Henry Ward Beecher, who, seeking relief from hay fever, spent a number of summers at the Twin Mountain House in the White Mountains. After he had accepted an invitation to hold informal Sunday services in the lobby of the hotel, more people came to hear him than the hotel premises could accommodate, and a big show tent was rented to shelter the crowd. Anyone familiar with Beecher's *Star Papers* or his *Eyes and Ears* can well imagine that his poetic inclination and his sincere love of nature made him especially suited to mold the minds of his summer audiences and make them appreciate nature. He would sway his hearers with words such as these based on his own experiences: "The sun feels your pulse daily, looks you all over, and tells you to come again tomorrow. Tomorrow he again inspects your case and puts you upon a full course of air. The great round blue heaven above your head is your medicine chest, and down drop from it every moment those restorative prescriptions which cure both soul and body." Or he would tell his congregation: "Even one day in the country is good. But not till you settle down, and cut the string that binds you to the city, shove out its cares, and rid yourself of its excitements, can you feel the genuine comfort and happiness of being in the country."[50]

Just as persons with literary tastes gathered about some spirited leader in peaceful summer resorts, so the artists congregated in places which to them had special pictorial interest. Since the 1850's the white umbrellas of artists, dotting the most interesting scenic spots of New England, had become a familiar part of the country scene. In the days of Cole, artists were explorers who went singly, or with a friend, to find picturesque subjects in areas which then were remote. Later, after most of the spots of artistic interest had been discovered, artists liked to go as a group and settle down in some small village to paint, discuss scenery and painting, and enjoy a summer season. Asher Durand loved to vacation near Lake George in the company of Casilaer, T. Addison Richards, Kensett, and others. Roswell Morse Shurtleff, an illustrator of *Leslie's Newspaper,* and the painters William Hart and Alexander Wyant, settled in Keene Valley near Lake Placid. If no comfortable quarters could be procured, tents were pitched and everybody gathered round the campfire in the evening.

For variety, Kensett went also to the White Mountains, where Benjamin Champney had settled in North Conway in 1850. The region attracted many other artists as well, among them Albert Bierstadt. By and by this American Barbizon on the Saco River became famous as an artists' colony, and attracted other visitors who liked the region and also wished to be in congenial company. Unfortunately for North Conway, before the end of the century, "fads and whims" turned the current to the seashore.[51]

Until the 1860's almost all the painters were men, but after William Morris Hunt accepted women in his classes, the lady artist began to win general recognition. Hunt's classes started the custom of going to the country and staying for the summer. There his students would work for a while and then the master would join them and criticize their work. Later, Theodore Robinson conducted classes in a similar manner. He liked to rent a house where the company could pass a pleasant summer and enjoy painting, picnicking, and excursioning. As art education grew in popularity through the establishment of a number of art schools in large cities, artists' summer schools and colonies became recognized institutions, much as they are today in Woodstock, Cape Cod, Provincetown, and many other places.

It would seem that Mrs. Hale of *Godey's Magazine* was right when she said that "circumstances have almost inevitably designed us as a nation of travellers."[52] Indeed, in the United States more than in any other country, summer was the preferred time for making a change in one's basic living conditions. Most of the winter-weary townspeople, by going to a resort or to their own country homes, or even by visiting city parks and participating in some kind of summer sport, could find respite from the city during the sultry months. For these summer pleasures the northern part of the country as far west as the Great Lakes was the favorite section.

During the second half of the nineteenth century the accumulation of visitors in comparatively small areas led to a great deal of congestion and made traveling uncomfortable. It became obvious that the existing resorts and the accommodations available in them were no longer adequate to satisfy the constantly growing desire of Americans to become acquainted with their homeland and enjoy every aspect of the out of doors. The obvious solution was to open the West for pleasure trips; but for the eastern nature lover and pleasure hunter just to "go West," as the slogan advised, would not have greatly eased the situation at this time. Before they could be accommodated in western towns a number of difficulties must be overcome and new methods of traveling must be introduced.

8

Western Reports

WHEN the Reverend Timothy Flint published his *Recollections of the Last Ten Years*, in 1826, the book immediately became popular. With his entire family Dr. Flint had left his home in New England to become a minister on the western frontier. He spent much of his time in St. Charles, Missouri, but he also traveled up and down the Mississippi and visited the Red and Arkansas rivers. Possibly Flint had read William Bartram's *Travels;* certainly he knew Chateaubriand and thus was familiar with echoes of Bartram as they resounded in the novel *Atala.* Surprisingly enough, Flint was also acquainted with Talleyrand and criticizes some of the derogatory statements about Maine fishermen that Talleyrand made before the French Academy in 1799.[1] To Flint all western lands were arcadian, and he thought it enjoyable to witness the "beginnings of social toil in the wide wilderness . . . springs burst forth . . . the trees and shrubs are of the most beautiful kind. The brilliant red-bird is seen flitting among the shrubs . . . flocks of parakeets are glittering among the trees . . . in the

VIGNETTE: A Steamboat Wooding on the Mississippi.

midst of these primeval scenes the patient and laborious father fixes his family . . ."² After the publication of his *Recollections,* Flint, though he was ill, remained in the West and did his best to convince Easterners that persons who lived on the frontier were more than backwoodsmen; indeed, a new society was emerging in the West, and a poem could be written as well on the banks of the Red River as in New York or Boston. To further his ideas Flint started the *Western Monthly Review* and, under extreme difficulties, managed to steer it through three years (1827–1829).

Judge James Hall, residing in Shawneetown and later (between 1820 and 1868) in Cincinnati, became well known as a prolific reporter of western matters second only to Flint. In books containing tales, statistics, and reports of various kinds, Hall endeavored to acquaint the eagerly waiting readers in the East with conditions as they existed in the new states. Like Flint, Judge Hall ventured to publish a magazine. This was the *Illinois Monthly Magazine* (1830–1832), which he renamed the *Western Monthly Magazine* (1833–1837) after he moved to Ohio. In order to boost circulation and whet the interest of his readers he announced a contest for the best essay concerning the West. The winning manuscript was a remarkable piece called "Themes for Western Fiction." In it the author recommended western scenery as a rewarding topic for a writer because

> none but the poet's pencil can adequately sketch its freshness and gorgeous beauties as it was gradually unfolded to the enraptured vision of the early pioneer. There was the prairie expanding far away into one boundless ocean of fragrance of bloom . . . there slumbered the landscape, over whose bosom danced crystal waters to the minstrelsy of birds . . .

This is only one example of the general conception that western territory was the Promised Land. The term "Promised Land," it will be remembered, had been used long before by Thomas Morton when he tried to promote New England as the new English Canaan. In spite of gross and often all too obvious misrepresentation, the country across the Mississippi, "beyond the hill and far away," was generally considered to be somewhat like the Garden of Eden, with boundless riches in pasture lands and untouched forests where, to quote Flint once more, "the moon, with her circumference broadened and reddened by the haze and smoke of Indian summer rose and diffused, as Chateaubriand so beautifully says, the 'great secret of melancholy' over these ancient forests."⁴

When Margaret Fuller set out across the lakes in 1843 for her trip West, she was fully aware that she would find the mushroom growth of the West distasteful, but she was resolved to "seek out the mighty meaning of the scene, perhaps to foresee the law by which a new order, a new poetry is to be evoked from this chaos." Thus prepared, she found rich compensation in the fruits she "gathered in the open field," and she began to love "the encircling vastness with the distinct feeling that the West once more might open the door to a paradise regained."⁵ Even as late as 1856, C. W. Dana, a promoter of railroad interests, gave the name *The Garden of the World; or, The Great West* to a handbook which he had published to assist potential immigrants in selecting their future home-sites. According to Dana, the vast deserts between the Mississippi and the Pacific would "blossom as the rose" after the Pacific Railway had brought new inhabitants; in fact, Dana felt that soon the country would be teeming with millions of people.⁶ It should be noted that Dana uses the term "desert," though he assumes that the waste land will be trans-formed into a garden by the coming of the settlers.

The desert theory contradicted the assumption that the West was the "Promised Land," but no one elaborated upon it to any great extent, and no one was very specific about it. Washington Irving spent a number of weeks on the prairie and described it quite realistically in his *Tour of the Prairies* (1835). As he stated in *Astoria* (1836), he felt that the western region was "vast and trackless as the ocean ... the great American desert ... where no man permanently abides." This "immense wilderness of the far west ... apparently defies cultivation and the habitation of civilized life."⁷ James Hall reviewed Irving's *Tour of the Prairies* favorably and praised it as being unusually graphic in spite of the fact that he him-self was one of those who maintained that the prairie, with the "unbounded fertility of its soil, stands without a rival,"⁸ and that there was water and timber enough to answer all reasonable demands of the present and even those of the future.

The uncertainty about the character of the West and the boundaries of the prairies is shown by the fact that Francis Parkman in the first edition (1849) of his *Oregon Trail*, called the barren trackless waste east of the Rockies between Arkansas and the Missouri "the great American desert" but omitted this term from the edition of 1872.⁹ The two concep-tions were subjects of dispute for decades, and the general public, at least, did not learn which was correct until after the Union and Central Pacific railroads had met, on May 10, 1869, at Promontory Point in what is now the state of Utah, and thus completed the transcontinental span.

Even before this period, when coast to coast travel was still a novelty, every new report from the West greatly excited the imagination of the public and was eagerly discussed. At the time Lewis and Clark returned from their expedition across the Rockies to the Columbia River in 1806, Jefferson had written that even the most humble citizen was taking a lively interest in the issue of the journey and was looking forward with impatience for the information it would provide.¹⁰ Although these reports

did supply a wealth of factual news and afforded the public a glimpse of
the highly adventurous character of the undertaking, they did not make
their readers really familiar with the western scene, for they were written
in a rather matter-of-fact way. Passages such as the following describing
a view near Billings, Montana, were not exactly inspiring: "On the southwest the Rocky Mountains covered with snow; a low mountain about forty
miles distant, bearing south 15° east . . . The north side of the river, for
some distance, is surrounded by jutting romantic cliffs; these are succeeded by rugged hills, beyond which the plains are again open and extensive . . ."[11]

Edwin James's report on Major Long's journey to the Rockies in 1819–
1820 was more interesting than most travel accounts, since it contained
a number of illustrations by Samuel Seymour, one of the two draughtsmen
who accompanied the expedition.[12] These pictures had been selected from
about one hundred fifty drawings by Seymour and more than one hundred
by Titian R. Peale, who accompanied the expedition as a scientist-
draughtsman. All of these drawings have been lost; but, as mentioned
earlier, Thomas Doughty had become interested in Seymour's sketches
and had painted a picture after one of them.[13]

The introduction of illustrated travel books was an important step
forward, for it gave the public the visual aid needed to grasp the idea of
these western lands which few people had yet seen. When Henry R.
Schoolcraft published a record of his travels in the central part of the
Mississippi Valley in 1821, he illustrated it with some of his own sketches
improved by Henry Inman. Unlike the earlier reporters, Schoolcraft gives
vivid descriptions of everything he saw, for his eye was "constantly employed in discriminating little objects that excite interest." His observations are reported with a naturalism that makes the reader "feel the full
sensation produced by one of the most beautiful of scenes."[14]

But a situation arose which promised to become critical. Western fron-
tiers were changing rapidly; numerous expeditions were undertaken to
chart and explore the country, and it was necessary to find artists to accompany these expeditions. This truly virgin territory, barren of traditions
or associations for the traveler—for the white man's knowledge of Indian
lore was still negligible—opened a vast new field which offered not only
new experiences but vistas of the American landscape never before seen
by a white man. Goethe had wished for just such an opportunity for the
people of the Western Hemisphere, hoping that, with "no past shadows,"
they would "use well the present." But unfortunately this was the time
when landscape artists of note were just getting established in the East,
and none responded. In the 1820's Cole and his friends were settling in
the Catskills or in New England; Inman saw no need to go into the

wilds himself, since Schoolcraft let him do the work for his *Travels* in the studio; Doughty was apparently satisfied to paint only one western scene; and Neagle and the rest of the minor painters were busy at their day to day work. All these men, whose training was more or less academic, were gradually becoming involved in the complicated business of exhibitions, competitions, reviews, and the whole scheme of competitive work modeled after the European pattern, apparently unaware of the unusual scenery that the West offered and that later aroused the enthusiasm of Albert Bierstadt, Thomas Moran, and S. R. Gifford.

What was needed was artist-explorers, men who besides being artists were seasoned travelers, and who could be useful to expeditionary forces in more than one way. Travelers even in colonial days had done more than merely travel or explore. Mark Catesby on his travels through Florida in 1712 had drawn the birds of the region; later, William Bartram, Alexander Wilson, Thomas Nuttall, and André and François Michaux had made their contributions to art and science. One French artist-scientist, Charles Lesueur, lived and traveled in this country for more than twenty years (1816–1837). The great Scottish-born geologist William Maclure had invited the Frenchman to come to this country to assist him in his explorations. Lesueur accompanied his friend for three years while "hammer in hand, wallet on shoulders," they visited almost every state and territory, wandering "amidst pathless tracts and dreary solitudes,"[15] and crossing the Alleghenies many times. Although the explorers were mainly concerned with geology, Lesueur devoted some time to studying fish life for a projected book on North American ichthyology for which, over the years, he prepared many exquisite drawings. In 1825 Lesueur settled in New Harmony, where Robert Owen and William Maclure intended to test their social reforms and where the artist-explorer was supposed to help establish life under natural conditions through his knowledge of the life of the aboriginal Indians and of the American continent in general. During the twelve years he taught at the agricultural school in New Harmony, Lesueur did much to place scientific learning on a high level and to acquaint a number of his pupils with the elements of scientific draughtsmanship. Among his students were Robert Owen's sons, David Dale Owen and Richard Owen, both of whom later headed important geological surveys in midwestern states and published the results, with illustrations from their own drawings. From 1825 to 1837, when the New Harmony experiment was drawing to a close, the little town was a representative center of American science and its scholars helped greatly in bringing the American scene to the attention of the public. Travelers such as Maximilian, Prince of Wied, and Constantine Rafinesque-Schmaltz went to New Harmony on their way West in order to confer with the little colony of scholars.

The majority of the traveling artists to whom we are indebted for knowledge of the western scene remain more or less obscure (see pl. 46). There was one named Joshua Shaw (see vignette, chap. 1; pl. 13) who traveled in the Ohio country and made paintings for a series of *Picturesque Views of the American Scene,* published in Philadelphia between 1819 and 1820. Shaw probably did not get any farther than Ohio and did not journey up the Mississippi as he had promised he would; the prints he published of the Falls of St. Anthony were after sketches by an otherwise unknown British captain named Watson. Many of Samuel Seymour's western paintings were on exhibition at the Peale Museum in Philadelphia, where Prince Maximilian became interested in them; but they disappeared in 1854 when the museum was discontinued. Only a few lithographs remain to give us an idea of the work of James Otto Lewis, who visited Prairie du Chien in the Wisconsin country in the 1820's and painted Fort Crawford. Basil Hall, a British captain (see vignette), deserves mention because of his excellent etchings from drawings perfected with the aid of the camera lucida, a drawing device he carried in a walking stick. Hall's trip took him from New England through Ohio to the Mississippi in 1827–1828.

Seth Eastman, a graduate of West Point and a nonprofessional artist, between 1829 and 1833 produced some of the best paintings ever done of the area around Fort Crawford and Fort Sumner. Later, Eastman supplied material for Schoolcraft's history of the Indian tribes, published between 1852 and 1857.[16] The most famous of all pictorial reporters of the western scene is John James Audubon, who has already been mentioned; his work, however, did not become popular until long after his death. George Catlin, one of his contemporaries, gained immediate fame through his beautifully illustrated accounts of his western travels. Like Audubon, he was a forceful writer and supplemented the work of his brush and drawing pencil with powerful and telling texts. Catlin began his career as a lawyer and continued as a miniaturist, but he found his true vocation in the study of the Indian tribes west of the Mississippi. His intention was to paint representative types of all Indian tribes between the Alleghenies and the Pacific, knowing that he was the first artist "who ever set out upon such a work . . . to carry . . . canvas and brushes and paint-pots to the Rocky Mountains."[17] In 1830 he began his roving mission, traveling up and down the Mississippi and from Minnesota to Florida.

Although it is not necessary here to trace Catlin's outstanding efforts in recording the "looks and customs of the vanishing races of the native man in America," his merits in another, related field should be recognized. Catlin had the vision to see that the primeval glories of nature in this country could not last forever. At a time when the plains seemed as unfathomable as the ocean, when pastures and grazing lands had no boundaries, and no one believed that the forests could be exhausted, Catlin felt that, if future generations were to enjoy this rich heritage, it was necessary to conserve, not squander and destroy, these natural treasures. He knew that more than mere love of nature and devotion to it were needed if the national domain were to be preserved; men would have to take definite action to keep the great fortune which nature had given them in trust.

Earlier, the magnitude of this problem had been seen by only a very few people. Judge William Cooper had been one of these. In 1806 he wrote a pamphlet setting forth the possibilities for settlers in this country, in which he stated flatly that a scarcity of timber was to be feared in the future, and that "the soil being all fit for culture, will be all cultivated, and the wood of course wasted."[18] Although Judge Cooper foresaw this situation, he made no remedial suggestions; nor did his son, James Fenimore Cooper, see much chance of relieving this evil when he had Leatherstocking argue this issue in *The Pioneers* (see chap. 3, above). At the time Catlin traveled up the Missouri River into the heart of the Indian country in 1832 he had an opportunity to behold the vast forests covering the banks of the river. Immediately his imagination made him realize that these regions

> might in future be seen (by some great protecting policy of government) preserved in their pristine beauty and wildness, in a magnificent park, where the world could see for ages to come, the native Indian in his classic attire, galloping his wild horse...amid the fleeting herds of elks and buffaloes. What a beautiful and thrilling specimen for America to preserve and hold up to the view of her refined citizens and the world, in future ages. A *nation's Park* containing man and beast, in all the wild and freshness of their nature's beauty![19]

Prophetic words, indeed, in regard to the national parks of a later day. This passage was first published in 1833 in one of the letters Catlin sent from the Indian territory to the *Daily Commercial Advertiser*, a widely read New York newspaper.

As might be expected, no one in the early 1830's paid much attention to this foresighted suggestion for the conservation of certain areas of the national domain. More than three decades passed before Congress was willing to consider this progressive idea; then, in 1864, the Yosemite grant was made to the State of California.

Assuming that the public would be interested in his western pictures, Catlin began to put them on show in 1836 and arrived with them in New York in 1837. Here he lectured about them with great success, and the *New-York Mirror* considered the occasion important enough to review his talk. Thereafter Catlin arranged many exhibitions of his pictures in this country and thus contributed greatly to the perpetration of a fresh and lively interest in western scenery.

The next voice which was raised in favor of Catlin's plan to conserve some of the national resources very likely was stimulated by his book. In 1844 Emerson delivered a speech under the title "The Young American," which was printed soon afterward in *The Dial*. In this address Emerson stated that "the interminable forests should become graceful parks for use and for delight," since the railroads had introduced a multitude of picturesque attractions into the pastoral scenery.[20] For reasons now unknown this passage was not included in later book versions of the speech. About three years later, in 1847, a somewhat similar idea was put on record by Cole, who felt that with "the wilderness passing away [there was] the necessity of saving and perpetuating its features."[21]

Following Catlin's example, Maximilian, Prince of Wied, accompanied by the distinguished Swiss painter Karl Bodmer, traveled in the region of the Rocky Mountains (1831–1834) in order to study the Indian tribes. Although he was not entirely successful in his quest, because of Indian wars and typhoid epidemics, Prince Maximilian went up the Missouri in the steamboat *Yellowstone* and studied the territory between Fort Clark, Fort Union, and Fort Mackenzie. On his return to Germany he published a report in German, French, and English editions, illustrated with a large number of pictures (see pl. 44) which were not only of high artistic merit but also of great scientific value.[22] This work became a standard source book and aided greatly in disseminating accurate information about the West and acquainting the public with some of the most striking features of that part of America. Publications of this kind were expensive and not easily available to the public, but they were of major importance. They almost invariably came to the attention of artists and writers and later reached the general public through magazine articles and reviews.

Fortunately, a large number of some of the best and most lively pictures ever made of the West have been left for posterity. When the gifted and well-trained artist Alfred Miller was in New Orleans looking for suitable work in 1837, he happened to meet William Drummond Stewart, a British army captain who was planning a trip overland to Oregon for the American Fur Company. Since Stewart was trying to find an artist to accompany him on his journey, to sketch and paint such scenes as might impress him, he asked Miller to join him. Miller wholeheartedly accepted this commission. As a result there exist today a great number of brilliant paintings of the West, particularly of the country west of the North Platte River and in the Rocky Mountains. Throughout his declining years Miller worked over the sketches he made on this journey and made copies of many of his paintings, for which he found a ready market. During his lifetime none of his work was published, and the artist was more or less forgotten until MacGill James arranged an exhibition of his work in Baltimore in 1923. Miller's work has given us much of the most accurate documentation ever made of the early West, picturing the life of the Indians and their rendezvous with fur traders and also fascinating grandiose scenes.[23]

In 1847, the year that found Miller in the West, a report of a trek across country on the trail to Oregon by two young men from Boston was printed in the *Knickerbocker Magazine*. This story immediately made an extraordinary impression on the American public and established the fame of its author, Francis Parkman. Happily, the author of this book about the West and the westward migration was a gifted and able writer who actually experienced all the adventures and hardships of the journey he wrote about. The book is especially impressive and convincing because in every event of the trip the author is always both hero and observer. There could have been no more stirring introduction to the West than *The Oregon Trail*, and many adventurous spirits of succeeding generations have found that Parkman expressed in this book ideas similar to their own.

This story by Parkman and stories about the West by other writers of lesser importance actuated in many a mind the desire to see what the author described. Miller's work was little known by his contemporaries, and Bodmer's was not easily accessible; but there was another kind of painting that came to the attention of the general public at this time— the panorama. The painters of panoramas were not as competent as the artists mentioned, but they were certainly resourceful.

Panoramas in general were not new to the American public, but before 1839 there was none that showed the West. In that year a western panorama was exhibited in Boston which proved to be a great surprise and success. This enormous panorama, designed by a little-known painter, John Rowson Smith, showed the whole course of the Mississippi River. The popularity of shows of this kind is indicated by the fact that in the years between 1845 and 1850 no less than seven panoramas of that river were painted. Among these, the one by John Banvard became one of the best known. Banvard had traveled down the Mississippi in 1840 sketching scenes along its banks and making a living by bartering goods. On his return to civilization he painted "the largest picture of the world" on a canvas three miles long, specially woven for him at Lowell. Later, Banvard converted his flatboat into a showboat and, floating down the river, exhibited his panorama to more than four thousand paying visitors.

When Charles Dickens saw the panorama in London in 1848, with its painter standing on a little platform by its side explaining it, he thought it

so extraordinary that he reported in the *Examiner* that it was "an indis-
putably true and faithful representation of a wonderful region—wood
and water, river and prairie, lonely log hut and clustered city rising in
the forest." It was full of great interest also, he thought, because of its
revelations of the different states of society yet in transition: "slaves and
free republicans ... immigrants ... Yankees ... Down Easterners ... alli-
gators, store-boats, show-boats, theatre-boats, Indians, buffaloes, deserted
tents of extinct tribes ..."[24] Another writer who viewed the panorama
with particular interest and who benefited greatly by the show was Longfellow, who was just then working on *Evangeline*. After looking at the
panorama, he wrote:

> one seems to be sailing down the great stream, one sees the boats and the
> sand banks crested with cottonwood and bayous by moonlight. Three miles
> of canvas, and a great deal of merit ... The river comes to me instead of
> my going to the river, and as it is to flow through the pages of the poem, I
> look upon this as a special benediction.[25]

Other artists, such as Henry Lewis and John Egan, produced similar
views. Egan's work, painted in 1850 and the only one of the western panoramas still in existence, was shown at the Mississippi Panorama Exhibition
held at the City Art Museum of St. Louis in 1949. With a commentator
announcing the various scenes in dramatic fashion, these early panoramas
were very impressive; it is understandable that the public, with appetite
still unspoiled by camera and movie, relished these firsthand views of the
western wilds. As a contemporary critic said, "we went to see it in the
same spirit that we are wont to ramble through the living forest with a
heart open to receive the delightful impressions which the beauties and
grandeur of nature never fail to impart."[26] The panorama was not high art,
it was never very true to nature, and it was frequently sentimental in
feeling; yet it stirred interest and stimulated the imagination of the public.
By providing some kind of picture of the West, it aided materially in
bringing the western theme into the purview of the townsmen of the East.

While the artists of the panoramas were touring the country with their
effective but somewhat complicated machinery, a competitive art was
slowly developing. This was photography. The new art would not only
give a more accurate representation of the scenery but in time would
altogether change the way in which the public obtained its visual knowledge of the outdoors—especially of the western United States. Traveling
in the West was still difficult, if not impossible, and would remain so for
a decade or two. Photography, almost from its introduction into this country in 1839, made rapid progress and quickly produced very acceptable
landscape views. In 1845 the brothers Langenheim took the first photographs of Niagara Falls, and these were much admired. Other pictures

of the falls taken a little later were shown at the Crystal Palace exhibition in London in 1851 and excited genuine interest.

It was obvious that this kind of reporting would be particularly useful for exploring expeditions. Isaac I. Stevens, in charge of one of the great surveys for the route of the Pacific Railroad, accordingly engaged the painter John Mix Stanley to join his force as a photographer. When John C. Frémont headed an expedition to Utah in 1854 which led him across the Rockies in the dead of winter, he chose the Baltimore painter S. N.

Photographer at Work in Northeastern Nevada

Carvalho to accompany him as photographer. The difficulties and hardships under which these photographers worked now seem almost unbelievable. Carvalho took photographs (see illustration) at the top of the Continental Divide while he was plunged waist deep in snow; but standing in the snow was not the worst of his troubles; he was kept busy "buffing, coating and mercurializing plates in the open air" in temperatures of 20° to 30° below zero." When Indians attacked, he was forced to abandon his equipment, though luckily he was able to save his plates and bring them safely to New York. Lieutenant Joseph C. Ives, when he went out to explore the upper Colorado River in 1857, took a camera along, but he broke it after taking only one picture. Unfortunately, the majority of the photographs taken by these early cameramen have completely disappeared, though many of them have come down to us in the form of lithographs or woodcuts. A photographic venture of which only a slight trace remains was undertaken by J. Wesley Jones, an investment broker in Brooklyn. Jones started out on a cross-country journey in 1851 with a daguerreotype carriage and a number of artists and cameramen. In the course of his travel from St. Joseph, Missouri, to San Francisco and back to St. Louis, Jones made 1,500 daguerrotypes, according to his own statement. These he used for a panorama of California for which he commissioned two painters, T. C. Bartholomew and Alonzo Chappell. This "Pantoscope," as it was called, was shown in the East about 1853 and won great acclaim. What happened to it later is not known.[28]

It is difficult to imagine the great sensation created by the first daguerreotypes of the western scene. We do know, however, that Longfellow, on seeing a daguerreotype of the Falls of Minnehaha taken by Alexander Hessler on his trip to the Minnesota territory in 1851, was tremendously stimulated by it and began to work on the poem which later became famous as *Hiawatha.*[29]

The first painter to seize the opportunity of participating in the exploration of the West and to use photography to supplement his own sketches and water colors was Albert Bierstadt (see pl. 47). After completing his studies in Düsseldorf, Bierstadt returned to America in 1857 and painted in the vicinity of Newport and the White Mountains. When he learned of Captain Frederick W. Lander's intention to cross the country, surveying for a railroad route from the Mississippi across the north fork of the Platte River and through Nebraska Territory and the South Pass toward San Francisco and Puget Sound, he asked and was granted permission to join the party, in company with the Boston photographer S. H. Frost.[30] In April, 1858, Bierstadt left New Bedford, Massachusetts, and he traveled with Lander as far as the Wasatch Range on the western side of the Rockies. There he and Frost left the party and traveled home in their spring wagon with a six-mule team. By midsummer of 1859 the entire Lander party had arrived safely at Fort Laramie. Lander later reported to Congress that Bierstadt and Frost, paying their own expenses, had taken "sketches of the most remarkable views along the route, and a set of stereoscopic views of immigrant trains, Indians, camp scenes, etc. which are highly valuable and would be interesting to the country."[31] Since Congress had not appropriated any funds, Lander had been unable to procure any of their works. Like the work of earlier photographers, none of Bierstadt's or Frost's material is extant today. On July 10, 1857, just before coming home, Bierstadt sent a letter to *The Crayon*[32] in which he recorded his impressions of the West. Excerpts from this letter were published again and again, showing that it was considered an important commentary on western scenery.

After settling down once more, Bierstadt sent pictures to the first National Academy exhibitions (1860–1863). These paintings were well received but did not arouse any particular interest or general discussion. But at the Sanitary Fund Fair which opened in New York in April, 1864,

Bierstadt's "Rocky Mountains—Landers Peak," a six- by ten-foot canvas completed in 1863, attracted such wide attention that the artist became famous overnight. Reproductions of it were widely distributed: J. D. Smillie made a steel engraving of the picture, and the Kell Brothers in London manufactured a chromolithograph of it. Also in 1863, but before his work was exhibited at the Sanitary Fair, Bierstadt had traveled across the continent accompanied by his friend Fitz-Hugh Ludlow, the writer; this time he reaped a rich pictorial harvest in California. Later, Bierstadt made several more journeys to the West. The enormous canvases resulting from these trips were so much in demand that a wealthy New York citizen, desiring to keep in step with the times, was almost forced to acquire a Bierstadt western scene. The less fortunate art lovers contented themselves with one of the chromolithographs printed in Boston or London.

All Bierstadt's pictures painted in his grand manner were done in his studio and were based on stereoscopic views, photographs, sketches, and water colors. Many of his pictures are composite scenes and are not views of the mountains, waterfalls, or other natural features that their titles name. In fact, the titles themselves sometimes give names of places which do not exist. Although most of the art critics were enthusiastic about these pictures and the public was completely hypnotized, there were a few persons who saw immediately that this grand manner of painting could not be considered great art. One of the most bitter critics was James Jackson Jarves, who wrote in his *Art Thoughts,* published in 1869, that

> the return to the spectator who thinks, or has the spiritual faculty, is not worth the cost. Yet they [Bierstadt's paintings] do address significantly the majority of Americans, who associate them with the vulgar ideas of "big things" as business. In reality, they are bold and effective speculations in art on principles of trade; emotionless and soulless ... nature's best is left out.[33]

Godkin, in *The Nation,* was also one of the few who disapproved of Bierstadt's paintings. He thought that his work was coarse and indecisive, and that his rocks did not really represent rocks.[34] An opinion of particular importance is that of Clarence King; because he had a sensitive spirit and in addition was a great mountaineer, his judgment on painting mountain scenery commands respect. In his book *Mountaineering in the Sierra Nevada,* King expresses himself through a young painter, who exclaims:

> It's all Bierstadt and Bierstadt and Bierstadt nowadays! What has he done but twist and askew and distort and discolor and belittle and bepretty this whole doggoned country! Why, his mountains are too high and too slim; they'd blow over in one of our fall winds. I've herded colts two summers in Yosemite and honest now, when I stood right up in front of his picture, I didn't know it. He hasn't what Old Ruskin calls for![35]

To a certain extent time has proved the validity of King's opinion. Bierstadt's pseudorealism has long since lost its impact, and his oversize pictures have fallen into disrepute.

Yet many of Bierstadt's smaller pictures and sketches, accurately representing specific localities and done under the impact of fresh impressions, have never lost their charm and still are well liked. The giant panoramas no longer have their old appeal, and most of them have now been retired to historical societies, museums, or halls of capitol dimensions. Bierstadt's panoramic view was a compromise between an accurate pictorial record and the artist's imaginative conception, which can now be achieved more satisfactorily by the process of photography without the use of brushwork. But with all their drawbacks, Bierstadt's paintings of the Rockies and the Far West played a more important role in making American scenery better known at home and abroad than any printed page could have done. Untold numbers of those who first saw the western scene through his eyes were enraptured by his epical mountain giants, or by the romantic views of lakes hidden in the depths of forests.

Turning again to the end of the 1850's and the time when the men of the railroad surveys were working their way across the Continental Divide, exploring a variety of possible routes, we find accounts of these expeditions in the reports of railroad surveys published by the U. S. War Department between 1855 and 1860,[36] in thirteen volumes. This outstanding work unfortunately was studied chiefly by those who were planning the railroads and went almost unnoticed by the general public. The colorful and well-designed lithographs based on drawings by J. Mix Stanley, Balduin Möllhausen, Freiherr von Egloffstein, R. H. Kern, and others were fairly accurate representations of the rugged scenery of the West. This series and the type of illustrations used in it established a precedent for the publication of scholarly surveys. Based on this pattern, the surveys of a later day, illustrated with photographs by men such as Alexander Hessler, William H. Jackson (see pl. 55), and T. H. O'Sullivan (pl. 56) became more popular.

Although news of the discovery of gold in California and the resultant gold rush was given prominent attention in the eastern newspapers, at first little was printed about the beauty spots of the newly acquired territory of California. In 1852, however, there did come a news story which did not mention gold. In the spring of 1852 the North Calaveras Grove of Big Trees (which since 1931 has been the Calaveras Big Trees State Park) east of Stockton was discovered by a hunter, who took some of his companions at Murphy's Camp to see it. Very soon after that, two unscrupulous men stripped one of the trees (*Sequoia gigantea*), the "Mother of the Forest" (315 feet in height and 61 feet in circumference), up to the height

of 116 feet and shipped the bark East for exhibition in some of the seaboard cities. In 1854 they sent the bark to the Crystal Palace exhibition
in Sydenham, London. A pamphlet printed and sold in London boasted
that the sight of a forest of such gigantic size would be ample reward for
the long and arduous journey to California. In spite of the fact that "the
trumpet-tongued press proclaimed the wonder to all sections of the State
and to all parts of the world,"[37] the exhibit was not successful; "owing to
the immensity of circumference, nobody would believe that the bark had
come off from one tree, and finally, being branded a humbug, they [the
exhibitors] had to shut up the exhibition."[38] While this was going on in
London, the widely read *Gleason's Pictorial* published a protest by a
Californian to whom it seemed a

> cruel idea, a perfect desecration to cut down such a splendid tree . . . in
> Europe such a natural production would have been cherished and pro-
> tected by law; but in this money-making-go-ahead community, thirty or
> forty thousand dollars are paid for it and the purchaser chops it down and
> ships it off for a shilling show. We hope that no one will conceive the idea
> of purchasing Niagara Falls with the same purpose.[39]

The complainant went on to praise the beauty of the tree at the time it
had been a "single sight, worth a pilgrimage to see." Another strong protest was raised in 1857 by James Russell Lowell, who became editor of
the *Atlantic Monthly* in the same year. His article on "Humanity to
Trees" proposed to establish a society for the prevention of cruelty to
trees, since "we are as wanton in the destruction of trees as we are barba-
rous in our treatment of them."[40] In the next year it was pointed out in
Harper's Weekly that the big tree was now fast decaying, having been
peeled "with as much neatness and industry as a troupe of jackals would
display in clearing the bones of a dead lion."[41] The same year (1858) saw
the publication of *The Autocrat of the Breakfast-Table*, which included
a "Talk on Trees" wherein Oliver Wendell Holmes professed his passionate
fondness for them. However insignificant Holmes's remark may seem now,
it undoubtedly stimulated great interest in the wonders of California
scenery. This and the destruction of the big tree aroused a great deal of
feeling in the East and caused people to ponder the duty of protecting
nature against the vandalism of all too enterprising businessmen.

News of the discovery of Yosemite Valley,[42] one of the greatest events
in California history, was accompanied by far less fanfare. The account
by the San Francisco *Daily Alta California* of the scenic wonders of the
valley discovered by the punitive expeditionary force of 1851 against the
"Yosemite" Indians created no stir outside the state. An article published
in the *Mariposa Gazette* of July 12, 1855, by James M. Hutchings, whose
activities from that time on were dedicated to the valley, was of wider

interest. But in the East hardly anyone was aware of the existence of this remarkable place until 1856, when the *Country Gentleman*[43] republished an article by the *California Christian Advocate* which declared the "Yo-hem-i-ty" Valley to be "the most striking natural wonder on the Pacific" and predicted that it would eventually become a place of great resort. In 1855 and 1856 a California pioneer artist, Thomas A. Ayers, made his first sketches of the valley; lithographs were made from some of them, and these were spread widely throughout the East. By 1858 Yosemite had become so well known throughout the nation that T. Addison Richards, who published the first illustrated handbook of American travel of general importance, allotted about 125 words and one illustration of Mirror Lake to the now celebrated "Valley of the Yosemite." Here the scenery was called "perhaps the most remarkable in the United States, and perhaps in the world."[44] With such nation-wide publicity, Yosemite was bound to grow more famous every year.

As one might have expected, Horace Greeley visited Yosemite Valley as soon as possible (1859) and made the most of it. He was overwhelmed by the grandeur of the "prodigious chasms" and called the valley "the most unique and majestic of nature's marvels." Greatly impressed by the giant sequoias, he expressed the hope that the state of California would immediately provide for the safety of the Mariposa Grove of Big Trees.[45]

In view of the difficulties of transportation in the early days, the taking of photographs in Yosemite Valley was a major enterprise. The first persons to attempt it were C. L. Weed and R. H. Vance. In 1859 these men took photographs and prepared stereoscopic slides which earned local applause when they were exhibited in Sacramento at the Fifth Annual Fair of the State Agricultural Society, May 21, 1859. About the same time, *Ballou's Pictorial Drawing-Room Companion*[46] published an illustrated article on Yosemite in which the author expressed regret that the valley was neither known nor appreciated as much as it should be. This implied criticism of the traveling public was not quite justified, since travel by eastern tourists to California was next to impossible and would remain so for at least another decade.

The first thorough description of an extended trip to Yosemite Valley appeared in a series of eight articles by Thomas Starr King which were published by the Boston *Evening Transcript* from December 1, 1860, to February 9, 1861. King, as the author of the book on the White Mountains, was an expert in writing such accounts, and his friends felt that "no one had really seen the Sierra Nevada, Mount Shasta, the Yosemite Valley . . . until his fine eye saw and his cunning brain and hand depicted them . . . you will find the newspapers in which his portraitures of these sublime and charming scenes are found carefully laid away in hundreds of New

England homes as permanent sources of delight."[47] These articles, little known today, acquainted the Easterners better than anything else could with the fabulous beauties of Yosemite.

The "Three Graces," Mariposa Grove

The most important photographic records of Yosemite made within the next few years were those of C. E. Watkins, in 1861 (see pl. 57).[48] In the eyes of Oliver Wendell Holmes these large and extraordinary views could be compared only with the finest work done in Europe.[49] They were constantly on exhibition at Goupil's Art Galleries in New York, and stereoscopic views made from them aided greatly in making them famous. By the end of the 1860's photographs had become one of the most effective methods of spreading knowledge of the scenic wonders of the West. Photography was a relatively cheap means of reproduction. Moreover it was said, in 1861, that it

> has worked like the engraving as an elementary instructor, while its truthfulness has been a constant lesson to the artist himself. Better pictures have, unquestionably, been painted through the hints of the daguerreotype and photograph; and many people who, but for them, would never have dreamed of pictures, have become intelligent lovers and liberal patrons of the art.[50] (See pl. 48.)

At the end of the 1850's and again soon after the Civil War, the scenic beauties of the West—of the Rockies as well as of the Far West—received their fair share of publicity. By the time peace came, the enjoyment of nature was becoming more popular each day and the West was attracting others besides the fortune-seekers and adventurers. Yet for most of the vacationists who had become weary of the congested highways and railroads along the Atlantic seaboard, leisurely travel in the West was not possible until several years after the war. In a popular book on summer resorts published in 1868, no trips across the continent were listed, because the author felt that they were "hardly yet practical for the ordinary summer tourist."[51] A trancontinental railroad was in the making, and though later competition lowered rail fares, these at first were enormous. But even after good transportation and reasonable security were assured, it was not easy to convince many people, even those who could afford the price of the journey, that they should travel West simply for the novelty or because they greatly admired that part of the country. The Great Lakes region probably was the westernmost point to which the fashionable crowd could be induced to go. The most outstanding summer resort was the Grand Hotel on Mackinac Island, which was opened on July 10, 1887, with a gala dinner for 1,000 society members, including the Vanderbilt, Astor, Bush, Palmer, and Field families—and Mark Twain. This hotel, with its 1,300 beds, had been made possible through the combined efforts of railway and navigation companies. Like the earlier hotels in Nahant and Newport, the hotel on Mackinac was built to cater to the select few—even if they numbered a thousand people.

Public interest in the West, however, could not be aroused until an important place was found that would compare favorably or even surpass the great scenic areas of the East, such as the Mammoth Cave, the Natural Bridge, or Niagara Falls. Undoubtedly Yosemite Valley was the place destined to be the great show place of the West. But the mere existence of some great natural wonder was not enough; it was essential that someone with both vision and initiative make the place attractive and acceptable to the public, and in addition provide means by which the public could reach it in convenience and safety. Fortunately, Frederick Law Olmsted, of whom we last heard when he gave up his position with Central Park in New York to accept, in August, 1863, a position with General Frémont in Mariposa County, California, was this type of man. Olmsted's imagination, perspicacity, energy, and good taste fitted him admirably for the task of establishing Yosemite as one of the great sites of the nation. When Olmsted saw the valley late in 1863 he immediately became interested in it, and he must have realized very soon the task that lay in store for him. It was a magnificent coincidence that for once the right man was in the right spot at the right time.

9

Yosemite, Yellowstone, and the Grand Canyon

IN 1864 some California gentlemen "of fortune, of taste and of refinement" asked Senator John Conness to introduce a bill in Congress granting to the state of California the tract of land including Yosemite Valley (see pl. 58) and the Mariposa Big Trees. This bill was subsequently passed and was signed by President Lincoln on June 29, 1864.[1]

A grant of this kind was nothing extraordinary, since the federal government often made grants to states, and undoubtedly the public paid little attention to such an action. There was, however, something out of the ordinary about this bill, and its passage set an important precedent. The gentlemen from California had requested the insertion of a clause stating that the grant was given "upon the express conditions that the premises shall be held for public use, resort and recreation and shall be held inalienable for all times."[2] These terms implied that no direct economic profit was expected from the new arrangement, though probably it was assumed that costs of upkeep would be offset by revenues from leases or privileges. This was indeed an innovation in legislation and spelled the end of an epoch. To protect an area and conserve it for recrea-

---

VIGNETTE: Cotillion on a *Sequoia gigantea* Stump.

tional enjoyment was a policy that had never before been adopted for the management of the public domain. Thus, the creation of Yosemite Park was an event for which men like Catlin and Thoreau had hoped and worked and for which the work of William Bartram, Alexander Wilson, and numbers of others had paved the way. There can be little doubt that Frederick Law Olmsted was the driving force behind this completely new idea of creating a park as a playground for the nation, to be administered by the state or, if necessary, by federal authority. It should be noted that the grant was given with certain stipulations, which required the state of California to act as trustee for the federal government; Congress expressly reserved all rights of control, so that the park could under certain circumstances revert to federal management at any time. This, indeed, did take place in 1906; but in 1864 administration by the state seemed practicable. The park was placed under a commission appointed by the governor of California, and Olmsted became its first chairman.

Believing that Yosemite was "far the noblest park or pleasure ground in the world," Olmsted immediately began to prepare a plan of management. Since he considered it his duty to give the public "the greatest practicable advantage over the natural scenery," he consulted with Virgil Williams, Thomas Hill, and C. E. Watkins, two artists and a photographer who had already explored the valley. Were there any conditions unfavorably affecting the scenery, he asked, and should something be done to facilitate better enjoyment of the valley by the public?[3]

The result of this report is not known. This lack, however, is compensated for by a report in Olmsted's own hand which has come to light only recently. Olmsted had sent it to the California Legislature in the fall of 1865, but it disappeared from the official files, perhaps suppressed by a group opposed to Olmsted's views.[4]

This appraisal, providing a description of the valley and evaluating the peculiarly attractive features of Yosemite, was no facile eulogy in the manner of Willis but one at which Olmsted had arrived only after a considerable searching of his heart. When he had first seen Yosemite in November, 1863, the falls had dried up, vegetation was sparse, and the generally rugged aspect of the area seemed so completely contrary to his taste that he felt unsure of his real feelings about it. He was not yet ready to endorse Yosemite wholeheartedly. To be sure, he was impressed. But did this scenery compare favorably with natural features he loved in the East? No aesthetic yardstick he had ever used could measure the California scene; but gradually, in spite of some hesitation and after a year of constant observation, Olmsted was overcome by the "union of the deepest sublimity and with the deepest beauty of nature" which made "Yo Semite the greatest glory of nature."[5]

Having arrived at this conviction, Olmsted started the movement to protect the unique valley of Yosemite and the country surrounding it. But this, as we may also gather from his report, was not the only purpose of his drive, since he realized that the conservation of Yosemite was only a beginning. These new public grounds, he felt, should be opened for "the use of the body of the people" and for their "free enjoyment"; he considered it the duty of the managers of Yosemite to make the park serve the people in their "pursuit of happiness." The document makes it evident not only that Olmsted envisaged the conserving of certain important natural features but also that he was the first to conceive the idea that "great public parks" must be managed "for the benefit and the free use of the people," which has become a fundamental policy of the National Park Service.

It was fortunate that just at the time Olmsted was pushing his idea, Schuyler Colfax, the Speaker of the House, led a group of friends from the East across the continent to see the country and study its resources before it was spanned by the railroad. Among these were Samuel Bowles, publisher of the Springfield *Republican,* and Albert B. Richardson, the distinguished war correspondent of the New York *Tribune.* The enthusiastic approval of the Yosemite park project by this group greatly encouraged Olmsted. In 1865 Bowles published an account of his travels in which he stated:

> The wise cession and dedication [of Yosemite] by Congress, and proposed improvement by California, ... furnishes an admirable example for other objects of natural curiosity and popular interest all over the Union. New York should preserve for popular use both Niagara Falls and its neighborhood and a generous section of her famous Adirondacks, and Maine one of her lakes and its surrounding woods.[1]

This was a remarkable statement, indeed, for here in unmistakable language is not only a formula for the protection of this or that place which was of interest to one particular group but an over-all approach for the protection of a system of areas, throughout the nation, embracing specific features of nature. Whether this was entirely Bowles's idea or whether it originated in conversations with Olmsted it is difficult to judge. At all events, it anticipated the pattern which was set up many years later when the National Park Service was established. It is well to note that in his statement Bowles referred to the cession of Yosemite to the state, which he must have considered the first step in the direction he recommended that the country take, and his counsel very likely represented the opinion of the distinguished group of men of which he was a member. The fact that Bowles felt that state legislatures should protect the areas is not important in an evaluation of his plan. Although one could hardly suppose that anyone in 1864 would anticipate the conservation of state areas by federal legislation, it is noteworthy that the objective of the grant was considered of nation-wide, if not of world-wide, importance.

Unfortunately, Olmsted could not wait to see his plans carried out, because he received a call in 1865 to return to New York and complete the task of establishing Central Park. In spite of this loss, the development of the Yosemite grant went on and the fame of the valley continued to grow (see pl. 61).

The year 1868 brought John Muir to California. Through his writings, in which he showed his deep devotion to the Sierra, the glory of Yosemite became still more widely known. Muir's enthusiasm is epitomized in his letter inviting Emerson to Yosemite. "I invite you to join me in a month's worship with Nature in the high temples of the great Sierra Crown beyond our holy Yosemite. It will cost you nothing save the time and very little of that for you will be mostly in Eternity.'" Despite his sixty-seven years, Emerson accepted the invitation and braved the hardships of a journey to Yosemite. In May, 1871, he arrived in the valley and jotted down in his journal his first impressions: "In Yosemite, grandeur of these mountains perhaps unmatched in the globe; for here they strip themselves like athletes for exhibition and stand perpendicular granite walls, showing their entire height and wearing a liberty cap of snow on the head."⁸

In the 'sixties and 'seventies, accounts of cross-country trips were eagerly bought, and almost all of them praised the scenic beauties of California. One of the first of these was written by Fitz-Hugh Ludlow, who traveled to Yosemite and Oregon with his friend Albert Bierstadt in 1863. His reports to the *Atlantic Monthly* reveal the great enthusiasm with which the two men had gone "into the vale, whose giant domes and battlements had months before thrown their photographic shadow through Watkins' camera across the mysterious wide continent, causing exclamations of awe at Goupil's window, and ecstasy in Dr. Holmes's study. . . . No Saratoga affair this!"⁹ This journey supplied Bierstadt with material for his first Yosemite picture, which Easterners found so impressive.

In 1867 Albert B. Richardson published a report of the trip he had made with the Colfax party in 1865, in which he confirmed Bowles's statement about Yosemite. Another book, published in 1872, which proved of great value was written by Clarence King about his mountaineering experiences in the Sierra Nevada. King was not only an outstanding scholar and expert in his own and several other fields, but he was also a great outdoor man and bold mountaineer who was able to put his experiences into forceful writing. Few works on mountaineering are as stimulating and as colorfully written as King's book on the Sierra, especially the accounts of his climbs of Mount Whitney and Mount Tyndall. After King had completed several years' work with the Whitney Geological Survey in California, the United States Survey of the Fortieth Parallel was undertaken on his initiative, and he was put in charge of it. Since Henry Adams was one of his closest friends, King invited him to go along on the expedition. Adams gratefully accepted this invitation, for he was only too happy to shed the worries that usually enveloped him at the end of the school term in Cambridge. In June, 1871, Adams set out for Fort Bridger in Wyoming Territory. In the wilderness, "geologizing, shooting, fishing or marching" as occasion required, the aesthete learned to appreciate the great outdoors. "To stand on the top of a lofty mountain and survey proudly the surrounding country with a haughty smile at civilization and a proud consciousness of my own savage freedoms was a gratifying experience . . . I never felt so lively and so much in the humor for enjoyment."[10]

Two huge tomes, entitled *Picturesque America*, also offered to the public in 1872, were the antithesis of King's spirited and now classic mountain book. William Cullen Bryant was the editor, and the illustrations were by some of the best artists, including S. R. Gifford, Washington Whittredge, and Thomas Moran (see pl. 53), who had been sent out West to provide authentic pictures. This monumental publication is representative of its period and is quite in keeping with the oversize canvases of Bierstadt. His pictures could not be observed in all their details at one time, and these books were not even intended to be read from cover to cover but rather to be perused now and again as they lay in state on the drawing-room table beside the stereoscope. Along with other reports and descriptions of western scenery, *Picturesque America* printed some striking news about "Our National Park," that is, Yellowstone,[11] which by act of Congress of March 1, 1872, had been placed under federal protection. The geysers had been known for many years, but precise information about the site and the wonders of Yellowstone had been spread only since a number of expeditions had explored the area between 1869 and 1872. The exploits of the Washburn-Doane expedition of 1870 were much discussed after one of its leading members, Nathaniel P. Langford, in 1871 had given talks on the subject in the East (a number of them for the benefit of the Northern Pacific Railway Company, the bond issue of which Jay Cooke was floating at the time). This private expedition was immediately followed by two official ones in 1871. The more important one, representing the Department of the Interior, was carried out under the leadership of the United States Geologist, Ferdinand V. Hayden. Hayden had invited the painters Henry W. Elliott and Thomas Moran and the photographer William H. Jackson to join his staff.[12] This foresight was well rewarded: the pictorial reports of these artists, two of whom were outstanding, later proved of great value. The spectacular geyser area, the tremendous falls, the canyon, and the lake became immediately known through Moran's paintings, with their striking and impressive colors, and through Jackson's superb photographs, which established his fame as the outstanding landscape photographer of the era. In addition, the firm of Prang in Boston made color lithographs from fifteen of Moran's paintings, and the government purchased (for $10,000 each) two huge canvases Moran had painted of the Canyon of the Yellowstone and the Grand Canyon of the Colorado. These are now in the office of the Department of the Interior in Washington, D.C. This extraordinary pictorial documentation was supplemented by a number of specimens Hayden collected on his expedition. All of this material was put on exhibition and aided materially in spreading the fame of Yellowstone and furthering the movement to appropriate it for public use.

The question who conceived the plan of establishing Yellowstone as a national park has been frequently discussed.[13] If we do not regard Catlin as the father of the idea, because his efforts were not immediately successful, we must consider David E. Folsom and his friends Charles W. Cook and William Peterson, who explored the region in 1869, the progenitors of the plan. Folsom discussed with General C. C. Washburn "the project of creating a park" just before the general, Nathaniel P. Langford, Cornelius Hedges, G. C. Doane, and others set out on their expedition of September, 1870. Soon after this trip, Hedges wrote an article in the Helena *Herald* of November 9, 1870, in which he followed up Folsom's idea by suggesting that the Yellowstone region be kept in such ownership as would secure its permanent use by the public. As far as the newly discovered area was concerned, Hedges' public-spirited plan undoubtedly was novel and startling, especially since he and his friends asserted that they were not fostering any personal business interests, as they might easily have done. A precedent for such a project had already been set. Only six years earlier, in 1864, Yosemite Valley, because of its nation-wide importance, had been established by Congress "for public use, resort and recreation" as a grant to the State of California. However, since Yellowstone was situated in a territory and thus could not be given in trusteeship to a state, the only way to segregate the vast area "as a public or pleasuring ground for the benefit and enjoyment of the people" (these words were later incorporated in the bill) was to establish it as a park under immediate federal administration. In spite of previous measures taken to protect Yosemite, the passage of the act creating Yellowstone National Park undoubtedly constitutes the legal beginning of federal administration of parks.

Although the establishment of every national park has been an important step forward on the road to a nation-wide conservation program, before 1916 the methods by which such parks were selected and brought into existence were rather imperfect and occasionally produced undesirable results. Also, there was no over-all policy, and either civil or military forces, depending on the circumstances, were employed to police the parks, or sometimes there was hardly any policing at all. Funds were appropriated only in response to local requests, which often represented a scramble for federal funds. The administration of the parks was handled by the office of the Chief Clerk of the Department of the Interior in Washington. This office handled the business of Yellowstone and Mount Rainier along with that of eleemosynary institutions and miscellaneous matters concerning the city of Washington, D.C. Decisions had to be made without any preliminary specialized studies. Because of the lack of coördination in the methods of selecting and administering national parks before the reorganization in 1916, that year can be considered the real birth date of the carefully organized and centralized National Park Service. Happily and most fortunately, national park work in the early period was carried on with an enormous amount of good will by officials like W. B. Acker. The parks from their very beginnings were much loved and enjoyed by the great majority of their visitors, and at an early date they became famous abroad as unique and essentially American creations, worth crossing the ocean to see.

Although Yellowstone (see pls. 51 and 52) proved an excellent testing ground for determining the best way of administering a park, the government when it created the park had no conscious intention of establishing a general policy concerning the purposes of this or any of the later parks. There was only the aim to prevent the destruction of the natural assets with which the area was endowed, and this indeed was no simple task. Congress wavered constantly in its opinion about the advisability of maintaining a park, since no one in Congress had expected all the difficulties which accompanied and resulted from the establishment of Yellowstone. The main trouble arose from the feeling that Congress should not spend the taxpayers' money on public lands which had been withheld from "proper" use. Since Congress at that time did not even acknowledge that it had any duty to further the fine arts with public funds, its negative attitude toward the parks was perfectly logical. Time and again, members of Congress expressed concern about the "doubtful" assets of Yellowstone; many members of the House felt that it would have been better to sell the area as was done with other public lands. After all, was it not "a very expensive luxury?" The federal government was not supposed to go into "show business," nor was it supposed to "raise wild animals." All these arguments are understandable if one considers that in the early days of its development the Yellowstone enterprise looked far from promising.

The park was rather inaccessible before the first railway reached it, in 1883; before 1885 there were only a few poor roads, there was scarcely a lodging place, and there certainly was no guide to advise visitors. Tourists could not have been expected to use the new "pleasuring ground" in any large numbers. More than once, efforts were made in Congress to rid the federal administration of its incubus. Had it not been for a group of senators faithful to the cause, the House would have yielded to those who wished to drop the project as unrewarding.

Yosemite was more fortunate in its beginnings. The Central Pacific Railroad touched Stockton as early as 1869, and as a result, the number of visitors jumped from 623 in 1868 to 1,122 in 1869. But gradually difficulties developed. Pretentious claims by individuals encroached on park territory, and the state administration began to give way to private interests and monopolies. A large part of the valley was fenced in for pasture and thus travel was blocked; overgrazing destroyed much of the beautiful growth; and mismanagement by the state had become so obvious as to invite an investigation by Congress. It also was becoming apparent that federal administration as it was carried out in Yellowstone might also be applied to Yosemite. In spite of all difficulties and even while the possibility of an investigation was being discussed, Congress created three new reservations in California: Sequoia, General Grant, and Yosemite national parks. Since the newly created Yosemite National Park of 1,600 square miles surrounded the old park in the valley, it was soon realized that this produced an awkward situation; yet fifteen years were to pass before it was remedied. California retroceded the valley land to the federal government in 1905, and both that and the surrounding park were merged to form the Yosemite National Park as it is today. By 1916 thirty-seven national parks and monuments had been established under federal control, among them Mount Rainier (1899), Crater Lake (1902), Mesa Verde (1906), Grand Canyon (1908, Monument; 1919, Park), Glacier Park (1910), and Rocky Mountain (1915). Although they all were and are cared for separately, much that was learned in the development of Yellowstone has been put to use in their administration.

Obviously travel to the national parks represented only a small part of the western tourist traffic which developed after the railroad proved to be a convenient method of transportation. From Whitman's "Specimen Days," which records the impressions the poet received on a transcontinental railway ride, we can get an idea of what it meant to journey leisurely across the vast expanse of the West. Traveling through the Rockies in 1879, Whitman experienced "a fierce weird pleasure to lie in my berth at night in the luxurious palace car." The view from the window made him wonder whether "the people of the West know how much of first class *art* they have in these prairies—how original and all your own—how much of the influence of a character for your future humanity, broad, patriotic, heroic and new." Although Whitman had no chance to see the Yellowstone and the "hoodoo," or Goblinland, of the region, he felt that he "wanted new words in writing about these plains, and all the inland American West, the terms far, large, vast, etc. are insufficient." Indeed, he knew that in order to write poetry, paint pictures, compose music—in fact to create anything expressing emotion—one needed a "feeding visit" in the West. In spite of those thoughts, which were far beyond the ken of his contemporaries, the poet was biased by and entangled in the ideas of his epoch. He stated that democracy can best flourish in the vastness of the American scene with all its infinite variety of mountains and plains and forests and rivers; yet he could not praise too highly man's great efforts to dominate nature. Civilization and progress date from the railroad, he believed, "it is the conqueror of crude nature, which it turns to man's use both on small scales and on the largest."[14]

Two generations later, Thomas Wolfe traveled abroad. As his train glided through the night and passed a dark forest in Germany his thoughts turned to his own country and he reflected on what it feels like when one looks out of the window of an American train. It is curious to note that Wolfe felt very much as Whitman did in an earlier day. He experienced pride, joy, and hope but not complete satisfaction or equilibrium:

> In America, the train gives one a feeling of wild and lonely joy, a sense of the savage, unfenced, and illimitable wilderness of the country through which the train is rushing, a wordless and unutterable hope as one thinks of the enchanted city toward which he is speeding, the unknown and fabulous promise of the life he is to find there.[15]

To most travelers the progress of the West did indeed look marvelous, and to many tourists accustomed to choosing New England as a vacation spot the West now became more alluring. Gradually, scenic photography had overcome the nearly insurmountable difficulties which had hampered it in the early days, and it now began to play a decisive part in publicizing the West. The stereoscope continued to play an extraordinarily important role. Photographs by Alexander Hessler, T. H. O'Sullivan (see pl. 56), William Bell, Jack Hillers, and others, most of whom had taken part in United States Geological or Railroad surveys, became well known throughout the country. Probably the most famous are the photographs by William H. Jackson, many of which have survived the years. Jackson first photographed the wonderland of Yellowstone in 1871 (pl. 52); he died in 1941 at the age of ninety-nine as the result of an accident. One of his especially interesting photographs was that of the Mountain of the Holy Cross (pl. 55) taken in 1873 when he accompanied Ferdinand V. Hayden on his geological survey of Colorado. What enthusiasm was needed to achieve results in those days can be gathered from the diary in which the photographer recorded his exploits. On Saturday morning, August 23, 1873, Jackson and two men started on their way to photograph the mountain, with very little food in their packs but with a load of one hundred pounds of equipment divided among them. After fording a river, struggling through underbrush, and being soaked by mist and water, the men worked their way up the mountain. "Clouds hung about all the summits" and the top of the Holy Cross was not to be seen, but they reached the peak. At sunset the party descended again to timberline and stayed overnight, "supperless, blanketless, on a bare rocky mountain side 12,000 feet above the sea." Climbing once more the next morning "on an entirely empty stomach ... was no fun."[10] But this time the weather favored them and the party succeeded in taking eight photographs. As a result, Jackson rose to fame through his photographs of the mysterious and hitherto almost unknown mountain. Longfellow was among those whose interest was attracted by a picture of the mountain, "upon whose lonely lofty breast the snow lies in long furrows that make a rude but wonderfully clear image of a vast cross." His thoughts then framed themselves into these lines (1879), which were found after his death:

> There is a mountain in the distant West
> That, sun defying in its deep ravines
> Displays a cross of snow upon its side.[11]

In 1876 Thomas Moran exhibited a large painting of the Holy Cross, based on studies he had made on the spot, and won a medal and nation-wide applause when the painting was shown at the Centennial Exhibition in Philadelphia.

Only occasionally was publicity for western travel as it appeared in magazine articles, books, or pictures countered by a warning not to go west. Olive Logan, writing for *Galaxy* in 1870, answered the question "Does it pay to go to Yosemite?" with a vehement "No." It appears from her article that distinguished travelers to San Francisco staying at one of the big hotels were all too persuasively solicited by agents to go to Yosemite. No doubt the agents played on the tourists' qualms about leaving California without having seen that famous place; members of smart society could not omit a trip to the valley without jeopardizing their reputation as cosmopolitan travelers. But, as Miss Logan asserted, punishment for being snobbish came quickly. After taking the boat from San Francisco to Stockton, travelers had to spend the next two days traveling by stage. But stagecoach travel had not improved since the time Horace Greeley had been shaken up so badly by his driver, Hank Monk, famous for his

constant exhortation, "Keep your seat, Horace," while driving at break-
neck speed over one of the roads of California.[18] After the stage ride, travelers to Yosemite must spend a day on horseback, after which the ladies had
to be lifted off their horses and revived by alcohol rubs. As a reward for

Descending the Mountain to the Yo-Semite Valley

all this hardship, what was there to be seen? "Tall rocks, a few tall trees,
a high and narrow waterfall" which looked "like a fireman's hose playing
over the top of Stewart's store." The travelers one met were "poor candle-
moth tourists"; the only people who really seemed to enjoy themselves
were the clergymen.[19] However, such dissenting voices were rare, and the
number of visitors continued to increase.

Interest in the western scene was greatly stimulated in the mid-seventies through reports by N. P. Langford, F. V. Hayden, T. C. Evert, and others which appeared in *Scribner's Monthly*. Between 1874 and 1875 John Wesley Powell wrote a series of articles that were later published as a book, which has since become a classic.[20] Up to the time he became a contributor to *Scribner's*, Major Powell had been known as a war hero who, in spite of the loss of his right arm at Shiloh, had served throughout the war as chief of artillery of the XVII Army Corps.

During his boyhood in Illinois, Powell had roamed the countryside from Wisconsin to Missouri and had traveled down the Des Moines, Ohio, and Mississippi rivers in his boat, always collecting artifacts and keenly observing nature. When war broke out, Powell enlisted, and after the war he became a professor of geology at Bloomington, Illinois. As a college professor, Powell introduced an entirely new way of teaching by organizing geological excursions for his students. Thus in 1867, before the railroad was in operation, he led a group of students and amateur naturalists under the protection of some troops, across the plains to the Rocky Mountains, which hitherto had been known as a field for adventure rather than for studies. In the summer of 1868 he repeated the trip, going into the region of the middle peaks, where he spent the winter alone, exploring the region of the Grand, Green, and Yampa rivers. In all these undertakings Powell was aided by the Illinois Natural History Society. Thoroughly prepared, the major started out in 1869 for the great task of his life, the journey down that part of the Colorado River which had never been successfully navigated.

Legend and hearsay had woven frightful stories about the river, and there was no knowing what fate might befall the explorers. One thing, however, was certain: there would be a descent of a mile on the route of travel, and this meant that they would encounter rapids, whirlpools, and cataracts, all of unknown size and force, where the river rushed through steep-walled canyons. To undertake such a journey was a risk which asked for tremendous boldness. Yet Powell dared take it because in his judgment the chances for success were great enough to justify the experiment. As it turned out, Powell approached imminent disaster again and again, but he faced all perils with courage and daring in spite of his constantly diminishing equipment and increasing handicaps. Toward the end of the journey, unaware of being near his goal, he came to the point where he had to decide whether to give up the boat trip and save himself and his crew by ascending the canyon walls, or go on to face further dangers. But Powell was intrepid and continued the journey. His courageous decision was rewarded, for he won immortal fame for a fearless group of men. In 1871 Powell repeated his trip; this time he took with him the artist Frederick

Dellenbaugh and photographers E. H. Beamann and Jack Hillers. The pictures made on this trip were used later to illustrate the reports.

Until Powell's trip, canyon country was almost unknown in the East. Once, in 1831, the Reverend Timothy Flint had prefaced and perhaps edited a narrative written by a trapper, James O. Pattie, who had crossed and recrossed Arizona and had visited one rim of the Grand Canyon. Pattie noted that "the river emerges from these horrid mountains, which so cage it up as to deprive all human beings of the abilities to descend to its banks and make use of its water."[21] Other trappers and traders had seen the region also and had either made unfavorable remarks, such as "the mountains were heaped together in the greatest disorder,"[22] or had thought it not worth while to comment on this barren land. In 1858 Lieutenant Ives, mentioned previously as having been in charge of a government expedition which explored the Colorado from its mouth, reached the point in Black Canyon where Hoover Dam is situated today. As he continued by land toward the southeast end of the Grand Canyon, he was greatly impressed by the strange beauty of the scene, judging by his captivating descriptions of the wondrous "chasms and fissures" he beheld. At one point near Diamond Creek, south of the Grand Canyon, he had a glimpse of the "Big" canyon, as he called it. Here he paused "in wondering delight, surveying the stupendous formations ... till the deep azure blue faded into light of cerulean tint that blended with the dome of the heavens." Nevertheless, Ives doubted that "any party will ever again pursue the same line of travel," because, in spite of the "strange sublimity of the region," it was a region of little value.[23] Ives's travel account, enshrouded in a government document, had almost been forgotten when, ten years later, Powell's report upset the earlier judgment completely and established the fame and glory of the canyon land overnight.

In his report Powell narrated his harrowing adventures and also described his observations made while resting and while exploring the banks and side canyons. Amid all the turmoil and in spite of the uncertainty about what experiences the next days would bring, Powell made entries in his diary which reveal the calm of a poet and the sensitivity of an impressionist painter:

> The reflected heat from the glaring surface produces a curious motion of the atmosphere; little currents are generated, and the whole seems to be trembling and moving about in many directions. ... Plains, hills, and cliffs and distant mountains seem vaguely to be floating about in a trembling wave-rocked sea, and patches of landscape will seem to float away, and be lost, and then reappear.

Subtle descriptions of this sort are interspersed with terse remarks reflecting the ideas of the times: "we are but pigmies, running up and down the sands, or lost among the boulders."[24] Little wonder that a book of such caliber fascinated the entire nation and stimulated more than one generation.

Powell's description of the land along the Colorado opened up an entirely new vista to potential travelers to the Southwest; yet it was not until a good deal later, when the railroad now called the Santa Fe spanned Arizona, that there was much opportunity to visit the region. Even railroad travel was not always safe, however, and robberies or holdups were frequent even as late as the early 'nineties. Travelers who did not mind hardship left the train at Williams for the stage, which took twelve hours and three changes of horses to negotiate the seventy-two mile run to the South Rim of the Grand Canyon (see pl. 54). In the early days, old-timer John Hance accommodated the traveler in his camp and guided him around the site, telling his famous tall tales. As one contented traveler was pleased to write in the guest book, "God made the Canyon, John Hance the trail; without the other, neither would be complete."[25]

Matters improved when the Grand View Hotel opened in 1897; but the pioneer phase did not end until 1901, when the railroad, branching out from Williams, brought the first train to the South Rim and Fred Harvey took over the care of the tourists, as he had been doing with much acclaim and success all along the Santa Fe route since 1876. Although Powell had also explored the canyons of Utah along the Virgin River now known as Zion and Bryce canyons, and though Zion had been established as Mukuntuweap National Monument in 1909, almost no tourists visited them before the 1920's when the Union Pacific Railroad began to make them accessible to the public.

Thus we see that far-western tourist travel toward the end of the nineteenth century was almost entirely limited to Yosemite Valley and Yellowstone National Park. However, eastern vacationists and sportsmen who wished to enjoy the outdoors without going all the way to the Pacific Coast could take advantage of the transcontinental railroad to go just to the Rocky Mountains. As early as 1852 a writer in *Harper's Magazine* had somewhat prematurely expressed the desire to see the "Valley of the Missouri form a pleasant tangent to summer travel."[26] After the completion of the railroad, the Rocky Mountains of Colorado were advertised as a fascinating place to go, and Colorado Springs, founded in 1871, was said to have a climate superior even to that of the Swiss resorts. And in 1880 a writer in *Harper's* expressed the belief that this part of the country was being overpublicized, that it was becoming crowded by visitors, and that the majority of those who went there returned disappointed. He thought that the only persons who should go there were the genuine lovers of mountains and those whose objective was business, health, or study. In any event, no one should expect pleasures like those of Nahant and Saratoga, because these were not to be found in the West in spite of all the advertising.[27] Among the most enthusiastic lovers of the out-of-doors who went to Estes Park and on to Yellowstone was the fourth Earl of Dunraven. After his return to England he wrote *The Great Divide* (1876), in which he recorded his hunting experiences in the Rockies and the glorious impressions he received at Yellowstone. He contrasted the freedom of move-

Shooting Buffalo on the Line of the Kansas Pacific

ment permitted in the park area with the restrictions prevailing in England and on the continent, where every step of the way in the outdoors was hedged in. This book, which publicized the all-American institution of the national park, was widely read, particularly in Europe.

Many hunters followed the Earl of Dunraven's example and visited the glorious hunting grounds of the Rocky Mountains. Here the outdoors could be enjoyed in a way not comparable to anything they had experienced in the East. But unfortunately the hunters and travelers began to include a sorry lot just like those who had roamed the Adirondacks earlier. These people brought real sportsmen into disrepute by "wearing weapons of defense and offense, carrying parlors upon wheels, kitchens in their carts, shooting rabbits, and Indians as the seasons vary and dining upon buffalo and corn bread à volunté."[28] After the railroad across the plains had been completed, "hunting" became even easier for buffalo butchers. One of their common pastimes was to shoot buffalo from the train (see text illus.

and pl. 50) just for the fun of aiming at a target. In time, buffalo killing became an industry, with the result that in the five-year period 1870–1875 almost six million buffalo were slaughtered, and the species—except for a negligible number of animals which escaped and fled to the north of the range, some of which crossed the Canadian border—was extinguished. No other resource of the country has ever been destroyed in so short a time, so deliberately and wantonly, and with so little protest. A passage from Philip Hone's diary written in 1835 may in part explain this complacency. Hone believed that "killing buffaloes, hunting wild horses . . . and depending from day to day for the means of subsistence on the deer, wild horses, and bears" were "events of ordinary occurrence to the settlers of the great West, but matters of thrilling interest to comfortable citizens who read of them in their green slippers, seated before a shining grate, the neatly printed page illuminated by a bronze astral lamp."[29] Such a passage emphasizes the fact that happenings on the plains were only thrilling stories for Easterners. As long as the West was not a part of their own experience, they could little understand the true significance of events which took place there.

Much information of considerable consequence about the West was derived from apparently casual sources. Gold mining, with its thrills and heartaches, and every other kind of western adventure produced a certain type of humor, perhaps uncouth and crude, but significant of the time and place in which it originated and interpretative of the western scene. Perhaps "Artemus Ward" (Charles Farrar Browne) with his famous talks on the Mormons, accompanied by a comical panorama based on photographs by Charles R. Savage,[30] was not the first to introduce frontier philosophy to the East; but certainly he was, next to Mark Twain (Samuel Clemens), the most successful humorist of the 'sixties. "John Phoenix" (George Horatio Derby), the author of some strange "official" reports on California, and Lincoln's favorite, "Petroleum V. Nasby" (David Ross Locke), were also popular humorists of the period; but the great success of these men was of course mild compared with that of Mark Twain, who was admired and lionized from coast to coast.

Both Twain's *Roughing It* and Bryant's *Picturesque America,* mentioned earlier, were offered to the public in 1872. Twain's book initiated a new era of writing, and Bryant's marked the approaching end of a period. When *Roughing It* came out, the transcontinental overland stage had just become a thing of the past, but the trip West was still adventurous and the characters Mark Twain portrayed so well were still to be found in the Rockies and the Far West. Twain not only told the human story well and with great vigor but from the beginning interpreted the western scene with keen perception. His style, unlike that of most magazine writers, was neither romantic nor sentimental. On going through the famous South Pass Mark Twain observed gathered about him

> a convention of Nature's kings that stood ten, twelve, and even thirteen thousand feet high—grand old fellows who would have to stoop to see Mount Washington, in the twilight . . . these Sultans of the fastnesses were turbaned with tumbled volumes of cloud, which shredded away from time to time and drifted off, fringed and torn, trailing their continents of shadow after them.[31]

Mono Lake, forlorn and silent in its desolation, Twain describes with realism and vitality, and his story of the poor raw-skinned dog that jumped into its alkaline waters is unforgettable in the precise and vivid account of the disaster that followed. A decade later Mark Twain wrote his great epic of the Mississippi. It was rare good fortune that a man who had gained the experience of a river pilot and who knew the river even at night "the same as he'd known his own front hall"[32] had the opportunity and the genius to tell his story of *Life on the Mississippi* to the applauding audience of an entire nation. In this was fulfilled the wish Walt Whitman had expressed in his "Specimen Days": an American writer had magnificently succeeded in distilling "American areas . . . in the alembic of a perfect poem" and treating "one of the great themes this continent had to offer."[33] Perhaps Mark Twain had no greater moment than when he came back to the Mississippi River in 1881, acknowledged and praised by his countrymen as a master of writing, and taking the wheel of a river boat demonstrated that he still knew "his" river. Backed by this kind of experience, and remembering his youth spent on and along the river, he wrote the stories of the adventures of Tom Sawyer and Huck Finn, which have been read and enjoyed by one generation after another. These books not only appealed to persons of an adventurous spirit but gave particular pleasure to readers who like Huck and Tom had experienced the novelty of "open-air sleeping" and "open-air exercise" and were feeling "wonderfully refreshed and gladhearted after enjoying the great outdoors in the wilds of the West."[34]

10

City Parks and Timberlands

IN THE period when the magnificence and the grandeur as well as the curiosities of the West were gradually being revealed, some of the large cities in the East became conscious of their duty to offer recreation to their citizens and began to develop city parks. This movement can be traced directly to Frederick Law Olmsted, who almost single-handed introduced large-scale landscape architecture to America. To be sure, Andrew Downing, one of Olmsted's predecessors, had stimulated interest in the art called "landscape gardening." Scenic rural cemeteries had become more or less common by the middle of the nineteenth century and

VIGNETTE: Central Park, New York.

country seats had been decidedly improved. In most cities there had always been some parks which offered possibilities for development, and occasionally a man like Thoreau had expressed the need for public parks: "Each town should have a park or rather a primitive forest of five hundred acres, where a stick should never be cut for fuel." This should be held as "a common possession forever, for instruction and recreation."[1] But the movement really started with the establishment of Central Park in New York, which owes its existence and successful development to the initiative and never-lagging efforts of Olmsted. This was only the first of a series of great projects he was to carry out. Olmsted became a noted landscape architect, and also a great humanitarian. On innumerable occasions he showed his deep interest in social conditions by making zealous efforts to improve them. After the great New York park was well on its way, Olmsted, with his stupendous energy, made plans for a large number of other parks. This work for cities, as well as his work for federal and private agencies, occupied him for many decades. An entry picked at random from his diary for 1882, November 9, mentions work in progress on public projects in Washington, D.C., Detroit, Boston, Providence, North Easton, Newport, Albany, Buffalo, Bridgeport, Niagara, Auburndale, Summit, Quincy, Dedham, and Wellesley, besides work for private clients in various places.[2] Americans were really following Downing's counsel, to "plant spacious parks in your cities, and unloose their gates of morning to the whole people."[3] Only two decades earlier, Charles A. Dana, once associated with the Brook Farm project and then (in 1860) the editor of *Appleton's New American Cyclopædia,* had invited Olmsted to write an article on "Parks," a subject which had not yet been treated in that work. In his article, published in 1861, Olmsted states that so far there is "scarcely a finished park or promenade ground deserving mention."[4] Later, as a result of his activities, there were few cities of importance which did not boast of one or two parks which had been planned by Olmsted or laid out in accordance with his advice or established through his influence. Perhaps his work was most conspicuous at the time he coöperated with Daniel Burnham in planning the setting of Chicago's Columbian Exposition of 1893. At the dinner given in honor of those artists who had contributed in making the fair an overwhelming success, Burnham expressed his admiration for the dean of landscape architecture, "not for his deeds of late years alone but for what his brain has wrought and his pen has taught for half a century." Charles Eliot Norton extolled Olmsted as the man whose work answered "the needs and gave expression to the life of our immense and miscellaneous democracy."[5]

Although big cities were improving greatly through the establishment of extensive parks (see vignette) they were losing rapidly in another respect. In the early machine age, mills were inconspicuous and sometimes not unattractive; but as cities mushroomed with uncontrolled growth, ungainly-looking manufacturing plants covered with soot and grime began to clutter up their neighborhoods. Cities with magnificent parks permitted industry, along the waterfront, not only to destroy the beauty of the scene but to pollute the water by dumping refuse. At the same time, a townsman who enjoyed his city park probably gave little thought to the wantonness with which the forests were being destroyed to provide for the needs of his city. On the contrary, he probably considered the utilization of natural material as a bonus to industry. A little story told by Margaret Fuller of her visit to Niagara seems apropos. While she was sitting on Table Rock, "a man came up to take his first look. He walked close up to the fall, and after looking at it a moment with an air as if thinking how he could best appropriate it to his own use, he spat into it."⁰ Why, indeed, in this age of utility should a prosperous businessman have cared about beauty values? Out in the countryside the situation was similar. A farmer would exhaust the soil of his property for a small monetary yield and then move on and mistreat another place. In short, mistreatment of the soil, wasteful cutting of timber, and improper usage of water were the rules. While nature enthusiasts and essayists continued to praise the beauties of nature in the traditional romantic manner, and painters with equal enthusiasm pictured their favorite forest retreats, the very objects of their delight were being rapidly destroyed.

Certainly there had always been some persons who advised restraint in the use of some natural resources, but these, for the most part, had spoken up only because they feared for the scarcity of one commodity or another, or perhaps because they felt that some species of wildlife was on the way to becoming extinct. Warnings of this kind, however, did not strike at the root of the evil. As mentioned earlier, William Penn, Dr. Nicholas Collin, and George Catlin many years before had warned against too lavish use of natural resources. Another sibylline voice was that of Noah Webster, for to some extent he too had become aware of the kind of forest devastation which caused floods. Also, in 1828 during the presidency of John Quincy Adams, live-oak timberland on the island of Santa Rosa, off the coast of Florida, had been purchased primarily for the use of the Navy, and some experimenting in sowing, planting, and nursing trees had been done there. But this venture was cut short under Adams' successor, Andrew Jackson, and the enterprise was abandoned in 1831. Occasionally there were outright warnings of the coming scarcity of trees, such as this: "the time is not distant when public attention must be drawn to the planting of forest trees in the country . . . we have destroyed our forests . . . and posterity must face the consequences."⁷ When this was written (1849) destruction had only just started, but it was growing more widespread each year. The basic trouble was that neither industry nor the general public had yet become conscious of the evil resulting from the exhaustion of soil, deforestation, the abuse of water, and the extermination of wildlife. The fact that there must be an interplay between these resources of nature to assure certain cyclic functions was ignored or grossly neglected. The few warnings that had been given had no force, and such knowledge as there was about problems of conservation was far from being practically applied in any large measure, because of the apparent abundance of trees and water and wildlife throughout the Western Hemisphere. Destruction, carelessness, and waste thus continued, to the detriment of all natural resources. Apparently this pernicious decline could not be arrested until man became aware of the fundamental principles governing his relations with nature. At one time Emerson's transcendentalist principles had seemed sufficient for their interpretation; now solid facts were needed to convince man that he would have to pay dearly for what he was wantonly wrecking. The plundering of natural resources meant courting disaster, which invitably would follow if warnings were not heeded.

At this crucial point George P. Marsh published his book *Man and Nature*, in 1864. The era of reconstruction, besides being a period of political readjustment, was one of reorienting industry and reëvaluating the potential of natural resources. It was therefore time to take stock of an entire continent. Marsh's book, because of its wide scope, offered abundant material on which to base a judgment about the future of the nation's resources. Marsh's purpose in writing the book was to indicate the enormous changes wrought by "human action in the physical conditions of the globe," and to point out that man must observe "caution in all operations which, on a large scale, interfere with the spontaneous arrangements of the organic or the inorganic world." He must take measures to restore the disturbed world and to bring about the "material improvement of waste and exhausted regions." Unfortunately, "man has too long forgotten that the earth was given to him for usufruct alone, not for consumption, still less for profligate waste." Marsh's study was conceived during the years he spent in Italy as United States ambassador. There he became convinced that to no small degree the depletion of the Mediterranean area of forest lay at the root of the fall of the Roman Empire. Marsh accordingly held up the collapse of this ancient empire as a warning to his own country to bring an end to the destruction and devastation of natural resources by the unstable and fluctuating population. It was time, he felt,

> for some abatement in the restless love of change which characterizes us, and makes us almost a nomadic rather than a sedentary people. We have now felled forests enough everywhere, in many districts far too much. Let

us restore this one element of material life to its normal proportions, and devise means for maintaining the permanence of its relations to the fields, the meadows and the pastures, to the rain and the dews of heaven, to the springs and rivulets with which waters water the earth.[8]

No one before Marsh had realized the basic importance of conservation and the nature of its extraordinary and complex pattern, and no one had ever presented overwhelming facts of this kind. The book made an extraordinary impression and was reprinted many times; an enlarged edition was published in 1874. Through many years to come, *Man and Nature* was to remain both a point of departure from old ways of thinking and a rallying point for new.

William Cullen Bryant was one of the first to recognize Marsh as an authority and quoted him extensively in an editorial in the New York *Evening Post* of June 20, 1864, on the utility of trees. By the time the Yellowstone problem was being discussed, Marsh was already preparing the second edition of his book and his ideas were well known. It is more than likely that his theories influenced public opinion in favor of Yellowstone. In the second edition (1874), published under the title *The Earth as Modified by Human Action*, Marsh discussed the idea of public parks and offered a definite program for a park policy which compares very favorably with the one adopted half a century later by the National Park Service.

> It is desirable that some large and easily accessible region of American soil should remain as far as possible in its primitive condition, at once a museum for the instruction of the students, a garden for the recreation of the lovers of nature, and an asylum where indigenous trees ... plants ... beasts may dwell and perpetuate their kind.[9]

This passage suggests that Marsh had been influenced by Thoreau, who had asked in 1858, "Why should not we ... have our national preserves ... in which the bear and panther, and some even of the hunter race, may still exist, and not be 'civilized off the face of the earth,' ... for inspiration and our true re-creation? or shall we, like villains, grub them all up, poaching on our own national domains?"[10]

That trees should be planted was one of Marsh's theories but by no means the principal one. He discussed the problems of reforestation but abstained from recommending any specific plan for reforesting, because he did not consider himself an expert on such matters. Nevertheless, tree planting, which was supposed to have a certain moral value, among other things, became a favorite practice of the 1860's and 1870's. Very likely it was not only the practical and moral aspect of the movement which made it so popular; back of it perhaps was a mystical or sentimental idea which defies precise analysis. It may be that because of this special appeal the protection of trees was more widely discussed than subjects that had apparently less romantic associations, such as the conservation of soil or water. Even Thoreau's thoughts quite frequently moved in this direction when he assailed the Anglo-American because he cannot "converse with

Horace Greeley at His Home in Chappaqua, New York

the spirit of the tree he fells . . . he cuts it down [and] coins a *pine tree shilling*" (as if to signify the value of the pine).[11] Susan Fenimore Cooper shows a related approach by stressing that "independent of market prices trees . . . have importance in an intellectual-moral sense." But she also gives some remarkably practical advice, stating that it would be better to thin woods instead of blasting them, and that woods on hilltops or on rough hillsides should be preserved, just as bushes and young trees should be allowed to grow along brooks and watercourses.[12] As might be expected, Oliver Wendell Holmes had an intense and passionate fondness for trees in general and a "romantic attachment to certain trees in particular."[13] The Autocrat's arduous interest in the destruction of the Calaveras big tree, as well as the general excitement about the incident, may also have been due to the romantic spirit that was prevalent at the time.

Undoubtedly the wave of tree planting was useful in opening the eyes of the public to matters of conservation, but the foresters of more recent times have doubted that it had any long-range usefulness. They contend that the idea of planting forests was fundamentally wrong and possibly retarded the only sound way, which is by self-perpetuation of timber growth. At all events, the celebration of "Arbor Day," which was inaugurated in most of the states in the early 1870's, was a great success. The idea originated with J. Sterling Morton, who started the custom of tree planting in Nebraska in 1872. Morton's name was later given to an arboretum established by his son Joy in 1921 for the benefit of Chicago and its surroundings. Another similar institution, the Missouri Botanical Garden, started in St. Louis in 1857 by Henry Shaw, had become important for the Middle West. Shaw, an ardent nature enthusiast, had established a hardware business, but only as a means to an end. After conducting his business successfully for a number of years, he retired and established the botanical garden. In time this was combined with a research laboratory.

The Arnold Arboretum, which was to become the most outstanding research institution of its kind, had its beginnings in 1873 as a bequest by James Arnold of New Bedford to Harvard University of a 260-acre site at Jamaica Plain, which is now a part of Boston. Plans were worked out through the combined efforts of Frederick Law Olmsted, Asa Gray, and Charles Sprague Sargent in the summer of 1878, and the first tree was planted in 1886. Sargent became the director of the Arboretum and held the post for fifty-six years. It served as a laboratory for his great work, *The Silva of North America* (1891–1902), and for his report on "American Forest Trees," published in a volume of the Tenth Census of the United States. These were indeed fundamental studies, which Gifford Pinchot praised as having given "eminent service to forestry through forest botany," and as providing "basic facts for all later conservation work."[14]

Although all discussions, theories, and experiments concerning the growth of trees were useful steps toward later moves of a more comprehensive pattern, there was one incident in the 'seventies which appeared as if it were Exhibit A for the illustration of Marsh's theory. This had to do with Niagara Falls. The "terrible loveliness" of these falls had awed and enchanted visitors throughout the 1820's and 1830's, but in the following period the area around the falls had suffered decided changes. As

early as 1843 Charles Dickens had complained that the surroundings of
the falls were ugly. Mills were constructed along the water's edge after
the establishment of the first power plant in 1853; thereafter the situation
went rapidly from bad to worse. Sheds, flumes, outbuildings, and refuse
dumps offended the eye and obstructed the view. In addition, tourists
were literally ambushed by hackmen, hucksters, and sharpers who used
any catchpenny device to press customers into "sight-seeing" in order to
get as much out of their victims as they could. Bryant in *Picturesque
America,* said that Niagara resembled "a superb diamond set in lead,"[15]
and described the surroundings as lamentably vile and completely destitute of beauty.

Americans, Canadians, and even foreign visitors complained about the
undignified and sordid conditions confronting visitors to the falls until
the protests finally took the form of a public petition requesting the
United States and Canadian governments to remedy the situation. In this
movement Frederick Law Olmsted and his friend Charles Eliot Norton
took an influential part. When the matter was brought before Congress
it became a fight based on principles, in which the advocates of the two
significant movements of the century were at loggerheads. In the early
days of the machine age there were businessmen and industrialists who
in their endeavors to attain success in their enterprises mined natural resources without regard to the aesthetic values that were thus sacrificed.
Opposed to these men and their methods there were the followers of a
new philosophy, which was nurtured on Darwin's studies and those of
biologists who recognized that in harnessing natural resources man must
not proceed arbitrarily, or, as Marsh had put it, must not interfere with
the harmony of nature.

The Niagara controversy, however, was not decided in one session.
Conditions changed from year to year; discussions were renewed again
and again. In the first round the fight was more or less concerned with the
aesthetic value of the surroundings of the falls. Although Olmsted had
suspected that the destruction or neglect of the natural beauties there
would be condoned on the ground that "the injury of the scenery has
been done" and that "the motion to profit and the profit realized is the
public's verdict of acquittal,"[16] his fears for once appeared unjustified.

Fortunately, with world opinion on one side and claims for riparian
rights on the other, the balance was weighted in favor of entirely doing
away with the clutter that disfigured the natural setting of the falls. It
was felt that its removal, after all, would not be detrimental to business
and might even draw a great number of tourists. At the time Olmsted
and Norton had taken sides in the dispute they had looked beyond the
early issue and realized that future increased demand for water power

would jeopardize the very existence of the falls themselves. For this reason, Norton from the beginning considered it his duty to plead for the preservation of the falls even though he doubted that the public could be induced to recognize any responsibility in this respect. Both Norton and Olmsted regarded the matter as a moral issue, although they felt that the actual saving of the falls was of great importance in itself. Niagara was more than a scenic phenomenon of which the nation was legitimately proud; it was "one of those works of nature which is fitted to elevate and refine the character and to quicken the true sense of the relations of man with that Nature of which he is a part, to the beauty of which he should be sensitive and of whose noble works he should feel himself to be the guardian."[17]

Much later, when the regulation of power was a matter of dispute, the Niagara problem became far more complicated; but for the time being, the conservationists were victorious. As a result, in 1885 the area around the falls on the United States side was placed under the care of the state of New York, as the New York State Reservation at Niagara, and that on the Canadian side was treated similarly. The protection of this area from further desecration established a precedent; the importance of aesthetic values had been recognized and, in addition, the possibility of their coördination with the use and regulation of water power and similar business activities had been acknowledged.

However fortunate the Niagara settlement was, it did not mean that principles of conservation were already generally accepted. Occasionally some small progress was made, but as far as forests were concerned, to say nothing of soil conservation, the situation was to become far worse before it would be allowed to improve. Throughout the 'seventies the demand for lumber increased prodigiously. Forests were decimated at an unprecedented rate, and the principal victims of this looting were the unprotected forest lands of the public domain. Big companies constantly trespassed upon these timber stands to an extent which now seems unbelievable.

One of the farsighted men who took the initiative in pointing out to the government that a timber famine would ensue unless the existing supplies were protected was the Reverend Frederick Starr. In 1865 Starr made a report to the Department of Agriculture asking the government to engage in research on the entire problem of timber reproduction and to establish plantations.[18] In the same year, the Chicago *Tribune* published a series of articles in which the author predicted that the woods around the Great Lakes would someday be exhausted. And in the next few years (1867–1872) the legislatures in Wisconsin, Maine, and New York made some inquiries about the forest situation, but did little of consequence

about it. Congress, stirred to some extent, passed the Timber Culture
Act in 1873 by which settlers were granted plots of 160 acres each under
the stipulation that they would plant trees on one-fourth of the land. But
apparently the settlers lost their enthusiasm for tree planting as soon as
they became owners of their homesteads, and there was no way of enforc-
ing the conditions set forth in the act under which the land had been
granted. Of the 38,000,000 acres granted under the act probably not more
than 50,000 acres were planted with trees.

It is thus apparent that most of the measures taken before the early
'seventies or soon after were of little effect in bringing about much real
progress in the policy of conservation of natural resources. Still lacking
were a systematic approach to the problems, competent guidance in all
practical matters, and the coördination of conservation problems throughout the entire country. A start in this direction, at least as far as timber
was concerned, was made in 1873 when Franklin B. Hough, who was not
an expert but just an interested citizen, addressed the American Association for the Advancement of Science convening in Portland, Maine,
"On the Duty of the Government in the Preservation of Forests." Hough
asked that the government adopt a pattern by which the care of forests
would be assured for all time and forest resources would be used con-
servatively. He considered that a knowledge of forestry was a basic necessity and recommended that the teaching of forestry be introduced in
appropriate schools.

As a result, the association resolved to request Congress and state legislatures to act upon matters of forest preservation, and Congress in 1876
invited Hough to write a report on the forest situation in the entire
country.[19] This report, in which he endeavored to show how knowledge
gained from the experience of European countries could beneficially be
applied to the forest problems in the Western Hemisphere, later was used
as a guide by all those who endeavored to bring about proper forest management in this country. Even before Hough's survey had been completed
another document of fundamental importance was placed before the
public and was widely discussed. Major Powell, who had earlier commanded attention because of his exploits on the Colorado River, now
issued his "Report on the Lands of the Arid Region of the United States,"
published in 1878. In the years in which he was preparing for his exploration of the Colorado, Powell had begun to investigate the arid regions of
Utah and Colorado and the possibilities for their rehabilitation. In his
survey Powell suggested ways to utilize the land of the arid region and
at the same time strongly recommended that this land be reclassified
before any decisive steps were taken for its use, and that for this purpose
the government enact certain legislative measures. The passing of such

measures, which conceivably might restrict the settlement of the semi-arid middle belt of the Great Plains, an area that had already begun to attract settlers, aroused a storm of protest from interested groups. Thus it happened that at the time Powell's treatise was published its fundamental importance was not generally recognized. Later this paper came to be a classic on the subject of conservation. It resulted in the creation of the Irrigation Division of the U. S. Geological Survey in 1888 and, in 1902, the passage of the Reclamation Act providing funds for irrigation purposes. Although Powell's ideas concerning forest matters were controversial, it must be recognized that Powell was one of the first to point out the danger of forest fires and ask for fire protection for the forests. This fact needs to be stressed because Pinchot in his *Memoirs* unfortunately makes some unjustified remarks concerning Powell, asserting that he "set fire to a great alpine tree just to see it burn." This was a strange accusation, for Powell had maintained that the protection of the forests of the arid region had been "reduced to one single problem—can these forests be saved from fire?"[20]

In spite of all the fine reports which were being written and the clarifying discussions they evoked, no practical measures were actually taken, though the loss in national property represented by timber alone was phenomenal. Lack of proper management of the forests not only encouraged large-scale trespassing, but it allowed for the recurrence of devastating fires. Perhaps worst of all, it did nothing to encourage or make possible rejuvenation of forest growth where it was needed, and so cut off all possible yield. Government management and control of nationally owned timberland was not secured without a long uphill battle. When Carl Schurz became Secretary of the Interior in 1877 he made serious efforts to attain this objective because he knew that the destruction of the forests would be "the murder of the country's future prospects and progress"; but Congress was deaf, since big western timber interests were influential and forestalled legislation calling for forest protection. Schurz's "outlandish notions" about forestry were sneered at, and his opponents declared that they might perhaps do for some "picayunish German principality but not for a free country."[21] Since 1882 the American Forestry Association, which had been established in 1875 under the able leadership of John A. Warder (who first used the term "conservation" in the sense in which it is now generally understood) and of B. E. Fernow, a Prussian trained in German forestry, took an active part in this campaign. Dendrologists, foresters, botanists, and geologists, including Joseph T. Rothrock, Charles S. Sargent, William H. Brewer, and other equally competent men, also fought valiantly for timber protection. In 1898 Carl A. Schenck established the Biltmore Forest School, the first of its kind in this country. Here he trained a number of men in a profession which was entirely new. When, half a century later, in 1951, this great pioneer who had gone abroad during the wars came back to the United States, one of the great California redwood groves was named for him and twenty men of his choice who had "helped blaze forestry's early trail."[22]

Colorado, California, New York, and Pennsylvania either took protective measures themselves or asked Congress to enact them, and the federal government finally made a start in 1886 by creating a Division of Forestry and placing Fernow at the head of it. In this long-drawn-out fight between private and public interests the *Century Magazine* coöperated with the conservationists wholeheartedly, from 1889 on, by publishing editorials by Robert Underwood Johnson which gained national approval and did much to form public opinion. Finally, a rider placed on the Sundry Civil bill slipped through Congress without debate and authorized President Harrison on March 3, 1891, to establish forest reserves from the public domain. This provision, drafted by Edward A. Bowers, a special agent in the General Land Office and an ardent enthusiast for the cause of the forests, had been recommended to the President by General John W. Noble, Secretary of the Interior. Noble had been in close touch with John Muir, through the good offices of Johnson. These were the men and this was the bill that laid the foundation for the establishment of forest reserves, which were later called national forests. The first area to receive protection was the Yellowstone Timberland Reserve, comprising 1,250,000 acres. More national forest reserves were created toward the end of the terms of Grover Cleveland and William McKinley.

All the acts reserving forest lands contributed to build up a system of nationally owned and nationally administered forests. But legal ownership did not always mean protection. Wholesale stealing, overgrazing, and other kinds of spoliation continued, because at that time and for a number of years thereafter the federal government did not employ even one forester. This grotesque situation was ended by an act of Congress, June 4, 1897, which provided for "the management of forest reserves to improve and protect the forest in order to furnish a continuous supply of timber." This, then, was the end of the battle. In 1898 Gifford Pinchot took office as Chief of the Division of Forestry, with the earnest desire "to get forestry out of the dark and into the woods." At that time, as Pinchot recalled in his autobiography, timber owners held him and "his little division" in amused toleration or open contempt, and the great public knew nothing about his work.[23] But since "breaking new ground" was Pinchot's life work, the situation changed rapidly, and timbermen and the public soon learned that Pinchot would not yield to any pressure group. Under his inspired leadership the staff of the Forest Service, organized in 1905, achieved extraordinary success in a few years and gained nation-wide recognition not only for their administration of government-owned forest lands but also for the advice and guidance they gave to private timber interests. In due time the Forest Service, and somewhat later the National Park Service, were recognized as being among the most effective agents in advancing the cause of conservation of national resources.

11

The Theodore Roosevelt Era

AFTER the importance of conservation of national resources had been recognized the question arose: How far should the government go in attempting to put the theory into practice? Even well-intentioned men, influenced by their special interests, differed in their interpretation of the fundamentals of conservation. For example, the first Chief Forester of the United States, Gifford Pinchot, to whom the nation owes everlasting gratitude for his services in saving the country's forests, was completely opposed to certain ideas held by John Muir, his great contemporary. Lest there should be any misunderstanding, let it be said here that both opponents and their friends were idealists who fought high-mindedly for the public good. Nevertheless, discussions of conservation matters were heated and dramatic clashes occurred. These differences of opinion were

VIGNETTE: The Cone and Foliage of the Mammoth Trees.

to have serious consequences. The problem to be decided was whether the goal of conservation should be the attainment of utilitarian benefits alone, or whether it should include intangible factors also. Should not the psychological aspects of man's well-being be regarded as an important factor in all calculations concerning conservation? Were not the sentimental, traditional, and aesthetic factors values which should not be disregarded in the complex business of conservation? In this competition between the utilitarian and idealistic aspects of conservation, no clean-cut decision to reconcile these opposed ideas was ever devised, nor is it likely that one ever will be. The best that can be hoped for in this effort to manage the resources of nature successfully is a reasonable compromise which, by coördination of the variety of divergent interests, will make comprehensive planning possible.

One of the most important events of the early period was a meeting held in California in 1903. In May of that year, John Muir wrote to Professor C. S. Sargent, then director of the Arnold Arboretum, that "an influential man from Washington wants to make a trip into the Sierra with me, and I might be able to do some forest good in freely talking around the campfire."[1] This man from Washington was none other than Theodore Roosevelt (see pl. 60) on his first trip to the Far West. Starting at the Mariposa Big Trees, Roosevelt and Muir disappeared into the woods of the Yosemite Valley for a week end. No report has ever been published about this meeting; but from what we know of later happenings, a good deal of Roosevelt's policy concerning conservation was probably devised then, based on the counsel John Muir gave the President, who was "not building this country of ours for a day," but "to last through the ages."[2] Roosevelt knew that to attain such a goal it would be necessary to use a farsighted economic policy in the management of the forests, forbidding senseless clear-cutting and calling for a wise use of the timberlands. He advocated that the giant sequoias, forming temples grander than any human architect could devise, be conserved in their entirety because they were monuments in themselves.

Muir and Olmsted had worked devotedly in behalf of the public interest at a time when such work was sorely needed; now Theodore Roosevelt shaped the policy of the conservation program. Roosevelt's mind was well equipped for his decisive role in preserving the natural resources of the country, but it is safe to assume that his meeting with Muir and their subsequent friendship had much to do with his conception of conservation as a measure which must be adopted lest "our civilization be put to shame."[3] In spite of his presidential duties, Roosevelt, always an ardent fighter for his ideas, took time to put his mark on some of the public discussions concerning nature which were held in the first decade of the century. As it became fashionable to be interested in nature, many voices were raised in its praise. Mingled in this chorus were the "nature fakers," as they were mockingly called, who colored and unduly sentimentalized their natural history by writing stories in which animals behaved in some heroic manner. One of the jokes current about 1903 told of a book which was supposed to come out under the title "How to Tell the Animals from the Wild Flowers." In 1905 this joke was still in vogue: the *Century* carried a cartoon showing a "dandy Lion" captioned with the title quoted above.' Discussions began to take a more serious turn after Theodore Roosevelt gave an interview on the subject of nature fakers to Edward B. Clark, who published it in *Everybody's Magazine* in 1907.' The President was quoted as complaining that the persons who were misinterpreting nature and replacing facts with fakes—for example, by endowing animals with anthropomorphic powers—were hindering the work of those whose love of nature and true knowledge of it made them interpret it in the right way. Denouncing the writings of William J. Long (now completely forgotten) and Jack London, Roosevelt maintained vigorously that real knowledge and appreciation of wild things gives "added beauty and health to life." Occasionally attacks of this kind went too far, especially when, strangely enough, Burroughs attacked the artist and naturalist Ernest Thompson Seton, much to the displeasure of Roosevelt, who was one of his friends. Seton was to become one of the country's foremost nature writers, whose name meant a great deal to the generations growing up after 1900. Through his writings, based on extremely careful studies of wildlife and journals kept throughout thirty years of extensive travel in all parts of the continent, Seton did a great deal to promote love and understanding of the outdoors. He is also well remembered as the founder, in 1902, of the movement called Woodcraft Indians; this was two years before General Baden-Powell introduced the rather similar Boy Scout movement in England.'

Burroughs, at the President's invitation, accompanied Roosevelt on a trip to the Yellowstone in 1903. Although the host with his cavalry escort went full speed ahead, old Burroughs, traveling military fashion in an ambulance drawn by mules, was not left far behind. He greatly enjoyed the camping and the tramping as well as the exchange of views with the President by the evening campfire. Burroughs was not entirely enthusiastic about "the novelties of the Geyser region," feeling that the novelties wore off rapidly and that nature had made a mistake in the whole matter. And when he and Roosevelt traveled in North Dakota, the Badlands seemed to him a strange, forbidding landscape, "utterly demoralized and gone to the bad—flayed, fantastic, treeless, a riot of naked clay slopes, chimney-like buttes and dry coulees.'" It could well be that the members of the presidential party discussed the causes of such utter destruction of a landscape, and that here T. R. reconfirmed his determination that conservation was to be one of the major achievements by which his term in office was to be remembered.

Conservation Tonic

The establishment of the Grand Canyon as a national monument in 1908 was one of the most significant actions of President Roosevelt. When the Santa Fe Railway made the canyon accessible by train (1901) there were many who regretted that this last of the great wonders of the New World could now be visited so easily. As Muir once said, with a railroad in the vicinity "the finest wilderness parches as if stricken by pestilence." But even Muir did not object to the railroad to the Grand Canyon, for there the seemingly illimitable space and gigantic formations dwarfed a train into nothingness. And what an opportunity this was for the tourist! "Wonders new and old, spread invitingly open before him, boring tunnels, moving hills out of his way, eager like the devil . . . spiritualizing travel for him with lighting and steam, abolishing space and time and almost everything else."[8] By 1908 many people feared that the Grand Canyon would soon become too commercialized, and since Congress was in no mood to establish it as a park, they believed that drastic action was imperative. Roosevelt took this action: under the authority of the Antiquities Act of 1906 he proclaimed the canyon a national monument. It took Congress ten more years to establish the site more appropriately as a national park; but long before that, the canyon had become one of the favorite points of interest not only of the nation but of the world in general.

The President's move in creating the Grand Canyon National Monument was a big step forward, but it was too much to expect that spontaneous actions of this kind would be taken whenever they were needed. Idealistic proposals, which frequently originated in the camps of Muir or Burroughs or in the *Century Magazine,* usually met with opposition. The *Century's* associate editor, Robert Underwood Johnson, over a period of forty years (1873–1913) valiantly defended these ideas. One of the greatest pioneers of the conservation movement was Enos A. Mills, who was self-taught, a pure idealist, independent, and endowed with extraordinary will power. Mills took up land in the Long's Peak area and turned his homestead into a resort for nature lovers. At his inn, opened in 1901, a poster made it known that there was to be "no music, dancing or card playing." Instead, the host would lecture to his guests in the evening and take them on climbing tours by day or night, summer or winter, on foot or on snowshoes. In 1905 Mills went East, at his own expense, to lecture on forest protection. Between 1907 and 1909, he came into the national limelight after Theodore Roosevelt named him federal lecturer on forestry. Mills spent the last part of his life in promoting the establishment of a Rocky Mountain national park. Although the plan was finally successful, it was for a long time bitterly opposed by federal forestry authorities. This is an example of the difficulties experienced by the conservation movement in its fledgling years.

It is obvious that the lumber industry and various speculative groups interested in the use of water power and other natural resources would oppose forest protection of any kind. However, opposition to it by the forestry group which was just gaining influence and was actively led by powerful Gifford Pinchot is less understandable. Their antagonism was directed against all varieties of conservation which were not strictly utilitarian or economic. Conservation without the utilization of natural resources seemed futile to the Chief Forester and his friends. Since Roosevelt had, as he said, put in the keeping of Pinchot all his conscience in the matter of forestry, and it can be presumed in other problems of conservation as well, this intimate friend of the President became the "brain trust" of conservation. Even though Roosevelt loyally backed men like Muir and Burroughs, the controversy between utilitarian and aesthetic issues became more acute. The fight came into the open when San Francisco asked permission to flood the Hetch Hetchy Valley, a part of the Yosemite area, in order to develop a source of supply for the city's water system and, as it was later discovered, for commercial purposes. Beginning about 1906, the *Century Magazine,* Muir, and many other men of high ideals, such as J. Horace McFarland and Frederick Law Olmsted Jr., fought for years against the project. George P. Marsh was quoted by opponents of such vandalism, and when *Scribner's* reprinted his book in 1907, the *Century Magazine* considered this a very valuable service to the public. However, all the agitation fanned into flame by the "nature fakirs," a term applied to those who had fought against the nature fakers a few years before, came to naught, for Pinchot and his group played into the hands of San Francisco. The long-drawn-out battle came to an end in 1913 when Congress passed an act granting San Francisco the use of Hetch Hetchy Valley as a reservoir. Interestingly enough, Pinchot in his memoirs, completed before his death in 1946, does not mention the Hetch Hetchy controversy, although he had been involved in it and it had been discussed for years—at times very heatedly. Johnson, however, Pinchot's opponent in the matter, in his memoirs published in 1923 printed a letter from Pinchot encouraging the city of San Francisco to go ahead in its pursuit of the project, which showed that Pinchot had played a prominent part in the affair.[9]

Perhaps one of the reasons for the loss of the Hetch Hetchy battle was the inability of the opponents of the measure to agree on principles and to coördinate their interests. One remarkable thing about the case was that, though the subject of the debate was a remote valley in California which few in the East had seen, interest in it became nation-wide. Very likely it had dawned on the public that what was happening in California today might be repeated in the East tomorrow. Indeed, as we shall see, Niagara was to be the next center of bitter argument.

In the early 1900's the public became increasingly aware of the dangers, tangible and intangible, threatening the natural resources of the country, and of the advisability of speedy adoption of conservation measures. To those who lived through the first decade of the century it later seemed that a real awakening had taken place in those years; indeed, never before had there been so widespread a realization of the need for spiritual and aesthetic values to bring the life of the people to a higher level. The names of the organizations which grew up at that time are indicative of the ideas which were fostered one after another. The American Park and Outdoor Art Society (established in 1897) and the American League for Civic Improvement (established in 1901) merged in 1904 into the American Civic Association, which became a powerful organization. In 1935 this society combined with the National Conference on City Planning (established in 1909) and became the American Planning and Civic Association. Under the leadership of Franklin Delano Roosevelt, Ulysses S. Grant III, and Horace M. Albright, this association was and still is "dedicated to the education of the American people to an understanding and appreciation of local, state, regional and national planning for the best use of . . . natural resources." The members of the association, most of whom are leaders in their communities, watch all developments in city planning and conservation and take action whenever they believe it to be necessary. Under such guidance, new city plans have been developed, zoning laws have been introduced, and parks for recreational and outdoor activities have been inaugurated. This group has also tried to keep down the growth of city slums and industrial enterprises on city land. In Washington the American Institute of Architects in 1901 promoted the revival of the original L'Enfant plan of the city; in Philadelphia the City Park Association began to bring city parks and parkways into a coördinated system, and in Chicago, Daniel Burnham presented his great and farsighted plan to improve and beautify the city.

One of the leading men in this magnificent campaign to make the country more livable through better utilization of land was J. Horace McFarland, who had founded the American Civic Association and was its first president from 1904 to 1923. McFarland began as a self-styled salesman, going from city to city and coast to coast trying to "sell" his "Harrisburg story"; that is, he told all who would listen how the city of Harrisburg had lowered the high mortality rate from typhoid fever by cleaning the polluted Susquehanna River. Speaking in more than five hundred towns, McFarland showed slides of the city before and after its replanning. In this way the so-called "city beautiful" idea was created and the slogan became nationally known. Although the expression was useful, McFarland did not like it because he felt that the aesthetic factor was not so important as the idea of making cities sound in every respect.

The people in villages, like those in the cities, began to feel the urge to improve their environment, and village improvement societies were founded. Large parts of the countryside close to cities had been divested of their original simplicity and beauty by inroads from the city. Industrial developments or cheap housing on the fringes of urban districts had not been built up in any coördinated way and had given these areas a mongrel aspect. Now in many places efforts were made to correct a situation which had long since gotten out of hand.

Also in the early 1900's the garden-club movement was started, and women in all parts of the country mobilized to improve residential sections and to rehabilitate run-down estates. In a few years many of these estates were again pleasant to live in, and in time a number of them paid for their upkeep by attracting tourists. Garden weeks held in Richmond, Nashville, Natchez, and many other places gradually became nationally known, and they still draw large crowds of visitors from all parts of the nation. Establishments such as the Biltmore Estate near Asheville, and later the Bellingrath Gardens near Mobile, since they have been opened to the public have attracted many visitors, some of whom have journeyed many miles out of their way in order to enjoy their singular beauty.

The garden clubs were farsighted enough to take an active part in the conservation movement; they published literature on the subject and in many other ways tried to acquaint the public with the principle of conservation. With garden clubs and civic associations working ardently to obtain green belts around the city and parks within it, and thus eradicate the open sores of slum districts, it was only natural that movements should develop for making larger units of the outdoors more accessible to nature lovers. The Appalachian Mountain Club, established in 1876, worked in this direction. Using voluntary help offered by enthusiastic nature lovers, it built camps and trails along the mountain ranges. On the Pacific Coast similar tasks were undertaken by the Sierra Club, which was established in 1892 under the leadership of John Muir. The more complex task of the American Scenic and Historic Preservation Society, founded in 1895, was carried out mainly through the initiative of Andrew H. Green, who had taken part in the action to protect Niagara Falls. In the days when the federal government was not in a position to act in such a capacity, this society was generally considered the legitimate adviser in all matters pertaining to the protection of scenic and historic sites.

All these movements, though fostered independently, were working toward a policy of conservation in which utilitarian and idealistic points of view were gradually becoming coördinated, not always by preconceived plan but rather as occasion demanded. Then came the epochal year of 1908, which marked the beginning of a concerted national policy of conservation. According to Gifford Pinchot, in that year he gave to the term "conservation" the connotation it is now generally understood to have: a comprehensive and well-planned management of natural resources of every character, based on sound ethical and economic grounds."[10] The great event of that year, as far as conservation is concerned, took place in May; this was the Conference of Governors at the White House, to which Theodore Roosevelt invited the governors of states and a number of other officials and interested men. The agenda for this conference embraced matters which in the mind of the President were the weightiest problems before the nation at that time. Roosevelt knew that the natural resources of the country were in danger of being exhausted if the old reckless and wasteful methods of exploitation were permitted to continue; the government must take action to bring about the renewal and rehabilitation of resources. Soil exhaustion, erosion, timber famine, scarcity of water, and diminution of wildlife were problems which were all closely connected. The interrelationship of these made it impossible to solve each problem singly; all must be treated as part of a comprehensive plan. If a way out of the great difficulties was to be found that would benefit the people as a whole, individual rights must be subordinated to the rights of communities and states. Here the President found himself of the same opinion as Oliver Wendell Holmes, Associate Justice of the Supreme Court, who a short while before had handed down the opinion that the State had the right to protect natural resources "irrespective of the assent or dissent of the private owners of the land most immediately concerned."[11]

Undoubtedly Pinchot made up the agenda of the conference, though it is very likely that the Inland Waterways Commission, which had convened the previous year, had been influential in determining what subjects would be discussed. But it should not be forgotten that in 1906 Robert Underwood Johnson had suggested to the President that a conference of governors be held to make decisions about protecting the watersheds of the Appalachians. Johnson repeated his suggestions in a number of letters to the President and to Pinchot; there can therefore be no doubt that the idea of interesting the governors in the matter of protection of natural resources came from Johnson. Pinchot elaborated upon the idea by making the entire matter of conservation a subject for deliberation and discussion.

Who first suggested that a conference of this kind be held is not of particular interest except for the fact that Pinchot directed that the discussion be confined to the utilitarian aspects of conservation and thus forestalled any suggestions that might have been presented by Johnson and his group. Yet there was one moment when the ideals of the other camp were brought brilliantly into focus. That Pinchot's action in thus limiting the discussion was deliberate is evident from the list of those other than governors whom he invited to participate; Johnson and his friends were not included in it. The names of John Muir, B. E. Fernow, director of the Forestry Department at Cornell University, Charles S. Sargent, director of the Arnold Arboretum, and E. A. Bowers, the author of the clause in the bill to put forests under protection, also were not on the list, nor were the names of any of the men who had fought for protective measures through the years. Johnson himself took part only by chance in his capacity as representative of the *Century Magazine*. Two other men had been invited as heads of their associations: J. Horace McFarland, President of the American Civic Association, and George F. Kunz, President of the American Scenic and Historic Preservation Society.

The conference was solemnly opened by the President with a speech which demonstrated his broad understanding of the scope of the conference. Then one meeting after another rolled on smoothly, and by the time of the fourth session there was no longer any doubt that the conference was to become the foundation stone of the future conservation policy. The subject scheduled for discussion at this session was land resources. After the speaker of the day had discussed problems of irrigation and the meeting had been opened for general discussion, the chairman announced a change in program. He said that Mr. McFarland would have the floor, but he did not announce the subject of his talk. Why McFarland was given the floor at this time is difficult to understand; certainly his subject had nothing to do with the current discussion. It may have been that the speaker had to be fitted in somewhere and this session seemed as good as any. McFarland's address was short but was so dynamic that it must have had an extraordinary effect. All the previous speakers had talked facts and had brought forth weighty figures based on sound commercial and scientific knowledge, but here was a speaker advancing ideas about intangible values: "I would urge this assembly to consider the essential value of one of America's greatest resources—her unmatched natural scenery." McFarland pointed out that it was all very well to discuss the possibilities of conservation, but to him "the true glory of the United States must rest, and has rested, upon a deeper foundation than that of her purely material resources. It is the love of the country that lights and keeps glowing the holy fire of patriotism. And this love is excited primarily by the beauty of the country." Continuing his speech, McFarland did not mince his words; he spoke of the "all too common unnatural scenery of man's careless commercial filth!" The iron manufacturers could get away from the ugliness they had created, but the working man had to live in the squalor of ugly and unhealthful cities. Although Andrew Carnegie sat in the audience, the speaker did not hesitate to mention that this gentleman found "the scenery about Skibo Castle much more restful" than his place of business. One sentence was addressed to Gifford Pinchot: "Hetch Hetchy Valley of the Yosemite region belongs to all America and not to San Francisco alone." The speaker closed with these words: "We have for a century . . . stood actually, if not ostensibly, for an uglier America; let us here and now resolve, for every patriotic and economic reason, to stand openly and solidly for a more beautiful and therefore a more prosperous America."[12]

How the speech was accepted is not known, except for the reaction of one person, the aged George Wilson, then the Secretary of Agriculture. Wilson went to McFarland after the meeting and said: "Those are good words, my boy. The world will forget what the rest of us say here, but the women and the children will read and remember those words."[18] McFarland had indeed put a great idea on record, and in time, like other previous suggestions made at the conference, it was incorporated in the code of conservation policies accepted by the nation.

In later sessions Governor Charles Evans Hughes spoke about conservation in the state of New York, and George F. Kunz set forth the relation between the conservation of the principal natural resources of the state and the preservation of landscape beauty. Both speakers presented their thoughts ably and gave added impulsion to the principles McFarland had put forward so forcefully. In the three-volume report issued by the National Conservation Committee appointed by the President to carry on the work of the conference were printed detailed reports on the suggestions and proposals made at the meetings. George Kunz was given a small space in it, but none was given to McFarland. Apparently he had been unable to convince the commission that his ideas had real value.

Undaunted, McFarland did not hesitate to take up a number of causes which had to do with conservation and which otherwise would have failed from lack of support. One of these was the continued fight to save the Hetch Hetchy Valley. Other causes for which McFarland worked in the next few years were the consolidation of the national parks and the saving of Niagara Falls. But before considering them in detail, let us turn our attention to a development which at the time of the governor's conference had already shown signs of becoming a problem.

The automobile had been introduced about 1895, and by 1909 the number of registered cars had soared to more than 3,000,000. The "tin Lizzy," which was first put on the market in that year, became so popular that, over the years, Ford sold 15,000,000 cars of this model alone. In 1955 there were 51,000,000 passenger cars averaging one car to 2.7 persons. For Thomas Wolfe and his contemporaries, riding in an automobile was "like soaring through the air, or finding wings you never knew you had before. It was like something we had always . . . dreamed of finding, and now we had it like a dream come true."[14] How the enormous sales of cars during the 1920's changed the entire life of the nation has often been discussed. Here it is pertinent only to consider the manner in which the automobile affected the behavior of the public toward nature.

After the introduction of the canalboat and the railroad, the turnpikes were all but deserted by those who went to the country for pleasure. Except for the people who had taken up permanent residence in the country, group entertainment in the rural resorts or at the seaside was about the only means of enjoyment of nature. Vacationists went to these places en masse and lived en masse. The difficulties arising from this kind of approach to nature have already been mentioned. The introduction of the car changed all this. True, it was a long time before roads became adequate or inns and hotels were able to offer sufficient facilities to house the new and steadily enlarging crowds; but to people who really wanted to enjoy the outdoors and enjoy it in their own fashion, these impediments were trifling. In a way, this attitude was similar to that of travelers of an earlier day, when the phrase "poetry of traveling" was popular. Then romantically inclined citizens explored the countryside by stage or on foot, like Thomas Cole, whom we remember as marching along the road, flute in hand. Now, however, there was a difference of real importance. The earlier traveler was not likely to disturb the beautiful scenery he saw, nor had he much opportunity to do so. His counterpart in the early twentieth century was of a different mold. Frequently lacking in tact or the instinct for doing things the proper way, he enjoyed the scene but did not stop to think of the damage he might do to it; nor did it occur to him to protest against the actions of speculators in building monstrous hotels or cheap shacks to accommodate tourists, or in using other ill-advised schemes in catering to the new crowds of customers. As the crowds grew, the landscape was marred still further. For instance, in many places, debris—such as bottles, cans, and paper left behind after a picnic on a mountaintop or at the lakeside—marred beauty spots to such a degree that the places were wholly objectionable to those who came later. In the countryside there was no army of cleaners like those in New York who pick up scattered sheets of the voluminous Sunday editions of the papers on a Monday morning in Central Park—or, for that matter, in any other city park.

But there was damage to more concrete things than aesthetic sensibilities. The new crowds were dangerous; they brought fire hazards, damaged underbrush, polluted streams, and made themselves a nuisance in many ways. Summer guests and campers of this type—particularly those from the cities who visited nearby recreational facilities—unprepared for life in the out-of-doors, became a potential danger in all parts of the country. The new outdoor movement was perfectly sound at its roots, but it needed to be channeled. It was essential that certain areas be designated for the use of the public; and to avoid friction, rules for the use of these sites must be made and certain facilities provided. In time this kind of regulation would improve the behavior of the crowds eager for outdoor recreation. There was no one who saw these needs more clearly than J. Horace McFarland. From his work in the rehabilitation of cities, McFarland knew that playgrounds were essential for city-weary citizens, and from the beginning he envisioned a great system of parks which would answer this need. The city and county parks were to be places to which the people could come to be refreshed; in these open spaces they could see the sky and delight in pure breezes. State parks—and even more so, national parks—would serve the even greater purpose of offering spiritual values to the visitors, for therein "lies the whole impulse of patriotism, on which the safety of the nation depends."[15]

Strangely enough, opportunity came in 1910 under President Taft when Richard A. Ballinger, the Secretary of the Interior whom Taft put into office in 1909, asked McFarland to confer with him on the preparation of a bill by which a special bureau to administer the national parks might be established. This invitation was a gratifying outcome of the proposals McFarland and his organization had made through the years concerning the codification of federal laws pertaining to national parks so as to provide for the uniform control and management of these parks. When the call came from Secretary Ballinger, McFarland immediately consulted with Frederick Law Olmsted, Jr., who, he felt, could give better advice about legislation for the organization of the national parks than any other man in the country. Olmsted had already devised and carried out a number of city plans and park projects in Boston, Pittsburgh, Baltimore, and elsewhere. Indeed, he has through the years been the top-ranking authority in park matters; still active, he is now serving as an adviser to the State of California in matters of parks and comprehensive city planning. Since Olmsted not only followed his father as a great landscape artist but also inherited his public-mindedness, he was glad to offer his counsel on this matter. Olmsted was much in accord with McFarland, for the Hetch Hetchy case and the problems of Niagara Falls had brought them together in the same camp. Olmsted recognized immediately that Ballinger's draft was merely a convenient instrument to centralize the administration of the parks in a way by which special-interest groups might be benefited. Nothing was said in it about the possibility of future development of the parks, nor was the purpose of the parks defined. At the same time, Olmsted felt that the President's attitude in the heated Ballinger-Pinchot controversy, which had been discussed from coast to coast on the front pages of newspapers throughout the whole year 1910, provided no guarantee that either President Taft or his Secretary of the Interior could be relied upon to hold firm on principles of conservation as they were understood by Olmsted and his friends. Therefore, to meet any possible challenge, Olmsted suggested the insertion of a passage which for all time clearly defined the purpose of the parks, monuments, and reservations; namely, that they shall not at any time be used in any way contrary to the purpose thereof as agencies for promoting public recreation and public health through the use and enjoyment by the people of the same parks, monuments and reservations, and of the natural scenery and objects of interest therein, or in any way detrimental to the value thereof for such purpose.

That McFarland, who had stressed the value of natural scenery so strongly at the governors' conference, would agree with this new version was to be expected, but it was rather surprising that Ballinger offered no objections to it. The passage therefore went into the draft and remained in the final bill of 1916, though with an improvement suggested by Olmsted himself. This amendment stressed the point that the characteristic values of a park or monument should be enjoyed by the public, but only through such means as will conserve these values "unimpaired," for enjoyment by future generations. In January, 1911, the original bill was presented to Congress in two little-differing versions, but neither of these passed. However, since there was hope for reintroduction of the bill, promotion of the measure was continued through the following years. At times, discussions assumed a rather dramatic character, though controversies were carried on at a high level owing to the fact that both those in favor and those against the bill were moved by entirely idealistic motives. As might have been expected, the strongest opposition came from the Forest Service. Although Gifford Pinchot was no longer active, he was still influential, and his successor, H. S. Graves, always remained close to him. Fortunately, Walter L. Fisher, formerly the president of the National Conservation League who had replaced Richard Ballinger, was willing to consider arguments brought forth by both parties. The point of view of the foresters who wished to combine the national forests with the national parks under the aegis of the Department of Agriculture was, of course, understandable. In many places, parks and forests were geographically close, and some even overlapped; problems such as maintenance of roads and fire protection were identical; and a separation of administrations seemed unnecessary duplication. As Graves pointed out, he had always clearly distinguished between an area which needed protection, such as the Grand Canyon, and others which did not suffer by being commercialized.

Up to the time President Taft left office the bill had not been accepted. Discussions went on for years, and the bill was reshaped several times. Finally, under Woodrow Wilson, it was passed on August 25, 1916.

Conservation

BEFORE we go on with the story of the National Park Service and discuss the conservation of natural resources in general, it would be well to evaluate the matter of conservation up to this point.

Until after the middle of the nineteenth century a great variety of individual trends of thought went to make up the American attitude toward nature. These were significant as long as the nature with which man came in contact was more or less in its virgin state and he had not impaired its balance in any way. However, individual causes of conflicts between man

VIGNETTE: What Man Does to One of the Most Beautiful Gifts of Nature.

and nature lost their importance as the two came more often into contact and the resultant disturbances became increasingly greater.

The turning point came when George P. Marsh published his book *Man and Nature*. With his comprehensive view of problems he showed that as long as the exploitation of natural resources for economic or political reasons was allowed to continue with scarcely any restrictions, man would never take into account aesthetic, scientific, and spiritual values in assaying the treasures of nature. As it became increasingly difficult for man to live in harmony with his surroundings, it became forcefully clear that the new idea of conserving natural resources was of basic importance in determining his attitude toward nature. This novel idea upset traditional thinking, and there was much bitter discussion, misunderstanding, and bad feeling throughout the first two decades of this century, with the result that until the early 'twenties the fostering of conservation was in the nature of a crusade. However, after the conservation movement began to rally its forces in the 'twenties, it rapidly acquired many new advocates. The importance of conservation was impressed upon the public by the disaster in the western Dust Bowl in the 1930's. This suddenly and forcefully taught the nation that nature could not be relied upon to produce and yield crops as an assembly line produced automobiles. Terrifying photographs and realistic paintings of abandoned farms and rotting carcasses brought the calamity to the attention not only of persons concerned with economic matters, but also of those more interested in aesthetic and spiritual values. As an immediate consequence, the Soil Conservation Service was established in 1935 and charged with the duty of conserving soil and water and assisting farmers and ranchers in matters of conservation.

The mass of literature on conservation published in the years following the calamity received nation-wide attention and served to keep the matter constantly before the public. But it took two wars and the dread feeling of uncertainty of the future to focus the attention of the country on the problem of conservation so clearly that the citizen as an individual came to consider the problem his own and not merely the responsibility of certain societies and agencies.[1] Books such as those by Richard Lieber, William Vogt, and Henry F. Osborn presented the basic formula of the problem, and popular magazines discussed the subject. Unfortunately there has been a tendency to belittle such efforts and to denounce writers who have pointed out the serious need for protective measures. These men have been accused of disturbing the peace, evoking unnecessary fear, and in general acting as if they were prompted by some strange, sadistic urge to prophesy doom although, according to some of their critics, there is really nothing to fear, because science will in due time take care of all of mankind's needs. Fortunately, this complacency is being counteracted by the work of a great number of agencies, committees, societies, and leaders who are taking part in the tremendous struggle to further the idea of conservation.

In order to coördinate ways and means of coping with present-day problems of conservation, a group of persons interested in such problems organized Resources for the Future in 1952 and named as its chairman Horace M. Albright. With only a small staff this agency set out immediately to arrange for a national resources conference. This conference was held in Washington, D.C., in December, 1953, and met with wide and enthusiastic response. As one of the results, the Ford Foundation gave a five-year grant to Resources for the Future for research and a program of education to foster better understanding of major problems pertaining to natural resources. Conservation[2] as generally understood means the husbanding of natural resources; that is, the developing of these resources in accord with the best public interest, restoring to productivity those that have been depleted and guarding them against further depletion. Some of these activities have been discussed in preceding pages, but there still remain for consideration myriad currents which shape the movement. These have been and are being treated in specialized literature in an ever-increasing number of publications. Here it is necessary only to convey a very general idea of the evolution of the conservation movement and to follow a few of the main lines it has taken.

We have considered the damage done to wildlife toward the end of the nineteenth century and the concern about it expressed by early sportsmen and nature lovers. The difficulties presented by this problem have increased over the years. When we realize that in 1950 alone the amount spent by hunters and fishermen for their activities was about $9,200,000,[3] there is no question that protective measures must be taken to insure the reproduction of wildlife.

Although forest conservation has been practiced ever since the Theodore Roosevelt era, it is obvious that the forests could not be fully protected all at once. As late as 1933 a comprehensive "National Plan for American Forests" was submitted to Congress by the Secretary of Agriculture. Prepared by the U. S. Forest Service and known as the Copeland Report, it presented an encyclopedic analysis of the forest situation and offered a complete program for the management of all forest resources on the principle of multiple use for the benefit of all concerned. The report met with a mixed reception. It did, to be sure, bring to the attention of the public the responsibilities of private stewardship. Since 1933 more studies and reports concerning the forest situation have been made. It cannot be said that the downward trends have been reversed, but it appears that they have at least been arrested, and measures have been taken for their reversal. Private owners no longer practice the "cut-out-and-get-out" policy through ignorance of the consequences.

The basic importance of soil conservation has become so obvious that to most people the work of the Soil Conservation Service represents the

"I WENT INTO THE VAST FOREST WITH NOTHING BUT SOME POWER-SAWS, BULL-DOZERS, AND LUMBER-JACKS, AND BY GEORGE, I CAME OUT WITH A FORTUNE!"

Lumber Business

essence of "conservation." Next to soil conservation, matters concerning water—flood control, power and irrigation projects, and the prevention of pollution—command a large part of the attention of the public. The Tennessee Valley Authority and some problems concerning Niagara Falls which fall in this category will be discussed in subsequent pages.

The federal government has the responsibility of managing and safeguarding public lands and national resources in such a way that, as President Eisenhower stated in his message to Congress on July 31, 1953, they will be available to the people "not only for this but for future generations." However, because of the frequently controversial character of matters concerning the public lands and natural resources it is difficult to shape policies for the necessary regulations. For instance, although "multiple use" of natural forests is legally allowable, it is quite obvious that not all of these forests can be put to such use. Sometimes compromises can be made. But all demands made by interested groups to have portions of the public domain turned over to them to serve their special interests cannot be satisfied or these lands will soon be depleted. Of the many problems which have to do with the complex subject of the public domain we will discuss only those that concern the wilderness areas.

Consideration of the various elements of the problem of conservation gives rise to the question whether a common purpose might not be found for conservation activities that is not a purely economic one. It is beginning to be understood that conservation is not solely a matter of technical or material importance, and that those sentimental and aesthetic points of view which were of great value in stimulating interest in nature throughout the nineteenth century no longer are the only ones to be taken into account. At present, social and ethical points of view have come into focus and must also be recognized as important.

The problem which presents itself is this: Will the people in general as well as those deeply concerned with the land, both individuals and groups, act in conformity with principles of conservation that are based on higher standards than materialism and personal likes and dislikes?

Among the great conservation organizations, the National Park Service is one of the most complex, since it touches on all the activities of conservation we have previously discussed. We have followed the efforts to establish an organization of this sort until about 1915 when McFarland was trying to steer the bill between opposing forces in Congress and Olmsted was securing support for it through his far-reaching influence with people and corporations.[1]

On August 25, 1916, the act to establish the National Park Service (H.R. 8668) was at last signed by President Woodrow Wilson. Franklin K. Lane, Secretary of the Interior (1913–1920), was to head the new bureau. Lane hailed from California and unfortunately was committed to the cession of the Hetch Hetchy Valley to San Francisco as a reward to California for giving its vote to Wilson. Although he was not greatly interested in matters of conservation, he appointed in 1916 as his assistant in charge of park matters a man who, as it turned out, later became the most inspired leader the fledgling National Park Service could have had. This came about in a strange manner. The Secretary had received a complaint from Stephen T. Mather about the administration of Sequoia National Park, and in reply Lane had told Mather simply that if he did not like the way the parks were being operated he should come to Washington and manage them in the way he saw fit. The surprising outcome of this exchange of views was that Mather was appointed assistant to the Secretary of the Interior and later was made director of the system of national parks and given the task of reorganizing them. Aided by his untiring assistant Horace M. Albright (who succeeded Mather after his untimely death in 1929), Mather went about his assignment with so much understanding and imagination that the system as it works today still shows the results of his clear vision and foresight. It has been reported that Mather in the first year of his appointment spent $40,000 of his own funds because of the lack of government appropriations. What Pinchot's name is to those interested in forests, Mather's is to all those who helped develop the park system and those who enjoy the parks—a potent and lasting inspiration. Just as Muir once talked about forest needs in his conversations with Theodore Roosevelt, so Mather and his staff began to tell the nation about the problems of the national parks. The main thought they tried to drive home was that "reserved places of great natural beauty were as important in everybody's daily life as those utilized areas that took care of physical needs," because "natural scenery . . . makes better men and women, physically, and mentally and spiritually."[5] As long as Muir lived he was one of the keenest propagators of the national park idea, and his book *Our National Parks* (which has been frequently reprinted since it was first published in 1901) spread the fame of these parks far and wide.

When Mather set out on his task he enlisted the services of Robert Sterling Yard, who carried on his park work with enthusiasm and devotion, writing much of the literature given out by the new bureau. Among the many ardent helpers who coöperated in the great task was Mrs. John Dickinson Sherman, who was chairman of the conservation committee section of the General Federation of Women's Clubs. Through her committee Mrs. Sherman had the opportunity of stimulating 2,500,000 women to active interest in park matters.

Mather well knew that in order to induce visitors to go to the national parks and repeat such visits it was necessary to improve physical conditions in the parks. Living accommodations and other facilities must be provided, and the road system must be improved. Congress, however, did not become accustomed to appropriating adequate sums for such purposes before 1924. In addition to making plans for the housing, feeding, and transportation of visitors, Mather and his imaginative assistant Albright conceived and developed the idea of a master plan for each area which not only made possible long-range planning of all improvements but also contained provisions for interpreting the park to the people. These plans represented the coöperative efforts of engineers, landscape architects, technicians, scientists, historians, and other specialists. Because the National Park system was conceived as one great unit, the Park Service was able to make full use of Civilian Conservation Corps camps and other agencies which offered their services to both federal and state conservation and preservation work during and after the years of depression (1933–1942). With this unexpected and efficient help the parks were able to carry out many of the programs incorporated in their master plans far more speedily than had been anticipated.

The master plan, however, was only one feature of the over-all policy Mather deemed necessary for the administration of the parks in accordance with the best public interest. Private rights, grazing, forestry, wildlife, and other matters—many of them highly controversial in character and affected by powerful lobbies—were gradually being regulated from the standpoint of public interest. The use of land in the national parks was regarded as in a completely different category from that in national forests. This distinction was necessary because even men like Gifford Pinchot often misinterpreted the principles established by Mather and his friends. Pinchot and his group believed that the forest areas which were completely protected from cutting were being mismanaged and were not being properly used. The leading men in the Park Service soon realized the need for a program of interpretation that would obviate misconceptions of this kind. It was necessary to educate the public to the idea underlying the conservation work in parks in general, and in each park in particular. Before this difficult and delicate task could be undertaken, it was necessary to determine the subjective value of each park and to find out whether the combined group of parks could be considered representative of the outstanding phenomena of nature in this hemisphere.

By 1917 the National Park Service had worked out a definite program, had issued guide folders, and had made conducted tours and lectures available in certain parks. In time, museums were established in some of the parks, each one being developed individually in accordance with the particular needs of the site. The "focal point" and "trailside" museum offered selected material in an attractive way near areas that seemed deserving of special attention. Quite different from the usual natural history museums with their morguelike atmosphere, these new museums in their fresh and unpretentious way prompted the visitor to observe his surroundings in the light of his newly acquired knowledge when he left the museum for the out-of-doors. All these experiments in visual education were made possible through the coöperation of the American Association of Museums and the Smithsonian Institution, and by funds from the Rockefeller Foundation and ideas offered by such men as Hermon C. Bumpus, John C. Merriam, and Harold C. Bryant. But museums alone were not sufficient to educate the park visitors or to make the public appreciate all that the parks had to offer. Only the spoken word could do this.

How successful this method could be had been demonstrated by university professors who had been visiting the parks and studying the great outdoors with their students ever since John Wesley Powell had started the practice in 1867. These men had found "books in the running brooks, sermons in stones . . ." But dealing with the general public was a different matter, because most of the visitors did not come to the parks in organized groups and, as Robert Sterling Yard expressed it, they wished to get their education wrapped in a "coating of pleasure and emotion."[6] The Park Service accordingly engaged young scientists to instruct the visitors to the parks and give them the kind of information they wanted. From this beginning and largely due to the advice given and the example set by Enos. A. Mills and Harold C. Bryant, the "ranger naturalist" emerged. This friend and teacher of the park visitor has become a popular figure, known to everyone from coast to coast. Youth especially is attracted to these trimly attired tutors and looks up to them. The adult also admires the pleasant way these men dispense their knowledge of geology, botany, zoölogy, and other branches of natural history at those informal gatherings around the evening campfire which visitors love to attend. In spite of the seemingly casual manner in which the ranger gives out his information, he is equipped with thorough academic knowledge and training. Mather did not limit his work to shaping the program of the national parks and putting it into effect. He believed that his bureau should also be a clearinghouse for park projects that were not part of the federal system. Many of the sites suggested to him for the establishment of parks did not measure up to the standard for national parks but had scenic and recreational value and other qualifications which made them perfectly suitable for state parks. By extending his interest to problems of this kind, Mather was able to make the National Park administration serve a double purpose. States might benefit from the experience of the federal administration, and the burden of too large crowds at national parks might to some extent be diverted to state parks. In 1921 Mather inaugurated the National Conference of State Parks as a forum for the discussion of these problems.

The idea of creating state parks was not a new one, for as far back as 1891 Minnesota had set aside Itasca Park, where the headwaters of the Mississippi originate. In the same year the park idea had been taken up by some public-minded men in Massachusetts, among whom were Charles W. Eliot, Oliver Wendell Holmes, Thomas Wentworth Higginson, Frederick Law Olmsted, and Francis Parkman. They established "The Trustees of Public Reservations" with the idea of providing by private endowment for the "preservation and dedication to public enjoyment of such scenes and sites in Massachusetts as possess either uncommon beauty or historical interest." With this organization as a pattern, years later the British National Trust was established.[7]

In New York State, Verplanck Colvin, a surveyor and scientist, had since 1865 enthusiastically explored the Adirondacks at his own expense. As Joel T. Headley had done much earlier, he drew attention to the scenic beauty of the region; he also tried to make the public recognize the necessity of setting aside a part of the area as a watershed. This campaign bore fruit several years later, when Olmsted worked for the same idea; as a result, the Adirondacks were made a state forest reserve in 1884. When New York State adopted a new constitution in 1894, conservation matters were deemed of enough importance to be incorporated in it. Thus the constitution directed that the reserve in the Adirondacks and another one in the Catskills be kept "as wild forest lands," and that the timber therein should never be sold, removed, or destroyed.[8] Although some sections of these reserves were established as state parks as early as 1892, the idea of the recreational value of the areas did not enter the project until 1903. Since then most of the other states have adopted this idea, and state parks for the purpose of recreation have been established in all parts of the country. The state of Indiana has given us one of the best examples. The movement took root there in 1916 under the enthusiastic leadership of Colonel Richard Lieber, who had the idea of making the state park system entirely self-supporting.

In California the efforts of influential groups to preserve some of the menaced stands of sequoias met with general approval. Stephen Mather was among the first to take action in behalf of the big trees, and the *National Geographic Magazine* also was an early sponsor of the cause. As a result, some groves of the big trees, notably the Giant Forest, were added to Sequoia National Park. In 1917 the fight for protection of the sequoias was taken up by the Save-the-Redwoods League under the inspired leadership of John C. Merriam and Newton B. Drury, who later served ably as director of the National Park Service during and after the very difficult years of World War II.

In spite of all complaints voiced about the "tree murder" in 1852, North Calaveras Grove with its more than 160 giants was not placed under protection as a state park until 1931. South Calaveras Grove with an even richer stand of almost a thousand big trees was until recently in the hands of a lumber company; but in 1954 this grove, too, was saved.[9] Fortunately, the *Sequoia gigantea* is not profitable for lumbering Since there may be as much as 80 per cent of waste when these trees are felled, the inducement to cut them is somewhat limited; yet 200 of the species were cut down in a privately owned stand in 1950.

The intensive and steadily rising demand for recreational sites could not be overlooked by the administrators of the national forests. The U. S. Forest Service, therefore, which had originally centered its attention on problems of economy and maintenance, established the Division of Recreation and Lands, which was to give attention to the needs of visitors and invite the public to seek recreation in the national forests. The effect was that 26,080,255 persons visited the national forests for recreational purposes in 1949. (In 1956 the number of such visitors was 52,556,084; the figure estimated for 1962 is 66,000,000.) The national forests did not relinquish any of their basic functions, such as supplying timber and protecting watersheds, but after Gifford Pinchot retired and Henry S. Graves became Chief Forester they provided accommodations for vacationists and offered well-balanced recreation programs in suitable areas. The decision to open the forests to visitors was not made lightly. There would be some risk in letting people roam the forests: they might start forest fires or damage signs, roads, underbrush, and forest soil; and they might disregard the rules of proper sanitation. Their carelessness in these and other ways was indeed a threat to both forests and wildlife. But awareness of the public to these dangers was increasing. All kinds of people, encouraged by the government to take advantage of the opportunities for recreation offered by the parks and forests, made use of outdoor facilities and began to observe greater care in doing so. It was not long before the visitors demonstrated that they were willing to accept and adhere to certain rules. Foresters began to have confidence in the public and, realizing that the forests had educational and inspirational values in addition to their utilitarian worth, decided to admit large numbers of tourists who were trying to escape the "abominations of mechanized life."[10]

It was recognized not only that under certain conditions a forest would yield profits when maintained as a smoothly running, sustained-yield project, but also that a fine stand of trees had, beyond its commercial value, a beauty value which attracted visitors and therefore might in time acquire added commercial value of a new kind. In some forests, therefore, it was advantageous to coördinate the business interests of forest management with the interests of tourist traffic. Although the administrators of publicly owned forests have come to this sound conclusion, most of the private owners of timberlands have not as yet adopted this principle. It would be possible and reasonable, however, for similar measures to be taken in at least some of the very large holdings, such as those of the paper industry.

One of the principal difficulties which stood in the way of the admittance of visitors to the forests was the lack of proper roads. The roads leading through and into the forests had been originally laid out for logging operations, with no idea of serving the heavy traffic of tourists' cars. This inadequacy existed throughout the entire road system of the country at the time the automobile first became popular. The needs of tourists grew at an amazing speed once the automobile came into general use; therefore it was necessary that a system of roads be developed which would run from coast to coast and cover the entire nation. Before this was possible a law had to be introduced in Congress to permit the allocation of federal funds to states as an aid to building highways. It took Congress four years to pass this bill. The act was finally passed in 1916, because of military needs as war threatened, and by 1955 there were 2,288,000 miles of surfaced highways. The number of tourists visiting twenty-four national parks by car increased from 2,500,000 in 1946 to 5,000,000 in 1955; that is, visits increased 112 per cent in nine years.

As a part of the great road scheme, scenic drives, or "parkways," have been built, from which heavy and speedy business traffic is excluded, so that the public can travel leisurely and enjoy the landscape en route. The National Park Service has built the Skyline Drive throughout the length of Shenandoah National Park and its continuation, the Blue Ridge Parkway. Other agencies devised the Mount Vernon Highway from the District of Columbia to Mount Vernon and have built a "thruway" from New York to Buffalo. Not planned for those who want to dash through the states as speedily as possible, this highway follows the contour of the country. In the Niagara area it has been laid out in such a way as to give the traveler on the road an opportunity to enjoy the country as much as possible and to leave his car whenever he feels so inclined.

The construction of these "thruways" has given rise to conflicts between private interests seeking to erect billboards and those who regard this kind of advertising as a public nuisance. Fortunately, the sort of high-pressure advertising which disregards the right of the individual to enjoy the scenery without being forced to look at hideous billboards is constantly assailed by the National Roadside Council in New York, whose aim is to protect the public against such infringements of its rights.

In all parts of the United States many persons and organizations are making every effort to rid the highways of these unsightly billboards; industry will no longer be permitted to spoil the beauty of the scenery as a result of public indolence. Admittedly the billboard abomination is a minor problem as compared with the destruction of entire landscapes, but the increase in the number and volume of protests against it shows that Americans have become more sensitive to defacement of scenery and the unpleasant appearance of neglected fringes of cities and of exploited or mismanaged areas. Into this controversy a new factor has recently entered—the threat billboards present to motoring safety. A number of surveys have shown that signs which divert the eye from the road are contributing causes of highway accidents.

The use of water for recreation has become an important problem second only to that arising from the use of lands and forests for recreation. Even at an early date it was generally recognized that lakes and waterways afforded opportunities for recreation and inspiration in addition to their utilitarian purposes, and in time it became apparent that if they were to be so used, they must be protected from pollution and misuse. Appropriate measures were advocated and propagated by powerful and representative bodies, such as the Izaak Walton League of America, with its almost 75,000 members; this organization (established in 1922), was known as the "defender of soil, vegetation, water, and wildlife." As a consequence of these efforts Congress in 1948 enacted a public law for the purpose of inducing the states to abate and control water pollution.[11] However, as the situation looks at present it seems unlikely that the goal will be achieved without a stronger federal law, because in most states legislation of this kind is lagging.

With ever-enlarging road systems and growing popularity of recreational facilities in national parks and forests, conflicting interests were bound to arise. Increased tourist traffic made it necessary over the years to build more roads, trails, cabins, and camps, and these began to encroach on sites theretofore untouched. This, of course, was a gradual process. In the early years of federal management of the parks there were few difficulties, and any visitor who wished to commune with nature could do so without interference from fellow tourists. But far-sighted conservationists envisioned what would happen in the not too distant future. Once the parks invited the public to make use of them, ways would have to be found to care for those who responded to the invitation. Administrators would have to plan facilities to accommodate visitors, and if they were good administrators they would try to anticipate future needs. The master plans of the parks provided for these future developments and showed that a conflict might result if authorities were too lenient in giving way to the so-called needs of the public. A case in point is the matter of concessions. The greater the influx of people, the more concessions seem to be necessary to take care of the needs of the crowds. Therefore, these "needs" must be very carefully defined so that they do not counteract the good work done by the National Park Service in preserving the natural scenery and wildlife. It was inevitable that, by permitting a road and allowing a filling station here, or improving a trail and providing a campsite there, protected areas would be worn away bit by bit. The visiting crowds certainly intended no harm, but trouble was bound to come when the juggernaut of tourism rolled on.

When the difficulties resulting from the great influx of tourists were discussed in forestry circles, one of the men participating in the discussions not only held definite views of his own on these problems but presented them forcefully and offered suggestions for coping with the situation. This was Aldo Leopold, originally a member of the Forest Service, who published an article expressing his thoughts about the place of the wilderness in forest recreational policy in 1921.[12] This article represents the first public statement of the philosophy underlying the "wilderness movement," which soon gained great momentum. Robert Marshall was another member of the Forest Service who devoted his life to furthering the idea of preserving as much as possible of the primitive areas still left in this country.[13] His official position in various government agencies gave him an opportunity to work for his philosophy and present his ideas so effectively that he finally succeeded in obtaining protection for certain wilderness areas. The activities and aims of these men and the circle of friends who held similar ideas are recorded in the files of *The Living Wilderness*, a periodical published by the Wilderness Society, which was founded in 1935.

More than a quarter of a century has passed since the beginning of the wilderness movement, and we can now realize how important that movement was in serving as a kind of counterbalance to the one that brought an influx of people into the parks and forests. In early discussions doubt was sometimes cast on the disinterestedness of the motives of park enthusiasts and friends of the wilderness, but the period of doubt has passed and protected wilderness areas have become an essential part of the conservation system. National forests, national parks, and Indian reservations give equal attention to the problem and regard the protected wilderness as land put to proper use. The ideas of Aldo Leopold, Robert Marshall, and their friends were novel in the 1920's and contrary to the general current of thought, but they were a continuation of the line of thinking expressed in the works of Catlin, Emerson, and Thoreau.

It is now commonly agreed that although the government has no intention of preventing the public from making the best possible use of recreational facilities in parks and forests and wherever else they are available, certain limitations must be accepted. Certain areas must not be opened for settlement but must forever be kept in as near their virgin state as possible. This reservation of wilderness areas must be recognized as a necessary and legitimate use of the land, because the "wilderness" has become scarce and is a commodity that cannot be renewed. Moreover, the wilderness is necessary for scientific study, much of which is comparative;[14] it also satisfies men's craving for recreation and inspiration as nothing else can do. And finally, it teaches man something which Aldo Leopold called "land ethic,"[15] the law which governs the relations between the members of an ecological society—that is, members of a "biotic community"—or in other words, the relations between man and his natural surroundings. Man's understanding of this law will give him greater insight into his place in the community—his position as a "biotic citizen."

In discussions concerning the wilderness idea and the proper management of public lands, national forests, or other areas which are made up in part of wilderness, the belief is often expressed that protection of a wilderness excludes its use. On the contrary, the wilderness area is to be "used," though in such a way that it is not "used up." Another argument advanced is that to reserve these areas for the few who are physically able to lead a rugged life in the wilds is undemocratic. One should not forget, however, that to provide recreation is not the whole function of the wilderness area, and that it is not undemocratic to serve the interests of a minority if that minority has high ideals and worthy aims that will benefit future generations.

The creed of the Wilderness Society states that "wilderness is a valuable natural resource that belongs to the people . . . its preservation is part of the balanced program essential in the survival of our civilized culture." The roadless tracts administered as wilderness areas by federal or state governments now cover more than 14,000,000 acres and stretch through many states. The largest of them is the Selway-Bitterroot Wilderness Area covering over 1,500,000 acres in Montana. The Gila Wilderness in southwestern New Mexico was the first to be protected. Since its establishment in 1924 this wilderness area has been cut down, and in 1952 the Forest Service wanted to reduce it still further for administrative reasons. A public hearing to investigate public opinion was held; what happened at this meeting is very significant. All those who were called on to make statements, whether or not they were speaking on behalf of the Wilderness Society, the Izaak Walton League, or similar organizations, based their theses on the same good reasons as have over the years been presented in similar cases by the conservation-minded agencies and authorities in the field. It became overwhelmingly clear that "the people" had understood the lesson taught by the wilderness movement; indeed, it was the local people who won the day by supporting the cause to prevent the whittling down of the protected area, even though it meant a reduction in the potential tourist trade.

A good example of the effects of advancing civilization on a wilderness region is found in the Quetico-Superior Area[16] on the border of Minnesota and Canada. For nearly half a century the fate of these public lands has been a matter of discussion. Persons who are trying to conserve the original character of the region have been combatting those who are trying to open up the region as a resort area for the tourist trade, and others who want to cut timber without regard to proper forest management or scenic effects.

In 1909 the two adjacent areas of Quetico Provincial Park (Canada) and Superior National Forest (Minnesota) were set aside to protect their unique wilderness character. The growing popularity of the unexplored canoe country induced local Forest Service authorities to promote a plan to build a "road to every lake." However, this plan was foiled largely through the efforts of the Izaak Walton League of America. Hardly had conservationists rejoiced in this success, when lumber interests made plans to dam a chain of border lakes in order to harvest the flooded timber stands. The Quetico-Superior Council was then founded, and another battle was fought. Conservationists, standing together for the first time in a cohesive group, won the battle. In the early days of World War II serious difficulties arose again when airplanes were used to transport guests to and from resorts which had grown up on private lands inside the protected area. This air traffic threatened to destroy the entire character of the country. Once more the battle was on. This time the Izaak Walton League raised funds with which to buy private properties which had begun to be a nuisance, but the task was too large for any private agency. Consequently, the League appealed to President Truman, and as a result he created an "air space reservation" above the roadless area, in spite of the strong opposing efforts of the exploiters. This restriction of air traffic now prevents the development of undesirable resorts by precluding service to them. Further progress in this program continues through the coöperative efforts of the Izaak Walton League and the U. S. Forest Service in purchasing land tracts and former resorts. The area is gradually returning to its virgin state. Here, it would seem, the conservation movement has at last won out.

In 1929 the American Legion and the Canadian Legion both endorsed the Quetico-Superior program and recommended that when an international forest should become a reality it should be dedicated in the name of peace to the servicemen of both countries in World War I. In 1948 the national convention of the American Legion adopted the idea that an "international peace memorial forest" be established as soon as possible. The victory in the Superior-Quantico and the Gila Wilderness matters is very encouraging in that it shows that the number of people who favor conservation has increased greatly and public opinion is on the side of the conservationists.

When water power is harnessed in an ill-considered way situations frequently arise which are comparable to those occurring when wilderness areas are threatened. Submission of the problems to arbitration can have fortunate results. For example, when additional water power was requested by companies which were already benefiting from the use of Niagara Falls, an international committee, of which J. Horace McFarland was a member, was set up to arbitrate the matter. In its final report the committee pointed out that government agencies had in the past paid little or no attention to scenic values, but that this time the committee had studied these values with infinite care. Optical effects had been measured with a special instrument called a "telecolorimeter." The precision with which observations had been made is evident from the following statement: "The optimum stream velocity to insure maximum persistence of the color curtain for the conservative minimum depth of 5 feet would be no greater than 15 feet per second." On the basis of these studies the committee concluded that the "scenic beauty" of the falls is, "in the main, dependent upon the volume of flow upon unbroken crest lines, upon their height, visibility, and color effects . . ." As a result, measures were taken to restrict the use of water power. Without neglecting the needs of industry, these new regulations respected the interests of the visitor, recognizing the fact that "more and more as the years go by the rights of the people to those things which contribute to recreation and to pleasure and to good health could no longer be contested."[17] Although it is doubtful whether it would always be opportune or even possible to use physical methods in measuring aesthetic values, the result in this case was satisfactory and served the purpose. The high aesthetic value of Niagara Falls was officially established. In the minds of the public the falls had always had a great sentimental value, but from this time on, attempts to exploit their water and thus spoil them would never be taken lightly either by the authorities or the public. It was also realized that a compromise must always be made in order to take adequate recognition of all interests involved, including industry. Once again, comprehensive planning and coordination of interests had happy results and served the common good.

The most outstanding example of comprehensive planning with reference to a conservation measure is the setting up of the Tennessee Valley Authority. This has been criticized by some as a socialistic project and praised by others because it was an achievement of the party which was in power. Without any doubt, projects of equally wide or even wider scope will become increasingly necessary in the future, regardless of who is in power. By what means measures will be authorized and supervised will be decided by public opinion. The quality of the achievement is the only thing to be considered here; or, as President Dwight D. Eisenhower put it in his Message on the State of the Union on February 2, 1953, the best natural resources program for America will result from "a partnership of the states and local committees, private citizens and the federal government, all working together." Of course, for all practical purposes, the success of the partnership will depend on how it is interpreted by the partners. If state legislation is remiss, as it was in the matter

of water pollution, or if forest ranges are depleted regardless of efforts
to conserve resources, and private forest owners do not coöperate in
proper forest management, then this partnership must be dissolved and
must be replaced by some other arrangement which will guarantee protective measures for the multiple use of all natural resources.

When the TVA was created in 1933 the idea was to rehabilitate a region
then existing under submarginal conditions. In the valley and in the
coves a whole population was living on a standard far lower than most
farmers or townsmen in other states could imagine, and there seemed to
be no hope for improvement. The betterment of living conditions for these
people meant the difference between economic life and death in the next
generation, or perhaps in their own. It was imperative that measures be
taken to control floods and to harness the Tennessee River in order to
generate power. The TVA electrified the valley, and electricity became
an easily available commodity. This achievement is usually extolled as
"the" main success of the project, but electrification was only one of many
factors that went to make the project a success. Agricultural experts taught
the farmer proper methods of soil conservation in order to improve his
production, stop soil erosion, and avoid loss of topsoil. Reforestation once
more became possible, watersheds were protected, floods were avoided,
and water supply was placed under control. National forests managed
under the sustained-yield system served as a pattern for private industry,
just as advice given by the Department of Agriculture for efficient farming
by means of rotation of crops, contour ploughing, terracing, and other
measures helped lift the level of agriculture. As a consequence, "a renaissance, manifest in a thousand ways," spread over the valley, although so
far only a minority of the people have had the opportunity to share in it.[18]

As a consequence of the economic improvement a bettering of social
institutions followed; churches and schools won a better standing in the
community. Since life has come to have a new meaning to the people of
the valley, and the relationship between man and nature has been established on a new and firm basis, the future no longer looks black to them.
Undoubtedly there is still much to be done, and the necessity for the
integration of plans is becoming increasingly evident; yet far more than a
beginning has been made, and the project will undoubtedly be carried
to its conclusion.

The TVA project is only one in the series of large-scale national projects.
In the Northwest the Columbia River is being harnessed. In the Southwest
the Hoover, Parker, and Davis dams have been completed and a number
of dams are yet to be built to provide complete control for the Colorado
and put it to a maximum use for Arizona and California. In the Middle
West the Missouri River is in the process of being brought under control.

Smaller plans are being carried out on the state level, such as the one by which the Wisconsin River is being regulated, and large-scale reforestation to serve the paper industry is being carried out in Wisconsin. Projects of this type may result in "multiple" danger to groups other than those concerned solely with power production, as we have seen from examples previously discussed. The proposed destruction of the Dinosaur National Monument on the Green and Yampa rivers in Utah and Colorado, widely recognized for its scenic values and world famous for its fossil beds, is a more recent case in point. After many discussions concerning the usefulness of including the area in a power project which would have destroyed the scenic value of the site, and extensive hearings in which conservation groups had a chance to voice their opinions, Congress rejected the bill and provided other means of carrying out the power project.

One of the great interstate conservation projects which originated during the administration of Franklin D. Roosevelt was the shelter belt begun in 1934 in the prairie states, which was planned to extend for more than 1,800 miles from North Dakota to Texas. Hundred-mile-wide windbreaks of drought-resisting trees and shrubs were to be planted in order to reduce excessive evaporation, prevent the soil from blowing away, and screen the land from damaging winds all year round. Much-needed work would thus be provided for men in the drought areas. The project was begun by the Forest Service and later was continued by the Soil Conservation Service. This gigantic task, never completely achieved, could not have been attempted without the assistance of the Civilian Conservation Corps. The idea of combining conservation work with this type of labor supposedly originated with the British forester and conservationist Richard St. Barbe Baker; at least Baker states that he was the first to discuss these matters with Franklin D. Roosevelt, and that he did so shortly before Roosevelt took office in 1932.[19] The rehabilitation of the prairie states made it possible for them to supply the great demands for foodstuffs during World War II.

Franklin D. Roosevelt throughout his entire administration devoted much of his energy to conservation problems; even during the war he was concerned with the project of the International Conservation Conference, an idea presented to him by Gifford Pinchot in July, 1944. Roosevelt believed that this was a "vital step toward permanent peace." Consequently, in October, 1944, he proposed to Secretary of State Cordell Hull that "all of the united and associated nations" hold a meeting in the United States "for what is really the first step toward conservation and use of natural resources—i.e., a gathering for the purpose of a world-wide study of the whole subject." "I am more and more convinced," he added, "that conservation is a basis of permanent peace."[20] Although President Roosevelt's death prevented the carrying out of this plan, conferences of similar nature were held in Denver and at Lake Success in 1948 and 1949. The United Nations has endeavored to carry on these discussions, since it is obvious that conservation has become indispensable and that only by concentrated global efforts can significant results be achieved.

Comprehensive methods and simultaneous planning are absolutely essential if nature is to be kept in balance. The term preferred by ecologists for this balance is "the biotic pyramid," which symbolizes the flow of energy between soil and plant and creature, and their dependence on one another for food; the idea being that on a layer of soil there rests a layer of plants and on that a layer of insects, and so on, each layer being smaller than the preceding one. The top layer consists of carnivores, including both man and beast. In the course of evolution the transitions in this system have become more subtle and the pyramid has become steadily higher. It is still growing, and the functions are increasing in complexity as changes are made in the circuit. There is thus ample reason for man to consider carefully before he brings about changes in his relations with nature.

Consideration of such changes is indeed everybody's business. No one has pointed this out more eloquently than Aldo Leopold, in "The Land Ethic," an essay in his *Sand County Almanac*. Here Leopold shows that to conserve natural resources to improve an economic situation is valuable, but it is not enough; conservation should be considered a moral obligation. Man's relation to nature should be governed by ethics. It is not the volume of conservation which is essential but rather the philosophy underlying its application. Land is not merely soil but a "fountain of energy flowing through a circuit of soils, plants and animals" in relation to which man must develop an "ecological conscience," or in other words, change his role as a conqueror to that of a citizen of the biotic community. Leopold considers it very unfortunate that as yet neither philosophers nor those concerned with religion have taken any interest in this mode of conduct. It is true, however, that the principles of ethics concerning the land no longer are problems merely for idealists. This is proved by the case of *Dexter* v. *The State of Washington*. An owner of forest property in that state who was about to denude his land by over-all logging would not agree to leave enough trees to ensure perpetuation of the stand of timber. The state authorities objected to this procedure, and the court found for the state. In his decision the judge quoted a passage from Edmund Burke which stated that there exists a great unwritten compact between the dead, the living, and the unborn. He held that "such an unwritten compact requires that we leave to the unborn something more than debts and depleted natural resources"; in fact, by "constitutional morality" we are required to utilize natural resources and at the same time perpetuate them for future generations. It is encouraging to know that this case was sustained by the United States Supreme Court (on November 7, 1949).[21] Undoubtedly, land ethic more than anything else will actually determine man's future and make the world more livable; it will, in fact, make it possible for man to continue to live in the world. This means that the great purpose of conservation is to bring about harmony between man and nature.

Conservation projects varying in size have been devised or are being considered in all parts of the world. The filling up of the Zuider Zee in Holland has produced more farmland; in the Austrian, German, Italian, and Swiss Alps power plants have been established which generate energy for bottom lands in both northern and southern Europe; in Russia the Stalin plan will provide gigantic shelter belts in the steppes and offer protection for watersheds; the Union of South Africa intends to take serious measures to stop the loss of topsoil, which has amounted to a staggering 30 per cent throughout the last seventy years.

On all the continents strong forces are at work to undo, or at least to lessen, the damage man has done; everywhere there is a growing conviction that man should no longer be allowed to disorganize nature and thus produce disastrous results. Let us accept as a grave warning and as a basic truth for international consideration some words G. M. Trevelyan addressed to the British nation when he viewed certain military threats the atomic age has released:

> natural beauty is the ultimate spiritual appeal of the universe, of nature, or of the God of nature, to their nursling man. . . . But science and machinery have now armed . . . man . . . with weapons that will be his making or undoing, as he chooses to use them; at present he is destroying natural beauty . . . unless he consciously protects it at the partial expense of some of his other greedy activities, he will cut off his own spiritual supplies, and leave his descendants a helpless prey forever to the base materialism of man and vulgar sights.[22]

This kind of insight, based on faith, common sense, and facts, is in no way related to pessimism or periodically recurrent fears of latter-day doom. The idea of conservation as the great need of our time has come to be a belief for which mankind must fight even against terrific odds. But it is a fight which can be waged in a spirit of optimism and in the firm belief that, if it is won, it will relieve man of many of his present-day tensions.

Although this is the world situation today, and basic conditions differ little in both hemispheres, we on this continent enjoy the privilege of frequenting the outdoors in many more ways than any other people anywhere else. According to our means and desires we can choose for our recreation the city park or the backwoods or any of a whole range of places in between. We may join the crowds on the beach or, traveling by canoe and pack train, lose ourselves in the wilderness; we may study the plains, the desert, or extensive forests, while the car travels for days without end; we may hike or climb, explore nature's phenomena, or admire scenic beauty. Yet, whatever road to nature we select, it is not the road which matters, but the mind and the way we have trained it to be receptive to the beauties and wonders of God's creation.

Notes

CHAPTER 1: *"Axes Leap and Shapes Arise"* (pages 1–13)

[1] *The Autobiography of Benjamin Rush*, ed. George W. Corner (Princeton: Princeton University Press, 1948), p. 72.

[2] Carl Sandburg, *Good Morning, America* (New York: Harcourt Brace, 1928), p. 27.

[3] Walt Whitman, *Complete Poetry and Selected Prose and Letters*, ed. Emory Holloway, pp. 170, 286, 191.

[4] John Ruskin, *Letters . . . to Charles Eliot Norton* (2 vols.; Boston: Houghton Mifflin, 1904), I, 28.

[5] Whitman, *op. cit.*, p. 79.

[6] "Répondez," *ibid.*, p. 512.

[7] Henry S. Burrage, ed., *Early English and French Voyages, Chiefly from Hakluyt, 1534–1608* (New York: Scribner, 1906), p. 228. Quoted by permission of Barnes & Noble, Inc.

[8] Lyon Gardiner Tyler, ed., *Narratives of Early Virginia, 1606–1625* (New York: Scribner, 1907), p. 16. Quoted by permission of Barnes & Noble, Inc.

[9] Thomas Morton, *The New English Canaan*, Prince Society, *Publications*, XIV (1883), 179.

[10] Edward Williams, "Virginia," in Peter Force, *Tracts and Other Papers*, III, No. 11 (1844), 11.

[11] Tyler, ed., *op. cit.*, p. 98.

[12] Albert Cook Myers, ed., *Narratives of Early Pennsylvania, . . . 1630–1707* (New York: Scribner, 1909), p. 170. Quoted by permission of Barnes & Noble, Inc.

[13] J. F. Jameson, ed., *Narratives of New Netherland, 1609–1664* (New York: Scribner, 1909), p. 170.

[14] John Josselyn, "New England Rarities Discovered," American Antiquarian Society, *Transactions and Collections*, IV (1860), 139.

[15] Louis Hennepin, *A New Discovery of a Vast Country in America* (London, 1698), pp. 29–30.

[16] Michael Wigglesworth, "God's Controversy with New-England," Massachusetts Historical Society, *Proceedings*, XII (1871–1873), 83–84.

[17] *The Diary of John Evelyn* (4 vols.; London, 1879), I, 239–240.

[18] Alexander V. G. Allen, *Jonathan Edwards* (Boston, 1889), pp. 355–356.

[19] Perry Miller, ed., *Images or Shadows of Divine Things by Jonathan Edwards* (New Haven: Yale University Press, 1948), pp. 41, 135, 137.

[20] Alice G. B. Lockwood, *Gardens of Colony and State . . . Before 1840*, II, 95.

[21] Myers, ed., *op. cit.*, p. 239.

[22] Samuel Hazard, *Annals of Pennsylvania from the Discovery of the Delaware* (Philadelphia, 1850), p. 519.

[23] Edward C. O. Beatty, *William Penn as Social Philosopher* (New York: Columbia University Press, 1939), p. 177.

[24] Myers, ed., *op. cit.*, p. 229.

[25] Beatty, *op. cit.*, p. 177.

[26] Anthony Ashley Cooper, Third Earl of Shaftesbury, *Characteristics, Men, Manners, Opinions, Times, etc.*, ed. John M. Robertson (2 vols.; London: G. Richards, 1900), II, 122, 125, 238.

[27] William Gilpin, *Observations on the River Wye, and Several Parts of South Wales . . .*
       1770 (London, 1792), pp. 1 and 2.
[28] *New York Magazine,* VI (1795), 503–504.
[29] *United States Magazine,* I (1779), 244.

CHAPTER 2: *Scientists, Philosophers, and Travelers* (pages 14–29)

[1] Michel Guillaume St. Jean de Crèvecœur, *Letters from an American Farmer,* p. 265.
[2] *The Writings of Benjamin Franklin,* ed. A. H. Smyth (10 vols.; New York: Macmillan,
       1905–1907), III, 99.
[3] Gilbert Chinard, "The American Philosophical Society and the Early History of
       Forestry in America," American Philosophical Society, *Proceedings,* LXXXIX
       (1945), 461.
[4] Charles C. Sellers, *Charles Willson Peale,* II, 229.
[5] "A Memorial of George Browne Goode," Smithsonian Institution, *Annual Report . . .*
       Year Ending June 30, 1897, Part II, pp. 443–448.
[6] *Ibid.,* p. 395.
[7] *The Complete Jefferson,* ed. Saul K. Padover, p. 581.
[8] *Ibid.,* pp. 578–579.
[9] William Bartram, *Travels Through North and South Carolina, Georgia, East and*
       West Florida, pp. 48, 187, 341, 156.
[10] Gilbert Chinard, *L'Exotism américain dans l'œuvre de Chateaubriand,* pp. 242–255.
[11] *Correspondence of Thomas Carlyle and Ralph Waldo Emerson,* II, 198.
[12] Michel Guillaume St. Jean de Crèvecœur, *Sketches of Eighteenth Century America,*
       p. 4.
[13] *Ibid.,* p. 54.
[14] *Ibid.,* p. 39.
[15] Philip Freneau, "On the Uniformity and Perfection of Nature," *Poems,* ed. H. H.
       Clark, p. 424.
[16] *Ibid.,* p. liv.
[17] Alexander Wilson, *Poems and Literary Prose,* ed. A. B. Grosart, I, 71.
[18] *Ibid.,* pp. 111–112.
[19] Joseph W. Krutch, ed., *Great American Nature Writing,* p. 89.
[20] Constantine S. Rafinesque, "A Life of Travels," *Chronica Botanica,* VIII (1944),
       pp. 291–360.
[21] Andrew Burnaby, *Travels Through the Middle Settlements in North America,* pp.
       101, 43–44.
[22] Timothy Dwight, *Travels; in New-England and New-York,* IV, 177.
[23] Manasseh Cutler, *Life, Journals and Correspondence,* I, 96.
[24] Robert Hunter, Jr., *Quebec to Carolina in 1785–1786,* pp. 98–99.

CHAPTER 3: *The Romantic Period* (pages 30–53)

[1] Parke Godwin, *A Biography of William Cullen Bryant,* I, 150.
[2] *North American Review,* V (1817), 338–341.
[3] William Wordsworth, *Poetical Works* (London, 1859), VII, 30.
[4] Howard Mumford Jones, *Ideas in America,* p. 297. See also Gilbert Chinard,
       L'Homme contre la nature; essais d'histoire de l'Amérique, p. 81 note.
[5] Godwin, *op. cit.,* p. 309.
[6] John G. Whittier, *Complete Poetical Works,* p. 232.
[7] *Port Folio,* 3d ser., II (1809), 101.
[8] *The Diary of Elbridge Gerry, Jr.* (New York: Brentano's, 1927), pp. 50, 69. "Sketches
       from Nature," *Port Folio,* 2d ser., IV (1807), 339.

[9] Godwin, *op. cit.*, p. 309.

[10] Susan F. Cooper, Introduction to *The Pioneers,* in J. F. Cooper, *Works* (Household ed.; New York, 1884), III, v.

[11] J. F. Cooper, *The Pioneers,* in *Works* (Mohawk ed.; New York, 1896), IV, 239.

[12] J. F. Cooper, *Home as Found, ibid.,* XIV, 125–126.

[13] The painting is now in the possession of the New York Historical Association, Cooperstown.

[14] Cooper, *Home as Found,* in *Works* (Mohawk ed.), IV, 295.

[15] Cooper, *The Pioneers, ibid.,* IV, 251, 265, 99–100, 300–302.

[16] Marcel Clavel, *Fenimore Cooper and His Critics,* pp. 142–175.

[17] Mark Twain [Samuel L. Clemens], "Fenimore Cooper's Literary Offences," *North American Review,* CLXI (1895), 1–12.

[18] J. F. Cooper, *Notions of the Americans,* p. 332.

[19] *Idem,* "American and European Scenery Compared," in Irving *et al., The Home Book of the Picturesque,* pp. 56, 61.

[20] Godwin, *op. cit.,* pp. 367, 271, 217.

[21] James R. Lowell, "On Board the '76," *Poetical Works* (Household ed.; Boston, 1860), p. 383.

[22] Godwin, *op. cit.,* II, 419.

[23] James K. Paulding, *Letters from the South,* II, 87, 54.

[24] Richard H. Dana, review of Irving's *Sketch Book* in *North American Review,* XXV (1819), 355.

[25] P. M. Irving, *The Life and Letters of Washington Irving,* I, 13, 14.

[26] Washington Irving, *Sketch Book,* in *Works* (Hudson ed.; 5 vols.; New York, 1891), I, 518, 58.

[27] *Foreign Quarterly Review,* XXXII (1844), 291–324. The article was generally but erroneously attributed to Dickens.

[28] *The Diary of George Templeton Strong, . . . 1835–1849* (4 vols., New York: Macmillan, 1952), I, 215.

[29] James T. Flexner, *First Flowers of Our Wilderness* (Boston and New York: Houghton Mifflin, 1947), pp. 150 ff. Hans Huth, "Pictures and Critics," in *From Colony to Nation: An Exhibition of American Painting, Silver and Architecture from 1650 to the War of 1812* (Chicago: Art Institute, 1949), pp. 7–9; review and letters to the editor in *Magazine of Art,* XLIII (1950), 152–233; XLIV (1951), p. 153. Lloyd Goodrich, *A Century of American Landscape Painting, 1800 to 1900,* p. 5.

[30] Alfred C. Prime, *The Arts and Crafts in Philadelphia, Maryland and South Carolina, 1721–1783* (Topsfield, Mass.: Walpole Society, 1929), p. 8.

[31] Kenneth Clark, *Landscape Painting* (New York: Scribner, 1950), p. 34.

[32] J. Hall Pleasants, "Four Late Landscape Painters," American Antiquarian Society, *Proceedings* (1942), LII, 3–146.

[33] Frank Weitenkampf, "Early American Landscape Prints," *Art Quarterly,* VIII (1945), 40–67.

[34] "The Deluge" is now in the Metropolitan Museum of Art, New York; "The Thunderstorm at Sea" is in the Museum of Fine Arts, Boston; "Elijah Feeding the Ravens," painted in 1818, is also in the museum at Boston.

[35] Jared B. Flagg, *The Life and Letters of Washington Allston* (New York, 1892), p. 204.

[36] *New-York Mirror,* III (1826), 364.

[37] Edwin James, *Account of an Expedition from Pittsburgh to the Rocky Mountains . . . 1819 and '20 . . . Under the Command of Major Stephen H. Long* (3 vols.; London, 1822–1823), III, 267.

[38] Frederick A. Sweet, *The Hudson River School and the Early American Landscape Tradition.*

[39] T. S. Cummings, *Historic Annals of the National Academy of Design,* pp. 12, 9, 11.

[40] Louis L. Noble, *The Course of Empire . . . Thomas Cole*, p. 202.

[41] Thomas Cole, "Lecture on American Scenery," *Northern Light*, I (1851), 25–26.

[42] Joshua Shaw, quoted in Weitenkampf, *op. cit.*, p. 61.

[43] *Ibid.*, p. 65.

[44] Nancy McClelland, *Historic Wall Papers . . .* (Philadelphia: Lippincott, 1924), p. 386.

[45] Mary Bartlett Cowdrey, *American Academy of Fine Arts and American Art Union 1816–1852* (New York: New-York Historical Society, 1953).

[46] Anna Jameson, *Memoirs and Essays Illustrative of Art, Literature, and Social Morals* (London, 1846), pp. 163, 164.

[47] Johann Wolfgang von Goethe, "Die Vereinigten Staaten," *Sämtliche Werke* (Jubiläums-Ausgabe; 40 vols.; Stuttgart and Berlin: Cotta, 1902–1907), IV, Gedichte (Zahme Xenien), 127; English trans. by Stephen Spender in *The Permanent Goethe*, ed. Thomas Mann (New York: Dial, 1948), p. 655.

[48] François René Vicomte de Chateaubriand, "Voyage en Amérique," *Oeuvres* (Paris, 1836), XII, 18. "Nothing is old in America but the trees, children of the soil, and liberty, the mother of all human society; these are worth as much as monuments and forebears."

[49] Cole, *op. cit.*, pp. 25, 26.

[50] Anna W. Rutledge, "Robert Gilmore, Jr., Baltimore Collector," *Journal of the Walters Art Gallery*, I (1949), 31.

[51] E. A. Poe, "The Elk," *The Works of Edgar Allan Poe* (10 vols.; New York: Scribner, 1914), II, 77–78.

[52] George W. Curtis, *Lotus-Eating*, pp. 137, 138.

[53] Edgar P. Richardson, *American Romantic Painting*, p. 21.

CHAPTER 4: *Play and Rest* (pages 54–70)

[1] Andrew Burnaby, *Travels Through the Middle Settlements in North America*, pp. 67–68.

[2] *The Diary of Philip Hone, 1828–1851*, ed. Allan Nevins (New York: Dodd, Mead, 1936), pp. 40, 737, 739, 771.

[3] *Massachusetts Missionary Magazine*, I (1803), 465.

[4] Catherine E. Beecher, *A Treatise on Domestic Economy* (3d ed.; New York, 1842), p. 244; Catherine E. Beecher and Harriet Beecher Stowe, *The New Housekeeper's Manual* (New York, 1873), p. 287.

[5] "The Fishing Season," *American Farmer*, IX (1827), 55.

[6] H. W. Herbert, *The Life and Writings of Frank Forester*, I, 10.

[7] John F. Watson, *Annals of Philadelphia, and Pennsylvania, in the Olden Time* (3 vols.; Philadelphia, 1891), I, 280.

[8] Burnaby, *op. cit.*, p. 11.

[9] William Dunlap, *Diary*, II, 377.

[10] Thomas Twining, *Travels in America 100 Years Ago* (New York, 1894), p. 163.

[11] *Thomas Jefferson's Garden Book*, p. 323.

[12] Watson, *op. cit.*, I, 43.

[13] François André Michaux, *Travels to the West of the Allegheny Mountains*, in Reuben G. Thwaites, ed., *Early Western Travels, 1748–1846* (Cleveland, 1904), III, 130.

[14] Robert Hunter, Jr., *Quebec to Carolina in 1785–1786*, p. 169.

[15] Manasseh Cutler, *Life, Journals and Correspondence*, I, 278.

[16] Nathaniel P. Willis, *American Scenery*, II, 73. Watson, *op. cit.*, I, 489.

[17] E. A. Poe, "The Elk," *Works* (New York, 1914), II, 80; "Landor's Cottage," *ibid.*, II, 113.

[18] Watson, *op. cit.*, I, 223.

[19] Timothy Dwight, *Travels; in New-England and New-York*, I, 490–491.

[20] Louise Hall Tharp, *The Peabody Sisters of Salem* (Boston: Little, Brown, 1950), p. 94.
[21] *Gleason's Pictorial Drawing-Room Companion* (Boston, 1851–1859), I (1851), 240.
[22] Charles Tracy, "Logbook."
[23] Cutler, *op. cit.*, I, 306.
[24] John Durand, *Life and Time of Asher B. Durand* (New York, 1894), p. 4.
[25] Hone, *op. cit.*, p. 155. Quoted by permission of Dodd, Mead & Company.
[26] *American Farmer*, VII (1825), 143.
[27] Durand, *op. cit.*, p. 40.
[28] Margaret Fuller Ossoli, *At Home and Abroad*, pp. 25, 43.
[29] Chicago Title & Trust Company records, Bushnell's Addition to Chicago Map S141842.
[30] Mrs. Caroline Kirkland, *Forest Life* (2 vols.; New York, 1942), I, 42.
[31] Mrs. Eliza R. Steele, *A Summer Journal in the West* (New York, 1841), pp. 198–199.
[32] Horatio Smith, *Festival Games and Amusements* (New York, 1831), p. 325.
[33] The painting is now in the Pennsylvania Academy of the Fine Arts, Philadelphia.
[34] Walt Whitman, *The Gathering of the Forces*, ed. Cleveland Rogers and John Black (2 vols.; New York: Putnam, 1920), II, 109, 118–121.
[35] F. L. Olmsted, Jr., and Theodora Kimball, eds., *Frederick Law Olmsted, Landscape Architect*, II, 18–19.
[36] *The Polynesian* (Honolulu), June 29, 1844.
[37] Cornelia W. Walter, *Mount Auburn Cemetery* (New York, 1850), p. 14.
[38] *Ibid.*
[39] *Atlantic Souvenir* (Philadelphia, 1826), p. 60.
[40] Edward S. Abdy, *Journal of a Residence and Tour of the United States of North America . . .* (3 vols.; London, 1835), I, 120.
[41] Frances Anne Kemble, *Records of a Girlhood* (New York, 1879), p. 590.
[42] Theodore Dwight, *Things as They Are*, p. 162.
[43] Andrew J. Downing, *A Treatise on . . . Landscape Gardening*, p. 63.
[44] *Idem, Rural Essays*, p. xxiv.
[45] "English and American Landscape Gardening," *Horticulturist*, II (December, 1847), 261.
[46] Downing, *Rural Essays*, p. 144.
[47] *Ibid.*, p. 146.
[48] *Ibid.*, p. 157.
[49] *Ibid.*, p. 152.
[50] Olmsted and Kimball, eds., *op. cit.*, II, 46.
[51] *Ibid.*, p. 14.

CHAPTER 5: *The Poetry of Traveling* (pages 71–86)

[1] William Dunlap, *Diary*, I, 65.
[2] Charles Lanman, *Recollections of Curious Characters and Pleasant Places* (Edinburgh, 1881), p. 15.
[3] George H. Davison, *The Traveller's Guide* (7th ed.; Saratoga Springs, 1837), p. xvi. Many editions of this guide were issued between 1822 and 1840.
[4] De Witt Clinton, *Letters on the Natural History and Internal Resources of the State of New York* (New York, 1822), pp. 10, 15.
[5] Caroline Gilman, *The Poetry of Travelling*, pp. 89–90.
[6] N. P. Willis, *American Scenery*, I, 119.
[7] Theodore Dwight, *Things as They Are*, pp. 232, 192, 215.
[8] Clinton, *op. cit.*, p. 7.
[9] Sarah J. Hale, *Traits of American Life*, p. 189.
[10] Willis, *op. cit.*, I, 1–2.

[11] Gilman, *op. cit.*, p. 103.
[12] *Ibid.*, p. 359.
[13] Willis, *op. cit.*, I, 10.
[14] Davison, *op. cit.*, p. 128.
[15] Willis, *op. cit.*, I, 14–15.
[16] Talbot Hamlin, *Greek Revival Architecture in America* (London and New York: Oxford University Press, 1944), p. 262.
[17] Davison, *op. cit.*, pp. 140–142.
[18] Timothy Dwight, *Travels; in New-England and New-York*, IV, 18.
[19] *Atlantic Souvenir* (Philadelphia, 1828), p. 281.
[20] Theodore Dwight, *op. cit.*, pp. 197, 198.
[21] Charles Lanman, "A Tour to the River Saguenay, 1848," in *Adventures in the Wilds of the United States and British American Provinces* (2 vols.; Philadelphia, 1856), I, 183.

In October, 1951, the Catskill Mountain House, after being closed for a year or two, was in a rather dilapidated state. Hoping to interest the public in having the building restored, I wrote a letter to the New York *Times*, which was printed on Nov. 20, 1951. Little enthusiasm resulted, and no actual help was provided. After the letter was published I approached Governor Thomas E. Dewey, and he referred the matter to the Joint Legislative Committee on Historical Sites. The chairman of this committee reported to me on Feb. 15, 1952, that "the property in question might have historical aspects that would be interesting to our committee, nevertheless our work is about completed and we are ready to make our final report to the Legislature and disband."

[22] *Autobiography, Reminiscences, and Letters of John Trumbull* (New York, 1841), p. 27.
[23] Lanman, *op. cit.*, I, 201.
[24] Lucy Crawford, *History of the White Mountains* (Portland, Me., 1845), pp. 61, 55.
[25] Joseph T. Buckingham, *Personal Memories* (Boston, 1882), I, 172.
[26] The sketchbook is now owned by the Detroit Institute of Art.
[27] Louis L. Noble, *The Course of Empire . . . Thomas Cole*, pp. 95–96
[28] Lanman, *op. cit.*, I, 250.
[29] Carol Brink, *Harps in the Wind: The Story of the Singing Hutchinsons* (New York: Macmillan, 1947), pp. 86–96. Material used with permission of The Macmillan Company.
[30] *Ibid.*
[31] Charles F. Hoffman, "Scenes at the Source of the Hudson," *New-York Mirror*, IV (1837), 118 ff.
[32] Noble, *op. cit.*, p. 373.
[33] *Ibid.*, p. 360.
[34] Willis, *op. cit.*, II, 36.
[35] Charles F. Hoffman, *A Winter in the West* (New York, 1835), II, 308–309.
[36] Edgar A. Poe, "The Literati," *Works* (New York, 1914), VIII, 126.
[37] Caroline Kirkland, *A New Home—Who'll Follow?*, p. 47.
[38] Eliza Steele, *A Summer Journey in the West* (New York, 1841), p. 14.
[39] George W. Curtis, *Lotus-Eating*, pp. 137, 140.
[40] "Artists' Railroad Excursion," *Harper's New Monthly Magazine*, XIX (1859), 1.

CHAPTER 6: *New Eyes* (pages 87–104)

[1] Ralph Waldo Emerson, *Journals*, III, 460–461.
[2] Thomas Carlyle and R. W. Emerson, *Correspondence*, I, 112.
[3] Harold C. Goddard, "Transcendentalism," *The Cambridge History of American Literature*, ed. W. P. Treat *et al.* (Cambridge: Putnam, 1931), I, 334

[4] Emerson, "Nature," *Works*, I, 9, 10, 78, 67–68.

[5] *Ibid.*, pp. 70, 79.

[6] Emerson, *Journals*, IV, 321.

[7] *Idem, Essays*, in *Works*, III, 171.

[8] Unpublished papers of President Andrew Johnson, MSS in Library of Congress.

[9] Emerson, *Journals*, IV, 130.

[10] Zoltan Haraszti, *The Idyll of Brook Farm* (Boston: Public Library, 1937), p. 13.

[11] *Passages from the American Note-Books of Nathaniel Hawthorne* (2 vols. in 1; Boston, 1875), II, 2–3.

[12] *The Journals of Francis Parkman*, ed. Mason Wade (2 vols.; New York: Harper, 1947), I, 3.

[13] Emerson, "The American Scholar," *Works*, I, 88.

[14] *Idem*, "Nature," *Works*, I, 77–78.

[15] Henry D. Thoreau, *The Maine Woods*, in *Writings*, III, 79.

[16] Emerson, "Thoreau," *Works*, X, 434–435.

[17] George Paston [pseud. Emily Morse Symonds], *Little Memoirs of the Nineteenth Century* (New York: Dutton, 1902), p. 344.

[18] Emerson, *Journals*, III, 460–461. Thoreau, *Familiar Letters*, in *Writings*, VI, 84.

[19] *The Journals of Bronson Alcott*, ed. Odell Shepard (Boston: Little, Brown, 1938), pp. 213–214.

[20] Henry Seidel Canby, *Thoreau*, p. 293.

[21] James R. Lowell, *My Study Windows*, in *The Complete Writings of James Russell Lowell*, II, 139.

[22] Hawthorne, *op. cit.*, p. 97.

[23] Emerson, "Thoughts on Modern Literature," *Dial*, I (1840), 150.

[24] William J. Stillman, *The Autobiography of a Journalist*, I, 198–216; *idem*, *The Old Rome and the New*, p. 205.

[25] Emerson, "The Adirondacs," *Works*, IX, 159–170; *Nature, ibid.*, I, 16.

[26] Charles E. Norton, *Letters*, I, 182–183.

[27] William J. Stillman, "The Philosophers' Camp," *Century Magazine*, XLVI (1893), 598–606.

[28] Emerson, "The Adirondacs," *Works*, IX, 166.

[29] Lowell, *op. cit.*, p. 153.

[30] *Idem, Poems*, in *Writings*, XII, 44.

[31] Wilson Flagg, *Studies in the Field and Forest* (Boston, 1857), p. 1.

[32] *Idem, The Birds and Seasons of New England* (Boston, 1875), p. 241.

[33] Thoreau, *Familiar Letters*, in *Writings*, VI, 311.

[34] Thomas W. Higginson, *Out-Door Papers* (Boston, 1863), pp. 249–267.

[35] Thomas Starr King, *The White Hills*, pp. 17, 57, 72.

[36] John Burroughs, *Wake-Robin* (Boston, 1895), p. ix.

[37] *Nation*, XXIII (1876), p. 66.

[38] John Burroughs, *A Year in the Fields* (Boston, 1875), p. 220; *Birds and Poets* (Boston, 1877), p. 41; *Indoor Studies* (Boston, 1891), p. 256.

[39] *John Burroughs Talks: His Reminiscences and Comments* as reported to Clifton Johnson (Boston: Houghton Mifflin, 1922), pp. 188, 210.

[40] Emerson, *Letters*, VI, 155.

CHAPTER 7: *Summer Migration* (pp. 105–128)

[1] Charles H. Sweetser, *Book of Summer Resorts*, p. 20.

[2] Timothy Flint, *Recollections of the Last Ten Years*, p. 394.

[3] *The Diary of George Templeton Strong*, ed. Allan Nevins and Milton Halsey Thomas (New York: Macmillan, 1952), I, 186.

[4] J. K. Paulding, *Letters from the South*, I, 196.

[5] John E. Cooke, "The White Sulphur Springs," *Harper's New Monthly Magazine,* LVII (1878), 337.

[6] Charles L. Brace, *Home-Life in Germany* (New York, 1853), p. 189.

[7] *The Complete Poetry and Prose of Walt Whitman* (2 vols.; New York: Pellegrini & Cudahy, 1948), II, 209.

[8] *Harper's New Monthly Magazine,* XIII (1856), 646.

[9] *The Works of Daniel Webster* (6 vols.; Boston, 1853), II, 412.

[10] *Nation,* IX (1869), 53.

[11] *Harper's New Monthly Magazine,* XLI (1870), 321.

[12] *Scribner's Monthly,* VIII (1874), 498; X (1875), 245–246.

[13] *Nation,* XXIV (1877), 240.

[14] *Extracts from the Diary of Jacob Hiltzheimer* (Philadelphia, 1893), pp. 217, 230, 231.

[15] John F. Watson, *Annals of Philadelphia and Pennsylvania* (Philadelphia, 1891), II, 542–543.

[16] Jacques Milbert, *Itinéraire pittoresque du fleuve Hudson et des parties latérales de l'Amérique du Nord* (Paris, 1829), II, 99–100.

[17] Theodore Dwight, *Things as They Are,* pp. 166, 40.

[18] G. W. Curtis, *Lotus-Eating,* p. 49.

[19] Henry James, *Notes of a Son and Brother* (New York: Scribner, 1914), p. 67.

[20] Henry Adams, *The Education of Henry Adams* (Boston: Houghton Mifflin, 1918), p. 242.

[21] Henry James, *The American Scene Together with Three Essays from "Portraits of Places,"* ed. W. H. Auden (New York: Scribner, 1946), p. 483.

[22] Thomas W. Higginson, *Old Port Days* (Boston, 1888), p. 13.

[23] C. E. Norton, *Letters,* II, 444.

[24] Curtis, *op. cit.,* pp. 154, 149, 158.

[25] Samuel T. Pickard, *Life and Letters of John Greenleaf Whittier* (2 vols.; Boston and New York, 1895), II, 595–596.

[26] Helen M. Knowlton, *Art-Life of William Morris Hunt* (Boston, 1899), p. 189.

[27] Charles Tracy, unpublished "Logbook" in the Pierpont Morgan Library, New York, pp. 110, 140.

[28] Robert Carter, *Summer Cruise on the Coast of New England* (Boston, 1864), p. 258. So many copies of this book were sold that it was reprinted in 1888.

[29] Clara B. Martin, *Mount Desert* (Portland, Me., 1874), p. 68. See also George B. Dorr, *Acadia National Park, Its Origin and Background* (2 vols.; Bangor: Printed by Burr Printing Co., 1942).

[30] John B. Bachelder, *Popular Resorts* (Boston, 1874), p. 68.

[31] Paul S. Buck, *The Evolution of the National Park System of the United States* (Columbus: Ohio State University, 1921; reprint for government use, Washington, 1946), p. 46. The Acadia National Park on Mount Desert was established in 1919.

[32] William Cooper Howells, "Camp-Meetings in the West Fifty Years Ago," *Lippincott's Magazine,* X (1877), 203–212.

[33] Dorothy G. Guck, "Prayer Trees of the Southwest," *American Forests,* LVII (January, 1951), 21, 45.

[34] "Harmony Grove, Framingham," *Gleason's Weekly,* II (1852), 384.

[35] "A Trip to the White Mountains," *Harper's Weekly,* I (1857), 536.

[36] Timothy Dwight, *Travels; in New-England and New-York,* IV, 162, 165.

[37] Henry B. Fearon, *Sketches of America* (London, 1818), p. 97.

[38] *Homes of American Authors* . . . [by various writers] (New York, 1853), p. 59.

[39] E. A. Poe, *The Domain of Arnheim,* in *Works* (London, 1914), II, 92–112; "Landor's Cottage," *ibid.,* pp. 113–119.

[40] H. D. Thoreau, *Walden,* in *Writings,* II, 100–101.

[41] Samuel G. Goodrich, *Recollections of a Lifetime* (2 vols.; New York, 1856), II, 415.

[42] R. W. Emerson, *Journals,* II, 494–495.

[43] Oliver W. Holmes, *The Autocrat of the Breakfast-Table* (Boston, 1858), p. 307.

[44] "Editor's Easy Chair," *Harper's New Monthly Magazine,* VII (1853), 129.

[45] A. J. Downing, *Rural Essays,* p. 131.

[46] Theodore Winthrop, *Life in the Open Air,* p. 6.

[47] Edwin L. Godkin, *Reflections and Comments, 1865–1895* (New York, 1895), pp. 304–305.

[48] William D. Howells, *The Landlord at Lion's Head* (New York: Harper, 1908), p. 64.

[49] Frederick W. Kilbourne, *Chronicles of the White Mountains* (Boston: Houghton Mifflin, 1916), p. 180.

[50] Henry Ward Beecher, *A Treasury of Illustrations,* ed. John R. Howard and Truman J. Ellinwood (New York: Revell, 1904), nos. 2563, 2554.

[51] Benjamin Champney, *Sixty Years of Memories* (Woburn, Mass., 1900), p. 160.

[52] Sarah J. Hale, *Traits of American Life,* p. 187.

CHAPTER 8: *Western Reports* (pages 129–147)

[1] Timothy Flint, *Recollections of the Last Ten Years,* p. 205. Cf. Hans Huth and Wilma Pugh, "Talleyrand in America as a Financial Promoter, 1794–1796, Unpublished Letters and Memoirs," American Historical Association, *Annual Report,* II (1942), 81.

[2] Flint, *op. cit.,* pp. 52–53.

[3] Isaac A. Jewell, "Themes for Western Fiction," *Western Monthly Magazine,* I (1833), 587.

[4] Flint, *op. cit.,* p. 285.

[5] Margaret F. Ossoli, *At Home and Abroad,* pp. 21, 261, 115.

[6] [C. W. Dana], *The Garden of the World; or, The Great West* (Boston, 1856), p. 14.

[7] Washington Irving, "Astoria," *Works* (Hudson ed.; New York, 1892), III, 301–303.

[8] James Hall, *Notes on the Western States,* p. 69.

[9] Francis Parkman, *The Oregon Trail,* ed. Otis B. Sperlin (New York: Longmans, Green, 1910), p. 60. The first book version was published in 1849.

[10] "A Memorial of George B. Goode," Smithsonian Institution, *Annual Report, 1897,* Pt. 2, p. 291.

[11] Meriwether Lewis and William Clarke, *Travels to the Source of the Missouri River, and . . . to the Pacific Ocean* (3 vols.; London, 1817), III, 331.

[12] Edwin James, *Account of an Expedition from Pittsburgh to the Rocky Mountains* (London, 1823), III, 267.

[13] An engraving after Doughty's painting is in *Port Folio,* 5th ser., XIII (1822), facing p. 179.

[14] Henry R. Schoolcraft, *Travels in the Central Portions of the Mississippi Valley* (New York, 1825), p. 63.

[15] "A Memorial of George B. Goode," *op. cit.,* p. 439.

[16] H. R. Schoolcraft, *Information Respecting the History, Condition, and Prospects of the Indian Tribes of the United States* (6 vols.; Philadelphia, 1852–1857).

[17] George Catlin, *North American Indian Portfolio* (London, 1844), Introduction.

[18] William A. Cooper, *Guide in the Wilderness* (Dublin, 1810; reprint Rochester, 1897), p. 23.

[19] George Catlin, *Letters and Notes on the Manners, Customs and Conditions of the North American Indians* (3d ed.; London, 1842), I, 261–262. Hiram M. Chittenden's assertion (*The Yellowstone National Park,* Cincinnati, 1895, p. 89) that Catlin in 1832 proposed that the government reserve the country around the Yellowstone geysers was omitted from later editions of his book. The Smithsonian Institution in 1952, in answer to an inquiry, stated that no proof that Catlin ever made such a proposal is to be found in any of the files or printed reports of the Institution.

[20] Ralph W. Emerson, "The Young American," *Dial*, IV (1844), 489, 486.

[21] Louis L. Noble, *The Course of Empire . . . Thomas Cole*, p. 398.

[22] Unpublished preliminary sketches by Karl Bodmer for Prince Maximilian of Wied, *Travels in the Interior of North America* (London, 1843; German ed., Coblenz, 1839–1841) are in the Ayer Collection of the Newberry Library in Chicago. Most of Bodmer's work and the entire correspondence of Prince Maximilian concerning his travels are preserved in the Archives of the Princes of Wied in Neuwied on the Rhine, Germany.

[23] Many of Miller's sketches and paintings were reproduced in Bernard de Voto, *Across the Wide Missouri*. A set of paintings now in the Walters Art Gallery, Baltimore, was reproduced by Marvin C. Ross in *The West of Alfred Jacob Miller* (Norman, Oklahoma: University of Oklahoma Press, 1951).

[24] Charles Dickens, "The American Panorama," *Works* (Centenary ed.; 36 vols.; London: Chapman & Hall, 1910–1919), XIX (*Miscellaneous Papers*, I), 139–141.

[25] Samuel L. Longfellow, *Life of Henry Wadsworth Longfellow*, II, 67–68.

[26] H. Lewis, *Das Illustrierte Mississippithal* (Dusseldorf, 1854–1858; reprint, ed. J. Bay, Leipzig, 1923), p. vii.

[27] S. N. Carvalho, *Incidents of Travel and Adventures in the Far West* (New York, 1857), p. 20.

[28] J. Wesley Jones, *Amusing and Thrilling Adventures of a California Artist While Daguerreotyping a Continent* (Boston, 1854). Sketches from Jones's daguerreotypes were published in the *California Historical Society Quarterly*, VI (1927), 109–129, 238–253.

[29] Robert Taft, *Photography and the American Scene*, p. 98.

[30] Ruth G. Hardy, "A Mountain Traveller: American Mountain Painters, VI, Albert Bierstadt," *Appalachia*, n.s., XVI (1950), 63–69.

[31] 36th Cong., 2d sess., House Ex. Doc. 64 (1861), *Maps and Reports of the Fort Kearny, South Pass, and Honey Lake Wagon Road*, p. 5.

[32] Albert Bierstadt, Letter signed "B," *Crayon*, VI (1859), 287.

[33] James J. Jarves, *Art Thoughts* (New York, 1869), p. 298.

[34] "The Domes of the Yosemite," *Nation*, IV (1867), 379.

[35] Clarence King, *Mountaineering in the Sierra Nevada*, ed. Francis P. Farquhar (New York: Norton, 1935), p. 223.

[36] U. S. War Dept., *Reports of Explorations and Surveys to Ascertain . . . Route for a Railroad from the Mississippi River to the Pacific Ocean* (12 vols. in 13; Washington, 1855–1869). Analysis of illustrations in the Railroad Surveys, in Robert Taft, *Artists and Illustrators of the Old West, 1850–1900*, pp. 1–35.

[37] James M. Hutchings, *Scenes of Wonder and Curiosity in California* (San Francisco, 1861) p. 13.

[38] "Remarkable Trees," *Ballou's Pictorial Drawing-Room Companion*, XVIII (1859), 264.

[39] "An Immense Tree," *Gleason's Pictorial Drawing-Room Companion*, V (1853), 216.

[40] James R. Lowell, "Humanity to Trees," *Crayon*, IV (1857), 96.

[41] "The Big Trees of California," *Harper's Weekly*, II (1858), 357.

[42] Carl P. Russell, *One Hundred Years in Yosemite*, pp. 1–8.

[43] "The Yo-hem-i-ty Valley and Falls," *Country Gentleman*, VIII (1856), 243.

[44] *Appleton's Illustrated Handbook of American Travel* (New York, 1857), p. 377.

[45] Horace Greeley, *An Overland Journey* (New York, 1860), pp. 307, 313, 381.

[46] "Yosemite," *Ballou's Pictorial Drawing-Room Companion*, XVI (1859), 325.

[47] Henry W. Bellows, *In Memory of Starr King* (San Francisco, 1864), p. 22.

[48] Ralph H. Anderson, "Carleton E. Watkins," *Yosemite Nature Notes*, XXXII (1953), 33–37.

[49] Oliver W. Holmes, editorial in *Atlantic Monthly*, XII (1863), 8.

[50] T. Addison Richards, "The Arts of Design," in *Eighty Years' Progress of the United States* (New York, 1861), I, 335.

[51] Charles Sweetser, *Book of Summer Resorts*, p. 14.

CHAPTER 9: *Yosemite, Yellowstone, and the Grand Canyon*
(pages 148–164)

[1] For details concerning the establishment of Yosemite as a state park, see Hans Huth, "Yosemite: The Story of an Idea," *Sierra Club Bulletin*, XXXIII, No. 3 (1948), 47–78.

[2] C. P. Russell, *One Hundred Years in Yosemite*, p. 148.

[3] Letter of Frederick Law Olmsted [Sr.] to his father, July 5, 1865, and letter to Messrs. Williams, Hill, and Watkins, Aug. 8, 1865, in Frederick Law Olmsted Papers, Library of Congress.

[4] Frederick Law Olmsted [Sr.], "The Yosemite Valley and the Mariposa Big Trees, a Preliminary Report (1865)," with an introductory note by Laura Wood Roper, *Landscape Architecture*, XLIII (1952), 12–25.

[5] *Ibid.*, p. 16.

[6] Samuel Bowles, *Across the Continent*, p. 231.

[7] R. W. Emerson, *Letters*, VI, 155.

[8] *Idem, Journals*, X, 354.

[9] Fitz-Hugh Ludlow, "Seven Weeks in the Great Yo-Semite," *Atlantic Monthly*, XIII (1864), 739–754.

[10] *Letters of Henry Adams* (1858–1891), ed. Worthington Chauncey Ford (2 vols.; Boston and New York: Houghton Mifflin, 1930–1938), I, 212.

[11] William Cullen Bryant, ed., *Picturesque America*, I, 292.

[12] Hayden's invitation to Moran was prompted by a letter from the firm of Jay Cooke & Co., "Financial Agents Northern Pacific Railroad Co.," which shows the railroad company's interest in the Yellowstone area. Dated at Philadelphia, June 7, 1871, and signed "A. B. Nettleton," the letter reads:

". . . My friend, Thos. Moran, an artist of Philadelphia of rare genius has completed arrangements for spending a month or two in the Yellowstone country taking sketches for painting. He is very desirous of joining your party at Virginia City or Helena, and accompanying you to the head waters of the Yellowstone. I have encouraged him to believe that you will be glad to have him join your party, and that you would in all probability extend to him every possible facility. Please understand that we do not wish to burden you with more people than you can attend to, but I think that Mr. Moran will be a very desirable addition to your expedition, and that he will be almost no trouble at all, and it will be a great accommodation to both our house and the road, if you will assist him in his efforts. He, of course, expects to pay his own expenses, and simply wishes to take advantage of your cavalry escort for protection. You may also have six square feet in some tent which he can occupy nights . . .

"It is possible, also that Bierstadt may join you in Montana, before you start for the Yellowstone . . . Mr. Moran will possibly go to Corinne by rail, and then cross over by stage to Helena in time to join you there.

"We shall be pleased to receive occasional letters from you telling of your expeditions, your discoveries, your opinion of things, etc., and if there is any way in which we can serve you be sure to let us know."

On Oct. 17, 1871, Nettleton addressed another letter to Hayden, telling him that "Judge Kelly has made a suggestion which strikes me as being an excellent one, viz: Let Congress pass a bill reserving the Great Geyser Basin as a public park forever—just as it has reserved that far inferior wonder the Yosemite Valley and big trees. If you approve this would such a recommendation be appropriate in your official report?" Hayden wholeheartedly approved this suggestion and in his article in *Scribner's Monthly*, VII (1872), 396, included a question which echoed Nettleton's words: "Why will not Congress at once pass a law setting it [i.e., the Yellowstone Park region] apart as a great public park for all time to come as has been done with that far inferior wonder, the Yosemite?"

These letters, which shed some interesting light on the motives which brought about the creation of Yellowstone Park, have not been published before. Copies of the letters are in the files of the National Park Service, Washington, D.C.

[13] Most books dealing with the origin of the national parks state that the birth of the national park idea took place at the "famous" campfire conversation of Nathaniel P. Langford and his friends in Yellowstone on Sept. 19, 1870, as related by Hiram M. Chittenden (*The Yellowstone National Park*, Cincinnati, 1895, p. 91). Although this conversation may have taken place, and Langford and his friends undoubtedly helped in many ways to promote the establishment of Yellowstone National Park, Cramton and I have proved that the idea of establishing national parks did not originate at that campfire (Louis C. Cramton, *Early History of Yellowstone National Park*, Washington, D.C., 1932, pp. 12–24; Huth, *op. cit.*, pp. 72–73; *idem*, "The American and Nature," *Journal of the Warburg and Courtauld Institutes*, XIII [1950], 146–147). The origin of the park idea should be looked for in the records of the circumstances which led to the setting up of Yosemite as a reservation in 1864.

[14] "Specimen Days," *The Complete Poetry and Prose of Walt Whitman* (New York, 1948), II, 155.

[15] Thomas Wolfe, "From Death to Morning," *The Portable Thomas Wolfe* (New York: Viking, 1946), p. 656. Quoted by permission of Charles Scribner's Sons.

[16] Mumey, Nolie, "William Henry Jackson: A Tribute," The Westerners, Denver Posse, *Brand Book*, III (1949), 262–263. The photograph of the Mount of the Holy Cross was published in a portfolio of Jackson's photographs prepared by the U. S. Geological and Geographical Survey of the Territories, *Photographs of Western Phenomena*, which is not indexed in any of the reference books of documents published by order of Congress. William Henry Holmes, one of the prominent geologists who explored the western territories, described the first ascent of the Mount of the Holy Cross in the *Ohio Archaeological and Historical Quarterly*, XXXVI (1927), 517–527.

[17] Samuel L. Longfellow, *Life of Henry W. Longfellow*, II, 372.

[18] Mark Twain, *Roughing It* (New York: Harper, 1913), I, 161, 162.

[19] Olive Logan, "Does It Pay to Go to Yosemite?" *Galaxy*, X (1870), 498–509.

[20] John W. Powell, "The Cañons of the Colorado," *Scribner's Monthly*, IX (1874–1875), 293–310, 394–409, 523–537; *idem*, "An Overland Trip to the Grand Cañon," *Scribner's Monthly*, X (1875), 659–678.

[21] *The Personal Narrative of James O. Pattie*, ed. Timothy Flint (Chicago: Donnelly, 1930), pp. 150–151.

[22] Roderick Peattie, *Inverted Mountains: Canyons of the West* (New York: Vanguard, 1948), p. 133.

[23] Joseph C. Ives, *Report upon the Colorado River of the West* (Washington, 1861), pp. 98–99, 5. The artist Balduin Möllhausen accompanied Ives on this expedition and published a book of his own: *Reisen in die Felsenberge Nordamerikas bis zum Hochplateau von New-Mexico* (2 vols.; Leipzig, 1861).

[24] John W. Powell, *Exploration of the Colorado River of the West and Its Tributaries* (Washington, 1875), p. 51.

[25] Peattie, *op. cit.*, p. 289.

[26] "Pleasuring in the Rockies," *Harper's New Monthly Magazine*, V (1852), 267.

[27] A. A. Hayes, Jr., "Vacation Aspects of Colorado," *Harper's New Monthly Magazine*, LX (March, 1880), 542–557.

[28] "Pleasuring in the Rockies," *Harper's New Monthly Magazine*, V, 267; Frank Gilbert Roe, *The North American Buffalo* (Toronto: University of Toronto Press, 1951), pp. 416–466.

[29] Quoted by permission of Dodd, Mead & Company from *The Diary of Philip Hone,* ed. Allan Nevins, pp. 155–156.
[30] Artemus Ward, *Panorama* (with illustrations) (New York, 1869).
[31] Mark Twain, *op. cit.,* pp. 84–85.
[32] *Idem, Life on the Mississippi* (New York: Harper, 1930), p. 123.
[33] Whitman, *op. cit.,* p. 148.
[34] Mark Twain, *Tom Sawyer* (New York: Harper, 1930), p. 123.

CHAPTER 10: *City Parks and Timberlands* (pages 165–177)

[1] Henry D. Thoreau, *Journal,* XII, 387.
[2] F. L. Olmsted, Jr., and Theodora Kimball, eds., *Frederick Law Olmsted, Landscape Architect,* I, 26.
[3] A. J. Downing, *Rural Essays,* p. 152.
[4] Olmsted, Jr., and Kimball, eds., *op. cit.,* I, 124–125.
[5] *Ibid.,* p. 37.
[6] Margaret F. Ossoli, *At Home and Abroad,* p. 5.
[7] *Aesthetic Papers,* Elizabeth P. Peabody, ed. (Boston and New York, 1849), p. 231.
[8] George P. Marsh, *Man and Nature,* iii, 31, 328–329.
[9] *Idem, The Earth as Modified by Human Action,* p. 327.
[10] H. D. Thoreau, "Chesuncook," *Atlantic Monthly,* II (1858), 317.
[11] *Idem,* "The Maine Woods," *Writings,* III, 253–254.
[12] Susan F. Cooper, *Rural Hours,* "by a Lady" (New York, 1850), pp. 202, 216.
[13] O. W. Holmes, *The Autocrat of the Breakfast-Table,* p. 269.
[14] Gifford Pinchot, *Breaking New Ground* (New York: Harcourt, Brace, 1947), p. 91; Olmsted, Jr., and Kimball, eds., *op. cit.,* I, 22. Olmsted had also participated in the publication of the weekly *Garden and Forest,* which Sargent had founded in 1887; this periodical helped greatly to spread interest in American forests and trees (Olmsted, Jr., and Kimball, eds., *op. cit.,* I, 29).
[15] W. C. Bryant, ed., *Picturesque America,* I, 435.
[16] *Special Report of the New York State Survey on the Preservation of Scenery, for 1879* (Albany, 1880), p. 27.
[17] C. E. Norton, *Letters,* II, 95 note.
[18] Frederick Starr, Jr., "America's Forests: Their Destruction and Preservation," U. S. Department of Agriculture, *Annual Report, 1865,* pp. 210–234.
[19] Franklin B. Hough, *Report on Forestry* (4 vols.; Washington, 1878–1884).
[20] Pinchot, *op. cit.,* p. 24. Pinchot does not give the source of his story; it is J. W. Powell, "The Non-Irrigable Lands of the Arid Region," *Century Magazine,* XXXII (1889–1890), 218. Here Powell tells about a fire he had caused unintentionally one snowy night in the Rocky Mountains; he wrote this as a warning to show how much damage can be done by man. Cf. J. W. Powell, *Report on the Lands of the Arid Region of the United States* (Washington, D.C., 1878), p. 17.
[21] Carl Schurz, *Speeches, Correspondence, and Political Papers* (6 vols.; New York: Putnam, 1913), V, 23. See also Hildegard B. Johnson, "Carl Schurz and Conservation," *American-German Review,* XXIII, No. 3 (1957), 4–8.
[22] *Trees for the Great, Honoring Carl Alwin Schenck* (New York: Privately printed, 1951).
[23] Pinchot, *op. cit.,* pp. 136–137.

CHAPTER 11: *The Theodore Roosevelt Era* (pages 178–191)

[1] W. F. Badè, *The Life and Letters of John Muir,* II, 409.
[2] *Ibid.,* p. 413.
[3] [Theodore Roosevelt], "We Americans and the Other Animals," *Century Magazine.*

LXVII (1903–1904), 626. In 1907 Robert Williams Wood, another physicist, published an amusing book of verses with drawings, under the title *How to Tell the Birds from the Flowers;* in 1908 he published a similar book, *Animal Analogies.*

⁴ Cartoon by E. M. Kemble, *Century Magazine,* LXX (1905), 320.
⁵ Edward B. Clark, "Roosevelt on the Nature Fakers," *Everybody's Magazine,* XVII (1907), 423–443.
⁶ Ernest Thompson Seton, *Trials of an Artist-Naturalist* (New York: Scribner, 1940).
⁷ John Burroughs, *Camping and Tramping with Roosevelt* (New York: Houghton Mifflin, 1916), pp. 63–64, 16.
⁸ John Muir, "The Great Cañon of the Colorado," *Century Magazine,* LXV (1902), 107.
⁹ Robert Underwood Johnson, *Remembered Yesterdays* (Boston: Little, Brown, 1923), p. 308.
¹⁰ Gifford Pinchot, *Breaking New Ground,* p. 326.
¹¹ *Presidential Addresses and State Papers by Theodore Roosevelt* (8 vols.; New York: Review of Reviews, 1910), VII, 1752.
¹² *Proceedings of a Conference of Governors . . . 1908* (Washington, 1909), pp. 153–157; *Report of the National Conservation Commission* (3 vols.; Washington, 1909).
¹³ National Park Conference, *Proceedings . . . at Washington, January 2 and 6, 1917* (Washington, 1917), p. 105.
¹⁴ Thomas Wolfe, "In the Park," *The Portable Wolfe,* ed. Maxwell Geisman (New York: Viking, 1946), p. 678.
¹⁵ National Park Conference, *op. cit.,* p. 107.

CHAPTER 12: *Conservation* (pages 192–212)

¹ Richard Lieber, *America's Natural Wealth;* William Vogt, *Road to Survival;* Fairfield Osborn, *Our Plundered Planet.*
² In dictionaries the words "conservation" and "preservation" are given as synonyms. They are indeed synonyms, but only so far as they mean "to protect" something. The term "conservation" has become limited in its scope and is no longer used to mean the care of historic (or man-made) objects; for this the term "preservation" is now used. Thus the act of Congress establishing the National Park Service in 1916 purposed to "conserve the scenery and the natural and historic objects and the wildlife herein"; whereas the Historic Sites Act, passed in 1935, stated as its purpose "the preservation of historic American sites, buildings, and objects." The meaning of the term "conservation" is likely to be still further contracted in the future, because of ideologic changes, and some of its meaning may be taken over by more closely defined terms. Even now, the meaning of "conservation" varies according to where and by whom it is applied. For instance, the creed of the Wilderness Society uses the term "preservation" in defining the measures for which this society stands. These measures, however, differ essentially from those that provide for the preservation of historic or man-made objects, which may need repair, stabilization, or some other physical attention. For a list of conservation agencies in the United States and charts pertaining to the matter of conservation, see *The Conservation Yearbook* for 1954, edited by Erle Kauffman.
³ Arthur H. Carhart, "Hunting and Fishing is Bigger Business," *Sports Afield,* CXXV (June, 1951), 31, 65–70.
⁴ The story of the origin of the National Park Service bill is based on the private papers of Mr. Frederick Law Olmsted, Jr., who very kindly gave permission for their use. These papers and those of Mr. J. Horace McFarland (now deposited with

the Pennsylvania Historical and Museum Commission, Harrisburg, Pa.) are basic for any study of the history of the National Park Service.

[5] *American Civic Annual*, I (1929), 16.

[6] National Park Conference, *Proceedings . . . at Washington, Jan. 2 and 6, 1917* (Washington, D.C., 1917), p. 83.

[7] J. Dixon-Scott, *England Under Trust* (London: Maclehose, 1937).

[8] Alfred L. Donaldson, *A History of the Adirondacks*, II, 191.

[9] Andrew H. Brown, "Saving Earth's Oldest Living Things," *National Geographic Magazine*, XCIX (1951), 679–695. The figures refer to trees more than 12 inches in diameter. A survey made in 1924 by Oscar Evans of the U. S. Forest Service showed 158 of these trees in the North Calaveras Grove and 947 in the South Calaveras Grove. Today "the corresponding figures . . . would probably be in the neighborhood of 175 and 1,000, respectively." Letter from Newton B. Drury, Chief of the Division of Beaches and Parks, California Dept. of Natural Resources, Feb. 20, 1957.

[10] Robert Marshall, "The Forest for Recreation," *A National Plan for American Forestry*, 73d Cong., 1st sess., Senate Doc. 12 (1933), p. 466.

[11] *Public Law* No. 845, 80th Cong., 2d sess., "Water Pollution Control Act of 1948."

[12] Aldo Leopold, "The Wilderness and Its Place in Forest Recreational Policy," *Journal of Forestry*, Vol. XIX, No. 7 (November, 1921), 718–721.

[13] Robert Marshall, "Bibliography of Robert Marshall," *Living Wilderness*, XVI, No. 38 (1951), 20–23.

[14] The Quetico-Superior Wilderness Research Center in Ely, Minn., privately financed, is designed to work for the advancement of the ecological sciences, with emphasis on wilderness problems. This project could well be used as a pattern for similar ones for the protection of other wilderness areas.

[15] Aldo Leopold, "The Land Ethic," in *A Sand County Almanac*, pp. 201–226.

[16] The President's Quetico-Superior Committee and Quetico-Superior Foundation (919 N. Michigan Avenue, Chicago 11, Ill.).

[17] "Preservation and Improvement . . . of the Niagara Falls and Rapids," *Message from the President of the United States* [Hoover], 71st Cong., 2d sess., Senate Doc. 128 (1931), pp. 31 ff. U. S. Congress, House, Committee of Foreign Affairs, *Preservation of Niagara Falls*. Hearings, 62d Cong., 2d sess., on H.R. 6746 and H.R. 7694 (Washington, 1912).

[18] Bernard Frank, and Anthony Netboy, "TVA's Unfinished Business," *Yale Review*, XI (1950), 549.

[19] Richard St. Barbe Baker, *Green Glory*, pp. 53–71. A hitherto unpublished letter to the Editor of *Time* from President Roosevelt's secretary and authorized by the President does not mention Richard St. Barbe Baker as the originator of the idea of the Civilian Conservation Corps. After elaborating on the theme of conservation and stating that no one "alive today can claim to have originated the idea," the letter states that the President "cannot find that the idea of the Civilian Conservation Corps was taken from any one source. It was rather the obvious conflux of the desire for conservation and the need for finding useful work for unemployed young men." (Letter from Miss M. A. LeHand, private secretary to President Roosevelt; quotation permitted by courtesy of the Franklin D. Roosevelt Library, Hyde Park, New York.)

[20] Gifford Pinchot, *Breaking New Ground* (New York: Harcourt, Brace, 1947), pp. 370–371.

[21] *State of Washington* v. *Dexter*, XXXII Washington Reports (1949), 2d ser., CCII, 906, per Mr. Justice Hill.

[22] James Lees-Milne, ed., *Britain's Heritage*, p. xii.

Climbing in Yosemite

Bibliography

The titles included are representative and selective and do not comprise all sources which have been consulted nor all the titles mentioned in the footnotes.

ADAMS, ANSEL EASTON. *My Camera in the National Parks.* Yosemite National Park: V. Adams; Boston: Houghton Mifflin, 1950.

ALBRIGHT, HORACE M., and FRANK J. TAYLOR. "How We Saved the Big Trees," *Saturday Evening Post,* CCXXV, No. 32 (February, 1953), 30, 31, 107, 108.

———. *Oh, Ranger!* Stanford, California: Stanford University Press, 1928.

American Forests. Washington, D.C.: American Forestry Association, 1895—

AMERICAN PLANNING AND CIVIC ASSOCIATION. *American Planning and Civic Annual.* Washington, D.C.: 1929—

AMERICAN SCENIC AND HISTORIC PRESERVATION SOCIETY. *Annual Reports,* 1896–1925. Albany, N.Y.

Appalachia. Boston: Published for the Appalachian Mountain Club by Houghton Mifflin, 1876—

Appleton's Northern and Eastern Traveller's Guide. New York, 1850.

Appleton's Southern and Western Traveller's Guide. New York, 1850.

Audubon Magazine. New York: National Audubon Society, 1899—

AVERY, MILTON H. "The Artist of Katahdin: American Mountain Painters III, F. E. Church," *Appalachia,* XXV (1944–1945), 147–154.

BABBITT, IRVING. *Rousseau and Romanticism.* Boston and New York: Houghton Mifflin, 1919.

BADE, WILLIAM FREDERIC. *The Life and Letters of John Muir.* 2 vols. Boston and New York: Houghton Mifflin, 1924.

BAKER, RICHARD ST. BARBE. *Green Glory: The Story of the Forests of the World.* London: Lutterworth Press, 1948.

BARBA, PRESTON A. *Balduin Möllhausen the German Cooper.* Philadelphia: University of Pennsylvania, 1914.

BARTRAM, WILLIAM. *Travels Through North and South Carolina, Georgia, East and West Florida . . .* London, 1792.

BEATTY, ROBERT O. "The Conservation Movement," *Annals of the American Academy of Political and Social Science,* CCLXXXI (May, 1952), 10–19.

BEECHER, HENRY WARD. *Star Papers; or, Experiences of Art and Nature.* New York, 1855.

BELKNAP, JEREMY. "Journal of a Tour from Boston to Oneida," Massachusetts Historical Society, *Proceedings,* XIX (1881–1882), 396–423.

BERGER, MAX. *The British Traveller in America, 1836–1860.* Ph.D. thesis, Columbia University. New York, 1943.

BIESE, ALFRED. *The Development of the Feeling for Nature in the Middle Ages and Modern Times.* New York: Dutton, 1905.

BIRD, ISABELLA L. *A Lady's Life in the Rocky Mountains.* New York, 1879.

BORN, WOLFGANG. *American Landscape Painting; an Interpretation.* New Haven: Yale University Press, 1948.

BOWLES, SAMUEL. *Across the Continent.* Springfield, Mass., 1865.

———. *The Switzerland of America: A Summer Vacation in the Parks and Mountains of Colorado.* Springfield, Mass., 1869.

BRECK, SAMUEL. *Recollections of Samuel Breck, with Passages from His Note-Books (1771–1862).* Edited by H. E. Scudder. Philadelphia, 1877.

BRIDENBAUGH, CARL. "Baths and Watering Places of Colonial America," *The William and Mary Quarterly*, 3d ser., III (1946), 151–181.

BROOKS, VAN WYCK. *The Flowering of New England, 1815–1865*. New York: Dutton, 1936.

———. *New England: Indian Summer, 1865–1915*. New York: Dutton, 1940.

———. *The Times of Melville and Whitman*. New York: Dutton, 1947.

———. *The World of Washington Irving*. New York: Dutton, 1944.

BROWNELL, WILLIAM C. *Newport*. New York, 1896.

BRYANT, WILLIAM CULLEN, ed. *Picturesque America; or, The Land We Live in*. 2 vols. New York, 1872–1874.

BURNABY, ANDREW. *Travels Through the Middle Settlements in North America in the Years 1759 and 1760*. 3d ed. London, 1798.

BURROUGHS, JOHN. *The Complete Nature Writings of John Burroughs*. New York: W. H. Wise, 1931.

CAMERON, JENKS. *The Development of Governmental Forest Control in the United States*. Baltimore: Johns Hopkins Press, 1928.

CANBY, HENRY SEIDEL. *Thoreau*. Boston: Houghton Mifflin, 1939.

———. *Walt Whitman, an American*. New York: Houghton Mifflin, 1943.

CARHART, ARTHUR H. *Water—or Your Life*. Philadelphia: Lippincott, 1951.

CARLYLE, THOMAS, and RALPH W. EMERSON. *The Correspondence of Thomas Carlyle and Ralph Waldo Emerson, 1834–1872*. Edited by C. E. Norton. 2 vols. Boston, 1883.

CHAMPNEY, LIZZIE W. "Summer Haunts of American Artists," *Century Magazine*, XXX (1885), 845–860.

CHINARD, GILBERT. "The American Philosophical Society and the Early History of Forestry in America," American Philosophical Society, *Proceedings*, LXXXIX (1945), 444–488.

———. *L'Amérique et le rêve exotique dans la littérature française au XVIIe et au XVIIIe siècle*. Paris: Hachette, 1934.

———. *L'Exotism américain dans l'œuvre de Chateaubriand*. Paris: Hachette, 1918.

———. *L'Homme contre la nature; essais d'histoire de l'Amérique*. Paris: Hermann, 1949.

CIRIACY-WANTRUP, SIEGFRIED VON. *Resource Conservation: Economics and Policies*. Berkeley and Los Angeles: University of California Press, 1952.

CLAVEL, MARCEL. *Fenimore Cooper and His Critics* . . . Aix-en-Provence: Imprimerie Universitaire de Provence, 1938.

COLLIER, SARGENT F., and TOM HORGAN. *Mount Desert, the Most Beautiful Island in the World*. Boston: Houghton Mifflin, 1952.

COLLOT, GEORGES HENRI VICTOR. *Voyage dans l'Amérique Septentrionale . . . le Mississippi, l'Ohio, le Missouri et autres rivières . . . 1796*. Paris, 1826.

Conservation Yearbook, The. Edited by Erle Kauffman. Washington, D.C., 1952—

COOPER, JAMES FENIMORE. *Notions of the Americans, Picked up by a Travelling Bachelor*. London, 1828.

———. *Pioneers; or, The Sources of the Susquehanna*. Vol. IV of *The Works of James Fenimore Cooper*. Mohawk ed. 32 vols. New York, 1896.

COWDREY, MARY BARTLETT. "William H. Bartlett and the American Scene," *New York History*, XXII (1914), 338–340.

———. *Winslow Homer: Illustrator*. Catalogue of an Exhibition at Smith College. Northampton, Mass., 1951.

CREVECOEUR, MICHEL GUILLAUME ST. JEAN DE. *Letters from an American Farmer*. Reprint of 1782 ed. London: Chatto and Windus, 1908.

———. *Sketches of Eighteenth Century America; More "Letters from an American Farmer."* Edited by Henri L. Bourdin *et al*. New Haven: Yale University Press, 1925.

CUMMINGS, THOMAS S. *Historic Annals of the National Academy of Design* . . . Philadelphia, 1865.

CURRIER GALLERY OF ART. *Artists in the White Mountains*. Exhibition Catalogue. Manchester, N.H., 1955.

CURTI, MERLE EUGENE. *The Growth of American Thought*. New York: Harper, 1943.

CURTIS, GEORGE WILLIAM. *Lotus-Eating: A Summer Book*. New York, 1856.

CUTLER, MANASSEH. *Life, Journals and Correspondence*. Cincinnati, 1888.

CUTRIGHT, PAUL RUSSELL. *Theodore Roosevelt, the Naturalist*. New York: Harper, 1956.

DARLINGTON, WILLIAM. *Memorials of John Bartram and Humphrey Marshall*. Philadelphia, 1849.

DARRAH, WILLIAM C. *Powell of the Colorado*. Princeton: Princeton University Press, 1951.

DELLENBAUGH, FREDERICK S. *A Canyon Voyage: The Narrative of the Second Powell Expedition down the Green-Colorado River* . . . New Haven: Yale University Press, 1947.

——. *The Romance of the Colorado River* . . . New York and London: Putnam, 1902.

DE VOTO, BERNARD AUGUSTINE. *Across the Wide Missouri*. Boston: Houghton Mifflin, 1947.

DINTRUFF, EMMA J. "The American Scene a Century Ago," *Antiques*, XXXVIII (1940), 279–281.

DOENHOFF, CHRISTIAN, GRAF VON. "Vom Wesen der National Parke," *Zeitschrift für Welt-Forstwirtschaft*, XII (1949), Heft 10–12, pp. 2–9.

DONALDSON, ALFRED LEE. *A History of the Adirondacks*. 2 vols. New York: Century, 1921.

DONDORE, DOROTHY ANNE. *The Prairie and the Making of Middle America: Four Centuries of Description*. Cedar Rapids: Torch Press, 1926.

DOUGLAS, WILLIAM ORVILLE. *Of Men and Mountains*. New York: Harper, 1950.

DOWNING, ANDREW JACKSON. *A Treatise on the Theory and Practise of Landscape Gardening Adapted to North America; with a View to the Improvement of Country Residences*. New York, 1841.

——. *Rural Essays* . . . Edited by George William Curtis. New York, 1854.

DRAPER, BENJAMIN P. "Albert Bierstadt," *Art in America*, XXVIII (1940), 61–71.

——. "John Mix Stanley," *Antiques*, XL (1942), 180–182.

——. "Thomas Moran," *Art in America*, XXIX (1941), 82–88.

——. "Washington Whittredge in the West," *Antiques*, XLV (1949), 50–57.

DUNBAR, SEYMOUR. *A History of Travel in America*. 4 vols. Indianapolis: Bobbs-Merrill, 1915.

DUNLAP, WILLIAM. *Diary of William Dunlap (1766–1839)*. 3 vols. New York: New-York Historical Society, 1930.

DWIGHT, THEODORE. *The Northern Traveller* . . . Routes to the Springs, Niagara, and Quebec . . . New York, 1831.

——. *Sketches of Scenery and Manners in the United States*. New York, 1829.

——. *Things as They Are; or, Notes of a Traveller Through Some of the Middle and Northern States*. New York, 1834.

DWIGHT, TIMOTHY. *Travels; in New-England and New-York*. 4 vols. New Haven, 1821–1822.

[ELIOT, CHARLES WILLIAM.] *Charles Eliot, Landscape Architect* . . . Boston and New York: Houghton Mifflin, 1902.

ELLIOTT, WILLIAM. *Carolina Sports, by Land and Water* . . . New York, 1859.

ELLIS, HAVELOCK. "The Love for Wild Nature," *Contemporary Review*, XCV (1909), 180–199.

EMERSON, EDWARD WALDO. *The Early Years of the Saturday Club, 1855–1870.* Boston and New York: Houghton Mifflin, 1918.

EMERSON, RALPH WALDO. *Emerson's Complete Works.* Riverside ed. 12 vols. Boston, 1833–1893.

———. *Journals of Ralph Waldo Emerson.* Edited by Edward Waldo Emerson and Waldo Emerson Forbes. 10 vols. Boston and New York: Houghton Mifflin, 1909–1914.

———. *The Letters of Ralph Waldo Emerson.* Edited by Ralph L. Rusk. 6 vols. New York: Columbia University Press, 1939.

FAGIN, NATHAN BRYLLION. *William Bartram, Interpreter of the American Landscape.* Baltimore: Johns Hopkins Press, 1933.

FARIS, JOHN T. *Old Gardens in and About Philadelphia and Those Who Made Them.* Indianapolis: Bobbs-Merrill, 1932.

FIELDING, MANTLE. *American Engravers upon Copper and Steel . . . A Supplement to David McNeely Stauffer's American Engravers.* Philadelphia, 1917.

FINLEY, RUTH E. *The Lady of Godey's, Sarah Josepha Hale.* Philadelphia and London: Lippincott, 1931.

FLINT, TIMOTHY. *Recollections of the Last Ten Years . . . in the Valley of the Mississippi.* Boston, 1826.

FOERSTER, NORMAN. *Nature in American Literature: Studies in the Modern View of Nature.* New York: Macmillan, 1923.

FORESTER, FRANK. *See* HERBERT, HENRY WILLIAM.

FRANK, BERNARD, and ANTHONY NETBOY. *Water, Land, and People.* New York: Knopf, 1950.

FRENEAU, PHILIP. *Poems of Freneau.* Edited by Harry Hayden Clark. New York: Harcourt, Brace, 1929.

FULLER, HIRAM. *Belle Brittan on a Tour, at Newport, and Here and There.* New York, 1858.

Garden and Forest; a Journal of Horticulture, Landscape Art and Forestry. 10 vols. New York: Garden and Forest Publishing Company, 1888–1897.

GILMAN, CAROLINE. *The Poetry of Travelling in the United States.* New York, 1838.

GODWIN, PARKE. *A Biography of William Cullen Bryant, with Extracts from His Private Correspondence.* 2 vols. New York, 1883.

GOODRICH, LLOYD. *A Century of American Landscape Painting, 1800 to 1900, . . .* New York: Whitney Museum of American Art, 1938.

GOULD, JOHN M. *Hints for Camping and Walking; How to Camp Out.* New York: 1877.

GREELEY, WILLIAM BUCKOUT. *Forests and Men.* Garden City, N.Y.: Doubleday, 1951.

GROSSMAN, JAMES. *James Fenimore Cooper.* New York: Sloane Associates, 1949.

HALE, RICHARD WALDEN, JR. *The Story of Bar Harbor . . .* New York: Washburn, 1949.

HALE, SARAH J. *Traits of American Life.* Philadelphia, 1835.

HALL, JAMES. *Notes on the Western States . . .* Philadelphia, 1838.

HAMILTON, ALEXANDER. *Gentleman's Progress: The Itinerarium of Dr. Alexander Hamilton, 1744.* Edited by Carl Bridenbaugh. Chapel Hill: University of North Carolina Press, 1948.

HARDING, WALTER. "Thoreau as a Lecturer," *Bulletin of the New York Public Library,* LX (1956), 74–80.

HARSHBERGER, JOHN WILLIAM. *The Botanists of Philadelphia and Their Work.* Philadelphia, 1899.

HAWTHORNE, HILDEGARDE, and ESTHER BURNELL MILLS. *Enos Mills of the Rockies.* Boston: Houghton Mifflin, 1935.

HAWTHORNE, NATHANIEL. *Mosses from an Old Manse.* 2 vols. Boston, 1854.

HENDRICKSEN, WALTER BROOKFIELD. *David Dale Owen, Pioneer Geologist of the Middle West.* Indianapolis: Indiana Historical Bureau, 1943.

[HERBERT, HENRY WILLIAM.] *The Life and Writings of Frank Forester*. Edited by David W. Judd. 2 vols. London, 1882.

HEWETT, DANIEL. *The American Traveller* . . . Washington, 1825.

HICKS, PHILIP MARSHALL. *The Development of the Natural History Essay in American Literature*. Ph.D. thesis, University of Pennsylvania. Philadelphia, 1924.

HIGGINSON, THOMAS WENTWORTH. *Cheerful Yesterdays*. Boston and New York, 1898.

HODGSON, ADAM. *Letters from North America, Written During a Tour of the United States and Canada* . . . 2 vols. New York, 1824.

HOLLEY, O. L., ed. *The Picturesque Tourist; Being a Guide Through the Northern and Eastern States and Canada* . . . New York, 1844.

HOLLIMAN, JENNIE. *American Sports (1785–1835)*. Durham, N.C.: Seeman Press, 1931.

HOLMES, OLIVER WENDELL. *The Autocrat of the Breakfast-Table*. Boston, 1858.

HONE, PHILIP. *The Diary of Philip Hone, 1828–1851*. Edited by Allen Nevins. New York: Dodd, Mead, 1936.

HOWELLS, WILLIAM DEAN. *Life in Letters of William Dean Howells*. Edited by Mildred Howells. 2 vols. New York: Doubleday, Doran, 1928.

HUBBARD, BELA. *Memorials of a Half-Century*. New York and London, 1887.

HUNGERFORD, EDWARD. "Our Summer Migration," *Century Magazine*, XX (1891), 567–576.

HUNTER, ROBERT, JR. *Quebec to Carolina in 1785–1786* . . . Edited by Louis B. Wright and Marion Tinling. San Marino, Calif.: Huntington Library, 1943.

HURLBUT, JESSE LYMAN. *The Story of Chautauqua*. New York and London: Putnam, 1921.

HUSSEY, CHRISTOPHER. *The Picturesque: Studies in a Point of View*. London and New York: Putnam, 1927.

HUTH, HANS. "The American and Nature," *Journal of the Warburg and Courtauld Institutes*, XIII (1950), 101–149.

———. "Pierre du Simitière and the Beginnings of the American Historical Museum," *Pennsylvania Magazine of History and Biography*, LXIX (1945), 315–325.

———. "The Poetry of Traveling," *Art Quarterly*, XX (1957), 17–33.

———. "Yosemite: The Story of an Idea," *Sierra Club Bulletin*, XXXIII (1948), No. 3, pp. 47–78.

INTER-AMERICAN CONFERENCE ON CONSERVATION OF RENEWABLE NATURAL RESOURCES (Denver). *Proceedings*, 1948. Washington, D.C., 1949.

INTERNATIONAL UNION FOR THE PROTECTION OF NATURE. *Bulletin* (Brussels, Belgium), 1948—

IRVING, PIERRE M. *The Life and Letters of Washington Irving*. 3 vols. New York, 1873.

IRVING, WASHINGTON. *The Western Journals of Washington Irving*. Edited by John Francis McDermott. Norman: University of Oklahoma Press, 1944.

IRVING, WASHINGTON, and OTHERS. *The Home Book of the Picturesque; or American Scenery, Art, and Literature*. New York, 1852.

JAMES, HENRY. *William Wetmore Story and His Friends* . . . Boston: Houghton Mifflin, 1903.

JANSON, CHARLES W. *The Stranger in America, 1793–1806*. London, 1807.

JEFFERSON, THOMAS. *The Complete Jefferson* . . . Edited by Saul K. Padover. New York: Duell, Sloan & Pearce, 1943.

———. *Thomas Jefferson's Garden Book, 1766–1824*. Annotated by Edwin Morris Betts. Philadelphia, 1944. Memoirs of the American Philosophical Society, Vol. XXII.

JONES, HOWARD MUMFORD. *Ideas in America*. Cambridge: Harvard University Press, 1944.

KAUFFMAN, ERLE. *See* Conservation Yearbook.

KILBOURNE, FREDERICK W. "A White Mountain Artist of Long Ago. American Mountain Painters, IV, J. F. Kensett," *Appalachia*, V (1946–1947), 448–455.

KING, EDWARD. "The Great South," *Scribner's Monthly*, II (1874), 1–31.

KING, THOMAS STARR. *The White Hills: Their Legends, Landscape, and Poetry*. Boston, 1860.

KIRKLAND, CAROLINE MATILDA (STANSBURY). *A New Home—Who'll Follow?* or, *Glimpses of Western Life*. By Mrs. Mary Clavers [pseud.] New York, 1850.

Knickerbocker New Monthly Magazine. New York, 1833–1865.

KNIGHT, SARAH (KEMBLE). *The Journal of Madam Knight [1704]*. With an introductory note by George Parker Winship. New York: P. Smith, 1935.

KRUTCH, JOSEPH W. *The Best of Two Worlds*. New York: Sloane Associates, 1953.

———. "Conservation Is Not Enough," *The American Scholar*, XXIII (1954), 295–305.

———. *The Desert Year*. New York: Sloane Associates, 1952.

———. *Henry David Thoreau*. New York: Sloane Associates, 1948.

———. *The Voice of the Desert, a Naturalist's Interpretation*. New York: Sloane Associates, 1955.

KRUTCH, JOSEPH W., ed. *Great American Nature Writing*. New York: Sloane Associates, 1950.

LAIGHTON, OSCAR. *Ninety Years at the Isles of Shoals*. Andover, Mass.: Andover Press, 1929.

Landscape. Santa Fe, N.M., 1951—

Landscape Architecture. Organ of the American Society of Landscape Architects. Boston: Landscape Architecture Publishing Co., 1910—

LANGFORD, NATHANIEL P. "The Ascent of Mount Hayden," *Scribner's Monthly*, VI (1873), 129–157.

———. "Yellowstone," *Scribner's Monthly*, II (1871), 1–17, 113–128.

LANMAN, CHARLES. *Essays for Summer Hours*. Boston, 1841.

———. *Haphazard Personalities, Chiefly of Noted Americans*. Boston and New York, 1886.

———. *Letters from a Landscape Painter*. Boston, 1845.

LARKIN, OLIVER W. *Art and Life in America*. New York: Rinehart, 1949.

LARSEN, ELLOUISE BAKER. *American Historical Views on Staffordshire China*. New York: Doubleday, Doran, 1950.

LEES-MILNE, JAMES, ed. *Britain's Heritage*. With Introduction by C. M. Trevelyan. London: Batsford, 1946.

LEOPOLD, ALDO. *A Sand County Almanac and Sketches Here and There*. New York: Oxford University Press, 1949.

LIEBER, RICHARD. *America's Natural Wealth: A Story of the Use and Abuse of Our Resources*. New York and London: Harper, 1942.

LILLARD, RICHARD G. *The Great Forest*. New York: Knopf, 1947.

LIPMAN, JEAN, and ALICE WINCHESTER. *Primitive Painters in America, 1750–1950: An Anthology*. New York: Dodd, Mead, 1950.

Living Wilderness, The. Published by the Wilderness Society. Washington, D.C., 1935—

LOCKWOOD, ALICE G. B., ed. *The Gardens of Colony and State . . . Before 1840*. 2 vols. New York: Scribner, for Garden Club of America, 1934.

LONGFELLOW, SAMUEL, ed. *Life of Henry Wadsworth Longfellow . . .* Boston, 1886.

LORD, RUSSELL, and KATE LORD, eds. *Forever the Land: A Country Chronicle and Anthology*. New York: Harper, 1950.

LOWELL, JAMES R. *The Complete Writings of James Russell Lowell in Prose and Poetry*. Riverside ed. 7 vols. Boston and New York, 1899.

McNAMARA, KATHERINE. *A Classified Bibliography of Landscape Architecture*. Cambridge, Mass.: Harvard University School of Landscape Architecture, 1934.

MANWARING, ELIZABETH WHEELER. *Italian Landscape in Eighteenth Century England . . . the Influence of Claude Lorrain and Salvator Rosa . . .* New York: Oxford University Press, 1925.

MARSH, GEORGE PERKINS. *The Earth as Modified by Human Action.* Rev. ed. of *Man and Nature.* New York, 1874.

———. *Man and Nature; or, Physical Geography as Modified by Human Action.* New York, 1864.

MARSHALL, ROBERT. *Arctic Wilderness.* Edited by George Marshall. Berkeley and Los Angeles: University of California Press, 1956.

MASON, GEORGE CHAMPLIN. *Newport Illustrated in a Series of Pen & Pencil Sketches.* Newport, 1854.

———. *Reminiscences of Newport.* Newport, 1884.

MESICK, JANE LOUISE. *The English Traveller in America, 1785–1835.* New York: Columbia University Press, 1922.

MEYER, HILDEGARD. *Nord-America im Urteil des deutschen Schrifttums bis zur Mitte des 19. Jahrhunderts.* Hamburg: Friederichsen, de Gruyter, 1929.

MILLER, ALFRED JACOB. *The West of Alfred Jacob Miller (1837).* With an account of the artist by Marvin C. Ross. Norman: University of Oklahoma Press, 1951.

MILLS, ENOS A. *The Rocky Mountain Wonderland.* Boston and New York: Houghton Mifflin, 1915.

MÖLLHAUSEN, BALDUIN. *Tagebuch einer Reise vom Mississippi nach den Küsten der Südsee.* Leipzig, 1858.

MOESCH, VASIL. *Naturschau und Naturgefühl in den Romanen der Mrs. Radcliffe und in der zeitgenössischen englischen Reiseliteratur.* Freiburg im Breisgau, 1924.

MONAGHAN, FRANK. *French Travellers in the United States 1765–1932: A Bibliography.* New York: New York Public Library, 1933.

MORAIS, HERBERT M. *Deism in Eighteenth Century America.* Ph.D. thesis, Columbia University. New York, 1934.

MOTT, EDWARD HAROLD. *Between the Ocean and the Lakes.* New York, 1899.

MOTT, FRANK L. *A History of American Magazines 1741–1885.* 3 vols. Cambridge, Mass.: Harvard University Press, 1930–1938.

MUIR, JOHN, ed. *Picturesque California and the Region West of the Rocky Mountains, from Alaska to Mexico.* 2 vols. San Francisco and New York, 1888.

MUMFORD, LEWIS. *Technics and Civilization.* New York: Harcourt, Brace, 1934.

National Parks Bulletin. Washington: National Parks Association, 1919–1930.

NATIONAL WILDLIFE FEDERATION, Washington, D.C. Various pamphlets.

Nature Magazine. Published by the American Nature Association, Washington, D.C. Baltimore, 1923—

NEUBERGER, RICHARD L. "How Much Conservation," *Saturday Evening Post,* June 15, 1940, pp. 12–89.

NEVINS, ALLAN. *America Through British Eyes.* New York: Oxford University Press, 1948.

NEWTON, ANNABEL. *Wordsworth in Early American Criticism.* Chicago: University of Chicago Press, 1928.

NEWTON, ROGER H. "Our Summer Resort Architecture—An American Phenomenon and Social Document," *Art Quarterly,* IV (1941), 297–318.

NOBLE, LOUIS L. *The Course of Empire, Voyage of Life, and Other Pictures of Thomas Cole . . .* New York, 1853.

NORTON, CHARLES E. *Letters of Charles Eliot Norton.* 2 vols. Boston and New York: Houghton Mifflin, 1913.

NORTON, CHARLES LEDYARD. *American Seaside Resorts . . . Atlantic Coast, from the St. Lawrence River to the Gulf of Mexico.* New York, 1871.

OAKES, WILLIAM. *Scenery of the White Mountains.* With sixteen plates from the drawings of I. Sprague. Boston, 1848.

OLD PRINT SHOP, INC. *Portfolio.* New York: H. S. Newman, 1941—

OLMSTED, FREDERICK LAW. *Walks and Talks of an American Farmer in England.* 2 vols. New York, 1852.

OLMSTED, FREDERICK LAW, JR., and THEODORA KIMBALL, eds. *Frederick Law Olmsted, Landscape Architect, 1822–1903.* New York: Putnam, 1922.

OLSON, SIGURD F. *The Singing Wilderness.* New York: Knopf, 1956.

Operation Outdoors, Part 1, *National Forest Recreation* (Part 2, *Wildlife,* to be published). Washington, D.C.: U. S. Department of Agriculture, 1957.

ORDWAY, SAMUEL HANSON. *A Conservation Handbook.* New York: Conservation Foundation, 1949.

OSBORN, FAIRFIELD. *Our Plundered Planet.* Boston: Little, Brown, 1948.

OSSOLI, MARGARET FULLER. *At Home and Abroad; or, Things and Thoughts in America and Europe.* Boston, 1856.

Outdoor America. Official publication of the Izaak Walton League of America, 1922–1923; 1935—

PANGBORN, JOSEPH G. *Picturesque B[altimore] and O[hio].* Chicago, 1883.

PARKINS, A. E., and J. R. WHITAKER. *Our Natural Resources and Their Conservation.* New York: Wiley, 1936.

PAULDING, JAMES K: *Letters from the South.* 2 vols. New York, 1835.

PEATTIE, DONALD CULROSS. *Audubon's America.* Boston: Houghton Mifflin, 1940.

———. *The Road of a Naturalist.* Boston: Houghton Mifflin, 1941.

PFEIFFER, EHRENFRIED. *The Earth's Face and Human Destiny.* Emmaus, Pa.: Rodale Press, 1947.

PINCHOT, GIFFORD. *Breaking New Ground.* New York: Harcourt, Brace, 1947.

Planning and Civic Comment. Washington, D.C.: American Planning and Civic Association and National Conferences on State Parks, 1935—

RAVEN, CHARLES E. *English Naturalists from Neckam to Ray: A Study of the Making of the Modern World.* Cambridge, [England]: University Press, 1947.

RESOURCES FOR THE FUTURE. *The Nation Looks at Its Resources.* Report of the Mid-Century Conference, December 2–4, 1953. Washington, D.C., 1954.

REYNOLDS, MYRA. *The Treatment of Nature in English Poetry Between Pope and Wordsworth.* Chicago, 1896.

RICE, HOWARD C. *Le Cultivateur américain: Étude sur l'œuvre de Saint Jean de Crèvecœur.* Paris: H. Champion, 1933.

RICHARDS, T. ADDISON. *American Scenery, Illustrated.* New York, 1854.

RICHARDSON, ALBERT D. *Beyond the Mississippi: From the Great River to the Great Ocean . . .* Hartford, Conn., 1867.

RICHARDSON, EDGAR PRESTON. *American Romantic Painting.* Edited by Robert Freund. New York: Weyhe, 1944.

———. *The World of the Romantic Artist.* Catalogue of an exhibition at the Detroit Institute of Arts, 1944.

ROBBINS, ROY M. *Our Landed Heritage; the Public Domain, 1776–1936.* Princeton: Princeton University Press, 1951.

RUSSELL, CARL PARCHER. *One Hundred Years in Yosemite.* Berkeley and Los Angeles: University of California Press, 1947.

ST. LOUIS, CITY ART MUSEUM OF. *Mississippi Panorama.* Catalogue of an art exhibition. St. Louis, 1949.

SCHOENICHEN, WALTHER. "Naturschutz als Aufgabe der europaischen Kulturgemeinde," in *Petermanns Geographische Mitteilungen* (Gotha, 1948), pp. 70–74.

SCHULTZE-NAUMBURG, PAUL. *Die Gestaltung der Landschaft durch den Menschen.* Munich: Callwey, 1918.

SCHWENKEL, HANS. *Naturschutz und Landschaftspflege.* Stuttgart: Ernst Klett, 1927.

SEARS, PAUL B. *Life and Environment: The Interrelations of Living Things.* New York: Teachers College, Columbia University, 1951.

SELLERS, CHARLES COLEMAN. *Charles Willson Peale.* American Philosophical Society, *Memoirs,* Vol. XXIII. 2 vols. Philadelphia, 1947.

SHANKLAND, ROBERT. *Steve Mather of the National Parks.* New York: Knopf, 1951.

SHELLEY, DONALD A. "George Harvey and His Atmospheric Landscape," *New York Historical Society Quarterly,* XXXII (1948), 104–113.

SHEPARD, PAUL. "The Nature of Tourism," *Landscape,* V (1955), 29–33.

Sierra Club Bulletin. San Francisco: Sierra Club, 1893—

SMITH, HENRY NASH. *The Virgin Land: The American West as Symbol and Myth.* Cambridge, Mass.: Harvard University Press, 1950.

SMITHSONIAN INSTITUTION. "A Memorial of George Browne Goode," *Annual Report of the Board of Regents . . . for the Year Ending June 30, 1897,* Part II (1901).

SPRINGER, JOHN S. *Forest Life and Forest Trees: Comprising Winter Camp-Life Among the Loggers, and Wild-Wood Adventures.* New York, 1858.

STAUFFER, DAVID MCNEELY. *American Engravers upon Copper and Steel.* New York: Grolier Club, 1907.

STEGNER, WALLACE E. *Beyond the Hundredth Meridian: John Wesley Powell and the Second Opening of the West.* Boston: Houghton Mifflin, 1954.

STILLMAN, WILLIAM JAMES. *The Autobiography of a Journalist.* 2 vols. Boston: Houghton Mifflin, 1901.

———. *The Old Rome and the New, and Other Studies.* Boston and New York. 1898.

STOKES, I. N. PHELPS, and D. C. HASKELL. *American Historical Prints.* New York: New York Public Library, 1933.

STREET, GEORGE E. *Mount Desert: A History.* Boston and New York: Houghton Mifflin, 1905.

SUTCLIFF, ROBERT. *Travels in Some Parts of North America in the Years 1804, 1805, & 1806.* York, England, 1811.

SWEET, FREDERICK A. "Asher B. Durand, Pioneer American Landscape Painter," *Art Quarterly,* XVIII (1945), 140–160.

———. *The Hudson River School and the Early American Landscape Tradition.* Catalogue of an Exhibition held at the Art Institute of Chicago, 1945.

SWEETSER, CHARLES H., comp. *Book of Summer Resorts . . .* New York, 1868.

TAFT, ROBERT. *Artists and Illustrators of the Old West, 1850–1900.* New York: Scribner, 1953.

———. *Photography and the American Scene, a Social History, 1839–1889.* New York: Macmillan, 1938.

TEALE, EDWIN WAY. "The Murder of a Landscape," *Natural History,* LX (1951), 252–256.

TELLER, JAMES DAVID. *Louis Agassiz, Scientist and Teacher.* Columbus, Ohio: State University Press, 1947.

TEMPLEMAN, WILLIAM D. *The Life and Work of William Gilpin (1724–1804).* Urbana: University of Illinois Press, 1939.

THACHER, MARY P. *Seashore and Prairie.* New York, 1878.

THOMAS, WILLIAM L., JR., ed. *Man's Role in Changing the Face of the Earth.* Chicago: University of Chicago Press, 1956.

THOMPSON, RALPH. *American Literary Annuals & Gift Books, 1825–1865.* New York: H. W. Wilson, 1936.

THOREAU, HENRY D. *The Writings of Henry David Thoreau.* 20 vols. Boston: Houghton Mifflin, 1906. Vols. VII–XX are Thoreau's *Journal,* edited by Bradford Torrey.

TILDEN, FREEMAN. *The National Parks, What They Mean to You and Me.* New York: Knopf, 1951.

TRACY, CHARLES. "Logbook." Unpublished MS in the Pierpont Morgan Library, New York City.

TROLLOPE, FRANCES. *Domestic Manners of the Americans.* London: Routledge, 1927.

TUCKERMAN, FREDERICK. "Early Visits to the White Mountains and Ascents of the Great Range," *Appalachia,* XV (1921), 112–126.

———. "The Golden Age of the White Hills," *Appalachia,* XVI (1924–1926), 291–297.

TUCKERMAN, HENRY T. *America and Her Commentators ... Travel in the United States.* New York, 1864.

TUNNARD, CHRISTOPHER. *The City of Man.* New York: Scribner, 1953.

UNITED STATES CONGRESS. *National Plan for America's Forests.* 73d Cong., 1st sess., Senate Doc. 12 (1933).

UNITED STATES DEPARTMENT OF AGRICULTURE. *Trees: The Year Book of Agriculture.* Washington, 1949.

UNITED STATES NATIONAL PARK SERVICE. *Study of the Park and Recreation Problems of the United States.* Washington, 1941.

VAUX, CALVERT. *Villas and Cottages.* New York, 1864.

VOGT, WILLIAM. *Road to Survival.* New York: Sloane Associates, 1948.

WADSWORTH ATHENEUM. *Thomas Cole, 1801–1848, One Hundred Years Later: A Loan Exhibition.* Hartford, Conn., 1948.

WAUGH, FRANK A. *Landscape Gardening ...* New York: Orange Judd, 1899.

WEITENKAMPF, FRANK. "Early American Landscape Prints," *Art Quarterly,* VIII (1945), 40–67.

WELD, ISAAC. *Travels Through the States of North America and the Provinces of Upper and Lower Canada ... 1795, 1796, and 1797.* 2 vols. London, 1807.

WESTON, EDWARD. *My Camera on Point Lobos.* Yosemite National Park: V. Adams; Boston: Houghton Mifflin, 1950.

WHITAKER, J. RUSSELL, and EDWARD A. ACKERMAN. *American Resources, Their Management and Conservation.* New York: Harcourt, Brace, 1951.

WHITCOMB, BELDEN X. "Nature in Early American Literature," *Sewanee Review,* II (1893), 159–179.

WHITMAN, WALT. *The Complete Poetry and Selected Prose and Letters of Walt Whitman.* Edited by Emory Holloway. London: Nonesuch, 1938.

WHITTIER, JOHN G. *The Complete Poetical Works of John Greenleaf Whittier.* Boston and New York: Houghton Mifflin, 1904.

WIEBKING-JUERGENSMANN, H. F. *Die Landschaftsfibel.* Berlin: Deutsche Landbuch-handlung, 1942.

WIED-NEUWIED, MAXIMILIAN, PRINZ VON. *Maximilian, Prince of Wied's Travels in the Interior of North America, 1832–1834.* Reuben G. Thwaites, ed., *Early Western Travels,* XXII–XXV. 3 vols. and atlas. Cleveland: A. H. Clark, 1906.

WILLEY, BENJAMIN G. *History of the White Mountains ...* North Conway, N.H., 1869.

WILLIS, NATHANIEL PARKER. *A l'Abris; or, The Tent Pitched.* New York, 1839.

———. *American Scenery; or, Land, Lake and River Illustrations of Transatlantic Nature.* 2 vols. London, 1840.

———. *Letters from Under a Bridge.* New York, 1844.

———. *Out-doors at Idlewild; or, The Shaping of a Home on the Banks of the Hudson.* New York, 1855.

———. *Pencillings by the Way.* London, 1839.

———. *Rural Letters ...* New York, 1849.

WILLIS, NATHANIEL PARKER, ed. *Trenton Falls, Picturesque and Descriptive.* New York, 1851.

WILSON, ALEXANDER. *Poems and Literary Prose.* Edited by Alex. B. Grosart. Paisley, 1876.

WILSON, FRED A. *Some Annals of Nahant in Massachusetts.* Boston: Old Corner Bookstore, 1928.

WINTHROP, THEODORE. *Life in the Open Air, and Other Papers.* Boston, 1863.

WOLFE, THOMAS. *A Western Journal; a Daily Log of the Great Parks Trip, June 20–July 2, 1938.* Pittsburgh: University of Pittsburgh Press, 1951.

WOODWARD, J. D. "Colorado," *Art Journal,* n.s., II (1876), 97–100, 129–130, 169–172.

WOOLLEY, MARY E. "The Development of the Love of Romantic Scenery in America," *American Historical Review,* III (1897–1898), 56–66.

Acknowledgments

I wish to thank the following publishers and libraries for permission to quote from books or periodicals or to reproduce illustrations bearing their imprint; or to quote from manuscripts in their possession:

AMERICAN FORESTRY ASSOCIATION, WASHINGTON, D.C.
American Forests, LVII (1951), 21, 45.
AMERICAN PHILOSOPHICAL SOCIETY, PHILADELPHIA, PA.
Charles Coleman Sellers, *Charles Willson Peale,* Memoirs of the American Philosophical Society, XXIII, 1947.
Thomas Jefferson's Garden Book, ed. by Edwin Morris Betts.
BARNES & NOBLE, INC., NEW YORK
Henry S. Burrage, ed., *Early English and French Voyages Chiefly from Hakluyt, 1534–1608,* 1906.
Albert Cook Myers, ed., *Narratives of Early Pennsylvania . . . 1630–1707,* 1912.
Lyon Gardiner Tyler, ed., *Narratives of Early Virginia, 1606–1625,* 1907.
B. T. BATSFORD, LTD., LONDON
James Lees-Milne, *Britain's Heritage,* 1946.
BOSTON PUBLIC LIBRARY
Zoltan Haraszti, *The Idyll of Brook Farm,* 1937.
THE CHRISTIAN SCIENCE PUBLISHING SOCIETY
Cartoon by Burr Shafer from *Christian Science Monitor,* May 17, 1951.
DES MOINES REGISTER, DES MOINES, IOWA
Two cartoons by J. N. Darling.
THE DIAL PRESS, NEW YORK, and MR. STEPHEN SPENDER
The Permanent Goethe, trans. by Stephen Spender, ed. by Thomas Mann, 1948.
DODD, MEAD & CO., NEW YORK
The Diary of Philip Hone, 1828–1851, ed. by Allan Nevins, 1936.
R. R. DONNELLY & SONS CO., CHICAGO
The Personal Narrative of James O. Pattie of Kentucky, ed. by Timothy Flint. Introd. and notes by Milo Milton Quaife, 1930.
DUELL, SLOAN & PEARCE, INC., NEW YORK
The Complete Jefferson, ed. by Saul K. Padover, 1943.
THE GARDEN CLUB OF AMERICA, NEW YORK
Alice G. B. Lockwood, *The Gardens of Colony and State . . . Before 1840,* 1934.
HARCOURT, BRACE & CO., INC., NEW YORK
Carl Sandburg, *Good Morning, America,* 1928.
Gifford Pinchot, *Breaking New Ground,* 1947.
HARPER & BROTHERS, NEW YORK
Thomas Twining, *Travels in America 100 Years Ago,* 1902.
William Dean Howells, *The Landlord at Lion's Head,* 1908.
Mark Twain, *Roughing It,* 1913; *Tom Sawyer,* 1913.
HOUGHTON MIFFLIN CO., BOSTON
Letters of Henry Adams, ed. by Worthington Chauncey Ford, 1930–1938.
William Frederic Badè, *The Life and Letters of John Muir,* 1924.
John Burroughs, *Camping and Tramping with Roosevelt,* 1916; *John Burroughs Talks: His Reminiscences and Comments* as reported by Clifton Johnson, 1922.
Henry Seidel Canby, *Thoreau,* 1939.
Journals of Ralph Waldo Emerson, 1909–1914.

Frederick W. Kilbourne, *Chronicles of the White Mountains,* 1916.
Letters of Charles Eliot Norton, with biographical comment by his daughter
    Sara Norton and M. A. De Wolfe Howe, 1933.
Letters of John Ruskin to Charles Eliot Norton, 1904.
William J. Stillman, *The Autobiography of a Journalist,* 1901.
The Journal of Henry Thoreau, ed. by Bradford Torrey, 1906.
The Writings of Henry David Thoreau, 1901.
The Complete Poetical Works of John Greenleaf Whittier, 1904.
HENRY E. HUNTINGTON LIBRARY, SAN MARINO, CALIF.
    Robert Hunter, Jr., *Quebec to Carolina in 1785–1786,* 1943.
LIBRARY OF CONGRESS, WASHINGTON, D.C.
    Papers of Frederick Law Olmsted, Sr.
LITTLE, BROWN & CO., BOSTON (also Mr. Frederic Wolsey Prattand Mr. Odell Shepard)
    The Journals of Bronson Alcott, ed. by Odell Shepard, 1938.
THE MACMILLAN CO., NEW YORK
    Carol Brink, *Harps in the Wind: The Story of the Singing Hutchinsons,* 1947.
    Diary of George Templeton Strong, ed. by Allan Nevins and Milton Halsey
        Thomas, 1952.
NEW YORK HISTORICAL SOCIETY, NEW YORK
    Diary of William Dunlap (1766–1839), 1930.
OXFORD UNIVERSITY PRESS, INC., NEW YORK
    Talbot Hamlin, *Greek Revival Architecture in America,* 1944.
    Aldo Leopold, *A Sand County Almanac,* 1949.
PRINCETON UNIVERSITY PRESS, PRINCETON, N.J.
    The Autobiography of Benjamin Rush, ed. by George W. Corner, 1948.
CHARLES SCRIBNER'S SONS, NEW YORK
    Kenneth McKenzie Clark, *Landscape Painting,* 1950.
    Henry James, *The American Scene,* 1946; *Notes of a Son and Brother,* 1914.
    The Portable Thomas Wolfe, ed. by Maxwell Geisman, The Viking Press, 1946.
WILLIAM SLOANE ASSOCIATES, NEW YORK
    Joseph W. Krutch, *Great American Nature Writing,* 1950.
VANGUARD PRESS, NEW YORK
    Roderick Peattie, ed., *The Inverted Mountains: Canyons of the West,* 1948.
E. WEYHE, NEW YORK
    Edgar Preston Richardson, *American Romantic Painting,* ed. by Robert Freund,
        1944.
YALE UNIVERSITY PRESS, NEW HAVEN, CONN.
    Perry Miller, ed., *Images or Shadows of Divine Things by Jonathan Edwards,*
        1948.

Index

Abbotsford, Scotland, 122
Acker, W. B., 154
Adams, Henry, 114, 152
Adams, John Q., 167
Adirondacks, N.Y., 77, 81 f., 96–98 *passim,* 110, 150, 200
Aesthetics, 11, 16, 21, 27, 94, 96, 101, 172, 179, 184, 187, 189, 196, 207. *See also* Beautiful
Agassiz, Louis, 90, 97
Albright, Horace M., 184, 194, 197
Alcott, Bronson, 94
Alleghenies, 45
Allston, Washington, 42 f.
American Academy of the Fine Arts, 44
American Art Union, 49
American Association for the Advancement of Science, 174
American Association of Museums, 198
American Civic Association, 184, 187
American Farmer, 56
American Forestry Association, 2, 175
American Gardener's Calendar, 60
American Institute of Architects, 184
American Landscape, 48
American League for Civic Improvement, 184
American Legion, 206
American Lyceum, 50
American Magazine, The, 13
American Museum, 26
American Park and Outdoor Art Society, 184
American Philosophical Society, 15 ff.
American Planning and Civic Association, 184
American Scenic and Historic Preservation Society, 185
Ames, Ezra, 43
Antiquities Act, 182
Appalachian Mountain Club, 111, 185

Appledore Island, Me., 115 f.
Arbor Day, 171
Arid region, 174
Arizona, 119
Arkansas River, 129
Arnold Arboretum, 171, 187
Arnold, James, 171
Art exhibitions, 44, 48, 135, 140
Artists, 48 f., 127 f.
Atlantic Monthly, 91, 100, 143, 151
Atlantic Souvenir, 48, 66, 78
Audubon, John James, 26, 102, 123, 134
Austin, the Misses, 79
Automobiles, 188, 201 f.
Awe, 7 f., 11, 25, 75
Ayers, Thomas A., 144

Bachelder, John B., 111
Baden-Powell, Robert S. S., 180
Badlands, N.D., 180
Baird, Spencer F., 90
Baker, Richard St. Barbe, 209
Ballinger, Richard A., 190 f.
Ballston, N.Y., 37, 73
Baltimore, Md., 190
Baltimore & Ohio Railroad, 86, 109
Balzac, Honoré de, 35
Banvard, John, 137
Bar Harbor, Me., 117 f.
Barlowe, Arthur, 4
Barnum, Phineas T., 90
Bartholomew, T. C., 140
Bartlett, William M., 74
Bartram, John, 14 ff., 28
Bartram, William, 15, 20–26 *passim,* 40, 88, 129, 133
Beaches, 82, 112, 118, 128, 189. *See also* Resorts
Beautiful, 11, 28, 96. *See also* Aesthetics
Beck, George, 41 f.

Beecher, Henry Ward, 90, 96, 127
Beecher sisters, 55
Belknap, Jeremy, 28
Bell, William, 156
Bellingrath Gardens, Ala., 185
Beamann, E. H., 160
Berkeley, Bishop, 10
Berkeley, Governor, 57
Berkeley Springs, W.Va., 85
Berkshires, Mass., 36
Bicycle, 112
Bierstadt, Albert, 128, 133, 140 ff., 151
Bigelow, Jacob, 66
Billboards, 202
Billings, Mont., 132
Biltmore Estate, N.C., 185
Biltmore Forest School, 175
Birch, Thomas, 42
Birds, 25 f., 103
Black Canyon, Ariz. and Nev., 160
Blackburn, Joseph, 40
Blue Ridge, Pa. to Ga., 27, 36, 41, 202
Bodmer, Karl, 136 f., 222 n. 22
Boston, Mass., 60, 63, 190; Common: 9, 60 f.,
    66 f.
Boston Magazine, 26
Botanical gardens, 15, 45, 61, 171
Bowers, Edward A., 176, 186
Bowles, Samuel, 150 f.
Brace, Charles Loring, 108
Brewer, William H., 175
British National Trust, 199
Brook Farm, Mass., 91 f.
Brooklyn, 63
Bryant, Harold C., 198 f.
Bryant, William Cullen, 24, 30–36 *passim*,
    65, 67, 69, 82, 90, 163, 169, 172
Bryce Canyon National Park, 161
Buffalo, N.Y., 73, 75, 202
Buffaloes, 162 f.
Bumpus, Hermon C., 198
Burke, Edmund, 11, 211
Burnaby, Andrew, 27, 55, 57
Burnham, Daniel, 166, 184
Burroughs, John, 53, 102–105 *passim*, 180,
    182
Burton, Warren, 91, 101
Byrd, William, 9, 15, 26, 57
Byron, Lord, 31, 37

Calaveras Grove, Calif., 142, 171, 200, 227
    n. 9
California, 135, 151, 153, 176, 200
California Legislature, 149, 153

Camp meetings, 118, 120
Campfire conversation, 224 n. 13
Camping, 111, 189
Canadian Legion, 206
Canals, 72 f., 110, 189
Canby, Henry Seidel, 95 ,
Cape Cod, Mass., 128
Cape May, N.J., 112
Carlyle, Thomas, 21, 88
Carnegie, Andrew, 187
Carter, Robert, 117
Carvalho, S. N., 139
Casilear, John W., 47, 127
Catesby, Mark, 133
Catlin, George, 134, 148, 153, 221 n. 19
Catskill Mountain House, N.Y., 77 f., 84, 218
    n. 21
Catskills, N.Y., 28, 38, 46, 50, 74, 77, 122,
    200
Cedars, N.J., 123
Cemeteries, scenic, 66 f., 69
Central Pacific Railroad, 131, 155
Century Magazine, 180, 183, 187
Champney, Benjamin, 127
Channing, William Ellery, 91, 101
Chappell, Alonzo, 140
Charleston, S.C., 40, 57
Chateaubriand, F. R. de, 21, 50, 129 f.
Chautauqua, N.Y., 119
Chesapeake and Ohio Canal, 73
Chesapeake and Ohio Railroad, 108
Chicago, 62, 166, 171, 184
Chocorua, Mount, 80
Christian thoughts, 10, 117, 119
Church, Frederick E., 47, 84, 97, 116 f.
Church gatherings, 118 f.
Cincinnati, Ohio, 62
City life, 22, 24, 89, 92, 187. *See also* Parks
Civilian Conservation Corps, 198, 209, 227
    n. 19
Clark, Edward D., 180
Clark, William. *See* Lewis and Clark
Cleveland, Grover, 176
Clinton, De Witt, 44, 73
Coates, E. C., 62
Cockneys, 111, 124 f., 162
Cohoes Falls, N.Y., 5, 7
Colden, Cadwallader, 15, 22
Colden, Jane, 15
Cole, Thomas, 12, 43–52 *passim*, 78–81 *pas-
    sim*, 116, 122, 127, 189
Coleridge, Samuel T., 31, 42
Colfax, Schuyler, 150 f.
Collin, Nicholas, 16, 35

Colman, Samuel, 120
Colorado, 119
Colorado River, 139, 153, 161, 174
Colorado Springs, 161
Columbia River, 131, 208
Columbian Magazine, 26, 42
Colvin, Verplanck, 200
Combe, William, 12
Conference of Governors, 186
Conness, John, 148
Conservation, 2 f., 16, 34 f., 118, 153, 169, 173, 179, 183, 185, 186, 190, 192–211 *passim*, 226 n. 2
Continental Divide, 139, 142
Cook, Charles W., 153
Cooke, Jay, 152, 223 n. 12
Cooper, James Fenimore, 31, 33–38 *passim*, 44, 63, 77
Cooper, Susan F., 33, 123, 170
Cooper, William, 34, 135
Cooperstown, N.Y., 62 f.
Copeland Report, 194
Cornell University, 186
Cottages, 118, 123 ff.
Country life, 22, 121 f., 123, 127, 184
Crater Lake National Park, 155
Crawford, Ethan A., 79, 123
Crayon, The, 97, 140
Crèvecoeur, St. Jean de, 15, 21
Cropsey, Jaspar F., 47
Croquet, 111 f.
Cumberland Gap, Tenn. and Va., 72
Curtis, George W., 36, 52, 83, 91
Cutler, Manasseh, 28, 59, 61

Dams, 160, 208
Dana, C. W., 131
Dana, Charles A., 166
Dana, Richard H., 30, 37
Davison, George H., 72
Dean, Bishop, 118
Deas, Charles, 82
Defiance, Mount, 78
Deforestation, 168 ff., 173, 175, 179, 186
Deism, 10 ff., 23 f.
Delaware River, 56
Delaware Water Gap, 36
Dellenbaugh, Frederick, 159 f.
Dennie, Joseph, 32
Dexter vs. *State of Washington*, 210
Dial, The, 91, 136
Diamond Creek, Ariz., 160
Dickens, Charles, 73, 137, 172
Dinosaur National Monument, 209

Division of Forestry, 176
Doane, G. C., 153
Dorr, George B., 118
Doughty, Thomas, 44, 48, 81, 132
Downing, Andrew J., 67–70 *passim*, 122–124 *passim*, 165
Drury, Newton B., 200
Dunlap, William, 33, 45, 58, 71
Dunraven, Earl of, 162
Durand, Asher B., 47 f., 62, 127
Du Simitière, Pierre, 18
Dwight, Theodore, 17, 67, 73, 78, 113
Dwight, Timothy, 27, 32, 48, 61, 73, 78, 121
Dyer, John, 28

Earl, Ralph, 39
East, 51, 102
Eastham, Mass., 118
Eastman, Seth, 82, 134
Ecology, 16, 210, 227 n. 14
Economic points of view, 187, 191
Edison, Thomas A., 103
Edwards, Jonathan, 7 f., 40
Egan, John, 138
Egloffstein, F. W. Freiherr von, 142
Eisenhower, Dwight D., 195, 207
Elgin Botanical Garden, 61
Eliot, Charles, 118
Eliot, Charles William, 118, 199
Elliot, Henry W., 152
Emerson, Ralph Waldo, 12, 21, 24, 36, 87–98 *passim*, 123, 136, 151, 168
Endicott, John, 63
Erie, Lake, 44, 109
Erie Canal, 44, 72, 75
Erie Railroad, 109
Erosion, 180, 208
Ethical points of view, 94, 196, 210
Evelyn, John, 7
Everett, Edward, 66, 82
Evert, T. C., 159
Exploitation, 35

Fabyan's Resort, N.H., 81
Fairmount Park. *See* Philadelphia
Fernow, Berthold E., 175 f., 186
Fisher, Alvan, 48
Fisher, Walter F., 192
Flagg, Wilson, 100 f.
Flint, Timothy, 107, 129
Florida, 108, 133
Flume House, N.H., 121
Follansbee Pond, N.Y., 97
Follen, Charles T., 109

Folsom, David E., 153
Ford, Henry, 188
Ford Foundation, 194
Fordham, N.Y., 122
Forest fires, 175, 201, 225 n. 20
Forest Service. *See* U. S. Forest Service
Forester, Frank. *See* Herbert, H. W.
Foresters, 10, 178
Forests, 16, 92, 174; multiple use of, 194, 196
Fort Bridger, 152
Fort Clark, 136
Fort Laramie, 140
Fort Mackenzie, 136
Fort Union, 136
Franconia Notch, N.H., 121
Franklin, Benjamin, 15 f., 56
Frémont, John C., 69, 139, 147
Freneau, Philip, 13, 23 f., 31
Frost, S. H., 140
Fourierism, 92
Fuller, Margaret, 62, 130, 167
Fulton, Robert, 45

Gainsborough, Sir Thomas, 40
Garden clubs, 185
Gardens, 9, 57 f., 60, 185
General Federation of Women's Clubs, 197
General Grant National Park, 155
Genesee Falls, N.Y., 75
George, Lake, 75, 77, 107, 127
Gifford, Sandford R., 133, 152
Gila Wilderness, N.M., 205 f.
Gilman, Caroline, 72 f., 75
Gilmore, Robert, 52
Gilpin, William, 11 f., 89, 94, 102
Glacier National Park, 155
Glen Mary, 122
Godey's Magazine, 128
Godkin, Edwin L., 110 f., 124, 141
Goethe, Johann Wolfgang von, 49 f.
Goode, George Brown, 90
Gould, John M., 111
Goupil's, 145, 151
Grand Canyon, 153, 161, 181; National Park, 181 f.
Grand objects, 41
Grand River, Colo. and Utah, 159
Grant, Ulysses S. III, 184
Graves, Henry S., 191, 201
Gray, Asa, 171
Gray's Ferry, 27, 59
Great Lakes, 128, 146, 173
Great Smoky Mountains, 82
Greeley, Horace, 90, 144, 157

Green, Andrew H., 185
Green River, Wyo., Colo., Utah, 159, 209
G.eenbriar White Sulphur Springs, W.Va., 107
Groombridge, William, 41 f.
Guy, Francis, 41, 42

Hale, Sarah J., 74, 128
Hall, Basil, 134
Hall, James, 83, 130
Halleck, Fitz-Greene, 33
Hamilton, William, 58
Hamlin, Talbot, 77
Hance, John, 161
Harmony Grove, Miss., 119
Harpers Ferry, 20, 86
Harrisburg Pa., 184
Harrison, William H., 176
Hart, William M., 127
Harvard University, 96, 114, 118, 171
Harvey, Fred, 161
Hassam, Childe, 116
Hawthorne, Nathaniel, 12, 92, 95 f., 115, 120
Hayden, Ferdinand H., 152 f., 159, 223 n. 12
Headley, Joel T., 97, 200
Health, 108 f. *See also* Recreation
Hedges, Cornelius, 153
Hennepin, Father Louis, 5
Henry, Joseph, 90
Herbert, Henry William, 56, 123
Hessler, Alexander, 140, 142, 156
Hetch-Hetchy Valley, Calif., 183, 188, 190, 196
Higginson, Thomas W., 100 f., 114 f., 199
Hill, John, 47
Hill, Thomas, 149
Hillers, Jack, 156
Hiltzheimer, Jacob, 112
Hoar, Ebenezer R., 97
Hoboken, N.J., 62
Hoffman, Charles Fenno, 81, 83
Holidays, 7, 56, 63, 106, 126
Holmes, Oliver Wendell (writer), 123, 143, 145, 151, 171, 199
Holmes, Oliver Wendell (jurist), 186
Holy Cross, Mountain of the, 156
Holyoke, Mount, 74, 76, 120
Homer, Winslow, 53, 98
Hone, Philip, 62, 163
Honolulu, 65
Horticulturist, The, 68
Hosack, David, 45, 61
Hough, Franklin B., 174

Howells, William D., 126
Howitt, William, 87, 94, 108 f.
Hudson River, 2, 37 f., 41, 44, 74, 122
Hudson River Portfolio, 48
Hudson River school, 39, 44
Hughes, Charles Evans, 188
Humphrey, Hubert H., viii
Hunt, William Morris, 114, 116, 128
Hunter, Robert, 28
Huntington, Daniel, 120
Hutchings, James M., 143
Hutchinson family, 80

Idealistic points of view, 179, 185
Idlewild, N. Y., 123
Illinois Monthly Magazine, 130
Illinois Natural History Society, 159
Indiana, 200
Indians, 50, 134 f., 136, 138 f.
Inland Waterways Commission, 186
Inman, Henry 47 f., 132
Innes, George, 53
International Conservation Conference, 209
Irving, Washington, 36 ff., 44, 50, 77, 82, 122, 131
Isles of Shoals, 115 f.
Italy, 32 f.
Itasca Park, Minn., 199
Izaak Walton League of America, 203, 205 f.

Jackson, William H., 142, 156, 224 n. 16
Jacksonville, Fla., 108
James, Edwin, 132
James, Henry, 114
James, MacGill, 137
James River, Va., 57
Jameson, Anna, 49
Jarves, James Jackson, 65, 141
Jefferson, Thomas, 15, 31, 37, 58, 60
Johnson, Robert Underwood, 182, 186
Jones, Howard Mumford, 31
Jones, J. Wesley, 139
Josselyn, John, 5
Juniata River, Pa., 27, 75

Katahdin, Mount, 82, 84, 93
Keene Valley, N.Y., 127
Kemble, Fanny, 60, 62, 67
Kensett, John F., 47, 127
Kentucky, 118 f.
Kern, Richard H., 142
King, Clarence, 141, 152
King, Thomas Starr, 101, 120, 144
Kingsess, Pa., 15

Kirkland, Caroline, 62, 83
Knickerbocker Magazine, 122, 137
Krimmel, John, 63
Kühn, Justus Engelhardt, 40
Kunz, George F., 187 f.

Ladies' Magazine, 26
Lafayette House, N.H., 121
Laighton, Henry B., 115
Lake Placid, N.Y., 127
Lake poets, 21 f., 31
Land ethic, 204
Lander, Frederick W., 140
Landscape painting, 3, 39, 44, 52, 120
Landscaping, 58, 65, 68
Lane, Franklin K., 196
Langenheim brothers, 138
Langford, Nathaniel P., 152 f., 159
Lanman, Charles, 80 ff.
Laurel parties, 127
Lawrence, David H., 35
L'Enfant, Pierre, 66, 184
Leopold, Aldo, 204, 210
Lesueur, Charles, 133
Lewis, Elisha J., 109
Lewis, Henry, 138
Lewis, James Otto, 134
Lewis and Clark expedition, 60, 131
Lieber, Francis, 109
Lieber, Richard, 193, 200
Lincoln, Abraham, 148
Lindley, Sir John, 68
Lipman, Jean, 39
Living Wilderness, The, 204
Livingston, Robert R., 45
Loch Katrine, 78
Logan, Olive, 157
London, 139, 143
London, Jack, 180
Long, Stephen H., 44, 132
Long, William J., 180
Long Branch, N.J., 73, 112
Long Island, 68
Longfellow, Henry W., 97, 138, 140, 157
Longs Peak, 182
Lowell, James R., 36, 95, 97 ff., 115, 143
Lowell, John, 66
Ludlow, Fritz-Hugh, 141, 151

McFarland, J. Horace, 183 f., 187 f., 196, 206
Mackinac Island, 146
McKinley, William, 176
Maclure, William, 92, 133
McMahon, Bernard, 60, 68

Madison, James, 24
Madison-on-the-Lakes, Wis., 110
Maine, 93, 150, 174
Mammoth Cave, Ky., 19, 146
Marcy, Mount, 81
Mariposa County, Calif., 69
Mariposa Grove, Calif., 144, 148, 179
Marsh, George P., 82, 168, 171 f., 183, 193
Marshall, Humphrey, 15 f.
Marshall, Robert, 204
Marshallton, Pa., 15
Marshfield, Mass., 82, 109, 123
Massachusetts Horticultural Society, 66
Massachusetts Magazine, The, 26, 42
Massachusetts Missionary Magazine, 55
Master plans for national parks, 197, 203
Mather, Cotton, 7
Mather, Stephen T., 196 f., 200
Megapolensis, Johannes, 5
Merriam, John C., 198, 200
Merrimac River, N.H., 127
Mesa Verde National Park, 155
Methodists, 118 f.
Michaux, André, 59, 102, 133
Michaux, François, 59, 133
Michigan, Lake, 83
Middle West, 26, 83 f.
Mifflin, Thomas, 56
Milbert, Jacques, 113
Miller, Alfred, 136
Miller, Perry, 8
Mills, Enos A., 182, 199
Minnehaha Falls, Minn., 140
Minnesota, 140
Mississippi River, 129 f., 132, 134, 137, 164, 199
"Mission 66," viii
Missouri River, 135, 161
Mitchell, Donald Grant, 22
Mitchell, Samuel L., 26
Möllhausen, Balduin, 142
Mono Lake, Calif., 164
Monthly Anthology, 32
Monticello, Va., 58
Moran, Thomas, 133, 152 f., 157, 223 n. 12
Morse, Samuel, 33 f., 45
Morton, J. Sterling, 171
Morton, Joy, 171
Morton, Thomas, 4, 130
Mount, W. S., 47
Mount Auburn Cemetery, 66 f.
Mount Desert, Me., 76, 81, 116 f.
Mount Rainier National Monument, 154 f.
Mount Vernon, Va., 57, 75

Mount Vernon Highway, Va., 202
Muir, John, 103 ff., 151, 176, 178 f., 185 f., 197
Multiple use of forests, 194, 196
Munich, 68
Munkuntuweap National Monument. *See* Zion National Park
Murray, William H., 110
Museums, 39, 90, 126, 134

Nahant, Mass., 73, 112–115 *passim*, 162
Nasby, Petroleum V., 163
Nation, 110 f., 141
National Academy of Design, 44, 140
National Conference on City Planning, 184
National Conference of State Parks, 199
National Conservation Committee, 188
National Conservation League, 191
National Forest Service. *See* U. S. Forest Service
National Geographic Magazine, 200
National Park Service. *See* U. S. National Park Service *and* names of individual parks
National Plan for American Forests, 194
National preserves, 169
National resources, 177 f., 187
National Roadside Council, 202
Natural Bridge, Va., 27, 37, 41, 48, 75, 146
Natural History Museum. *See* Philadelphia
Natural resources, 2 f., 9, 16, 34 f., 167, 168 f., 172, 183 f., 186, 193
Nature: essays, 26, 35, 103, 167, 180; fakers, 180, 183; fakirs, 183; philosophers, 16, 88
Neagle, John, 43
Nebraska, 140
Newburgh-on-the-Hudson, 15, 68
New England, 4, 9, 28, 39 f., 54 f., 57, 80, 83, 94, 127, 156
New Harmony, Ind., 92, 133
New Haven, Conn., 67
New Mexico, 119, 205
Newport, R.I., 114 f.
Newport, Mount, 117
Newton, Isaac, 8
New York City, 38, 44, 56, 57, 60, 61, 63, 135, 140; Battery, 61, 67; Central Park, 65, 70, 147, 151, 166, 189
New York Magazine, 13, 26, 42
New-York Mirror, 44, 135
New York State, 38, 83, 173, 176, 199 f.
New York State Reservation at Niagara, 173
Niagara, 2, 5, 24, 27 f., 43, 48, 72, 75, 146, 167, 171 f., 188, 190, 202, 206 f.
Noble, John W., 176

Noble, Louis, 46
Nogal Mesa, Ariz., 119
North, 9, 36, 55, 72, 84, 107 f.
North American Review, 30, 37
North Carolina, 4
North Conway, N.H., 127 f.
North Dakota, 180, 209
North Woods Walton Club, 109
Northern Pacific Railroad, 152
Northern Railway, 109
Norton, Andrew S., 114
Norton, Charles Eliot, 3, 98, 114, 166, 172
Nuttall, Thomas, 102, 133

Ocean Grove, N.J., 118
Ohio, 37, 45, 72, 134
Old Point Comfort, Va., 112
Olmsted, Frederick L., 69, 147, 149, 166, 171 ff., 179, 199 f.
Olmsted, Frederick L., Jr., 183, 190, 196
Ontario, Lake, 72, 75
Oregon, 131, 137
Osborn, Henry F., 193
O'Sullivan, T. H., 142, 156
Oswego, N.Y., 75
Otsego Lake, N.Y., 33 ff.
Owen, David Dale, 133
Owen, Richard, 133
Owen, Robert, 92, 133

Pacific Coast, 83
Pacific Railroad, 139
Palisades, N.Y., 36
Pamunkey River, Va., 36
Panoramas, 137 ff.
Pantheism, 24
Park movement, 108
Parker, J. Mason, 115
Parkman, Francis, 92, 131, 137, 199
Parks: city, 63, 65, 67–70 *passim*, 166 f., 190; European, 65 f., 68; national, 118, 135, 149 f., 152 f., 190, 221 n. 19, 224 n. 13; state, 149, 190, 199
Parkways, 202
Passaic Falls, N.J., 27, 75
Patapsco River, Md., 58
Pattie, James O., 160
Paulding, James Kirke, 33, 36 f.
Pawtucket River, Mass., 27
Peabody, Sophie A., 61
Peale, Charles Willson, 17
Peale, James, 40
Peale, Titian R., 44, 132
Pell family, 78

Penn, William, 9, 58
Pennsylvania, 45, 176; fireplace, 16
Penobscot River, Me., 81 f., 84
Percy, George, 4
Père-Lachaise, Paris, 66 f.
Peterson, William, 153
Philadelphia, 17, 24, 44, 55, 57, 60, 63, 157, 184; city plan, 9, 15, 58 f.; tree planting, 16, 58; Natural History Museum, 17; Fishhouse, 55; Fairmont Park, 55, 59 f., 60; Gray's Ferry, 27, 59
Philosopher's Camp, 96–98 *passim*
Phoenix, John, 163
Photography, 138 f., 144 ff., 156 f.
Picturesque, 11, 27, 33, 41, 47, 67, 78, 81, 84 ff., 88, 94, 97, 136, 152
Picturesque Views of the American Scene, 47
Pinchot, Gifford, 2, 171, 175 f., 182, 186 f., 197 f., 200, 209, 225 n. 20
Pine Orchard, N.Y. *See* Catskill Mountain House
Platte River, Colo., 136, 140
Poe, Edgar A., 12, 52, 60, 83, 122
Pope, Alexander, 11, 23, 57
Port Folio, The, 25 f., 31 f., 44
Portico, The, 32
Potomac River, Md., 27, 41
Powell, John Wesley, 159, 174, 199, 225 n. 20
Prairie du Chien, Wis., 134
Prairies, 130 ff., 134 f., 138, 175
Prang, Louis, 153
Preservation, 173 f., 226 n. 2
Princeton, N.J., 57
Profile House, N.H., 121
Promised Land, 130 f.
Promontory Point, Utah, 131
Protection of resources, 9
Provincetown, Mass., 128
Public domain, 196
Public use of parks, 148, 150, 153
Puget Sound, Wash., 140
Puritans, 7 ff., 11, 40, 57

Quetico Provincial Park, Canada, 206
Quetico-Superior Area, Minn. and Canada, 205

Radcliffe, Ann, 12, 32
Rafinesque-Schmaltz, Constantine Samuel, 26, 133
Railroads, 110, 131, 146, 156, 161, 181, 188; surveys for, 139, 142
Rangers, park and forest, 126, 199
Rappahannock Falls, 27

Rappists, 92
Rationalism, 10
Reclamation Act, 175
Recreation, 57, 59, 67, 148, 165, 189, 200 f., 203
Red River, N.M. and La., 129
Reed, Luman, 47
Reforestation, 164, 173
Resorts, 37, 65, 75, 107, 117 f., 127 f., 148, 189. *See also* Beaches
Resources for the Future, 194
Rhine River and valley, 2, 48
Richards, T. Addison, 83, 127, 144
Richardson, Albert B., 150 f.
Richardson, Edgar P., 52
Ripley, George, 91 f.
Roads, 72, 110, 201
Robinson, Theodore, 128
Rockefeller Foundation, 198
Rockaway Beach, N.Y., 112
Rocky Mountain National Park, Colo., 155, 182
Rocky Mountains, 35, 44, 112, 131 f., 134, 159, 161 f.
Romanticism, 28, 47, 59, 67, 73, 88, 95, 97, 142, 170
Roosevelt, Franklin D., 184, 209 f.
Roosevelt, Theodore, 2, 179, 181, 183, 186, 197, 227 n. 19
Rothrock, Joseph, 175
Round Lake, N.Y., 118
Rousseau, J. J., 31
Ruisdael, Jacob van, 42
Rumford, Count (Benjamin Thompson), 68
Rush, Benjamin, 17, 26, 56
Ruskin, John, 3, 141
Russia, 211

Saco River, Me., 128
Sacramento, Calif., 144
St. Augustine, Fla., 108
St. Charles, Mo., 129
St. Louis, Mo., 62, 110, 138
Sandburg, Carl, 1
San Francisco, 140, 157, 183
Sanitary Fund Fair, 140
Santa Fe Railway, 161, 181
Santa Rosa Island, Fla., 167
Saratoga, N.Y., 37, 78, 106 f.
Sargent, Charles Sprague, 171, 186
Savage, Charles R., 163
Savannah, Ga., 57
Save-the-Redwoods League, 200
Scenery: American, 3, 19, 32, 35, 37 f., 40 f.,

44–52 *passim*, 68, 71, 74, 86, 98, 106, 134, 154, 156, 187; European, 6, 10, 32, 35 f., 40, 49–52 *passim*, 65, 68, 81, 85, 106
Schenck, Carl A., 175
Schenectady, N.Y., 58
Schoolcraft, Henry R., 8, 31, 132, 134
Schurz, Carl, 175
Schuylkill Fishing Company, 55
Schuylkill River, Pa., 14 f., 58
Scientific value of wilderness, 204
Scientists, 14–29 *passim*, 90, 96
Scott, Sir Walter, 31, 37
Second Mutual Fire Insurance Company, 59
Secretary of the Interior, 176, 196 f.
Selway-Bitterroot Wilderness Area, 205
Sequoia gigantea, 68, 142 f., 200, 227 n. 9
Sequoia National Park, 155, 196, 200
Seton, Ernest Thompson, 180
Sewall, Samuel, 60
Seymour, Samuel, 44, 132, 134
Shaftesbury, Earl of, 10
Shaw, Henry, 171
Shaw, Joshua, 47, 134
Shelter belt, 209
Shenandoah National Park, Va., 202
Shenandoah Valley, Pa., 75
Sherman, Mrs. John D., 197
Sherman, Roger, 45
Shurtleff, Roswell Morse, 127
Sierra Club, 185
Sierra Nevada, 151
Skyline Drive, Va., 202
Slabsides, N.Y., 103
Smith, John, 4
Smith, John Rowson, 137
Smith, Sydney, 38, 49
Smithson, James, 90
Smithsonian Institution, 198
Snow Flake, The, 48
Social points of view, 196
Soil: conservation, 208; exhaustion, 186
Soil Conservation Service, 193, 195, 209
Somes Sound, Me., 117
Somesville, Me., 116 f.
South, 9, 36, 40, 55, 57, 75, 83 f., 107, 112
South Pass, Wyo., 140, 164
Southey, Robert, 31
Southwest 119
Spiritual values, 94, 183
Sports, 7, 16, 35, 55 f., 63, 96, 109, 111 f., 161, 194
Staffordshire pottery, 48
Stanley, John Mix, 139, 142, 171
Star Island, N.H., 116

Starr, Frederick, 173
Steele, Eliza, 83
Stevens, Isaac I., 139
Steward, Joseph, 39
Stewart, William Drummond, 136
Stillman, William J., 96 ff.
Stockton, Calif., 157
Story, Joseph, 66
Stratford, Va., 57
Strong, George Templeton, 38, 107
Sublime, 11, 21, 24, 41, 50, 88, 117, 149
Suburbanism, 123 f.
Sugarloaf Mountain, Conn., 5, 28
Summer books, 82, 96
Summit House, N.H., 121
Sundry Civil bill, 176
Sunnyside, N.Y., 122
Superior National Forest, Minn., 206
Susquehannah River, Pa., 184
Sustained-yield system, 201, 208

Taft, William H., 190 f.
Talisman, The, 48
Talleyrand, Charles Maurice de, 129
Tennessee, 118
Tennessee Valley Authority, 195, 207 f.
Tennis, 112
Texas, 119, 209
Thaxter, Celia, 115 f.
Thaxter, Levi, 115 f.
Thomasville, Ga., 108
Thoreau, Henry Walden, 12, 53, 82, 89, 91–100 *passim,* 149, 169
Thruways, 202
Ticonderoga, N.Y., 78
Timber Culture Act, 174
Tip Top Mountain House, N.H., 121
Token, The, 48
Topographical views, 43
Tourists, 72–79 *passim,* 155, 161, 172, 182, 201
Tracy, Charles, 116 f.
Trailside museum, 126, 198
Transcendentalism, 88 f., 91, 95 f., 168
Travel, 65, 71 f., 91, 106, 110; books about, 27
Trees, 9, 15 f., 34, 50, 58 f., 65, 143, 171, 227 n. 9
Trenton Falls, N.Y., 2, 75, 120
Trevelyan, G. M., 211
Trollope, Frances, 62, 119
Truman, Harry S., 206
Trumbull, John, 32, 43, 45, 78
Trustees of Public Reservations, 199

Twain, Mark, 36, 146, 163 f.
Twin Mountain House, N.Y., 127
Twining, Thomas, 58
Tyndall, Mount, 151

Ugliness, 3, 5, 40, 66, 167, 172, 181, 187, 189, 202
Union Pacific Railroad, 131, 161
Union of South Africa, 211
United Nations, 210
U. S. Congress, viii, 45, 135, 140, 148 ff., 152 f., 172–176 *passim,* 182, 191, 194, 196 f., 202, 209, 223 n. 12, 226 n. 2
U. S. Department of Agriculture, 173, 191, 194, 208
U. S. Department of the Interior, 153 f., 176
U. S. Forest Service, 176, 177, 191, 198, 200 f., 209
U. S. Geological Survey, 152, 175
United States Magazine, 13
U. S. National Park Service, 150, 154, 169, 177, 192, 196, 198 f.
U. S. Supreme Court, 211
U. S. Survey of the Fortieth Parallel, 152
U. S. War Department, 142
Utah, 131, 139, 174
Utilitarian values, 3, 179, 185

Vacations, 106, 161, 189. *See also* Holidays
Vance, R. H., 144
Vanderlyn, John, 33, 43
Vaughan, Samuel, 59
Verplanck, Gulian C., 45
Virgin River, Utah, 161
Virginia, 4, 37, 57
Virginia Hot Springs, W. Va., 73
Vogt, William, 193
Vulgarity, 61 f., 63, 108, 110 f., 117, 121, 124, 141

Walden, Mass., 95 ff., 123
Wall, William G., 48
Ward, Artemus, 163
Warder, John A., 175
Wasatch Range, Utah, 140
Washburn, Henry D., 153
Washburn [Henry D.]-[G. C.] Doane Expedition, 152 f.
Washington (state), 210
Washington, D.C., 66, 68, 154, 184
Washington, George, 41, 55
Washington, Mount, 79 ff., 120
Waste, 2, 9, 34, 135, 167 f.
Water: for recreation, 203; pollution; 184,

189; for power, 206. *See also* Niagara, Tennessee Valley Authority, Dams
Watkins, C. E., 145, 149, 151
Watson, Captain, 48, 134
Watson, John F., 59
Webster, Daniel, 66, 82, 109
Weed, C. L., 144
West, 2, 37, 51, 83, 104, 119, 128, 130–147 *passim*, 155, 179
West Ossipee, N.H., 126
West Virginia, 107
Western Monthly Magazine, 130
Western Monthly Review, 130
Western Review and Miscellaneous Magazine, 32
Westover, Va., 9
Wheeling, W.Va., 72, 86
Wheelman, The, 112
White, Gilbert, 94, 100
White Mountains, N.H., 28, 75, 79 ff., 92, 101 f., 120, 127, 140
White Sulphur Springs, W.Va., 107, 108
Whitman, Walt, 2 f., 22, 63, 109, 155 f., 164
Whitney, Josiah D., 152
Whitney, Mount, 151
Whittier, John Greenleaf, 31 f., 115 f., 120, 126
Whittredge, Washington, 53, 152
Wied, Maximilian, Prince of, 133 f., 136, 222 n. 22
Wigglesworth, Michael, 6
Wilderness, 5 f., 10, 35, 46, 50, 84, 92, 96 f., 103, 110, 131, 136, 196, 204, 226 n. 2
Wilderness bill, viii
Wilderness Society, 204 f.
Wildlife, 26, 34, 134, 168, 186, 194
Willey Cottage, N.H., 79, 120
Williams, Edward, 4
Williams, Virgil, 149
Williams, William, 40

Williamsburg, Va., 9, 36, 40, 57
Willis, Nathaniel P., 59, 72, 74, 100, 113, 122
Wilson, Alexander, 22, 24–29 *passim*, 31 f., 40, 133
Wilson, George, 188
Wilson, Richard, 41
Wilson, Woodrow, 191, 196
Winchester, Alice, 39
Winnepesaukee, Lake, 28, 48, 75
Winstanley, William, 41 f.
Winthrop, Theodore, 83 f., 116 f.
Wisconsin, 173
Wisconsin River, 208
Wolfe, Thomas, 53, 156, 188
Wood, Robert William, 225 n. 3
Woodchuck Lodge, N.Y., 103
Woodcraft Indians, 180
Woodlands, Va., 58
Woodstock, Conn., 96
Woodstock, N.Y., 128
Wordsworth, William, 31, 46
Wyant, Alexander, H., 47, 127
Wyoming, 119
Wyoming Valley, Pa., 75

Yale College, 10, 27
Yampa River, Colo., 159, 209
Yard, Robert Sterling, 197, 199
Yellowstone National Park, 112, 152–169, 221 n. 19, 223 nn. 12, 13
Yellowstone River, 153
Yellowstone Timberland Preserve, 176
Yosemite National Park, 180
Yosemite Valley, 70, 102, 135, 143–146 *passim*, 148–169 *passim*

Zion Canyon, Utah, 161
Zion National Park, 161
Zuider Zee, Holland, 211